'99

RENEGADE TRIBE

The Palouse Indians and the Invasion
of the Inland Pacific Northwest

RENEGADE TRIBE

*The Palouse Indians and the Invasion
of the Inland Pacific Northwest*

**CLIFFORD E. TRAFZER
and
RICHARD D. SCHEUERMAN**

**Washington State University Press
Pullman, Washington**

Printed and bound in the United States of America
Washington State University Press
Pullman, Washington
First printing 1986
Second printing 1987
Third printing 1993

Library of Congress Cataloging-in-Publication Data

Trafzer, Clifford E.
    Renegade tribe.

    Bibliography: p. 177.
    Includes index.
    1. Paloos Indians—History. 2. Indians of North America—Washington
(State)—History. I. Scheuerman, Richard D. II. Title. III. Title: Palouse In-
dians and the invasion of the inland Pacific Northwest.
E99.P22T72   1986   979.7'00497   86-23398
ISBN 0-87422-028-9
ISBN 0-87422-027-0 (pbk.)

Cover photo: Harlish Washomake

This book is printed on pH neutral, acid-free paper.

Research grants for this study were provided by
The American Philosophical Society
College of Arts and Letters, San Diego State University
The Pettyjohn Endowment, Washington State University
Office of Affirmative Action, San Diego State University
E. O. Holland Grant, Washington State University

For Lee Ann and Lois, and for the many Palouse Indians
who shared their history, especially
Mary Jim, Andrew George, and Emily Peone

Contents

PREFACE

Renegades, outlaws, and outcasts. These were all words used to describe the small tribe of Palouse Indians that inhabited village sites along the Snake River from present-day Clarkston to Pasco, Washington. The Palouses greeted Lewis and Clark with peace and friendship, but soon thereafter they experienced a violent encounter with a party of fur trappers that led to a negative image of the tribe among early whites. This image of the Palouses as an aggressive group composed of outcasts from surrounding tribes greatly influenced the course of their history. The image was bolstered by Palouse involvement in the "Whitman Massacre," when whites charged that the Palouses harbored the Cayuse killers of the missionaries and openly attacked the Oregon volunteers commissioned to punish the murderers. Furthermore, most Palouse leaders refused to enter into a formal agreement with the United States in 1855 during the treaty council at Walla Walla.

War was the harvest of the 1855 treaty, and the Palouses had become deeply involved by 1856. Bands of Palouse Indians joined in the Yakima War, and the tribe was singled out as one of the most belligerent during the Steptoe fight of 1858 which resulted in the deaths of several soldiers and a colossal embarrassment for the army. When soldiers returned to conquer the inland tribes, several Palouses were hanged and the tribe was threatened with extermination by Colonel George B. Wright who refused to negotiate a peaceful settlement with them. With no reservation to call their own, and with increasing demands by white settlers to remove the Palouses from the public domain, the Palouses became outcasts in their own land.

The Palouse Indians would certainly disagree with the image given them by the white men. It was, they believed, applied to justify the invasion and settlement of the Palouse Country. The Indian view of their own history differs in many ways from that chronicled by whites, and we have attempted here to present, interpret, and analyze both dimensions of the past. In doing so we have relied heavily on traditional scholarly sources which were scrutinized with an understanding of both the white and the Indian communities. We have also relied on oral histories of Indians and whites, and we have found that tribal descendants remember their history well; even minute details that were handed down by tribal elders correspond exactly at times with written records left by whites. Parents and grandparents had imprinted on their children's minds unforgettable images of the loss of their homeland, the physical invasion of their environment, and the resettlement of their homelands by whites. The Palouses remember their removal to reservations and the demand by whites to change every aspect of their culture, from their religion and customs to their politics and economy.

Like so many American Indians, the Palouses were significantly affected by whites who generally viewed Indian lands as wild domains, awaiting the hand of progress, development, and civilization. Of course not all whites considered Indians "uncivilized" people, nor were all whites aggressive, land-hungry thieves. The history of the Palouses and their relationship with whites was far too complex to be treated in such simplistic terms as good versus evil. The Indians were no more "noble savages" than whites were "dirty dogs." Indians and whites were human, functioning within the framework of their own unique societies, and their past must be interpreted within the context of the time with an understanding of both the white and Indian worlds. This study details and analyzes the Palouse past using evidence left by Indians and whites alike, and it is therefore more than a chronicle of the impact of whites on Palouse Indian society and culture. It presents Indians as "actors" in the historical process and demonstrates the way in which Indian initiatives and decisions influenced the course of history. Thus, both Indians and whites determined the history of the Palouses, and the sources left by both cultures—written and oral—have been instrumental in this work.

This work was completed with the assistance of many people and numerous institutions. Several Indians from the Yakima, Colville, Nez Perce, Umatilla, Warm Springs, Spokane, and Coeur d'Alene reservations shared their oral histories with us. In particular, we wish to thank Mary Jim, Andrew George, Emily Peone, Arthur Kamiakin, Isaac Patrick, Joe Thompson, Wendell Jim, Patricia Jones, Karie Nightwalker, and Charlie Jim. Non-Indians as well shared their oral histories including Ray DeLong, Charlie Jenkins, Leonard Jones, and Bill McNeilly. Written sources comprise the bulk of this study, and these have been accumulated from several historical repositories including: the National Archives, the Federal Record Center of Seattle, Library of Congress, Smithsonian Institution, Huntington Library, Bancroft Library, Yakima Valley Regional Library, Umatilla County Library, Spokane Public Library, Maryland Historical Society, Oregon Historical Society, Idaho State Historical Society, Washington State Historical Society, Washington State Archives, Oregon State Archives, Archdiocesan Archives of Seattle, and Hudson's Bay Company Archives. Numerous university libraries contributed source materials, including those at San Diego State University, Washington State University, Harvard University, Yale University, and Gonzaga University. Numerous staff members at these institutions provided us with assistance, especially Steve Balzarini, Jary Anderson, Richard Crawford, Marie Jones, Clifford Carroll, John Guido, Terry Abraham, Robert Eddy, Deirdre Malarkey, Nancy Prior, and Valerie Franco.

Several colleagues provided source materials, criticisms, and encouragement, including Raymond Starr, Richard Griswold del Castillo, Larry Leach, Marilyn Boxer, Steve Schlesinger, and Robert Detweiler of San Diego State University, and Herman Deutsch, David Stratton, Raymond Muse, Thomas Kennedy, Steven Leibo, Fred Bohm, Glen Lindeman, William Willard, and Steven Gill of Washington State University. We express a special thanks to Bud McKenna and Thomas Cox who read the manuscript thoroughly, offering constructive criticisms. Other individuals helped us gather materials and organize our work, including Cindy DeGrosse, Dorothy Garceau, Wendy Williams, Margery Sharkey, Bruce Wendt, Rayner Thomas, Ellen Reinsch, Rhonda Yandle, Josy Drury, Susan Elrod, and Barbara Schloss. Donald Fixico, R. David Edmunds, and Arrell M. Gibson provided us with significant insights into the history and interpretations of Indians. Special thanks are extended to Kathy Peck, Helena Basye, Carla Fourneir, Janet Hamann, and Helene Cweren for helping us complete the last stages of this manuscript. We received additional support from Mary Lou Trafzer, Don and Mary Scheuerman, Louise, Richard, and Kerry Smith, Steven Foley, Carl and Mildred Repp, Wilma Fletcher, Glen Adams, and Jack Briggs. We also thank Veryl Kaiser, Dorothy and Joe Riggan, Ray Reich, Clifford Cook, Jerry Peltier, Jerry and Ann Vanderhowen, and Henry Reimers.

The works and help of other scholars have been important in our study. We thank Alvin Josephy, Jr., John Brown, Robert Ruby, Grace Bartlett, A. J. Splawn, Edward Kowrach, Alex McGregor, Donald W. Meinig, Verne Ray, Alfred W. Shulmeyer, Clifford Drury, Kent Richards, and Albert Thompson. We acknowledge our parents for their encouragement, and we thank our wives, Lee Ann and Lois, for their kind support of our seven-year journey through the Palouse past.

INTRODUCTION

The Snake River runs its course swiftly across present-day Washington, from its confluence with the Clearwater to its junction with the Columbia River. Over the years, the Snake cut a spectacular canyon, exposing the black basalt left by a large lava flow that covered the Inland Northwest.[1] In recent geological time the rocky shores of the river and its tributaries provided shelter from inclement weather from the Plateau above and a home for a group of American Indians known as the Palouses.[2] The various bands of Palouse Indians had much in common with one another and with their neighbors, the Nez Perces, Wanapums, Walla Wallas, Yakimas, and others who possessed a common language known as Sahaptin. Palouse Indian life was intimately tied to the rivers, mountains, and plateaus of the region. The earth provided them with every necessity of life, including nutritious roots, berries, game, and fish.[3] But their life and environment would change radically and rapidly after the arrival of the first whites.

When Meriwether Lewis and William Clark canoed down the Snake River in 1805, they misidentified the Palouse Indians who lived between Alpowa Creek and the Snake's confluence with the Columbia.[4] They believed that the Nez Perces inhabited this vast region, and their error has been repeated many times since. Explorers and trappers, soldiers and surveyors made the same mistake. Scholars continued to publish the error in their studies, and much confusion has resulted.[5] The Palouse Indians, not the Nez Perces, lived along this portion of the Snake River, sometimes sharing their villages with the Nez Perces, Walla Wallas, and Wanapums. The Palouses claimed this vast domain drained by the Snake River and characterized by rolling hills, steep canyons, and arid plateaus. This is a study of the Palouse Indians and their relationship with whites and other Indians of the Columbia Plateau.

Palouse Indian history cannot be separated from that of other Plateau Indians, because of the intimate relationship between the Palouses, other Sahaptin-speaking Indians, and the interior Salish-speaking peoples of the Plateau. All of these people shared a common heritage to some extent, and all were influenced by the flow of historical events after the arrival of whites.[6] The Palouses shared a common language with the Nez Perces, Yakimas, Wanapums, and others. But just as these Indians considered themselves separate peoples, so too did the Palouses consider themselves a distinct group. White observers and scholars typically think of Indians in terms of tribes that function as unified political units. The Palouses and other Plateau Indians did not fit into such convenient molds, for they lived, worked, fought, and married each other in a fluid social world. Each was distinct with their own dialect and "tribal" identity, but they moved freely in and out of the other tribes. Thus, a person considered a Yakima Indian for over fifty years could move to the Palouse Country where the people would consider that person a Palouse Indian, particularly if that person had one or more parents of Palouse ancestry. The Palouse tribe must be viewed as the Indians of the nineteenth century viewed the "tribe," not as white scholars have labeled these people.[7]

The Palouses were never a unified entity with a single leader but were composed of numerous bands who shared a common culture, language, religion, and way of life. They lived in a defined area along the Snake River, sharing their villages at both ends of their territory with the Wanapums and Nez Perces. The Palouses claimed three geographical areas. To the east, the Upper Palouses lived near—and sometimes with—the Nez Perces at the villages of *Alpowa, Wawawai,* and *Almota* (or *Alamotin*). The Middle Palouses lived near *Palus,* their largest village at the junction of the Palouse and Snake Rivers. The Lower Palouses lived near the confluence of the Snake and Columbia Rivers, inhabiting the major villages of *Tasawiks, Sumuya,* and *Qosispah.*[8] Whites often identified the Palouses as members of other, better known Sahaptin tribes, particularly Nez Perces. Yet, in 1853 when George Gibbs made his first estimate of the Indian population of eastern Washington, he suggested that the Palouse Indians comprised the third largest group among the Sahaptin-speaking Indians—third only to the Nez Perces and Yakimas.[9] In the last century, Gibbs considered the Palouses a distinct people, and the Indian Claims Commission judged them to be a separate tribe in this century.[10] The Palouse Indians living today believe themselves to be a separate people apart from the other tribal peoples of the Inland Northwest.[11]

The basis of this study is numerous documents written by whites living in the nineteenth and twentieth centuries. In addition, oral histories of Indians have been employed. Both sources have been analyzed with an understanding of nineteenth century white America and the Plateau Indians of the period. Some scholars may discredit oral histories, labeling them as "fish tales that grow with the telling."[12] But like written documents, oral histories tell us a great deal about the American Indian communities and the people who made up those communities. Oral histories reveal internal matters within families, bands, and tribes that help explain the course of Indian events, decisions, and actions. Oral histories provide another dimension to a complicated past that should not—indeed cannot—be interpreted as good versus evil or civilized versus savage. Those who view the past using white documents alone, ignoring Indian sources, especially oral histories, fail in their tasks as scholars. Those who do not study the Indian cultures about whom they are writing cannot provide the thorough job required of them. For without an understanding of the Indians and their sources, scholars cannot presume to interpret the American Indian past.[13]

Religion provided the basis of the Palouse Indian communities, and it guided many events associated with their history. The Palouses shared their spiritual beliefs with the other Sahaptin-speaking Indians, emphasizing the "chieftanship" of the earth, plants, and animals. The Palouses believed that the Creator had given them specific lands upon which to live, and this idea formed the basis of their religion. The Palouses were guardians of the lands, not owners, and for them to surrender their lands to the whites was literally against their religion. The land that held the bones of their ancestors was considered sacred.

The traditional religion of the Palouses was the *Washani,* and in the mid-1850s the Wanapum Prophet, Smohalla, formalized and revitalized the religion, preaching a return to the "old ways" and a rejection of white culture, rule, and reservations. Smohalla's message was non-violent, but in the 1870s, some Palouses preached the destruction of all whites and the unification of the tribes against them. Although most Palouses rejected Christianity, some chose the Christian way, which created a religious schism that persists to this day. Religious factors influenced the path of Palouse history many times, notably in 1855 when treaties were made at the great Walla Walla Council.[14] Few Palouses participated in the council, but the outcome of the proceedings forever changed the Palouses who lost all of their lands and were ordered to remove to the Yakima Reservation.

The era of treaty making ushered in the most destructive element of the white invasion, for the treaties limited the freedom and sovereignty of the Palouses. The government concentrated the Palouses onto reservations where they were controlled, to varying degrees, by the social, political, and judicial mandates of the United States. Commissioners, superintendents, and agents assumed control of Indian affairs in the Northwest, and bound the Palouses to an agreement which the vast majority did not support. Four months after the treaty council, Indians and whites clashed in the largest Indian war in the history of the Northwest. This war and the subsequent Nez Perce War resulted in disaster for the Palouses. These conflicts became watersheds in Palouse history, and both contributed to their military conquest. Whether or not Palouses fought in every engagement of these wars, they were significantly influenced by the outcomes.

During the last three decades of the nineteenth century, whites expanded into the region in ever-increasing numbers, and with the growth of the white population came a rapid decline of the native population. A few Palouses filed for homesteads, but most of them moved or were removed to one of the neighboring reservations. As a result, the Indians lost every inch of their land, and forever lost control of their destiny. Yet the whites did not totally destroy the Palouses or their culture. Today various pockets of them survive and maintain elements of their culture, including kinship networks, language, and religion. They have not forgotten their uniqueness or their heritage. They have persevered. These tenacious people, descendants of individuals who met Lewis and Clark, retain their cultural identity as Palouse Indians.[15]

CHAPTER 1

VANGUARDS OF CHANGE

This country would form an extensive settlement.
—Meriwether Lewis

Thomas Jefferson had long been interested in the exploration of the American West. As president he appointed Meriwether Lewis and William Clark to explore the region from the Mississippi River to the Pacific Coast. Called the Corps of Discovery, the expedition was important to the lives of all northwestern Indians, inaugurating a new era for peoples of the Plateau and setting into motion a series of events that culminated in the destruction of the Palouse Indians as free and independent people. The Corps of Discovery acted as the first wave of the invasion, but neither the Palouses nor their Plateau neighbors perceived the danger. Initially the Indians viewed the coming of the white men as a good omen, because they brought useful technological items to trade, such as guns, metal knives, fish hooks, pots, and pans. The Indians reasoned that whites had acquired the knowledge to create these wonderful items from their God. Intrigued by both the strangers and their goods, the Palouses greeted the white men, or *suyapo* as they called them, with peace and friendship.[1]

A few white men, one black man, and a Shoshone woman and her baby were not a threat to the Palouses. The Corps of Discovery presented a curious bunch, traveling down the Snake River making notes and observations. Lewis and Clark logged much of what they did and saw, providing the first written accounts of the Palouse Indians. From the region of present-day Lewiston, Idaho, the expedition traveled swiftly past several Indian lodges. They arrived in *Hophlulh,* "Time of Yellow Falling Needles," October 1805. At that time of year the explorers recorded the grandeur of the Snake River Canyon, noting that the farther west they traveled, the higher the canyon walls became, the sides curving skyward in a long, steep upward motion. The brown from the sun-parched brush and the grey-black of the basaltic rock met the explorers' weary eyes. Few trees or bushes grew in the canyon, except for the trees lining the narrow crevices that snaked down the canyon walls, draining the plateau above.

As Lewis and Clark moved closer to the first Palouse village, they stopped to trade with Indians, Palouses and Nez Perces, bartering for fish, dogs, and roots, a portion of that day's fare. The Upper Palouses lived in this region, often sharing their villages with the Nez Perces and inter-marrying with them. The explorers passed the village of *Wawawai* and stopped at the mouth of Almota Creek, where they found two lodges standing and one Palouse man. The Indians who lived at the village of *Alamotin,* meaning "the soaring flame," had dismantled and cached their homes before leaving for their fall trip to the root and hunting grounds. The Palouses had left their village to complete the final phase of their "seasonal round" before the coming of winter. At the time Lewis and Clark arrived, the Palouses were in the Blue Mountains hunting deer, elk, bear, and antelope. Palouse women were busy picking fall berries and digging nutritious roots to be stored for winter. The lone Palouse villager sold the explorers "three dogs and a few fish." The *suyapos* continued downstream past many "rapids all of them great fish places."

Periodically they noticed Palouse houses and "near each of those houses we observe grave yards picketed, or pieces of wood stuck in permiscuesly [promiscuously] over the grave or body which is covered with earth." Despite the fact that wood was a precious commodity to the Palouses, they used it to fence their cemeteries and mark their graves. They had a deep respect for their dead and considered grave sites sacred places. An important axiom of the Palouse social system centered around this reverence for the dead and their burial grounds. This fact weighed heavily with the Palouses and con-flicted with the white man's future demand for the Indians to move from their homes onto reservations.[2]

When word reached the Palouses that strange visitors had arrived in their country, the people returned to the river. Long before white contact, holy men and women had prophesied the coming of the whites, and some Indians had learned special songs to honor the newcomers when they arrived.[3] As the explorers moved down the Snake, some Indians traded with them, sup-plying a variety of "provisions those Indians could spare." More important, the Palouses provided information about the rocky rapids downstream, rapids found to be "long and dangerous about 2 miles in length, and many turns necessary to Stear Clare of the rocks, which appeared to be in every direc-tion." A few Indians who knew the river and were accustomed to shooting the rapids, guided Lewis and Clark through the Snake's torrential waters.[4]

On October 13 the Corps of Discovery passed two major tributaries of the Snake, the Tucannon and Palouse Rivers. After passing through a rapid twenty yards long, the explorers neared another "great fishing place." They had reached the site of *Palus,* the largest village of the Palouses, located at the mouth of the Palouse River. The Indians had disassembled their mat lodges before moving onto the plain to hunt and gather. If Lewis and Clark had passed the village later in the year, they would have seen as many as fifty mat-covered lodges. The Nez Perces called the site *Pelutpe,* but the Palouses knew it as, *Palus.* The place was literally the heart of the Palouse Country, a sacred site where a legendary beaver named *Wishpushya* had been killed by Palouse warriors. The heart of the animal had turned to stone and was known as Standing Rock. Lewis and Clark rested at Palus before con-tinuing downstream away from the Middle Palouses.[5]

Despite aid given by their Indian scouts, Lewis and Clark overturned a canoe in the Snake on October 14. While passing through a boiling rapid, George Drouillard (also spelled Drewyer), for whom the "Drewyers," or Palouse River, was named, struck a rock and upset the canoe. Those men tossed out of the canoe reached a rock and were rescued. The dugout canoe did not fare as well. It "took in water and she sunk." The explorers recovered their goods and paddled to shore, landing at another Palouse village. They dried their provisions by the warmth of fires made from the logs of Palouse lodges. The explorers noted that the Palouses had dismantled their mat lodges before leaving and had hidden the wooden planks and poles in piles of rocks. During the winter or *Ahnumkapus,* "The Cold Time," most Palouse lived in A-framed or conical-shaped mat lodges. When they temporarily abandoned their villages, they stored their mat lodges and lived in tipis like the Plains Indians. The explorers used the lodge poles to fuel their fire, exonerating themselves by recording that the Nez Perces allowed them to do so.[6]

At Palus, as well as at the site of the canoe accident, the explorers noted the Palouse practice of digging large holes in the river banks for storage of their fish. The Indians took trout, whitefish, squawfish, sturgeons, suckers, chubs, and eels in great numbers. More important, they caught blueback, chinook, and steelhead (sea-run trout) from rocks, platforms, and canoes, using dip nets, seines, gill nets, spears, and hooks.[7] Fishing had begun in early summer, *Latitme,* "Time of Blossoming," and a large catch had been made.[8] The pits served as natural refrigerators which preserved the fish. Lewis and Clark were "cautious not to touch" realizing that the fish was necessary for the winter survival of the Indians. After making a few notes about the accident and the Palouse pits, the explorers continued down the Snake. The day proved hazardous as the Corps of Discovery passed through a series of choppy rapids, described by William Clark as being "verry bad."[9]

Short on fresh provisions, the explorers supplemented their diet of roots and fish by hunting. One "fair morning" in the heart of the Palouse Country, Lewis set out with his best hunters in search of game. They made the arduous climb over the layers of basalt, ascending the steep canyon of the Snake River to reach the plain above. A rolling landscape greeted their eyes, a prairie that reminded them of the Great Plains. They found no signs of large game, and they saw no Indians. To the south lay the Blue Mountains where many Palouses were hunting and gathering, and to the north and west were the foothills of the jagged Cascade Range. The hunters killed two ducks and two geese before rejoining their cohorts. After eating the fowl, they continued downstream, passing several small islands consisting of stone and sand. As they paddled down the Snake, the explorers ran a series of rapids, but these did not pose a dangerous threat to them. However, on one occasion, Lewis and Clark "over took the three Indians who had Polited [piloted] us thro the rapids from the forks." These Indians, probably Palouses, knew the river well, and they had waited "to warn us of the difficulties of this rapid."[10]

Lewis and Clark found the rapids "more dificuelt to pass than we expected from the Indians information." For this reason, they encamped at a Palouse village on the night of October 15. According to Clark, they "landed at a parcel of split timber, the timber of a house of Indians out hunting the *Antelope* in the plains; and raised on scaffolds to save them from spring floods." The night was cold and the villagers were away. Clark wrote that the explorers were "obliged for the first time to take the property of the Indians without the consent or approbation of the owner." They split some of the poles and planks of the Palouse houses and burned them. The next day the Corps of Discovery shot the rapids which proved to be "a sucksession of sholes" which ran "from bank to bank for 3 miles . . . with large rocks Sticking up in every direction, and the channel through which we must pass crooked and narrow." A Palouse Indian guide took the first canoe through the rapids, and the others followed. All of the canoes got through safely, except the last one which ran "fast on a rock." With the assistance of "the Indians, who was extreamly ellert" the men in the canoe were saved. They and their provisions were wet, but not much the worse from the accident.[11]

On October 16, the whites reported seeing Indians on horseback riding on the south side of the river. Five of them approached the whites "in great haste." The Palouses showed no signs of hostility, but instead smoked tobacco with the white men and received from them a "piece of tobacco." After exchanging this greeting, the Indians rode off to join the others and "continued to go as fast as they could run as far as we could see them." The Indians rode off to tell everyone about the white men, likely encouraging others to meet the white men at *Qosispah,* an important village of the Lower Palouses located at the confluence of the Snake and Columbia (near present-day Pasco, Washington). This group of Palouses called themselves *Nahahum* — people of the Snake River.[12]

The junction of the two rivers had long been an important meeting place for the Palouses and others who gathered there to sing, worship, dance, and race horses. Two Nez Perce scouts waited for the explorers at this location, along with a large number of friendly Indians. They had been informed by others of the expedition's "approach and friendly intentions towards all nations."[13] The Palouses who had smoked with Lewis and Clark a few days before were present, including an important Palouse chief who was "a man of great influence." All of the Indians treated Lewis and Clark with kindness, entertaining the explorers with a pow wow on the night of October 16, when two hundred men assembled to drum, sing, and dance. The Indians "formed a circle around us and Sung for Some time," providing a ceremony that was possibly linked to the old prophecy, foretelling the coming of whites. The Indians and whites assured each other of their "friendly disposition to all nations." As tokens of goodwill, Lewis and Clark presented medals bearing the inscription, "Peace and Friendship." The explorers gave one large medal to a "principal chief" and two smaller ones to other chiefs, one of whom was a Palouse who had come "down from the upper villages." The Indians reciprocated with presents of their own, including a quantity of fish. Grateful for the medals, the Palouses proudly exhibited these tokens of American friendship for some time to come.[14]

The gifts given to the Indians were more than equaled by those presented to the whites. The Indians gave presents of fish, prickly pears, dogs, and twenty pounds "of verry fat Dried horse meat." The Indians sold the explorers everything the whites needed and provided them with accommodations while they remained on the western edge of Palouse territory. Before descending the Columbia River, the explorers rested and reconnoitered the region, traveling up the Columbia a few miles. Clark did not go far up the swift Columbia, but he observed a few "verry large mat lodges" as well as a few fish racks upon which the Indians dried salmon. The explorers recorded the fall run of salmon, a run considerably smaller than that of the spring. Nevertheless, the Indians collected "emence quantities of dried fish." Clark visited the Indians living up the Columbia River a short distance from its junction with the Snake, including some Palouses and Wanapums. Both were Sahaptins, related to one another by language and family, but the explorers called the Palouses "Choppunish" and referred to the Wanapums as "Solkulks."[15]

The white men camped and rested at the junction of the Snake and Columbia Rivers for two and a half days, preparing for their journey down the

Columbia. While in the region, Clark observed the Palouses and other Indians who had ventured to the area to get a glimpse of the newcomers. The Palouses, he wrote, appeared "to live in a State of comparitive happiness" and were "of a mild disposition and friendly." Like many later travelers, the explorers mistakenly thought the Palouses to be a band of Nez Perces, and in fact compared the Indians of the lower Snake River with the Nez Perces. 'The Dress of those natives," wrote Clark, "differ but little from those on the Koskia and Lewis's [Snake] rivers." The black eyes and hair of the Palouses matched that of the Nez Perces, and the Palouses wore beads, bracelets, and necklaces. The Indians dressed, spoke, and lived in a similar fashion, making it impossible for Lewis and Clark or other whites to distinguish between the Palouses and Nez Perces. Indeed, the Palouses were culturally and linguistically related to the Nez Perces, but the Indians recognized them as distinct people.[16]

While camped near the junction of the Snake and Columbia, Lewis and Clark made the first notes regarding Palouse and Wanapum villages. On October 17, Clark traveled up the Columbia a short distance and visited one of the villages located near the present-day tri-city area of Pasco, Kennewick, and Richland, Washington. As Clark paddled toward the Palouse village, "great numbers of Indians on the banks" watched with growing enthusiasm and curiosity. Eighteen canoes filled with Indians followed the explorer as he glided across the Columbia to the villages. The clear Columbia ran in front of the village, and Clark could see salmon at a depth of fifteen to twenty feet. This was another "place of fishing" for the Palouses, who inhabited several lodges in the area, often sharing them with Wanapum friends and relatives. Clark approached one of the dwellings, and as he neared the entrance, he studied the manner in which the women split the salmon and dried them in the sun. Like so many white observers, he was impressed with the role of the Palouse women as providers. A family invited him into a large mat house, a dark dwelling, except for the sun rays that radiated through the openings between the wooden poles and planks. These formed the skeleton of the A-shaped lodge, covered with tightly-woven mats that formed the body of the dwelling.[17]

The Palouses kindly received the unusual guest who "was furnished with a mat to set on." Men, women, and children crowded around, and one man "set about me [Clark] something to eate." The Palouse man first brought a pine log, and split it apart with an elk horn and stone mallet. He used the small pieces of wood to start a fire, into which he tossed round stones. As the fire grew and the rocks got hot, the smoke curled up to the top of the lodge, escaping through openings in the corners of the roof. A woman handed the host "a basket of water and a large Salmon about half Dried." He dropped the hot stones from the fire into the basket which boiled the water immediately. The salmon "was soon sufficiently boiled for use" and the Indians placed the fish "on a platter of rushes neetly made." When Clark finished the meal, he departed, traveling to another village where Indians told the explorers about another river which flowed into the Columbia from the west. This was the Yakima, along the banks of which lived a powerful tribe of the same name.[18]

Clark returned to the junction of the Snake and Columbia Rivers accompanied by twenty Indians. Along the way, he killed a few game birds and several ducks, commenting on the large number of birds along the

Columbia. While Clark was upriver, great numbers of Indians had congregated around Captain Lewis and his men who were busy tanning hides, "mending their clothes and putting their arms in the best order" in preparation for their journey down the Columbia River. The Palouses who gathered at the confluence were interested in seeing these curious white men and in acquiring their fine gifts and trade goods. The explorers and Indians had gotten along well with each other. Like the inscription on the Lewis and Clark medals, the newcomers had displayed only peace and friendship. In exchange, the explorers had received an equal measure of good will from the *Nahanum,* the Palouses of the lower Snake River.[19]

On the afternoon of October 18, 1805, the Corps of Discovery left the Palouse villages and "set out down the Great Columbia." They continued their journey, arriving at their long-awaited destination, the Pacific Ocean, spending a miserable winter on the Oregon Coast, dreary with rain and fog that dampened their spirits. Winter could not end soon enough for members of the expedition, and in the early spring, they journeyed up the Columbia, passed through The Dalles, and soon after reached Quosispah at the mouth of the Snake River. Rather than travel east by way of the Snake River, Lewis and Clark headed overland along the southern portion of present-day Washington through the land of the Wallas Wallas, Umatillas, and Cayuses. As the expedition traveled past the sage-studded lava beds of southeastern Washington, the explorers saw "Great numbers of the nativs pass us on hors back." They met many Indians, including Palouses, all of whom proved friendly.[20]

Lewis and Clark chronicled their journey across the Walla Walla Country with the same attention to detail they had shown throughout their expedition. Much of what they reported in this region reflected upon the life and character of the Indians. The explorers had not seen much of the Columbia Plain north of the Snake River. They probably were not aware that much of the land lying south of the Snake was similar to that north of it. They considered the soil sandy and unproductive, but as they moved east, they noted that the earth produced "a low grass on which the horses feed very conveniently." The rolling hills south of the Snake River, like those above it, produced "the bunch wheat grass, with its varied cover — from the scattered tufts of the desert margins to the luxuriant carpet of the eastern hills — which reflected all the variations of sun and rain, slope and elevation." Lewis and Clark noted the value of the bunchgrass to the Indians, for the grass supported huge herds of horses. The Palouses and their Sahaptin neighbors were well known for their horses, which they used as a means of exchange with white traders and immigrants. By the time Lewis and Clark had arrived, horses constituted an integral part of their economic well-being.[21]

Lewis observed the relationship between the bunchgrass and the Indian horses, stating "it astonished me to see the order of their horses at this season of the year when I knew that they had wintered on the drygrass of the plains." That the rolling hills of the region provided an excellent range for stock, Lewis had no doubt. The Palouse herds had grown large since the mid-eighteenth century when horses first arrived on the Columbia Plateau. Their horses were of a good quality, wrote Lewis, despite the fact that the Indians apparently used their animals "with greater severity than is common among ourselves." Lewis commented that he "did not see a single horse which could be deemed poor and many of them were as fat as seals." The explorers viewed the inland Northwest as a splendid region in which to raise stock, a fact that would have an important bearing on the future course of Palouse history. In years to come, the Indians faced an increasing number of white people who brought with them sheep, cattle, and horses. Indeed, the rancher would be the precursor of the farmer. Both would occupy, alter, and resettle the Palouse region, destroying the natural habitat of the area and thereby destroying the economic life of the Palouses.[22]

The explorers described in some detail the methods of fishing used by the Palouses who depended so much on fish for their survival. This point is well known, but the role of plant foods in the Plateau Indian diet has been often overlooked, although Lewis and Clark noted the importance of plants as sources of food. Lewis, for example, commented that "this plain as usual is covered with aromatic shrubs, herbaceous plants and a short grass. Many of those plants produce those esculent roots which form a principal part of the subsistence of the native." As the expedition moved south of the Snake along the Touchet River of southeastern Washington, Captain Lewis wrote that, among the many varieties of plants used by the Indians, "there is one which produces a root somewhat like the sweet pittaitoe." Surely he was referring to camas.[23]

On May 2, 1806, the explorers moved along the Tucannon River, through the southern reaches of Palouse Country. There, they "observed considerable quantities of quamash [camas] in the bottoms through which we passed this evening now in blume." It was the spring of the year, and Lewis and Clark correctly ascertained that at this time the Indians moved to their favorite root grounds. Indeed, Lewis commented on the seasonal round of the Palouses, stating that "a great portion of the Choppunish . . . are now distributed in small villages through this plain collecting the quawmish and cows [kouse]." The Palouses and others ate "bread of cows" and showed the explorers how to eat "the inner part of the young and succulent stem of a large course plant with a ternate leaf, the leafet of which are three loabed and covered with a woolly puberence." Clark, more adventuresome than Lewis on this occasion, "tasted of this unidentified plant" and "found it agreeable and eate hartily of it without feeling any inconveniance."[24]

Across the luxurious grasslands, the Palouses traveled north and south of the Snake River in search of roots. The Upper Palouses gathered the potato-like camas south of the Snake along the Grande Ronde River of present-day Oregon and Washington, while the Lower Palouses usually traveled north along the Columbia River to Soap Lake, Badger Mountain, and Moses Lake. In the rough and rocky terrain in this region, this staple grew profusely just as it did near the rocky areas around present-day communities of Washtucna, Dayton, and Colfax, Washington. Abundant camas of a large size grew near present-day Pullman, Washington, and Moscow, Idaho.[25]

Using digging sticks, called *kapon*, "the women gathered great quantities of camas during the short season," collecting them in large woven bags known as *ta-khon-ta*. The camas, sweet and nutritious, could be eaten raw or cooked as a mush. Most, however, was cooked in large pits or preserved by drying on scaffolds in the sun. When the Palouses found a good camas ground, they made camp, remaining until they had gathered all they desired. In a good field, a woman could gather enough camas in three or four days to feed a large family for an entire year. These industrious workers gathered twenty or thirty bushels before they dug a deep pit and lined it with rocks.

They built a huge fire in the pit, adding rocks. When the fire died down, the Indians threw dirt and bunchgrass on the coals. The women then dumped the roots into the pit and covered the vegetables with more grass and dirt. Before the camas was completely covered, they poured water into the pit to steam the camas. The women kept their camas covered from one to three days, depending on the quantity to be cooked.[26]

Palouse women also dug kouse or biscuit root. Like the camas, they gathered it in the spring and summer. Kouse grew in rocky areas, usually along well-drained ridges and canyons. The Indians ate kouse raw or prepared it in pits like camas. They dried the white tuberous root, grinding it into meal and making it into fist-sized biscuits. The women mixed the nutritious biscuit root into a batter and squeezed a quantity of batter in the hand, forming a small white, grainy biscuit that had a sweet, nutty flavor.[27] They also collected stringy bitterroot. It "served both as a food and as a sort of condiment," and grew in the same areas as camas.[28] Women collected wild onions, rhubarb, strawberries, carrots, and parsnips as well as seeds and stalks of wild sunflowers which they ate raw or dried and pounded into meal. The Palouses liked to mix ground sunflower meal with cooked bone marrow and fat, a tasty and nutritious mixture formed into cakes.[29] In addition, the women took at least seven varieties of *Lomatium* that grew in the rocky terrain of the Palouse Country. The Palouses ate roots, like the *Lomatium salmoniflorum* and the *Lomatium greyi,* boiled or dried.[30] They ate the stems of many of these plants and the moss from evergreens. They cooked the moss underground like camas and pounded it into a treat which tasted much like licorice. The profusion of plant foods led one Palouse woman to remark that "there were lots of roots; it was like in the water, all kinds of fish; it was the same with the roots; there were all kinds, all fixed in different ways, you know."[31]

Their observations of native plants, along with their comments regarding fishing and hunting, showed an understanding of the relationship between the Indians and the land. Lewis and Clark noted that nature provided well for the Palouses, for the earth provided an abundance of natural foods that the Indians gathered, but did not cultivate. Palouse Indian life and culture was so closely tied to their environment that one authority has suggested, "their land was their religion and their religion was the land."[32] The explorers reported that the Indians gathered roots because the salmon had "not yet arrived to call them to the river." In the near future other white men would come into the region. Some recognized and approved of the patterns of life known to the Palouses. Others, however, refused to understand the Indian way, demanding that they change every aspect of their lives from their food to their dress, and from their social customs to their religious beliefs. Only in this way, some said, could the Indians progress, survive, and be saved in this life and the next.[33]

Lewis and Clark did not advocate such extreme measures; their mission was to observe and explore, not to civilize and convert. The expedition passed through the Palouse Country on its way westward. On Sunday, May 4, 1806, Lewis and Clark reached the Snake River about seven miles west of Alpowa Creek. From there they moved southeast along the river in the region inhabited and shared by Palouses and Nez Perces. The whites made few notes regarding the people of the area, as the explorers moved quickly eastward into the heart of Nez Perce Country. Five days after leaving the Snake River,

Lewis made his last entry regarding the lands south of the Snake, lands inhabited by some Palouses and used by many. He described this country as being "extremely fertile and in many parts covered with a tall and open growth of the longleafed pine, near the watercourses the hill steep and lofty tho' . . . covered with a good soil not remarkably stony and possess more timber than the level country." In a prophetic manner, Lewis stated that "this country would form an extensive settlement; the climate appears quite as mild as that of similar latitude on the Atlantic coast if not more so and it cannot be otherwise than healthy." These regions, Lewis wrote, "possess a fine dry pure air" and a thick carpet of tall grass, which, "if cultivated would produce in great abundance every article essentially necessary to the comfort and subsistence of civilized [white] man." This view reflected that of other whites who believed that the Indians would one day give way to white "civilization" and surrender their lands to white Americans.[34]

The Corps of Discovery concluded its expedition on September 23, 1806, when it arrived in St. Louis, but its impact on Palouse Indian history and the Pacific Northwest continued for years to come. For example, Lewis and Clark claimed the region for the United States, and they were harbingers of a new concept of land use and ownership. By opening the region to other whites, Lewis and Clark provided the foundations for a new social, economic, and political order. It was a familiar process in American history, but it caught the Palouses by surprise. Lewis and Clark also made a contribution to regional history, including their comments on the Palouses and others in the form of journals, maps, field books, and documents relating to Indian life on the Columbia Plateau.

Published in 1814, the *Journals of Lewis and Clark* quickly became the leading source of information on the Northwest and its people. The report included rich sources on the life of the Indians, but the importance of the expedition went far beyond these ethnographic accounts. To the Palouses, meeting these whites held out the promise of a new era of friendship and trade. Lewis and Clark had been generous people who either gave away articles or provided a fair exchange for goods. They presented a positive image of white people, and eager to engage in trade, the Indians asked the whites to return with guns and powder, pots and kettles, knives and axes, blankets and tobacco. Like on so many frontiers, the Indians invited more trade, opening a new chapter in their history.[35]

CHAPTER 2

BLOOD ON THE LAND

You have spilt blood on our lands!
— Tummeatapam

The romantic era of fur trappers and traders was shortlived, but it had great influence on the history of the Palouses. The quarter of a century after the Lewis and Clark expedition brought the Palouses into contact with British and American trappers who armed the Indians and introduced them to manufactured goods. Indians and trappers enjoyed relatively peaceful relations, and the Indians formed fairly good impressions of the whites. Indians quickly adopted items offered in trade. Since God provided all power and all things, the Indians reasoned that God had given whites the power to create magnificent trade items. The Indians ultimately grew interested in acquiring knowledge of the white man's spirit power or *wyak*. The trappers and traders entered the region to exploit the bountiful resources, but most did not wish to transform the Indians. Inadvertently, however, they laid foundations for great changes.

While journeying through the Columbia Plateau, Lewis and Clark had promised Indians that white men would return to trade. But the British, not the Americans, first opened trade with the Indians in the inland Northwest. To be sure, the Indians had a long tradition of trade, journeying regularly to barter horses, fish, and roots with Indians west of the Cascades and east of the Bitterroots. The British and Canadians of the North West Company became the first non-Indian traders in the inland Northwest. Initially, the Palouses welcomed them. The British concern was headquartered in Montreal, and David Thompson was the company's agent in the far Northwest. Thompson built Kootenay House, Kalispell House, Salish House, and Spokane House, and through these factories, the British traded with Indians living along the present international border of British Columbia and the states of Washington, Idaho, and Montana.[1]

Thompson faced little competition his first few years except for the "mystery Americans" who reportedly arrived in the Northwest in 1807 and disappeared almost as quickly as they appeared.[2] Like Lewis and Clark before him, Thompson lumped the Sahaptins together, and adopted the term used by the French Canadians, calling them *Nez Perces*. Some Palouses traveled to his trading posts to gawk at and trade for the many fascinating items available to them. Guns, blankets, knives, iron arrowheads, hats, cloth, and awls found their way back to Palouse Country. The Palouses carried on limited trade with David Thompson, or with Indians who had dealt with the British trader, which resulted in greater interest to acquire goods.

As the fur trade expanded, Thompson decided to find an outlet for his merchandise using the Columbia River. In July, 1811 he set off down the Columbia "to explore this river in order to open out a passage for the interior trade with the Pacific Ocean."[3] Accompanied by nine men in a large cedar canoe, Thompson journeyed down the river, traveling six days before arriving at the confluence with the Snake at Quosispah. When Thompson arrived, he scribbled a few lines on a half sheet of paper, hoisted the Union Jack, and claimed the land for Britain. At the "Junction of the Shawpatin River with the Columbia," Thompson took possession of the Palouse village, announcing that the region was "claimed by Great Britain as part of its territories, and that the N.W. Company of Merchants from Canada, finding the factory for this people [the Palouse and other Sahaptins of the region] inconvenient for them, do hereby intend to erect a factory in this place for the commerce of the country around."[4]

Thompson traveled down the Columbia a few miles. He again put ashore where he "met the principal chief of all the tribes of Shawpatin Indians." This headman, probably a prominent Cayuse named Ollicott or Yelleppit as Lewis and Clark had called him, greeted Thompson.[5] This "stately good looking man of about 40 years" upset the trader when he showed him the Lewis and Clark medal and the Stars and Stripes the Americans had left with the Indians. Thompson and Ollicott "discoursed a long time and settled upon the Junction of the Shawpatin River for a House."[6] Although the North West Company never established a trading post in this region, another British concern did. Thompson traveled to the Pacific Coast where he met Americans agents of John Jacob Astor's Pacific Fur Company. Like Thompson, the Astorians wanted to extend the trade to the interior tribes, and to this end, the Astorians under David Stuart accompanied Thompson on his return trip up the Columbia.[7] On July 22, 1811, the American and British traders left Astoria, traveling together until Thompson took an alternate route to Spokane House. When he reached Quosispah, he turned east along the Snake River, passing several Palouse village sites.[8] Thompson described the enchanting landscape of "black rude rock" which the trader speculated had been "broken or cracked by a violent blow." He saw pillars of basalt which appeared "like flutes of an organ at a distance." Thompson found it difficult to understand how the river had cut its course through such a barrier, musing that "the finger of the Deity has opened by immediate operation the passage of this river through such solid materials as must forever have resisted its action."[9]

On the evening of August 5, Thompson camped among two hundred Palouses who gave him a gracious welcome of feasting, drumming, dancing, and singing. Thompson remarked that the Indians "behaved very well," and he offered his thanks to "Heaven for the favors we find among these numerous people." The morning after the celebration, Thompson hired a Palouse scout to guide the British party upriver against a "very strong current."[10] Thompson traveled past several Palouse villages, making his second camp on the Snake River, where the Indians entertained him with a pow wow. Over twenty enthusiastic men sang, danced, and drummed for the trappers who spent a pleasant night on the narrow banks of the Snake River before continuing their journey the next day. "A fine clear morning, a little distant thunder" greeted Thompson and his men on August 7, but the British traders continued up the Snake, fighting the swift current. As the party moved along, Thompson recorded that to the southeast he could "see the Blue Mountains."

This was the first time in written history that anyone had called the mountains of Washington and Oregon the Blue Mountains.[11]

Thompson's trappers met more Palouses as they continued up the Snake, passing numerous villages including the main village of Palus. On August 8 Thompson's party "put ashore at the mouth of a small brook and camped." The trader had reached the confluence of the Palouse River with the Snake where Thompson met fifty enthusiastic Palouse men. The Palus villagers celebrated the arrival, dancing "till they were fairly tired and the Chiefs bawled [sang] themselves hoarse." The Indians expressed their warm wishes to Thompson and demonstrated their generosity by giving the trader eight horses and a leather war garment. Although the Palouses "did not wish for any return for the present of Horses," Thompson presented the headmen paper notes to be redeemed when the traders returned.[12]

On August 9 Thompson started his journey out of the Snake River Canyon by way of the Palouse River, which he followed through a deep gorge running north for about three miles. Thompson arrived on the Columbia Plain and crossed the rolling hills of the Palouse Country, reaching the Spokane River two days later. While the trader traveled up the Snake, the Astorians, whom he had left behind, struggled against the Columbia's currents. These Americans, under the leadership of David Stuart, met a huge gathering of "fifteen hundred souls" at the junction of the Walla Walla River with the Columbia. 'The tribes assembled," wrote Astorian Alexander Ross, "were the Walla-Wallas, the Shaw Haptens, and the Cajouses." The "Shaw Haptens" were Palouses who lived along the Snake River.[13] All of the tribes were pleased to meet the traders, whom they sometimes called *pacten,* that is Bostonmen.[15]

The Palouses and others displayed numerous "symbols of peace and friendship," dancing and singing to celebrate the arrival of the Astorians. Ross recorded that the Columbia Plain was "literally covered with horses, of which there could not have been less than four thousand in sight of camp." This Astorian left this vivid portrait of the Indians assembled at the pow wow.

The men were generally tall, raw-boned, and well dressed; having all buffalo-robes, deer-skin leggings, very white, and most of them garnished with porcupine quills. Their shoes were also trimmed and painted red;—altogether, their appearance indicated wealth. Their voices were strong and masculine, and their language differed from any we had heard before. The women wore garments of well dressed deer-skin down to their heels; many of them richly garnished with beads, higuas, and other trinkets—leggings and shoes similar to those of the men. Their faces were painted red. On the whole, they differed widely in appearance from the piscatory tribes we had seen along the river.[15]

Two days after Thompson arrived in Spokane Country, the Astorians reached the junction of the Snake and Columbia, where they discovered the British flag Thompson had erected. "On the 14th early in the morning," wrote Alexander Ross, "what did we see waving triumphantly in the air, at the confluence of the two great branches, but a British flag." There, fluttering in the middle of the Palouse village, was a visual edict declaring that Britain claimed Palouse land. Ross feared that the Palouses were acting under instructions from Thompson who had "attempted to incite the Indians against us, in our helpless and almost forlorn state." If this was the case, Thompson never mentioned it in his journal.[16]

The Palouse villages near the confluence of the Snake and Columbia were located at a strategic location. Indians traveling to and from the Pacific Coast often passed through the Palouse Country, and individuals traveling overland into the interior mountains or plateaus usually passed through the area. Ross recognized the significance of the "open and very pleasant" country surrounding the confluence. It appeared "to be a great resort, or general rendezvous, for the Indians on all important occasions." Many different Indians frequented the area surrounding Quosispah, making the Lower Palouse Country an important geographical spot.[17]

Before leaving the area, Ross commented about the trade items the Palouses had already acquired. "The only European articles seen here with the Indians," he wrote, "were guns, and here and there a kettle, or a knive." This proved that the Palouses had traded with the Nor'Westers and with coastal tribes. This also demonstrated a willingness of the Palouses to possess trade goods. This should have enticed the Astorians, but Ross was wary of the Palouses, stating that "the more they get of our manufacture the more unhappy will they be." According to the trader, "the possession of one article naturally creates a desire for another, so that they are never satisfied." These were strange words from a businessman interested in expanding trade with the Indians.[18]

Shortly after Thompson, Stuart, and Ross left the Palouse Country, another party of Astorians led by Wilson Price Hunt entered from the east. Hunt's Astorians had traveled overland from St. Louis but had met with grave difficulties while traveling along the Snake River in southern Idaho. A canoe accident resulted in the dispersion of the group, and one party led by the three hundred-pound trapper, Donald McKenzie, made their way through Hells Canyon before the Nez Perces rescued them. Like Lewis and Clark, McKenzie canoed past the Palouse villages along the Snake River, but unfortunately he made no detailed record of his trip.[18] From Quosispah, McKenzie traveled down the Columbia to Astoria, where he outfitted a party and returned east to the junction of the Clearwater with the Snake.[20] McKenzie was accompanied by John Clarke and Ross Cox. The latter left an account of the expedition, stating that the Astorians "proceeded up Lewis' [Snake] River in order to establish a post on the upper parts of it." As the party moved along the Snake, "Some on land with the horses, but the greater part still in the canoes," the Astorians met several Palouses. Like other travelers, Cox identified the Palouses as Les Nez Perces, carefully recording some of their cultural characteristics and noting correctly that the Palouses were much like the Walla Walla Indians.[21]

McKenzie, Clarke, and Cox arrived at Palus on August 7, 1812, exactly one year after David Thompson had been there. The Astorians recorded their arrival, stating that "we reached a small stream which falls into the Lewis' River from the north; the mouth is wide, and forms a kind of semi-circular bay, but suddenly narrows to about ten or twelve yards." The village of this "small and friendly tribe [the Palouse] of the great Nez Perce nations" was composed of forty large mat-covered lodges. "In their dress, language, and dwellings," Cox commented, "these people differed little from those at the mouth of Lewis' River." Indeed, this was true, for both people—those at Palus and Quosispah, were Palouse Indians.[22]

The Astorians split at Palus, Clarke heading north to the Spokane Country and McKenzie continuing up the Snake to the Nez Perce Country. Because

Clarke was embarking on an overland journey, he bought fifty horses from the Palouses who "were hard to deal with." Clarke and his men stored their canoes, leaving "them to the care of the chief, who promised that they should be carefully preserved until our return the following spring." The Astorians paid this Palouse headman with an axe, a knife, and a length of blue cloth, and they gave his wife strings of blue and white beads as well as some hawk bells. With their business concluded, Clarke set out on his journey north across the "steep rugged hills" of the Palouse Country.[23]

Meanwhile, McKenzie hurried up the Snake to the Clearwater, where he established a post on the north bank of the Clearwater, across from the present-day Lewiston, Idaho. This location was in the heart of Nez Perce Country but close enough to the Upper Palouse villages for them to trade with the Astorians. The Palouses and Nez Perces welcomed the white men in their typically cordial manner. However, the Indians soon learned that the trader wanted high prices for his goods and wanted to be paid in beaver skins. The Palouses and Nez Perces expressed no interest in trapping, no desire to "submit to the drudgery of killing beaver." To have done so would have required an abandonment of their way of life, based on the seasonal round, in favor of fur hunting. Simply put, the Indians refused to spend their time "crawling about in search of furs."[24] The Astorians refused to trade their goods except for furs. McKenzie maintained this hard line until food became scarce, and then he asked the Nez Perces for food. The Indians demanded high prices for their horses, forcing the white men to trade their manufactured goods for horse flesh, not beaver pelts. McKenzie had to trade on the Indians' terms or starve. He traded.[25]

Conditions became so acute that McKenzie "resolved to abandon that post, and proceed further up the river." In the fall of 1812 he traveled overland to the Spokane Country to discuss his plans with John Clarke. Unfortunately, McKenzie made no account of his journey through the bunchgrass hills of the Palouse Country, but he made his way safely to Spokane House where he and Clarke learned that the United States and Britain had declared war. McKenzie hurried back to his post, cached his goods, and headed down the Snake to warn the Astorians. He arrived at Astoria on January 15, 1813, and the trappers abandoned the post.[26] In February, 1813, McKenzie and John Reed returned to the Nez Perce Country to retrieve their possessions, only to find that Indians had plundered their cache. McKenzie recovered some of the goods and worked out his differences with the Nez Perces. He bartered for horses and moved overland to meet his cohorts at the junction of the Walla Walla and the Columbia Rivers. Soon after McKenzie arrived at the confluence, he learned that trouble had developed between Clarke and the Palouses.[27]

While McKenzie hastened away from the Nez Perces, John Clarke loaded thirty horses with furs and traveled south from the Spokane River across the heart of the Palouse Country, arriving at Palus on June 30, 1813. Clarke recovered his canoes at Palus and repaired them in preparation for the journey down the Snake and Columbia Rivers. While encamped there, Clarke took the opportunity to impress the Indians with two silver goblets which he carried in a delicate case. The trapper allowed the Indians to inspect the shiny vessels, even to touch one of them. Clarke ceremoniously poured a little wine into one of the goblets, telling a chief to take some spirits. When the headman had finished his drink, the trapper told him "that he was a greater man now than ever he was before."[28] When the fanfare ended, Clarke retired to his tent with his wine and precious goblets. The next morning he discovered that someone had stolen one of the silver goblets and that "the pearl of great price was gone!" The trapper made a thorough search of the camp, turning the village "topsy-turvy."

Clarke assembled the Palouses to tell them of the theft, and "declared if the property was returned, he would pardon the offender, but added, if it were not, and that should he find the thief, he would hang him." The trapper tried every means to retrieve his lost article, for "he coaxed, he flattered, he threatened to bring down his vengeance upon the whole tribe for the loss of his goblet, and, in his wrath and vexation, denounced death upon the offender." Two accounts have survived regarding the recovery of the goblet. Ross Cox, present at the time, stated that the trappers caught the thief on the night of May 31, making his escape in a canoe. Alexander Ross, who was not there but who heard about it soon after, stated that the Palouses met in council, made their own search, and recovered the goblet. The Palouse chief, according to Ross, stepped forward "and spreading out his robe, laid the precious vessel before him." It will never be known, and it matters little, which of these accounts is more accurate. The climax of the event was the same.[29]

Clarke had sworn that the thief would be hanged, and since "white men never break their word," he set out to execute the Palouse. The trappers quickly bound the arms and legs of the man while others devised a gallows from "the poles of his own lodge." The overbearing trapper, "like Herod of old, for the sake of his oath . . . instantly commanded the poor, unsuspecting wretch to be hung." According to Cox, the Palouses were not concerned about the man's fate, but Ross stated that the Palouses "could not believe that the whites were in earnest, till they beheld the lifeless body." Following the hanging, one of the headmen threw "his robe on the ground, a sign of displeasure, harangued his people, who immediately after mounted their fleetest horses, and scampered off in all directions to circulate the news and assemble the surrounding tribes, to take vengeance on the whites."[30]

Cox, an accomplice to the murder, exonerates Clarke, maintaining that the thief was to be "launched into eternity" and that the Palouse simply "acquiesced in this decision." The Indians "declared that the prisoner did not belong to their tribe, but was a kind of outlaw, of whom they were all afraid." Cox suggests that he did the Palouses a favor by executing the man who, so he said, belonged to another tribe. Yet the unfortunate man was definitely from Palus, for Ross stated that he had a permanent lodge in the village, the dwelling from which he was hanged. This was no trifling incident, as Cox led his readers to believe, for it provoked hostility with all the nearby tribes, marking the first recorded killing of an Indian by a white man in the inland Northwest. The incident had long-term effects. The Indians never forgot, and for many years reminded whites of the deed. For the whites, the Palouse hanging created a tense situation which endangered many lives.[31]

At the time of the hanging at Palus, various groups of Astorians rendezvoused where the Walla Walla flowed into the Columbia. When David Stuart and Alexander Ross arrived at the appointed spot, they "were at a loss to account for the unusual movement and stir among the Indians." The trappers had not yet learned of the hanging and could not understand why the Indians had assembled "from all quarters in great haste." McKenzie arrived at the rendezvous, unable to explain the hostile atmosphere. "The mystery was," Ross recorded, "soon cleared up when Mr. Clarke joined us, and related the affair of the silver goblet." The Astorians could not understand such a "reckless deed" and all of the fur hunters raised their "voice of disapprobation . . . against him." Palouse warriors spread their resentment far and wide, and Indians from the surrounding area gathered to challenge the whites.[32]

John Jacob Astor had once called Clarke, "the brightest star in the Columbian constellation," but the traders on the Walla Walla River believed that Clarke's star had fallen. They became increasingly alarmed as the Indians grew bolder in their demonstrations. The Palouses and others "kept flying to and fro, whooping and yelling in wild commotion." At one point Tummeatapam, a leader of the Walla Wallas and friend of the Astorians, rode in yelling, "What have you done, my friends?" The chief exclaimed: "You have spilt blood on our lands!" He pointed toward a large dust cloud, "There, my friends," said the exasperated chief, "do you see them?" Tummeatapam gave his warning, wheeled his horse, and galloped off "like a shot." The Astorians astutely took "the hint" and made ready to leave. Soon after, they canoed down the Columbia "with all haste from the inauspicious shore."[33]

Because of the War of 1812, the Astorians had previously decided to travel to the Great Plains. The hanging at Palus altered their plans, deciding instead to return to Astoria rather than risk their lives crossing the Plateau. The Astorians remained on the coast for a month before traveling to the Walla Walla River where they met Tummeatapam who "appeared much agitated, and sat for some time without uttering a single word."[34] The Palouses and others knew that the *suyapo* had returned. To illustrate the dangerous situation, Tummeatapam took a handful of sand and threw it into the air, explaining that the Indians were "as numerous as the grains of sand; the Indians have bad hearts." The Astorians remained, displaying their arsenal of "a brass four-pounder, some hand-grenades, and skyrockets." The trappers traveled north toward Quosispah where the Palouses and others waited, "mounted in numerous squadrons . . . flying backwards and forwards, seemingly bent on some great design." On the north bank of the Snake, the Indians assembled, to block the passage of the trappers. Ross stated that there "could not have been less than two thousand, with a fleet of one hundred and seventy-four canoes along the beach." The "imposing and formidable" force of Indians sang and danced in preparation for the impending battle.

The volatile situation was diffused, however, after a delegation of Indians met the *suyapo*. One of the trappers argued that the "peaceable behavior" of the Indians was due to "Tummeatapam's account of our big gun." In addition, the Palouses became "peaceable" after learning that the trappers would move up the Columbia rather than the Snake. Clarke planned to return to Spokane Country by way of the Snake and Palouse Rivers, passing through Palus, but the "demonstration of the Indians prevented Mr. Clarke from proceeding to his destination by the usual route." Clarke wisely remained with the other Astorians, traveling to Spokane House by way of the Okanogan Country.[35] The nature of Palouse culture insured that the incident remained a vivid memory for future generations, for oral tradition transferred the event. Older members of the tribe taught children the history of their people, relating religious stories and historic incidents again and again;

the youngsters in turn repeated the tales for their elderly instructors until they knew them in precise detail. Oral tradition, rather than written history, provided the means for relaying accurate representations of incidents such as the murder at Palus, an event that is remembered to this day.[36]

On October 16, 1813, the Astorians sold their interest in the Columbia trade to the North West Company. Some of the Astorians, including Ross Cox, joined the North West Company. As a Nor 'Wester Cox moved inland to the Walla Walla Country in late October 1813. He had received orders to take provisions and horses to Spokane House, and to this end he proceeded north, crossed the Snake River, and entered Palouse lands. He learned from the friendly Walla Wallas that the Palouses were still vengeful because of the hanging "and had declared their determination to have satisfaction for his death." Concerned about the news, Cox instructed his men to carry pistols and daggers in addition to their muskets. He traveled swiftly, but on the third day out from the Walla Walla Country, three Palouses spotted him. "They were mounted," Cox stated, "and, on perceiving us, stopped a few minutes in order to ascertain our numbers." Cox and his three companions had good reason to fear the Palouses.[37]

The Indians eyed Cox for some time before galloping off toward the Snake. "Being now of [the] opinion that their intentions were not friendly," Cox reported, "we increased our speed, and for upwards of three hours none of them made their appearance." Soon after "large clouds of dust in a south-westerly direction, which, on clearing away, displayed to our view between thirty and forty of the savages on horseback." The Palouses gave chase. Cox and his men spent the next two hours running for their lives. Some of the Palouses gave up, but about ten of them persisted, forcing the whites to dismount and make their stand. At this point the Indians ended the fight having made their point, warning the Nor'Wester's to stay out of the Palouse Country.[38]

The last group of Astorians left the Plateau in April of 1814, but the Nor'Westers inherited the ill will generated by the Palouse hanging. Trouble erupted in May 1814, when Alexander Ross and five companions traveled to the Yakima Country to buy horses, despite a warning from the Wenatchee Indians that the Palouses spoiled for revenge. The Salish-speaking Wenatchees had told the trappers that the Sahaptins would kill them, and when the Nor'Westers arrived in the valley, the hostile Indians greeted them. The Indian camp was huge, for the trappers "could see its beginning but not the end!" This "grand and imposing sight" included a six-mile camp containing "3,000 men, exclusive of women and children, and treble that number of horses." Palouses attended, reminding the others that "These are the men . . . who kill our relations, the people who have caused us to mourn."[39] The Indians detained the trappers but ultimately allowed them to leave unharmed.

Late in 1814, another clash occurred between the Palouses and the Nor'Westers. In November of that year, the Palouses intercepted a large party of trappers as they canoed up the Columbia. A number of Indians paddled out to meet the white men, and a fight ensued after the Indians, according to Cox, tried to take a few items out of the canoes. The Indians and trappers exchanged blows with their fists and clubbed each other with their canoe paddles. One of the Indians tried to take a bale of tobacco, but Finan McDonald struck the Indian with the butt of his gun. The warrior retaliated, fixing an arrow to his bow, but before he could fire, McDonald reached out breaking the arrow in two.[40]

Fighting continued. "The savage," recorded Ross, "ordered his canoe to push off, and was just in the act of letting fly another arrow, when M'Kay fired and hit him in the forehead." Two other Indians prepared to shoot their arrows, but the trappers shot them with a double barreled gun, killing one and wounding the other. "The moment they fell," Ross wrote, "a shower of arrows was discharged at us." The trappers escaped unscathed and headed for the shore to regroup. The Palouses did not attack, and the trappers relocated to an island, "the safest place to withstand an attack, or prevent a surprise." As the trappers paddled toward the island, the Palouses attacked, wounding two men with arrows. However, the Palouses and their allies held off their major attack, and the whites reached the island. The Nor'Westers dug foxholes and trenches in preparation for the fight, and they spent a gloomy November night on the island, composing their wills and preparing for death.[41]

The Indians waited and watched, making one feeble attack that night. The next morning, the trappers decided to leave the island but a storm prevented them from doing so. They anxiously waited another day before moving to the banks of the Columbia, where they hoped to "offer a certain quantity of goods to appease the relations of the deceased." The *suyapo* canoed to shore, met the Indians, and asked "to have a 'talk' with them on the late disagreeable affair." The trappers parleyed with the Palouses and other Sahaptins and handed out gifts of clothing, blankets, tobacco, and other items. The situation was tense at first, until a powerful war leader reminded the people that the whites provided guns to the people which helped prevent incursions by Shoshones. The leader asked the people to allow the trappers to pass unharmed, proclaiming that "no hostile foot shall again be set on our lands." This leader and his Palouse followers vowed to protect their lands and to prevent the unwanted incursions into their country by whites. From this time on the Palouses vowed to fight any whites who invaded their lands.[42]

The attack on the trappers in 1814 signaled the last act of aggression initiated by the Palouse Indians against the fur hunters. In 1816 Donald McKenzie returned to the Northwest in the employ of the North West Company, and the next year he visited the Upper Palouses to patch up his differences and to trade. He successfully established friendly relations with the Indians and likely told them of his plans to build a trading post on the Columbia, just south of its confluence with the Snake. McKenzie planned to construct his post near the lower Snake River on the southwestern parameters of Palouse Country.[43]

On July 11, 1818 McKenzie, Ross, and ninety-five men camped "on a level point upon the east bank of the Columbia, forming something like an island in the flood, and by means of a tributary stream, a peninsula at low water."[44] On this site, the North West Company hoped to construct a factory, calling it Fort Nez Perces and locating it between the mouths of the Walla Walla and Snake Rivers. The spot designated was land used by three different Sahaptin people—the Cayuses, Walla Wallas, and Palouses. Ross wrote that the site selected was "commanding" owing to "a spacious view of our noble stream in all its grandeur, resembling a lake rather than a height." To the east and north was an "expanse of boundless plain," and to the south "wild hills and rugged bluffs on either side of the water." Beside the river to the east were "two singular towering rocks similar in colour, shape and height called by the natives 'Twins.' "[45] The trappers planned to settle in, because they believed that "the country must be secured, the natives awed and reconciled, buildings made, furs collected, new territories added." The trappers considered this strategic site "the most hostile spot on the whole line of communication." It was here that the trappers had fought the Indians, and when the *suyapo* arrived to build their factory, the Indians withdrew from the Columbia and "Not a friendly hand stretched out; not the least joy, usual among Indians on such occasions, was testified to invite or welcome our arrival." The Indians were worried and asked themselves, "Are they going to kill more of our relations?"[46]

McKenzie and Ross dealt diplomatically with the Indians who "flocked about us in very suspicious numbers, often through curiosity to see our work." Some Palouses and others discouraged the traders from building their post, insisting that the white men pay for the timber they gathered. The Indians prohibited the whites from hunting and fishing and charged them "exorbitant" prices for horses, fish, and roots. In these ways the Indians conveyed their sentiments. The Nor'Westers had no desire to fight the Indians, so they identified the Indians who desired the trade, entertaining them with food, drink, and gifts. In this manner "the seeds of dissension were artfully sown among them [the Indians] to hold the balance equal and prevent their uniting against us." By dividing the tribes and creating factions within various groups, the white men successfully assured peace with the Indians.[47] Anxious as he was to leave Fort Nez Perces in search of beaver, McKenzie stayed at the post to meet an Indian war party returning from a victory over the Shoshones. Nearly five hundred warriors, among them Palouses, returned to celebrate with a victory dance. They met McKenzie and negotiated a peace agreement. With assurances from the Indians, McKenzie moved overland to the upper reaches of the Snake River, leaving Ross in charge of the post.[48]

In 1821 the North West Company merged with the Hudson's Bay Company, and McKenzie became the governor of the Red River region for Hudson's Bay Company. The company appointed George Simpson the new governor of the Columbia Department who wanted to maintain peace with the Palouses, Cayuses, Walla Wallas, and Nez Perces. As he stated in his journal, the Indians "identify us with their enemies the Snakes on account of our furnishing them with the Sinews of War." Simpson and his chief factor, John McLoughlin, set about to make the department efficient and economical.[49] To this end Simpson reduced the number of men at Fort Nez Perces and limited the operation of this post to one chief trader and eight men. In 1825 he proposed to move Fort Nez Perces, "The Gibralter [sic] of the Columbia." He felt that the post had "never been very productive, as the country in its neighbourhood is not rich, and the Natives who are a bold Warlike race do little else than rove about in search of Scalps, plunder and amusement."[50] The governor could not abandon the post, however, because the Palouses and their neighbors "from their numbers and daring character command the main communication." Furthermore, the Hudson's Bay Company depended on the Indians "for an annual supply of about 250 Horses, and finally, the Trade in Furs altho' falling off pays tolerably well."[51]

The Palouses enjoyed the trade goods they received from Fort Nez Perces, but they resented the post being located so close to their homelands. They remained fairly independent of the trading company, "requiring but few of our supplies," Simpson wrote, and did not use the post "until absolutely in need."[52] Nonetheless, the Palouses became tied to the trade and affected by it.[53] Ultimately, Dr. McLoughlin decided not to move Fort Nez Perces, for to have done so against the will of the Indians would have exposed the company and communication up and down the river to great danger and "would Greatly Injure the Whole of the Columbia Trade of the Interior." The trappers of the Hudson's Bay Company were not enamored by the Palouses, Indians they considered "capricious and treacherous." However, the site commanded the routes leading through the inland Northwest, and the Indians provided excellent horses. Fort Nez Perces was the "jumping off" place for Hudson's Bay trappers to the Rockies and the Great Basin, and for these reasons, the company did not close or relocate it.[54]

Like the other Sahaptins, the Palouse Indians crossed the Bitterroot Mountains to fight the Shoshones and hunt buffalo. In describing the Palouses, Cayuses, and Walla Wallas, Ross wrote that the "Indian tribes inhabiting the country about Fort Nez Perces often go to war on their southern neighbours, the Snakes: but do not follow war as a profession." The Palouses "likewise frequently go to the buffalo" where they lived by hunting the great beasts. The Palouses were "known from their roving propensities, their dress, cleanliness and independence." They were "rich in horses . . . expert hunters, good warriors." Indeed, the Palouses often traveled with the Nez Perces to the buffalo country, where they met American trappers.[55] In 1824 the Iroquois hunters of Hudson's Bay Company met Jedediah Smith west of the Teton Mountains in what was later called Pierre's Hole. Nez Perces and Palouses dealt with the first American they had met since the Astorians. The Americans had acquired equal rights with the British to work the region, and it appeared to both the Indians and the English that the Americans might make inroads into the Northwest trade.

Many of the Indians hoped for such development, especially after sharing with the Americans a wild, jovial, and exhilarating rendezvous on the Snake Plains of southern Idaho. They considered American mountain men different in behavior and attitude from the staid and stuffy British. Americans loved to race horses, gamble, tell jokes, and drink. The Indians became part of the rendezvous, and most welcomed trade with the Americans. This certainly was the case with bands of buffalo-hunting Palouses, who were included among the "Nez Perces." The Indians liked the Americans and through this contact, developed a positive image of them. Impressed with manufactured goods, the Indians believed such items were tied to the "power" or "medicine" of whites. Since all power came from the spirit world, the Indians reasoned that whites possessed special religious strengths. Some became interested in the nature of the white man's religion, and this curiosity, coupled with a positive view of Americans, led some Indians to invite Christian missionaries into the inland Northwest.[56]

CHAPTER 3

THE SPIRIT AND THE FAITH

*They seemed more like demons from the
bottomless pit than human beings.*
— Asa Smith

During the first three decades of the nineteenth century, American and British explorers and trappers laid claim to the Northwest, kindling numerous cultural changes among the tribes. Bit by bit, the social, political, and economic life of the Palouses and their neighbors were inexorably altered. Perhaps the most basic result of contact was a change in the religious beliefs of many Indians, especially after the arrival of Christian missionaries. The missionaries had two distinct effects on the Indian communities. First, Christianity split tribes into factions — Christian versus non-Christian, Catholic versus Protestant. Second, it pushed many Indians toward a revival of old traditions and religious beliefs. The Palouses took the latter path. The members of the various Palouse bands were not attracted to Christianity during the nineteenth century and instead turned for solace to the traditional teachings of their elders and religious leaders.[1]

Despite the fact that trappers had not entered the Northwest to proselytize, some of their number hoped to advance the Indians along the road of white "civilization," Christianity, and formal education. In an attempt to further the process, George Simpson selected two boys to be educated and Christianized at the Canadian mission school on the Red River. The sons of prominent Spokane and Flathead chiefs, Nicholas Garry and J. H. Pelly, spent four years at the mission school before returning to their people in 1829 to spread the gospel. Within their own communities, these boys created a stir when they read from the Bible in English and preached in their native languages. Word of these boys and their new-found spirit power spread to the Palouses. The young preachers did not influence the Palouses immediately, but many shared an interest in learning something of the white man's "book" of knowledge. The words of Garry and Pelly titillated the interest of many Indians, and as a result, the Nez Perces and Flatheads sent delegations to Missouri to inquire about the new religion.[2]

In the company of Lucien Fontenelle and Andrew Drips of the American Fur Company, the Nez Perces and Flatheads traveled to St. Louis where they met Superintendent of Indian Affairs William Clark. The famous explorer introduced the Indians to Bishop Joseph Rosati. The Catholics had a long tradition of missionizing peoples throughout the world, but they were not the first denomination to send missionaries to the Columbia Plateau. Instead, the Protestants led the northwestern endeavor, largely due to the efforts of a Wyandot chief from Ohio. In 1831 William Walker visited St. Louis on unhappy business, to locate a suitable site for his people who Americans planned to remove from Ohio. Chief Walker, a devout Methodist, wrote to G. P. Disoway, a Christian friend, about the Nez Perce delegation. Disoway composed a romantic essay in the *Christian Advocate and Journal and Zion's Herald* about the "wandering sons of our native forests." He appealed for missionaries to save the Indians of the Great Columbia Plain—"inquirers after the truth." Disoway's zealous appeal bore fruit, as three missionaries answered the call almost immediately.[3]

Jason Lee, a tall, well-built, determined man first responded to the challenge presented in the *Christian Advocate*. But after a brief introduction into Indian life, Lee turned to other pursuits. Two other missionaries, Samuel Parker and Marcus Whitman, followed Lee in 1835, meeting their first Plateau Indians at the annual rendezvous of fur trappers. At the confluence of the New Fork and Green Rivers, the missionaries met Palouses attending the yearly gathering. Whitman and Parker advanced their missionary endeavor. Whitman returned to the East to plan and organize the northwestern missions, while Parker traveled to the Plateau to locate suitable mission sites. In the company of Jim Bridger and a band of Nez Perces, Parker journeyed to the inland Northwest by way of a rugged route known as the Nez Perce Trail. He nearly died on the trail, but he survived to reach the Hudson's Bay post of Fort Vancouver. Parker traveled throughout the inland Northwest, compiling several descriptive notes on the Indians and their land, but he sailed for home in June, 1836, before Whitman and his party entered the Pacific Northwest.[4]

While Parker explored, Whitman assembled a party of missionaries, consisting of Narcissa Prentiss Whitman, Henry Harmon Spalding, Eliza Hart Spalding, and William H. Gray. During the summer of 1836, they traveled across the plains and mountains in the company of Thomas Fitzpatrick. They reached South Pass on Independence Day, and not long afterwards, a band of riotous Indians and trappers greeted the missionaries. The Whitmans and Spaldings attended the rendezvous before continuing their journey in the company of John McLeod, a Hudson's Bay employee, and a small band of buffalo-hunting Nez Perces, including Kentuck and Lawyer. The missionaries journeyed through the hard and rocky basalt country of southern Idaho, across the rough, broken hills of the upper Snake River region, over the Blue Mountains in eastern Oregon, and finally into the Walla Walla Valley. While the Spaldings struggled to keep up, McLeod, Gray, and the Whitmans advanced to Fort Walla Walla [formerly Fort Nez Perces] where they received a hearty welcome from Pierre C. Pambrun, the factor of the Hudson's Bay post. In early September 1836, after the Spaldings had reached the Walla Walla Valley, the party traveled down the Columbia River to Fort Vancouver where they learned from Dr. John McLoughlin that Parker had departed for Hawaii the previous June. The missionaries were extremely disappointed to learn that Parker had left the Northwest without providing them with his notes.

Undaunted, Whitman and Spalding returned to the inland Northwest to establish their missions. Whitman selected a spot twenty-two miles up the Walla Walla River from the Columbia in Cayuse Country, known to the Indians as Waiilatpu, "the place of rye grass." Spalding chose a site on the Clearwater River called Lapwai, "the place of butterflies" located twelve miles above its confluence with the Snake in the Nez Perce Territory. Thus began the Protestant missionary endeavors among the Sahaptin tribes. During their early years in the Northwest, the missionaries contemplated erecting a church among the Palouses but none was ever built. Still, the Palouse bands lived close to Waiilatpu and Lapwai and had frequent contacts—joint religious, social, hunting, and war affairs—with both the Cayuses and Nez Perces. They were well apprised of the missionary systems operating on the Columbia Plateau.[5]

The Whitmans, Spaldings, and other missionaries who followed them were devout Christians who believed they were doing God's work. They sought to bring Christianity to the Indians, but the social and cultural heritage of the Indians impeded their efforts. Many whites considered Indian culture backward, indeed, savage, and the missionaries worked to destroy those elements of Indian society which they considered to be primitive, replacing them with the Christian, white culture of nineteenth century America. The Indians did not understand these goals, and in 1836 the Cayuses and Nez Perces fought with each other over the honor to host these new holy men. Most of the Indians received Whitman and Spalding with deference, according the whites the same respect they gave their own religious leaders.[6]

Within Indian communities, religious leaders—men and women alike—were powerful individuals. Today such people are called Indian doctors, medicine men and women, or shamans. Known for their spirit power, their psychic abilities, and their physiological and psychological knowledge, the Indians believe they derived their power from God. During the nineteenth century Indians interested in acquiring the white man's spirit power gravitated to the missionaries. Moreover, new and serious illnesses spread among the Indians, but the whites were largely untouched by epidemics that ravaged the Indian communities. To the Palouses and their neighbors, the white men possessed desirable powers. Thus, many Indians were drawn to Christianity, while others, like the Palouses, shunned the missionaries. None of them had a clue as to the actual workings of a mission system or the ultimate missionary goals.[7]

The religious beliefs of the Palouses and their manner of worship were markedly different from those of white men. The Palouses believed that God had created all things—the earth, stars, animals, and plants. The Creator had made the earth for use by all, providing the means of survival. The Palouses often thanked God for the roots, fish, game, and berries, and because the earth provided them with so much food, they did not cultivate the earth. The Indians held religious ceremonies in thanksgiving of their Creator, and they revered the earth and its bounty. Before the arrival of whites, they shared common spiritual beliefs and ceremonies with their neighbors. However, their faith was not formalized or organized until the late 1850s, when the pressures of white expansion stimulated a renaissance of native religion and the creation of formal worship. Religious leaders living within the Palouse communities, were affected by the spiritual change.[8]

Palouse spiritual leaders, like those throughout the Plateau, were influenced by the religious experiences of a Wanapum Indian *yantcha,* or religious leader, named Smohalla (teacher). Born at the village of Wallula, located on the Columbia River not far from the Palouse village of Quosispah, Smohalla shared a common heritage with his Palouse neighbors. Smohalla had numerous followers among the Palouses who were attracted to his teachings, ceremonies, and songs. The Wanapum Prophet did not fit the white man's image of a great leader, for he was considered "to be a rather under-sized Indian with a form inclining toward obesity." Added to this, the "peculiar" holy man was born with a hunchback and a large, oversized head. But what he lacked in appearance, he made up for with his ability as an orator who could hold his listeners "spellbound" with his "magic manner." Smohalla had the ability to predict the future, foretelling the coming of storms, the run of the salmon, and the eruption of volcanoes. Today, Smohalla would be considered a psychic, but to the people of his time, he was a famous and powerful spiritual leader who derived his power directly from the Creator.[9]

Many Palouses followed Smohalla's teaching, because they believed that he had undergone two afterlife experiences. Over the years, Smohalla had become depressed about the polarization of the Indian communities between the "progressives," who became more white-like, and the "traditionalists," who doggedly adhered to the religious beliefs of their forefathers. According to Smohalla's nephew, Puck Hiyah Toot, the *yantcha* died, traveled to the "land in the sky," and conversed with God. Not permitted to enter eternal life, *Nami Piap* (God) told Smohalla to return to his people and tell them to reject white culture and return to the Indian social, economic, political, and religious traditions. When the Lower Palouses learned of Smohalla's experience and his apparent return from the "land in the sky," they gravitated to the spiritual leader and his conservative message. Smohalla's following among the Palouses grew dramatically after the holy man had a second afterlife experience. On this journey to the "land in the sky," Smohalla visited the Creator, learning a special *washat* or dance and over 120 religious songs to add to the old Washani repertoire. The Palouses performed the dance and the songs, conducting the washat ceremony in the manner prescribed by God.[10]

In accordance with Smohalla's doctrines, Palouses performed the *washat* using seven *kookoolots,* or drums, seven singers, and several *qualal qualal,* or brass bells. The women and men used eagle and swan feathers to symbolize flight from earth to heaven, and wherever the ceremony was held, the Palouses flew a triangular flag displaying a five-pointed star and a red circle with a white, yellow, and blue background. Smohalla had taken traditional religious beliefs of the Palouses and others and formalized the old Washani faith. Since the Prophet had received his message directly from God, his teaching had a powerful effect on the Indian communities, particularly among the conservative, non-Christian Palouses.

The Palouses embraced the doctrines of Smohalla without significantly altering their old belief systems. Smohalla's *washat,* songs, and ceremony were more a return to traditionalism than a break from the old ways. Many Palouse followers of Smohalla's teachings were militant in their religious fervor, but only a few ever advocated violence or the extirpation of whites. Thus, unlike the teachings of Tenskwatawa, the Shawnee Prophet, Smohalla's doctrines were non-violent; but the Wanapum Prophet did demand a rejection of the white work ethic, the reservation system, and American Indian policies. During the mid-nineteenth century, when Christianity first came to the Indians of the Columbia Plateau, the Palouses turned their backs on the new religion, steadfastly embracing the old Washani faith and the innovations introduced by Smohalla.[11]

The Palouses sometimes visited Lapwai and Waiilatpu and, perhaps, attended religious services. However, the missionaries never baptized any Palouses. From the white perspective, Spalding and Whitman offered to uplift their red brothers from the depths of savagery and barbarism. The Indians would then be able to follow a new life, guiding them into eternal life with Christ. From their perspective, the Palouses watched the destructive work of the missionaries, as factions emerged in Indian communities and infectious diseases spread among many tribes. Coinciding with the establishment of missions came a flood of white emigrants along the Oregon Trail. Opened in the fall of 1840 by Joe Meek, William Craig, Robert Newell, John Larison, Caleb Wilkins, and other former trappers with their families, the trail provided a wagon route into the Northwest over the Blue Mountains to the Willamette Valley. With their arrival, a new era emerged, one which brought violence to the doorstep of the Palouses.[12]

Between 1836 and 1847, Whitman and Spalding diligently worked at their missions. Spalding was more successful than Whitman in dealing with the Indians, although his treatment of many Nez Perces was harsh, drawing the condemnation of his white contemporaries. The Cayuses did not tolerate Marcus and Narcissa Whitman who were never able to establish a working relationship with the Indians of the Walla Walla Valley. When Whitman failed to attract Indians to his cause, the missionary turned his attentions to promoting white emigration and the economic development of the Northwest. He invited emigrants from the Oregon Trail to visit his mission and in 1843 guided a wagon train across the Blue Mountains to the Grande Ronde River. The Palouses and their neighbors were concerned about Whitman's activities and alarmed that the Indians of the Willamette Valley had been ravaged by horrible illnesses. Some feared that Whitman was inviting similar problems onto the Plateau. As the years passed tensions and ill-feelings grew to such a pitch that conflict was unavoidable. Indians living near the missions and the Oregon Trail were drawn into conflicts, but others, including the Palouses, also became involved in the violence.[13]

By the winter of 1846-1847, hostility among the Indians toward whites became widespread. At Lapwai the Nez Perces became more outspoken, ordering the Spaldings to stay out of their affairs and to leave. To demonstrate their contempt for the missionary, the Nez Perces destroyed Spalding's fences, the mill dam, and the windows in his meeting house. Not realizing the degree of Nez Perce resentment, the missionary stepped out one night ordering the Indians to stop singing and dancing. Some of the Nez Perces grabbed him, and one wrestled him to the ground. Extremely upset, Spalding wept but refused to heed the warning. At Lapwai the non-Christian Nez Perces, labelled "heathens" by the missionaries, assumed power as the number of Christian Indians declined.

Whitman's situation was no better. Several Cayuses and Walla Wallas had grown to hate Whitman and his wife. The Indians blamed Whitman, rightfully or not, for their troubles, particularly problems resulting from the migration of thousands of whites through the Cayuse Country. The white immigrants, the Indians argued, depleted the game and destroyed their grazing lands. Small war parties, consisting of Cayuses, Walla Wallas, and some Palouses, attacked a few wagon trains in the summer of 1847. Conflict intensified when Indians attacked the emigrants with increasing regularity, plundering slow-moving wagons and killing a few settlers. The Cayuses and their allies struck at the whites, hoping to scare them and to turn them away. Their effort failed.[14]

There was good reason to fear white men, for whites brought deadly ill-nesses. Disease, the scourge of Indians since Columbus, caused a crisis in 1847. The white man's diseases, "more terrible than any Black Death known to Europe's history," were not new to the Palouses, for they had known of diseases for years. However, they knew little about the causes of the dread-ed epidemics. As early as 1782, smallpox had spread from the coast up the Columbia River system. Fevers of many types and with numerous symptoms, had spread among the northwestern Indians, especially in 1831. Smallpox struck in 1835 and again in 1846. In 1847 whites brought measles to the in-land Northwest. Although American immigrants contracted measles, they rarely died of it. The Palouses and their neighbors perished in large numbers, because they lacked natural immunities. In addition to measles, fever and dysentery spread through the inland Northwest, and Indians blamed the whites for their maladies.[15]

Mixed-blood Indians, embittered by the treatment accorded them by whites, seem to have been especially active in circulating rumors that whites were poisoning the Indians. Whitman tried to help the Indians by giving them medicine, but his efforts failed. Indians died in alarming numbers. The Cayuse, living so close to Whitman's mission, were especially hard hit. Many Palouses believed that Whitman had maliciously murdered the Cayuses with his poison, and one "old Palouse Indian," reported "that at the time Dr. Whit-man used to administer medicine to sick Indians, all who took his medicine died. There was one volunteer, an oldish man who was not healthy and knew he wasn't going to live but two or three years, [who] told other Indians that he was going to take Dr. Whitman's medicine to find out if it contained poison." When Whitman visited the elder, as was customary for the doctor, the Indian took the medicine. He died the next day, leading his friends and relatives to believe that Whitman had poisoned him.

Measles, like other diseases, was an indiscriminate killer of men, women, and children, and the Indians were outraged by the deaths of their loved ones.[16] The Palouses considered Whitman a "medicine man," endowed "with supernatural powers for working them harm, besides it was known to them that he was using poison against the wolves." The Palouses knew that in 1837 American traders on the upper Missouri River had spread smallpox among the Blackfeet, and they believed Whitman had done the same thing with measles. It is impossible to measure the number of Palouses who died from measles in 1847, but a Palouse Indian reported that the disease decimated at least one Palouse village along the Snake. The long-term effects of measles were tragic enough for the Palouses to remember the devastation in their oral traditions. Like the Palouses, the Cayuses were outraged by the epidemic, and on November 29, 1847 a few Cayuses took matters into their own hands, precipitating the Whitman murders.[17]

The Whitmans received many warnings that their lives were in danger. Word spread among the Cayuses and others that some Cayuses had plotted to kill them, and the Whitmans heard the rumors. But they remained at Waiilatpu with seventy-two other people. On a cold November day, in an atmosphere charged with doom, Tilokaikt, who owned the land on which the mission stood, entered the Whitman home to ask for medicine. While Whitman's back was turned, another Cayuse named Tomahas struck

Whitman in the head with a tomahawk. The attack began, and once it was under way, the uprising became a brutal bloodletting that continued off and on for several days. The Cayuses killed Marcus and Narcissa along with eleven other whites. Three other people died of illnesses, because they went unattended, including Helen Mar, the daughter of Joe Meek. The Indians burned and plundered the mission, then set out to kill Spalding who had been visiting nearby. Spalding reached Lapwai where William Craig, a former mountain man who had long opposed Spalding, saved the preacher's life.[18]

When word of the Whitman murders reached the Willamette Valley, the cry went out to raise and equip an army to punish the Indians. Hudson's Bay traders, fearful that the Americans would incite a general Indian war on the Upper Columbia River, interceded and cooled the situation. Peter Skene Ogden, a seasoned trapper who understood the Indians, traveled to Fort Walla Walla where he worked to free the hostages from the Whitman mission. Catholic missionaries on the Umatilla River aided Ogden who successfully ransomed the hostages, including Spalding's daughter. On January 2, 1848, Ogden left Fort Walla Walla with the Spaldings and the captives, and in due course safely reached the Willamette Valley. Some Cayuses, particularly the younger men, remained hostile and tried to draw other tribes into a confederacy. The Palouses refused to join the Cayuses in a war against the whites, instead remaining neutral just as Kamiakin chose to do among his Yakima band. The Nez Perces split and could not decide on a unified path; the Spokanes also declined to join the confederacy. Even most Cayuses do not seem to have supported the attackers, for only a few Cayuses had acted independently of the others. The white population perceived a great danger in the Whitman attack, and they would not allow the killings to go unanswered.[19]

While Ogden attempted to defuse the explosive situation, whites in the Willamette organized a volunteer army bent on avenging the Whitman deaths. Led by Major Henry Lee, a former teacher at the Lapwai mission and member of the famous Lee family of Virginia, the army joined a force commanded by Colonel Cornelius Gilliam, a veteran of two prior Indian wars, the Black Hawk War and the Seminole War. An avowed Indian hater who believed that all Indians should be exterminated, Gilliam was a bigoted Baptist minister who had helped chase the Mormons from Missouri. He believed that Catholics had conspired to incite the Cayuses, and he had no interest in cooling the situation. Gilliam deliberately tried to foil attempts by a peace commission authorized by the provisional government of Oregon. The commission consisted of a three-member party composed of Joel Palmer, the newly-appointed Superintendent of Indian affairs, Henry Lee, and Robert Newell. The commissioners were instructed to assure the Indians that Gilliam's troops would leave the region as soon as the Cayuses surrendered the murderers. The three men were to tell the Indians that the Americans wanted only to punish those Cayuses responsible for the killings and not all Indians.

The whites drew the Palouses into the controversy after the peace commission failed in its intended mission. The peace commission met with Gilliam at The Dalles, where the commissioners asked the colonel for a small escort to accompany them to the Walla Walla River where they hoped to negotiate a settlement. Uninterested in peace, Gilliam refused the request, saying he had come to fight the Indians, not to talk. This refusal was an unfortunate turn of events for whites and Indians alike, for it added fuel to the growing fire of hatred between the conflicting parties. Most of the Indian tribes had turned their backs on the hostile Cayuses, and most would have preferred peace. Moreover, some of the racial tensions that developed in years to come might have been avoided. But Gilliam became impatient with the peace commission and too eager to engage the Indians. His callous approach increased racial hatred and brought conflict to the Palouse Indians.[20]

By February 10, 1848, when the peace commission first met Gilliam, the Oregon volunteers had already fought a few skirmishes with Indians. More fighting occurred as the troops moved up the Columbia River on their way to Waiilatpu. Approximately three hundred warriors and one hundred women and children met the Americans south of the Walla Walla River. Palouses living with or near Cayuses may have fought alongside the Cayuses who engaged the whites in an indecisive battle which lasted several hours. The warriors rode to and fro shouting and shooting, while the whites charged and regrouped. Despite the Indian attempts to force the Americans to retreat, Gilliam's men pushed forward toward Waiilatpu, arriving at the burned mission on March 2. The mutilated bodies of those slain had been dug up by wolves, and soldiers were nauseated by the gruesome scene. Gilliam and his men reburied the mutilated corpses. When the colonel left Waiilatpu, he was more determined than ever to punish the Indians. Gilliam tried to prevent the peace commissioners from negotiating a settlement with the Nez Perces who had traveled to Waiilatpu to parley. The commissioners held their council, securing a peace with the powerful Nez Perces. No known Palouses attended the council, and except for a few younger men, most remained neutral.

Gilliam remained "altogether against" a peaceful solution to the Cayuse question. In fact, during the negotiations with the friendly Nez Perces, "Col. Gilliam left the council in a huff, and declared he has come to fight and fight he will."[21] According to one account of Gilliam's attitude, "All this talk was an irritation" and he ruined an opportunity to negotiate a settlement. Gilliam pressed his position to such a degree that after dealing with the Nez Perces, the peace commission withdrew. Gilliam, the impatient warrior, had his way, ordering his men to march north toward the Palouse Country. He and his volunteers headed toward the Tucannon River, hoping to surprise their enemy. Along the way they met three Indians riding to Waiilatpu to council for peace and to return some horses belonging to the army. The soldiers learned that Taiutau, or Young Chief as he was called, had separated himself from the other Cayuses and that his band desired peace. They also received word that two of the Whitman murderers, Tamsucky and Tilokaikt, had fled across the Snake River. Apparently Tamsucky rode into the Palouse or Nez Perce Country, having crossed the Snake at Red Wolf's Crossing. However, Tilokaikt and a large group of Cayuses had traveled down the Tucannon River, reportedly planning to cross the Snake River near Palus and seek sanctuary with the Palouse Chief Hasilsuiates. Gilliam set out immediately to intercept and engage the Cayuses.[22]

Gilliam believed that the Cayuses were making their escape into Palouse Country. He forced his men to march throughout the night in order to catch the illusive Indians. By dawn the troops neared the mouth of the Tucannon River where they found a village of tipis. This was a camp shared by Walla Wallas and Palouses, both of whom had moved onto the Plateau to dig spring roots. When Gilliam rode within four hundred yards of the camp, an elderly Indian approached the soldiers "with one hand on his head and the other on his heart." The Indian man told Gilliam that the camp belonged to Peopeo Moxmox (known to the soldiers as Yellow Serpent, but literally translated as Yellow Bird). The tribal elder assured the Americans that the people were friendly and that they meant the soldiers no harm. Gilliam entered the village, despite the reassurances, and the Indians left. Gilliam found only a few warriors milling around the tipis, men who were "painted and armed, but who appeared friendly." According to one account, the elderly Indian pointed to a herd of cattle and horses grazing on a nearby hillside and said that the animals had been left there by Tilokaikt. No evidence exists to support this assertion, and it is probable that the story was fabricated to excuse the soldiers for their actions.[23]

Gilliam ordered his soldiers to round up the stock then grazing on the steep slopes of the canyon walls. The whites set out to drive the animals off the hills and into the valley of the Tucannon River. But after riding a short distance up the slopes, they saw Indians moving most of the stock across the Snake River. Gilliam, who was continually distrustful of the Indians, believed that he had been deceived and that the Cayuses were slipping out of his grasp. Instead of pursuing the Indians, he ordered his men to collect the horses and cattle, about five hundred in number, and drive them to the Touchet River. The horses belonged to Palouses, and they protested the theft. Gilliam ignored the Palouses, pushing them aside. The Palouses reacted swiftly, responding in a defensive manner and attacking the soldiers.[24]

Before Gilliam drove the herd far, the Palouses attacked him. Four hundred Palouse Indians raced off the hills and caught the seasoned Indian fighter totally by surprise. The warriors were experienced, thanks to their fights against the Blackfeet and Shoshones. They struck at the rear of Gilliam's troops and nipped at their flanks in a running battle that ensued throughout the day. The Indians continually fired into the company of confused volunteers, and at dusk the soldiers set up a camp where the men spent "a wretched night" without food or fire. The Palouses kept up intermittent firing throughout the night, harassing the colonel to such an extent that he ordered his men to release the stock he had stolen. Not satisfied with this gesture, the Indians continued to strike. The soldiers received no relief the next day, as "the Indians swarmed about their heels and hung upon their flanks." The running battle continued into the second day in the same manner as it had the day before. The soldiers hurried forward, hoping to cross the Touchet River before the Indians could cut off their retreat, but the Palouses, well aware of Gilliam's intentions, dashed forward to secure the crossing before the soldiers arrived.

In the bottom lands of the Touchet River, thick with brush and trees, the Oregon volunteers and the Palouse warriors fought a spirited skirmish. For an hour, two hundred and fifty Palouses fired at the fleeing troops, as they watched Gilliam's men cross the Touchet. The younger men, eager to prove themselves, wanted to pursue the white men, but the older men, leaders experienced from warfare on the Plains, gave up the fight. Such was the nature of Plateau Indian warfare. They had had their day and had drawn blood. With the army fleeing from their lands, the warriors, accompanied by one hundred and fifty women who had ridden with the fighting men, returned to their tipis. Four Indians, the white men reported, had been killed and fourteen injured, while the soldiers suffered ten wounded. For the first time the white men had invaded the Palouse Country in a military fashion, and the soldiers had been soundly defeated. The victory, so it seemed in March of 1848, belonged to the Palouses, but the battle along the Tucannon and Touchet Rivers had grave consequences for the Indians. Whites would not soon forget that the Palouses had fought and defeated the Oregon volunteers, an embarrassment to American military prowess. Justifiably or not, the white men would remember the Palouses as the only tribe that had fought as an ally of the Cayuses, murderers of the Whitmans. Whites branded the Palouses renegades and outlaws, enemies of all Americans.[25]

On March 16, Gilliam and his defeated troops arrived back at Fort Waters, a military post the colonel had established at Waiilatpu. Four days later Gilliam set out for The Dalles to resupply his bedraggled troops, but on the first night out, the colonel accidentally shot and killed himself. While pulling a rope from a wagon, the rope caught the trigger of a loaded gun, discharging and killing Colonel Gilliam instantly. His body was taken to The Dalles, and his command was given to Colonel James Waters. The new leader of the Oregon volunteers prepared for another campaign against the Cayuses. Waters believed that Gilliam had stirred up a full-scale war with all the interior tribes, for he had seen Gilliam at work with his reckless, unprovoked attack on the Palouses and Walla Wallas. Anxious to find and punish the guilty Cayuses, Waters regrouped his four hundred soldiers at Waiilatpu and set out for the Nez Perce Country. Waters divided his troops, sending Lee and 121 men to Red Wolf's Crossing. He took the remainder of the soldiers to the confluence of the Palouse and Snake Rivers. Neither group found the Cayuses, and Water's campaign, like that of Gilliam, only created more suspicions and animosities. When an Indian protested the theft of his cattle, the soldiers gunned him down.[26]

The volunteer soldiers never succeeded in locating the Cayuses accused of the Whitman killings, but the Cayuses themselves, with the encouragement of some Nez Perces, secured five men, handing them over to the whites. The Indians included Tilokaikt, Tomahas, Kiamasumpkin, Isiachalakis, and Klokamas. The Americans took these men to Oregon City where the citizens tried and sentenced them to death. On June 3, 1850, the five Cayuses were hanged, dying at the hands of their enemies because of the stance they had taken. The other Cayuses wandered on the Plateau and in the mountains, choosing to live with other tribes rather than return to their homes. A few gradually moved back to their homelands.[27]

The Cayuse War ended during an era of great change for the Palouses, particularly in the realm of political matters outside their control. In 1846 the United States secured its claim on the Pacific Northwest and would soon take official control of the region south of the 49th parallel. In fact, the United States sent its first agent to the northwestern Indians as early as September 1842. Dr. Elijah White was appointed subagent of the Indians of Oregon. The Palouses never "officially" met White, but they learned that the Americans planned to dictate Indian policy. Yet, the Palouses did not feel the full weight of American Indian policy until 1853 when the United States appointed the first governor to the Washington Territory. For Palouse Indians born in 1800, many drastic changes had occurred within their own lifetime. But what occurred after those individuals reached their fiftieth birthdays was much more radical. For the Palouses, the world turned upside down during the decade of the 1850s.

CHAPTER 4

PRELUDE TO WAR

I confidently expect to accomplish the whole business,
extinguishing the Indian title to every acre of land.
—Isaac I. Stevens

On March 2, 1853 President Millard Fillmore split the Territory of Oregon, creating the Territory of Washington. Following the March inauguration of Franklin Pierce, the new president appointed Isaac Ingalls Stevens the first governor of Washington Territory. By the mid-nineteenth century, the United States was experienced in dealing with new territories and Indians inhabiting those regions. Policies followed by the United States in the New Northwest were in keeping with those which had evolved for more than half a century in the eastern portion of the country, including liquidation of Indian land title, drafting Indian treaties, and the removal and concentration of Indian people onto prescribed lands. American Indian policy was designed for the benefit of whites, not Indians, and was carried out by determined agents far more concerned with their professional duty and the destiny of their nation than they were with Indians. These policies were generally executed by governmental representatives selected more for their political loyalties than their experience in Indian matters. This included the newly-appointed governor of Washington Territory.

Isaac Stevens was only thirty-five at the time of his appointment but was well qualified for the post. A loyal Democrat, a graduate of West Point, and a veteran of the Mexican War, Stevens was a hard-driving, ambitious young man who believed in Manifest Destiny and the superiority of American civilization. In addition to his selection as governor, Stevens campaigned for and won appointment as the head of the Pacific Railroad Survey. The Secretary of War assigned him the task of finding a feasible northern transcontinental route running from St. Paul, Minnesota, to Puget Sound. Stevens had received valuable experience as a member of the United States Coast Survey and in the Army's Corps of Engineers. He was qualified as governor and surveyor but not for the third position he assumed, that of Superintendent of Indian Affairs for the Washington Territory. Stevens was a trained military man who knew nothing about Indians except what he had heard in lectures or read in books. However, in keeping with the political traditions of the Indian Bureau, Stevens—a loyal Democrat, and territorial governor—received the appointment to handle Indian affairs in the newly-created territory.[2]

The Palouses witnessed many changes in their homeland and knew of others during this period. They learned, for example, of the California Gold Rush, the onslaught of white immigration to the Pacific Coast, and the flood

of whites to the Far West.[3] The white population in the Northwest expanded,
and like spokes from a hub, they radiated out in all directions in search of
new lands and opportunities. This movement of whites into new areas was
facilitated by the Donation Land Law of 1850 which granted half a section,
320 acres, to every white male (or half-blood) over eighteen years old. If the
male citizens of Oregon married before December 1, 1851, a man and his
wife could claim another 320 acres, provided that they "occupy or cultivate"
it. The Palouse Indians may have been unfamiliar with the details of the
Donation Land Law, but they felt its effects. In increasing numbers, white
settlers moved out of the Willamette Valley and into the wooded regions north
of the Columbia River. In 1849 approximately three hundred whites lived
north of the Columbia; a year later, over one thousand lived there. By 1853,
the year Washington became a territory, an estimated four thousand whites
inhabited Washington between the Columbia and Puget Sound.[4]

The Palouse knew something of white men through their assocation with
the railroad survey parties. In June of 1853, while Stevens and the major
segment of the Northern Pacific Survey made its way west across the Great
Plains from St. Paul, Minnesota, Captain George B. McClellan, the future
commander of the Army of the Potomac, surveyed eastward from Fort Vancouver across the Cascades to the Great Columbia Plain. The Palouses knew
of McClellan's movements near their homelands, and some believed that the
white men planned a full-scale war against them. The soldiers under
McClellan, who had arrived at Fort Vancouver in June 1853 with sixty-five
men to survey possible passes through the Cascade Mountains, had no such
intentions. Included in the party were George Gibbs, a geologist and
ethnologist, who compiled the first survey of the Indians of the interior, and
Dr. J. G. Cooper, a surgeon and a naturalist who commented extensively
about the effects of disease on the tribes. McClellan was embarrassed about
the large number of men with him and wrote Stevens explaining that the
reason he did so was to counter "the disposition of the Indians among whom
we were able to travel." McClellan and his men moved up the Columbia,
but because of the high waters, they changed their route, moving in "a direct
trail" from Fort Vancouver to Mt. St. Helens. The party marched into the
rugged Cascades but moved farther north toward Mt. Rainier before swing-
ing his party east over the mountains into the Yakima Valley.[5]

As the soldiers moved out of the thick forests of the Cascades, a scenic
panorama of bunchgrass and sagebrush greeted them. McClellan marched
through the Simcoe Valley, reaching Ahtanum Creek on August 17, camping less than a mile above the Catholic mission of St. Joseph. Before the
troops had arrived, rumors spread quickly among the interior Indians who
speculated that the soldiers intended to take Indian lands forcefully and
remove them to a far-off land. According to Father Durieu a Ricard, stories
circulated that the Palouses and others would "be banished to the Arctic,
i.e to a land where the sun never shines, where eternal night reigns." Such
a tale was not too far-fetched for the Indians to believe, because they knew
that the whites had overrun the Indians in the eastern states, the Willamette
Valley, and north of the Columbia River. Many believed that white men
would push them onto "a corner of land" where they would be hemmed in
by an enclosure." Some of the holy men and women had foretold a time when
the *suyapo* would force every Indian to a specific area. To some, it seemed
that time was at hand. The Indians were suspicious of McClellan's large force,

heavily armed but professing peace. The last large body of Americans had arrived during the Cayuse War, and the Indians remembered well the trouble they had brought.[6]

Since then, the Indians had become increasingly alarmed at the number of whites moving into the Northwest via the Oregon Trail, and they became more concerned in the summer of 1853 when they learned of "a party of citizens . . . engaged in cutting a road through the Nahches [Naches] Pass." The new road ran through the Yakima Valley, across the Cascade Mountains along an old Indian trail to Puget Sound. These activities worried the Palouses who approached Kamiakin at his home near St. Joseph Mission.[7] Kamiakin was a respected Yakima leader, but because he was a half-blood Palouse, members of that tribe as well looked to him for guidance. Kamiakin distrusted whites. Even before McClellan arrived, the chief had sent his younger brother, Skloom, into the Cascades to "learn of their intended movements and purposes." For the first time, the Indians heard that the white men "wished to buy their lands and open them up for white settlement."

Through Kamiakin, the Palouses first learned of McClellan's intentions. Many looked to him for advice because of his influence among the tribes and because of his diverse and complex family ties. He was related to the Palouse, Nez Perce, and Spokane Indians through his father, Tsiyiak, and to the Yakimas through his mother, Kamoshnite, the daughter of Weowicht, the powerful chief of the upper Yakimas. Through the family ties of his five wives, Kamiakin also enjoyed the strong political support of a large extended family structure. Born around 1800, Kamiakin grew up among his mother's people in the Yakima Country.

Even during his youth, Indians recognized Kamiakin's potential as a leader. When he went forth to seek his *wyak* during his vision quest, he did so on the majestic slopes of Mount Rainier. During his ordeal, "the severest feat of his life," a buffalo visited Kamiakin, and the great animal imparted power to the young man. The buffalo, a strong spirit helper among the Plateau and Plains tribes, blessed Kamiakin with considerable spiritual strength. As a young man Kamiakin distinguished himself as a fine warrior and buffalo hunter, and over the years he earned the respect of young men and women alike. He grew rich in horses and took his first wife at the age of twenty-five. This woman was Kamiakin's cousin, Sunkhaye, the daughter of Chief Teias and the granddaughter of the regal and respected Weowicht. As was the custom, Kamiakin married within his own family in order to consolidate political, social, and economic power within the family of Weowicht.[8]

Kamiakin had other attributes which made him an important leader. In appearance he was an imposing figure, described by one white man as "a tall, large man, very dark, with a massive square face, and grave, reflective look." He was a noted orator and a natural leader whose bearing was one of strength and honesty. Kamiakin had a manner "strikingly distinguished, quiet, and dignified." As Kamiakin advanced in years, he became wealthy and powerful among the Yakimas, and several Sahaptin and Salish-speaking peoples sought him out for counsel and advice. Through his own abilities as well as through his family ties, Kamiakin emerged as one of the most prominent leaders in the region. Although a man of considerable influence among the Palouses, neither Kamiakin nor any other chief was considered the "head chief" of any of the Sahaptin tribes on the Great Columbia Plateau.[9]

Kamiakin had his adversaries. His principal rivals were members of his own family. Among them were Teias—leader of a portion of the lower Yakimas and both Kamiakin's uncle and father-in-law—and Owhi, leader of the Yakimas living upstream along the Yakima River, and another of Kamiakin's uncles. Teias and Owhi were jealous of a nephew whose economic, social, and political star outshowed their own. Over the years Kamiakin traveled widely, acquiring several head of cattle and horses. At his summer home on Ahtanum Creek, near the site of St. Joseph Mission, he had begun a small farming enterprise, raising vegetables in small garden plots, irrigated by the waters of the creek. Like some interior Indians, Kamiakin initially believed that he and his people could benefit from the spiritual power and practical knowledge of the white man. But Kamiakin refused to surrender his freedom and autonomy or that of his people. However, he welcomed some whites into the Yakima Country in order to learn aspects of white culture which he considered advantageous. He invited William Gray to establish a mission among the Yakima people, but when the Protestants failed to build a mission, Kamiakin turned to the Catholics. Consequently, in 1847 the Oblate missionaries established St. Joseph Mission on Ahtanum Creek.[10]

When McClellan rode into St. Joseph Mission, Fathers Charles M. Pandosy and Louis D'Herbomez greeted him. Through the priests, Kamiakin met McClellan who called the headman, "the principle chief of this country." McClellan believed him to be the "Head Chief" of the several Indian groups in the region, an honor which Kamiakin could not and would not have claimed. Kamiakin camped with McClellan and had a long conversation with the captain regarding the purpose of the American expedition. McClellan truthfully explained that the white men sought suitable trails over the Cascade Mountains for highways to the Puget Sound. McClellan did not explain a railroad, but he assured Kamiakin that the whites would not settle the interior, because, as the captain wrote, "it is difficult to imagine" that the Columbia Plain could serve any "useful purpose." McClellan, of course, failed to foresee the dryland farming or irrigation techniques that in time were to transform so much of the region.[11] McClellan was much impressed with Kamiakin, arguing that the chief "expressed very friendly feelings, and I have no reason to doubt his sincerity, for, in a number of instances, he displayed an honesty not often found among Indians."[12]

Disturbed by McClellan's survey, Kamiakin rode to Owhi's village to converse with his uncle. Owhi, who resided in the Kittitas Valley, shared Kamiakin's concerns, telling his nephew that he would accompany the survey party to the Wenatchee Country and learn more about the army's intent. Owhi had friends and relatives among the Salish-speaking Indians to the north and thought that they, perhaps, had learned something. On his way to visit the Wenatchees, Owhi was joined by a prominent chief of the Columbias (or Sinkiuses), named Quiltenenock. Owhi and Quiltenenock received some alarming intelligence as a result of their trip: the "Great Father" in Washington, D.C., planned to take their lands and that, "if they refused to sell, soldiers would be sent to drive them off and seize the lands." Owhi returned to tell the Indians what he had learned. This information "went out to all the tribes in the Northwest," confusing the Indians who did not know what course to take in response to the white threat. It was from his reports that the Palouses were informed of the white man's intent.[13] Within a short time each tribe and band would decide on its policies toward the whites, including the Palouses.[14]

|While Kamiakin acted to ascertain the design of McClellan's explorations, the Palouses spied on the survey party operating near the Snake River.| The Palouses, Cayuses, Walla Wallas, and Umatillas were as surprised as the Yakimas, Columbias, and Wenatchees when American soldiers marched into their lands. While McClellan moved through the Yakima Country, other American soldiers, under the command of Lieutenant Rufus Saxton, marched into the interior. With a party of fifty-one men and a large packtrain loaded with provisions for Governor Stevens, the lieutenant moved up the Columbia River, reaching The Dalles on July 18. Seven days out from The Dalles, Saxton approached the Umatilla River where he was "met by a delegation of Cayuse braves, sent by the chief of the Nez Perces [Palouses], to ascertain our object in passing through their country." Rumors spread that the soldiers "were coming to make war upon them, and take away their horses." The lieutenant told them that he "had been sent by the great Chief of us all, at Washington, on a mission of peace to all the Indian tribes on both sides of the mountain." The Indians listened, smoked a pipe of tobacco with the soldier, and at least one of them "said that he was glad that our 'hearts were good.' " Lieutenant Saxton failed to mention that he was surveying a railroad which would ultimately carry hundreds of whites to the Pacific Northwest.[15]

Saxton's men traveled to Fort Walla Walla where Andrew Pambrun hospitably received them. Pambrun, a former factor for Hudson's Bay, often acted as an interpreter. Several Indians visited Saxton at his encampment, including the venerated chief of the Walla Wallas, Peopeo Moxmox, whose village had been raided during the Cayuse War. The Indians "expressed a great deal of friendship" toward the whites, stating that they were much "delighted to find that the reports of our hostile intentions were false." Peopeo Moxmox arranged for the soldiers to cross the Snake River. The chief sent a runner to Palus to ask the Indians to meet the soldiers "with men and canoes, to transport . . . [them] across the river." On the last day of July 1853, Saxton's party left the Hudson's Bay fort and began its journey northeast across a vast, rolling prairie "entirely destitute of trees and water." Several Indians visited the soldiers along the route, including Palouses who treated the whites with courtesy and received an equal measure in return.[16]

\Saxton's party rode all day and night, arriving at "Camp Peluse" on August 1. Not long after reaching the southern bank of the Snake River, Saxton received "a delegation of fifty Peluse and Nez Perce warriors, who came in full costume, and with great formality, to hold a grand 'war talk.' " The Indians did not converse with the soldiers immediately but talked among themselves about the policy they should follow.\The Palouse headmen "seated themselves in a circle, the head chief in the centre [sic], and the braves and warriors, according to rank, on either side." Behind the circle of headmen were six men who were "dressed in very fantastic style" whom Saxton believed to be "medicine men." The Palouses talked among themselves for a time before announcing to the lieutenant that they were willing to speak with the soldiers.[17] However, Saxton replied that we were then too much tired." He wrote, "but that after we had eaten and slept we should be in a better condition to hold a council." The Palouses waited patiently. The Palouse council with Saxton began the next morning with everyone shaking each other's hand. One of the Palouse headmen lit a pipe, and after "smoking a few whiffs himself, passed it to each member of the council, in the direction of the sun."

Smoking the pipe in this fashion symbolized a pledge of friendship between the survey party and the Palouses.[18]

After everyone smoked, one Palouse chief inquired about the object of the soldiers' passing through Palouse Country and why the whites had "so many animals and such a quantity of merchandise." They learned that the party was heading east over the Bitterroot and Rocky Mountains to the land of the Blackfeet. They also discovered that the soldiers were "to meet the chief of all the country between the mountains and the Pacific ocean." Saxton told the Palouses "to be in readiness, when Gov. Stevens should arrive, to give him any aid he would require." In addition, the lieutenant informed the Palouses that the "great chief in Washington was their friend, and would protect them."[19] The Palouses had learned earlier from Peopeo Moxmox that Saxton's troops wanted them to help him cross the Snake River. Saxton said as much to the Palouses, telling "them to be ready with their men and canoes to help us in crossing the river." He also requested that the Indians send their men to "bring in all our horses that had strayed." The Indians discussed these matters among themselves before one of them "made an eloquent speech to the others." The "fine young Indian" who made the presentation told the others that his father had "extended the hand of friendship to the first white man who was seen in that country, and they must follow his example." The Palouses who had met Lewis and Clark had treated the first Americans with peace and friendship, they helped the whites on this occasion. Pleased to learn of the Palouse decision, Saxton handed out tobacco and beads before ordering his men to fire their new Sharp's and Colt rifles. He told the Indians that he would be ready to cross the Snake the next day at sunrise.[20]

As the next dawn first broke, Antoine Plante, a mixed-blood Indian then serving as a scout for Saxton, woke the entire camp with a "war-whoop" when he saw the Palouses crossing the Snake in dugout canoes. Several Palouses aided the whites in the crossing, and within a few hours the horses, baggage, and men were moved safely to the north side of the Snake River, except for two horses that drowned while swimming the swift stream. The soldiers paid the Indians for their services with presents provided by the Bureau of Indian Affairs. These were the first such "gifts" that the Palouses received from the Indian Office, but they accepted them as payment for their labor, not as a sign of dependence on or allegiance to the United States. The Palouses may have expressed their good faith by helping the *suyapo*, but they had originally anticipated trouble. Saxton commented on this when he reported that he "found all the grass burned on this side of the Peluse River." The lieutenant learned that the Palouses had burned the prairie, because they had heard that "a large body of American soldiers were coming to cut them off, and take possession of their homes."[21]

After helping the whites cross the Snake, the Palouses watched them make the long, arduous climb out of the canyon. They exhibited no hostile feelings toward the soldiers or the white settlers who had most recently crossed the Plateau. The Palouses had heard that the first white immigrants—between one to two hundred men and women in fifty wagons—had successfully crossed the Cascade Mountains from Fort Walla Walla to Puget Sound. While the older men and women pondered these developments, some younger men rode north across the Palouse Hills to spy on Saxton whose troops traveled north to the Spokane Country where they met the famed Spokan Garry who feared that the soldiers had come to make war. Saxton had heard the same concerns expressed among the Cayuses, Walla Wallas, and Palouses. Anxiety ran high among the various tribes. The councils held between Saxton, McClellan, and the Indians did little to reassure the tribes that they had nothing to fear. Rather, the talks increased their suspicion.[22]

Saxton traveled east from the Spokane River across the Bitterroot and Rocky Mountains, finally arriving at Fort Benton, located near the junction of the Missouri and Teton Rivers in northern Montana. Stevens had already reached that trading center of the American Fur Company before Saxton's arrival and was busily preparing to cross the mountains. In late September Stevens headed west, arriving in the lands of the Coeur d'Alenes on Columbus Day, 1853. The governor held a council with a few Indians at the Coeur d'Alene Mission and told them that he had "come four times as far as you go to hunt buffalo, and have come with directions from the Great Father to see you, to talk to you, and to do all I can for your welfare." As Superintendent of Indian Affairs, Stevens promised the Indians that he would see that "every family will have a house and a patch of ground, and every one will be well clothed."[23] He gave a similar speech to the Spokane Indians after arriving at the Hudson's Bay post of Fort Colvile, "telling them of the interest the government took in them, and that measures had been taken to secure peace between the Blackfeet and all the other Indian tribes." The Coeur d'Alenes and Spokanes were pleased to learn that the Blackfeet had pledged peace, but the Indians wondered about Stevens' talk of a Great Father and his plan to assist, clothe, and shelter all of the Indians as well as to place them on "a patch of ground." Stevens told the Indians "that the government would do for them what it had done for the other Indians." This proclamation did not ease the minds of the Indians, for some of them knew from their own experience and from the stories told to them by whites and Eastern Indians that the United States government had forced thousands of Indians to give up their homes and move far from their traditional homelands. Stevens' message reached all of the Indians, including the Palouses who were keeping track of his activities in the inland Northwest.[24]

After leaving Fort Colvile, Stevens traveled into the Palouse Country. Accompanied by Spokan Garry, Stevens journeyed across the rolling hills of southeastern Washington where two Palouses intercepted the governor, telling him that Palus was abandoned. It was November 1, 1853, when the survey party entered the "deep canyon, surrounded by isolated volcanic buttes," and the men were, at that time of year, in the mountains hunting deer and elk while the women gathered roots and berries. The Palouses remained in the mountains, completing the last phase of their seasonal round. The two Indians who had met Stevens on the Palouse River joined the soldiers, offering to help them cross the Snake River. Other Palouses, whose village was up river, also joined Stevens' party. Together they traveled to the mouth of the river where they crossed the Snake. The governor and his Palouse friends arrived safely on the southern bank of the river where they set up camp. Among the "several Peluse Indians accompanying us," Stevens stated, was "a chief from a band but a few miles distant from our camp." The chief was Witimyhoyshe whose ancestor had been presented a medal by Lewis and Clark, one of those that had been given to the Palouse chiefs in 1805 at Quosispah. According to Stevens, Witimyhoyshe "exhibited a medal of Thomas Jefferson, dated 1801, given to his grandfather, as he alleges, by Lewis and Clark." On two occasions, one with Saxton and one with

Stevens, the Palouses made references to Lewis and Clark and the message
of "Peace and Friendship" they had received from the first white men.[25]
Governor Stevens spent little time in the Palouse Country, but he left
a few observations about one of the most striking features of the region,
Palouse Falls, located nine miles upstream from the junction of the Palouse
River with the Snake. Palouse Falls cascades over a hard, dark basalt for-
mation, dropping two hundred feet into a pool of clear, green water which
settles for a moment at the base of the falls before rushing downstream
through a deep, black gorge of volcanic basalt. Stevens recorded that the
Palouse Indians told him that the falls were created by the Great Spirit because
of his displeasure with the wicked Indians who lived further upstream. They
were created to halt further ascent of the salmon. According to the governor, the Palouses depended on fishing for their livelihood and that Palus
was situated at a place of good fishing where the Indians "devote much of
their time to salmon fishing."[26] Unfortunately, the governor and the officials
who followed, did not understand that salmon was more than food; the fish
were part of their religion and an integral part of their cosmology.[27]

On November 2, Stevens and Spokan Garry rode from the Snake River
to Fort Walla Walla across a luxurious landscape characterized by "high rolling prairies." At the Hudson's Bay post Stevens held a meeting with Frederick
W. Lander, a civilian employee working with the railroad survey, instructing him to take a small party across the Cascade Mountains via the Naches
Pass to Puget Sound. Before leaving the Walla Walla Valley, Stevens
"endeavored to impress him with the entire feasibility of the enterprise."[28]
Lander never made the proposed journey across the mountains. Similarly,
Stevens ordered McClellan to make a survey across Snoqualmie Pass, but
the future commander of the Union forces during the Civil War gave up the
trip over the mountains because of snow. The governor then instructed his
trusted friend, Abiel W. Tinkham, to travel from the Nez Perce Country
to Puget Sound by way of Snoqualmie Pass. Stevens found a man equal to
the task, and despite snow and foul weather that thwarted McClellan,
Tinkham made it across Snoqualmie Pass in January 1854. Stevens was
delighted to hear that Tinkham "was satisfied that it [Snoqualmie Pass] af-
forded fair facilities both in ascent and descent for a wagon and railroad."
As head of the railroad survey, Stevens had found a feasible route for a northern Pacific railroad, a transportation system that would significantly influence
the future course of Indian history.[29]

Not long after leaving Fort Walla Walla on his way to Olympia to assume
his duties as the first territorial governor, Stevens was faced with a new problem, one different from any he had encountered while working on the railroad
survey. At The Dalles he was informed by Major Gabriel J. Rains that trouble
brewed east of the Cascades, as more and more whites traveled through the
region. The Indians had long feared that once the whites secured all the land
they desired west of the Cascades, they would turn their attention to the other
side of the mountains. The activities of the various parties of the railroad
survey had not put their minds to rest. Indians worried over additional wagon
roads and settlers. Before reaching The Dalles, Stevens had been preoccupied
with this survey and had not given much thought to the growing unrest in
the interior, but after talking to Rains, the governor remarked that he had
"met several gentlemen — men who had crossed the plains, and who had made
farms in several States and in Oregon or Washington — who had carefully

examined the Yakima country for new locations." These white men "impressed" the governor "with the importance of it as an agricultural and grazing country."[30] Before whites could settle in the inland Northwest, however, the government was obligated to make treaties with the Indians and secure title to the land. As the Superintendent of the Indian Affairs, Stevens negotiated such treaties in the Pacific Northwest. A few agreements had already been made between some coastal tribes and the United States, but these treaties had never been ratified. If Stevens were to open the Northwest through treaties, he had to look elsewhere for precedents.[31]

When the new governor and his men arrived in Olympia, they assembled their notes, journals, and maps pertaining to the railroad survey and compiled a comprehensive document regarding a northern railroad route. This massive work — the finest of all of the railroad surveys — contained significant information that would be beneficial to white settlers migrating to the Pacific Northwest. The volumes contained convincing evidence that the rolling hills of the Palouse Country were fertile and conducive to American agriculture. Contained in its pages were descriptions of "virgin and free lands" in eastern Washington that contained "fertile soil" which the Indians had never cultivated extensively. While it was true that the Palouses and their neighbors were not farmers, some of them had small gardens where they raised corn, potatoes, and other vegetables. Years after the survey was made, whites would claim that there was no indigenous agriculture among the Plateau Indians, but there is evidence to prove otherwise. This was, to a degree, a justification for taking Indian lands. Therefore, some argued that the Indians were backward and shiftless obstacles to civilization and progress. Indeed, some whites justified their encroachment onto Indian lands by maintaining that the white man offered the Indians a new way of life, one that God had ordained the Americans to spread from shore to shore. During the two decades following the railroad report, white settlers moved into the Palouse Country and transformed the billowy hills, once graced only by huge horse herds, into some of the most productive farm lands in the nation.[32]

The invasion of the white man would, unlike some other inland tribes, result in the total loss of the traditional Palouse homeland. The developments that brought this about were varied; prominent among them was the policy toward the Indians shaped by Governor Stevens. Since his principal concern was the opening of Indian lands for the expansion of the American empire, Stevens devoted himself to extinguishing Indian title to the land. His attention first focused on the tribes west of the Cascades where the Indians were already alarmed at the number of whites moving into the Cowlitz Valley and onto the land around Puget Sound. Whites seemed to move into the region in what appeared to the Indians a never-ending stream. Most of these newcomers were farmers, but all of them wanted land — land that belonged to the Indians. In time, Stevens would redirect his efforts at extinguishing Indian title to the interior tribes. When he did, the Palouses felt the full brunt of his policy's effects.[33]

From the first, Stevens spent time traveling about reassuring the Indians that he would protect them and their property, while at the same time seeking to implement his Indian policy. Unschooled in Indian affairs, Stevens followed policies already adopted in other parts of the country. He relied heavily on the instructions sent to him by the Commissioner of Indian Affairs;

he appointed agents for the tribes, including one to implement Indian affairs for the tribes east of the Cascades. He urged the Indians to be peaceful and to live like white people. In this manner, the Indians could become "civilized" human beings. Stevens, his men, and most whites of the mid-nineteenth century believed that Indians were wild, uncivilized, primitive people whose only hope of emerging from their savagery was to live and think like whites. There was nothing new in what Stevens set out to do. The United States had pursued such a course since the birth of the nation. Stevens was simply a product of a peculiar system and a particular time. The Indians had little to say about their own destiny, and they had no unified white policy to counter Stevens.[34]

Traditionally the various tribes communicated regularly, sharing news of importance and interest. According to Andrew Jackson Splawn, an early white settler in the Yakima Valley who personally knew many of the Indians, the Yakimas had learned that the governor planned to return to the east side of the mountains in the summer of 1855 and hold a council "to talk over the purchase of Indian lands." Apparently, a chief had replied that the Indians were not interested in selling their lands and simply "wished to be left alone." Stevens reportedly told some Yakimas in 1854 that "if the Indians would not sell, the whites would take the lands anyway and the Indians would get no return; also, that if they refused to make a treaty with him, soldiers would be sent into their country to wipe them off the earth." Stevens never held a meeting with the Yakimas and never told the Yakimas any such thing, at least to their faces. The governor was in Washington, D.C., during the summer of 1854 working out details of the forthcoming treaties. Nevertheless, it is possible that someone in a survey party made these statements. And even if the statements were mere rumors, they were important since the Indians believed that Stevens wanted to take their homes and resettle whites on them. Indians also believed that if they refused to submit, war would break out. In this, they were certainly correct.[35]

Kamiakin also informed the Palouses of the intentions of the whites. In response to the white problem, he and others decided that their best hope was to band together. Kamiakin was a prominent organizer of the confederacy, and some of the strength which resulted was drawn from Palouses. The idea of forming an Indian alliance on the Plateau was a novel one. The Indians had organized themselves for hunting, gathering, and war parties, but never had they attempted a large political confederation of Salish- and Sahaptin-speaking peoples. According to Splawn, Kamiakin met with several of the prominent leaders of the region and urged them to join him in a huge inter-tribal council to discuss the white problems. Evidence that such a meeting occurred is sketchy, but the council reportedly met along the Grande Ronde River of northeastern Oregon, far removed from white interference. The proceedings were to be kept secret; thus little is known about the council. The main discussion supposedly centered around the question of whether or not to meet with Stevens. Most of the chiefs were in favor of boycotting such a meeting, except for Lawyer of the Nez Perces, Stickus of the Cayuses, and Garry of the Spokanes. These leaders took "the view that if all were in a position to hear directly what the emissary of the whites had to say, war might, perhaps, be avoided."[36]

According to Splawn, the Indians at the council finally agreed that they would meet with Governor Stevens but refuse to cede any of their land. The Indians would "mark the boundaries of the different tribes so that each chief could rise in council, claim his boundaries and ask that the land be made a reservation for his people." In this manner, the Indians felt that "there would be no lands for sale, the council would fail, and the contentions of Lawyer and Sticcas, at the same time, be met." Splawn's written account of the great council of 1854 is the only one to survive, perhaps because he received his information directly from the Yakimas who shared with him their oral histories. Some historians have suggested that the meeting took place in the summer of 1855 after Stevens had concluded the Walla Walla Council. The Indians likely had such a meeting since inter-tribal gatherings were common. Certainly there was good reason to have such a conference in 1854; this was an extraordinary period in the history of the inland tribes, a time of suspicion, fear, and change; a gathering was logical. But whether or not they met and reached a decision to attend the treaty council and refuse to sell their land cannot be ascertained. Whatever the case, word reached all of the tribes that Stevens planned to hold a council east of the Cascades, just as he had among the Indians of the Puget Sound. The Palouses knew he wanted to "purchase" their lands and concentrate them on reserves; this much, at least, the Palouses had heard.[37]

From Kamiakin the Palouses learned of events in the Puget Sound. Leschi, a prominent chief of the Nisquallys, was Kamiakin's cousin. This family relationship was not an isolated case. More than one Indian of the interior had relatives west of the Cascades, including some of the Palouses. From these and other sources the Palouses learned a great deal about the situation in Puget Sound, for many problems had emerged in the Sound resulting from white contact. Disease became a major concern, and this grave problem was not isolated to the Pacific Coast, although the diseases there were more acute. The Palouses and their neighbors suffered from the scourges of disease. According to Doctor George Suckley and Doctor J. G. Cooper, members of the railroad survey, diseases had spread up the Columbia, infecting and killing many Indians. "The Indian tribes on the Columbia river, below Fort Colville [sic]," wrote Suckley, "are rapidly becoming depopulated by the smallpox, intemperance, and syphilis." All three of these diseases — and others — had been introduced to the Pacific Northwest by whites, and the sicknesses were killing Indians by the hundreds. According to one Palouse, the diseases killed everyone in one village along the Snake River. Diseases killed men, women, and children indiscriminately, infecting members of all tribes, including Palouses.[38]

Measles had been the major killer among the Cayuse and other inland tribes during the epidemic of 1847. Six years later smallpox swept up the Columbia River to the inland Northwest, prevailing "in every direction, carrying off the natives by hundreds." Some of the Indians living along the Columbia River, which included some Palouses, "buried more than one-half of their numbers." Dr. Cooper noted that "of the diseases prevalent among the Indians, the smallpox was the most common and fatal in its effects." Cooper maintained that "Whole tribes have been exterminated by it on the Columbia river." The doctor had personally witnessed the influence of the disease along the Columbia where, he said, "we met with it among all those inhabiting" the region.[39]

George Gibbs also reported that smallpox had spread among the Yakimas, Klickitats, and Wishram in 1853 and that the Indians had "suffered severely." In fact the major Indian village at The Dalles had "been depopulated." Gibbs suggested that smallpox was not new to the region, commenting that "this disease, the greatest scourge of the red man . . . has passed through this region more than once, and was probably the first severe blow which fell upon the Oregon tribes." Smallpox had made its appearance in the inland Northwest "before any direct intercourse took place with the whites," and by 1853 had contributed to a good many deaths among the Indians. As Gibbs traveled through the Yakima Valley, he reported that the entire "course of the Yakima [River] is lined with the vestiges of former villages now vacant." As the epidemics swept up the Columbia River and its tributaries, it often left too few alive to bury the dead.[40]

The Indians east and west of the mountains suffered the disastrous results of smallpox and other diseases which became more acute among the Indians in relation to the growth of white population. The migration of white men into the Northwest was the chief cause of the epidemics in the region and "those creatures who have been longest in isolation suffer most" from the disease. The "genetic material" of the Palouses and others had not been "tempered" by smallpox, measles, and fever. Therefore, the Palouse Indians, who had had comparatively little contact with whites, were still vulnerable to the disease. They had few natural immunities, and they died as a result.[41] No one will ever know the number of people who died from the epidemics, but clearly, the Palouses were affected by the smallpox epidemic of 1853. They and other Indians were terrified to watch their friends and family suffer the horrors of disease. Smallpox spread through the air, and quickly transformed a healthy Indian into a disfigured, crying mass of oozing pustules. The Palouses, like other victims, felt a great sense of helplessness as they watched their people die from a disease which they suspected had been introduced by whites.[42]

Diseases also weakened the Indians by decreasing their numbers, demoralizing their populations, and destroying their political, military, and economic strength. This was true on both sides of the Cascade Mountains, particularly along the coast and in the Puget Sound where Indians had more contact with whites than those of the interior. Cooper, Gibbs, and Suckley say as much in their reports, and Leschi told Kamiakin about the devastating harvest of the diseases in the Puget Sound. Kamiakin learned this and much more from his cousin.

Kamiakin knew that Stevens had made treaties with the Coastal Indians and had forced them to accept the terms dictated by the United States government. In late 1854 and early 1855, Stevens made a whirlwind tour of Puget Sound, making formal agreements with the Indians, including one with Leschi's people. These treaties included that of Medicine Creek, Point Elliott, and Point No Point. They were important measures that influenced the Indians of Puget Sound as well as the people of eastern Washington. Stevens, who had virtually no experience in treaty making, simply studied the treaties which had recently been concluded with Oto, Omaha, and Missouri tribes. He and his staff, particularly George Gibbs, drafted documents for the Indians of Puget Sound based on these models.[43] By and large the coastal treaties were nearly identical, each calling for the end of tribal warfare, the surrender of the Indian lands, and the establishment of reservations. The government recognized the Indian right to fish "at common and accustomed places" as well as their right to hunt. It promised to establish an agency on each reservation as well as to build a school where the students would learn farming and trades. In addition, medical care was guaranteed. Although Stevens and his agents said that the treaties would benefit Indians, the native peoples were not fooled. Some openly defied the governor. Such was the case of Kamiakin's cousins, Leschi and Quiemuth, whose names were forged on the Treaty of Medicine Creek.[44]

On March 7, 1855, a small party of men, consisting of James Doty, Andrew Jackson Bolon, and Dr. Richard H. Landsdale, left The Dalles for the interior. These men were under instructions from Stevens "to organize a party with a view to vigorous action in the Indian country east of the Cascades, explaining to the Indians the objects of the Government in proposing to treat with them, and collecting them at some point favorable for holding Treaties."[45] During the last week of March the *suyapo* met with Peopeo Moxmox of the Walla Wallas who learned that "Stevens was coming to hold a treaty with his tribe." They reportedly received the consent of the headman "to meet Gov. S. at a Council to be held near Wayelatpoo [Waiilatpu]." Word spread quickly among the interior tribes, for they had been expecting the conference with Stevens. The Palouses, who had relatives among the tribes south of Snake River, particularly among the Walla Wallas who recognized Peopeo Moxmox as their leader, also learned of Doty's message. When the whites had completed their parley with Peopeo Moxmox, they turned northwest toward the Yakima Country.[46]

On the last day of March, Doty dispatched an Indian to Skloom's camp, asking Kamiakin's younger brother to meet with him on Ahtanum Creek. Doty arrived at St. Joseph Mission on April 1, 1855, and Kamiakin and his father-in-law (and uncle), Teias, were at the mission to meet Doty. Following a short discussion with Father Charles M. Pandosy, an Oblate missionary, Doty talked with the two chiefs for some time, explaining the purpose of his mission and asking them to meet with him again after Owhi and the other headmen arrived. Doty was favorably impressed with Teias, an old man by this time who "was cordial in expressions of friendship and readily acceded" to deal with the whites. Kamiakin, however, "was either silent or sulky and declined meeting the whites or discussing the subject of a Treaty." Like many Indians, Kamiakin disliked and distrusted the whites, but because he was embroiled in several family feuds and jealousies, he remained near the mission to hear first hand what the whites wanted and what the other chiefs would decide.[47]

Doty recognized the divisions among the Yakimas, and he determined to secure "the friendly presence of all the other chiefs and if Kam-i-a-kun, then stood aloof, it would be alone." Doty was correct about the intra-tribal divisions, because "there was a very considerable amount of family rivalry existing between Kamiahkin and his wife's people." Kamiakin was only half Yakima through his mother, and there were those Yakimas who reminded the chief that he was not a full blood and thus had less claim to power than Owhi or Teias. Then too there were "smoldering family discords" because Kamiakin was a wealthy and powerful figure who overshadowed other Yakima leaders, including his own uncles, Teias and Owhi. To make matters worse, Kamiakin had married women outside the extended family of Teias and Owhi. Four of his wives came from the family of Tenax, a Klickitat

chief and rival to the family of Kamiakin's first wife. The details of all of
this were unknown to Doty, but he easily perceived that the Yakimas were
divided along family lines. Like so many government agents before, he determined to make the best of this division to foster his objective and that of
his government.[48]

The second day Doty was at Ahtanum, he met with Kamiakin's brothers,
Skloom and Showaway, who were also mixed-blood Palouses. Teias was present, and the three headmen reportedly "were very friendly." But Kamiakin
was not interested in socializing with Doty and therefore camped about a
quarter of a mile from the mission, paying "no attention to an invitation"
to visit Doty's camp. The chief remained at his own camp and awaited the
arrival of Owhi before they all met in council. All of the important chiefs
met with Doty, including Owhi, Teias, Showaway, Skloom, and Kamiakin,
and everyone listened patiently as Doty explained the objectives of his government. The proposals presented were pertinent to the Palouses, for Doty told
the Indians that Stevens wished to meet with them "to purchase all their country." Then the government would give back a portion of the land as reservations which would "belong to them forever." The Indians "would be required
to live" on the reservations where "they could build their houses, cultivate
farms, and pasture their cattle and horses." In addition, the Indian bureau
would "manage them [the reservations] for the exclusive benefit of the Indians." The Indians were promised a "schoolhouse, blacksmith and carpenter
shop, farm house and mills."

All this was to be "given" to the Indians "without charge." Doty felt that
he and the government were doing the Indians a favor, by helping the Indians along "the white man's road." Indeed, Doty believed that the "beneficial
results" would soon be seen among the Indian "children, who would learn
the trades of a blacksmith, carpenter, miller, farmer, in addition to learning
to read and write, and thus qualify themselves to take a position among the
whites, and earn for themselves and families a comfortable subsistence."
Clearly, Doty did not understand the Indians with whom he was dealing.[49]
According to him, Kamiakin asked "that a treaty Council might be held at
that point [Walla Walla] and the Nez Perces, Cayuses, Walla Wallas,
Palouses, Okin-e-kanes and Pisqouse, assemble there." This statement seems
uncharacteristic of a man opposed to selling his lands. Kamiakin had previously said that "He had never had much to do with the Whites," and "he knew
but little of them; he had heard that the soldiers were coming to take their
lands and had believed it, but was glad to hear that we [the Americans] wished
to treat fairly for them, and that it was all a lie about the soldiers." Perhaps
Doty convinced Kamiakin that it was in his own best interest to meet with
Governor Stevens. More likely, Kamiakin agreed to meet with Stevens because
he did not trust Teias, Owhi, or his brothers. The chief feared the loss of
his own power, and he worried that Stevens would make an unacceptable
agreement with the other chiefs. The Palouses learned about the meeting at
Ahtanum Creek and the upcoming council at Walla Walla. Like Kamiakin,
they opposed the cession of their lands or the establishment of reservations.
But unlike Kamiakin, most refused to attend the Walla Walla Council.[50]

Before leaving the Yakimas, Doty distributed gifts of clothing, tobacco,
and cloth, a common practice for government agents. Kamiakin was aware
that Indians from other parts of the country had lost their lands by accep-
ting gifts, and for this reason, he refused to accept any, stating "that he had

never accepted from the Americans the value of a grain of wheat without paying for it." He refused to accept the goods offered him, maintaining "that the Whites gave goods in this manner, and then claimed that the Indian lands were purchased by them." Doty denied that this was true, telling Kamiakin that the presents "were given to indicate our friendship." The other leaders followed Kamiakin's example and did not accept gifts until the next day when Teias received some, because "he did not wish to offend them [the president and the governor] and make them think his heart bad."[51] Both Teias and Owhi accepted gifts, stating at the time of acceptance that they were slaves of no man, referring of course to Kamiakin. Skloom and Showaway likewise received gifts in spite of Kamiakin's objections. Kamiakin had decided to meet with Stevens and hear what the white man had to say, but the chief was not willing to sell his lands or permit whites to displace his people.

Kamiakin had learned his lessons well, and he refused to compromise his principles. Doty left the Yakima Country believing that Kamiakin was the "head chief" of the Yakimas. This was a serious error, for Kamiakin was "chief" of only one band of Yakimas and not a "head chief." Certainly he never would have said that he could speak "on behalf of and acting for" the fourteen different tribes and bands that Stevens claimed were under Kamiakin's leadership. The Palouses were included in this number, but as a whole they never supported the treaty. True, the Palouses looked to Kamiakin as a leader, but he was neither the "head chief" of that tribe nor any other. Such was contrary to the political makeup of the Plateau people, but Kamiakin's designation as "head chief" created a grave problem for the Palouses because it led to their being considered a party to the Yakima Treaty of 1855.[52]

CHAPTER 5

THE WALLA WALLA COUNCIL

*Shall I give the lands that are part of my body and
leave myself poor and destitute?*
—Owhi

American Indian policy, executed in Washington Territory by Governor
Stevens, called for the creation of treaties between the United States government and each of the tribes; these treaties would establish formal relationship between the Indians and the national government. From the outset, few,
if any, Palouses were interested in making a treaty with Stevens and most
Palouse leaders refused to attend the governor's regional treaty council when
it met. Nevertheless, the Walla Walla Council, as it became known, and the
subsequent signing of the Yakima Treaty were significant events in Palouse
history. The Palouses were drawn into the flow of events, and as a result
of the council and the treaty, they lost all of their land and were ordered
onto the Yakima Reservation. But they would immediately defy this order,
and because of armed conflicts in the Yakima Country, they found themselves
engaged in a disastrous war which would lead to their military conquest. These
events were set in motion in May 1855 when the Great Treaty Council was
held in the lush, green Walla Walla Valley.[1]

Governor Stevens arrived on May 21, accompanied by Joel Palmer,
Oregon's Superintendent of Indian Affairs. By the time these men reached
the meeting ground, they were "thoroughly drenched in the soaking rain
through which they had ridden all day."[2] The council was held on Mill Creek,
near the present-day city of Walla Walla; there Stevens's men built a large
log and brush structure. Another structure of poles and boughs was built
as a council chamber where the leaders would be protected from the elements.[3]
Upon arriving at Walla Walla, Stevens exchanged ideas with various white
officials, including Nathaniel Olney and Richard Landsdale. These territorial
officials talked of many things, but the policies they were about to present
were not discussed that rainy May night. Rather, Stevens and Palmer followed
instructions sent to them by the Commissioner of Indian Affairs, to be im-
plemented as they saw fit.[4]

By the time the Stevens party arrived at Walla Walla, they had considerable experience dealing with Indians. Stevens in particular had learned
from his negotiations with Puget Sound tribes, and he arrived at the council
with a plan for drawing up the treaties. First and foremost, Stevens said,
"I confidently expect to accomplish the whole business, extinguishing the Indian title to every acre of land in the territory."[5] Of course, he was acting
under the direction of the Commissioner of Indian Affairs who had instructed
him to do precisely that, as well as to concentrate "the tribes and fragments
of tribes on a few reserves of limited extent, naturally suited to the

requirements of Indians, and located, as far as practicle [sic] so as not to interfere with the [white] settlement of the Territories." Stevens was to use his own methods to accomplish these ends.[6]   *reservations*

The governor and other whites professed that another objective was to "civilize" the Indians. Some policy-makers believed that whites had a duty to uplift their red brothers from "savagery" to "civilization." As Commissioner of Indian Affairs George Mannypenny put it, "the Indian may be domesticated, improved, and elevated." The commissioner believed that there was a chance that Indians were capable of becoming more white-like and one day might become "completely and thoroughly civilized, and made a useful element of our population." The commissioner and many others believed that Indians could become "civilized" if they lived in "a fixed, settled, and permanent home." The reservation was viewed as the vehicle through which Indians would become acculturated. Indians would learn to farm on reservations and, through formal and informal education, acquire white values, beliefs, and attitudes. As the older Indians died, so would native culture. As young Indians were raised in an environment controlled by whites, they would become more white-like. To some degree this attitude was reflected in speeches by Stevens at the Walla Walla council; but his interest in "civilizing" the Indians was secondary to his desire to extinguish land claims, concentrate Indians on reservations, and open their lands to white settlement. He was an expansionist, an ardent advocate of Manifest Destiny.[7]

While Stevens had a plan of action and a policy, the Indians had no unified agenda to match. Indeed, there was little agreement, either within individual tribes or among the various groups represented at the treaty council. Far from being unified, they appeared confused by the talk of treaties and reservations. Unanimity among the tribes represented at the council developed only on a few points as time passed and as the council's purposes became clearer. Concerned that the Palouse Indians would boycott the council, Stevens dispatched Patrick McKenzie "to the Palouse to invite them to the Council." Two days later, on May 26, McKenzie returned, reporting that most Palouses were "simply indifferent to it." Yet he came into camp in the company of "a Palouse Chief who says his people will not come to the Council."[8]

According to Judge William C. Brown, an authority who gathered oral histories for fifty years, there was no way of knowing "how far he [McKenzie] went, what Palouse Indians he got word to and the identity of this 'Palouse Chief.' " Evidence suggests that Kahlotus was the Palouse who returned with McKenzie, but little is known about him, except that he was the only person to sign the Yakima Treaty specifically in the name of the Palouses. Because of the nature of their "tribal" organization, which was composed of several bands and numerous headmen, rather than a single chief, Kahlotus did not represent all Palouses. However, Stevens recognized Kahlotus as spokesman for all Palouses and claimed that he and Kamiakin spoke for the entire tribe.[9]

The Nez Perces arrived en masse at the council, and they "came in with considerable ceremony," making an impression on Stevens and his small party. As far as the eye could see, the Nez Perces rode onto the grounds, across the gently rolling prairie. When they were about a mile from camp, some of the chiefs rode forward with William Craig who introduced them to the governor. Included in the group was Lawyer, Old Joseph, Metat Waptass, James, Eagle from the Light, Utsinmalikin, and Red Wolf. After the introductions, they joined Stevens and Palmer at the flagpole where they watched the colorful entry of the rest of the Nez Perces. The Americans and Indians peered across the valley as the party rode into camp, "a thousand warriors mounted on fine horses and riding at a gallop, two abreast, naked to the breech-clout, their faces covered with white, red, and yellow paint in fanciful designs, and decked with plumes and feathers and trinkets fluttering in the sunshine."[10] The Indians "sat upon their fine animals as if they were centaurs," Indians and horses alike "arrayed in the most glaring finery. They were painted with such colors as formed the greatest contrast; the white being smeared with crimson in fantastic figures, and the dark colored streaked with white clay."[11]

The proud Nez Perces and their colorful horses rode to the flagpole. The long stream of mounted Indians charged "at full gallop in single file . . . firing their guns, brandishing their shields, beating their drums, and yelling their war whoops, and dashed in a wide circle around the little party on the knoll." After surrounding the Americans perched on the small hill, they charged "as though to overwhelm it, now wheeling back, redoubling their wild action and fierce yells in frenzied excitement." Finally, the younger men dismounted, formed a circle, and danced to the loud beat of drums. Stevens felt that the grand show was performed in his honor, but it was more than a "specimen of . . . Prairie chivalry." The demonstration was a message to Stevens that the Nez Perces were powerful people whose rights were to be respected. Stevens had an escort of forty-seven soldiers under the command of Lieutenant Archibald Gracie, but in an armed conflict, they would have been no match for the Indians. Stevens was not worried about a threat from the Nez Perces, however, because he believed that the "malcontents" were to be found among the Cayuses, Palouses, Umatillas, Walla Wallas, and Yakimas.[12]

Two days later, the Cayuses arrived, numbering about three hundred strong. "They came in whooping and singing in the Indian Fashion," wrote Lawrence Kip, a professional soldier who had taken a leave of absence to attend the council. In their show of force, they rode around the Nez Perce camp a few times before riding off to set up their own encampment. The few Cayuse chiefs who visited Stevens were friendly, though most resented the whites for the Cayuse War and its aftermath. Nor did their former allies, the Umatillas or Walla Wallas, demonstrate a liking for the Americans. Tauitau (Young Chief) and Peopeo Moxmox (Yellow Bird), Cayuse and Walla Walla chiefs respectively, mirrored the distrust of their people, sentiments that were also shared by many Palouses. The Palouses, Walla Wallas, Cayuses, and Umatillas had all been involved in the Cayuse War and resented the opening of the Cayuse Country to white settlement. To demonstrate their disapproval, representatives from these tribes refused provisions offered by Stevens. They also refused tobacco, "a very unfriendly sign."[13]

The Yakimas traveled to the council by way of the Palouse village of Quosispah and visited their neighbors at the mouth of the Snake River before departing. Kamiakin explained his reluctance to attend the council, but he felt compelled to do so in order to protect his own interests and those of his band. Kamiakin had long been opposed to negotiating with whites, and his steadfast position worsened his relations with his uncles, Teias and Owhi. The Walla Walla Council and its aftermath caused a major schism within the Yakima Tribe, one that persists to this day.[14]

Kamiakin's disposition toward the treaty concerned Stevens. His anxiety grew as the council progressed. When Father Charles M. Pandosy, a priest at St. Joseph Mission, arrived with the Yakimas, he reportedly told Stevens "that these Indians were generally well disposed towards the whites, with the exception of Kam-i-ah-kan." The priest told Stevens that Kamiakin had said, "If the governor speaks hard, I will speak hard, too." Some of the other Indians allegedly warned the governor that "Kami-a-ah-kan will come with his young men with powder and ball." Although the governor knew that Kamiakin opposed the treaty and land cession, and some were worried that Kamiakin planned hostilities, no evidence exists to prove that there was in fact any such plan.[15]

Before the council, Stevens confidently stated that: "There is scarcely a doubt that the negotiations will be successful."[16] As deliberations began, the governor reassessed his position, concerned that Young Chief, Peopeo Moxmox, and Kamiakin were opposed to treaties and land sales. Kamiakin's dislike for the whites was subtle. He was cordial when he talked and smoked with the governor. He "shook hands in the most friendly manner." But the chief purposely refused the tobacco offered to him, fearing that Stevens would say that he had accepted the tobacco in payment for his lands. The April before, Kamiakin told Doty that he had never accepted gifts from Americans and would never do so. Kamiakin distrusted Stevens, but he was unsure of himself with regard to his position during the proceedings.[17]

The day before the council opened, Peopeo Moxmox and Kamiakin asked tribal leaders to assemble. They hoped to organize a united front, but the Nez Perces were unwilling to join the assembly. The Cayuse leaders approached Utsinmalikin, a noted Nez Perce chief, to ask the Nez Perces to attend the meeting. "What are their hearts to us? Our hearts are Nez Perce hearts," Utsinmalikin reported, "and we know them. We came here to hold a great council with the Great Chief of the Americans, and we know, the straight forward path to pursue and are alone responsible for our actions." He concluded by saying that the Nez Perces "will not have the Cayuse troubles on our hands."[18]

On May 29, 1855, the Walla Walla Council commenced with a brief meeting. About 5,000 Indians attended the first meeting, including three Palouse Chiefs—Kahlotus, Slyotze, and Tilcoax. They played no role in the official meeting, but undoubtedly spoke at the Indian councils held each night. The Palouse bands knew about the council, but most chiefs made a conscious choice not to attend, believing that if they were not in attendance then they would not be bound by any agreement made there.[19] Tragically, the Palouses did not understand that white negotiators regularly drafted treaties without the consent of all members of a tribe. By 1855 this was a well-established axiom of American Indian policy, and one which Stevens employed at the Walla Walla Council.[20] But even if a number of Palouse chiefs had attended the council, the results would have been the same.

Indians and whites met near Stevens's tent, under the brush arbors built for the occasion. Stevens and Palmer sat on a wooden bench, "while the Indians were seated on the ground in front in semicircular rows forty deep, one behind another." After smoking a pipe filled with tobacco, the meeting commenced. The Americans and Indians recorded the proceedings. One of the Nez Perces, Timothy, "acted as a crier for his nation" and kept a record of the meeting so that it would "be preserved among the archives of the nation and handed down to future generations." Unfortunately, Timothy's notes have not surfaced, leaving only those minutes kept by the Americans. These, however, are revealing.[21]

The first order of business was to appoint and swear in the interpreters, including William Craig, Andrew Pambrun, Nathan Olney, and John Whitford. Indians in the Puget Sound and on the coast had been forced to conduct their treaty proceedings in Chinook, a trade jargon, not their native languages. At the Walla Walla Council various dialects of Sahaptin were employed. Peopeo Moxmox insisted on having "more than one interpreter at the Council, that we may know they translate truly." But even with good interpreters, language problems resulted since Stevens and Palmer could not speak with the Indians directly. Inevitably something was lost in translation, and several times the Indians made note of the fact.[22] During the early discussions, Stevens revealed his paternalistic attitude, often referring to men much older than he as "children." Stevens believed himself to be superior, and he assumed from the outset that whites had a right to direct Indian policy, thus determining their future—regardless of what the Indians thought. Those present knew something about white attitudes but were patient, listening to what Stevens had to say.[23] They attended the first session despite a pouring rain, returning the next day to listen to the governor speak in circles about Lewis and Clark, William Penn, Chief John Ross, and Andrew Jackson. Stevens talked to them as if they were ignorant and knew absolutely nothing about past American Indian policies.

He spoke of the Eastern Indians as if the Plateau tribes were unaware of the removal of the Cherokees, Choctaws, Delawares, Wyandots, and others. All of the Plateau tribes had known Eastern Indians—many of whom had worked for Hudson's Bay and had married Plateau women. At least one Eastern Indian, Jim Simonds, known as Delaware Jim, attended the Walla Walla Council. The Plateau tribes may not have been familiar with the techniques of treaty making, but they understood the effects of American Indian policy. They were not "foolish children," and they did not believe that the white man had "been for many years caring for his red children across the mountains." Many treaties had been made, and despite Stevens's reassurances, they knew that many had been broken. The Eastern Indians were not happy about their relocation to the Indian Territories west of the Mississippi. Stevens suggested that the government had done "much for John Ross and his people [Cherokees]," asserting that before the Cherokees had met the whites, "they were as blind men." After white contact, however, the tribe learned a great deal about white civilization which made them "a great and happy and good people." Stevens told those present that government officials felt it was only fair that "what had been done for John Ross should be done for you, and more, as I will tell you." Such a proposition was not reassuring.[24]

Stevens, an impatient man and, according to a recent biographer, a "young man in a hurry," did not understand Indians, and prematurely revealed his objective. "What shall we do at this council? We want you and ourselves to agree upon tracts of land where you will live; in those tracts of land we want each man who will work to have his own land, his own horses, his own cattle, and his own home for himself and his children." Stevens asked the Indians to become reservation farmers, ruled by agents of the Bureau of Indian Affairs. He offered them a new way of life, progress, and prosperity. Stevens wanted the Indians "to learn to make ploughs, to learn to make wagons, and everything which you need in your house." He offered Indian women the chance to learn "to spin, and to weave and to make clothes." Someday, the governor stated, the Indians would "be farmers and mechanics, or you will be doctors and lawyers like white men." In addition to "all these things, these shops, these mills and these schools," the governor promised to pay the Indians "for the land which you give to the Great Father." He guaranteed to pay the people "a fair sum." Stevens stated that all this would be "done with your free consent."[25] Stevens said too much too quickly. Realizing his mistake, he concluded, saying "I am tired of speaking, you are tired of listening." He then turned to Palmer who reassured the Indians that the whites did not really expect them to make an agreement "with one day's talk."[26]

Stevens and Palmer had spoken of some things of interest, particularly promising to end raids by the Blackfeet "who stole your horses and murdered your grown people and your children." Palmer promised to prevent white Americans from encroaching on Indian land, despite the fact that whites "were as numerous as the leaves on the trees." To prevent hostilities, Palmer proposed "a line of distinction drawn so that the Indians may know where his land is and the white man where he is." The Indians supported boundaries, so that people could "say that this is mine and that is yours." Palmer explained: 'If there were no other whites coming into the country we might get along in peace; you may ask, why do they come? Can you stop the waters of the Columbia river from flowing on its course? Can you prevent the wind from blowing? Can you prevent the rain from falling? Can you prevent the whites from coming? You are answered No!" There were far too many whites, Palmer continued, and no one could prevent them from entering the West — not the president and not the Indians.[27]

The Indians said little until the third day, when pent-up anger surfaced. Five Crows, a Cayuse chief and the half-brother of Old Joseph, asked Stevens and Palmer if they were truly friends since they were asking the Indians to commit a sin. "Do you speak true that you call me brother? We have but one Father in Heaven; it is He (pointing upward) who had made all the earth; He made us of earth on this earth; He made our Fathers; when he gave us this earth. He gave us gardens also." Five Crows responded to white proposals by expressing his spiritual view of the land. To northwestern Indians the land was sacred, a gift from God, and as such, could not be sold. Peopeo Moxmox explained that the goods that had been offered were not worth the value of the land, because, "Goods and the Earth are not equal." The Indians believed that the earth was their mother and provider, the burial place of their ancestors. The earth was a gift from God whose law required the Indians to protect the lands.[28]

To prevent the Indians from gaining momentum and to observe the Sabbath, Stevens announced that the council would not be held on Sunday, June 3. To this proposal Peopeo Moxmox asked, "why not speak tomorrow as well as today? We have listened to all you have to say, and we desire you should listen when any Indian speaks." The Walla Walla chief expressed his anger when he declared that he knew the value of the white man's words from his experiences in California where his son had been murdered in cold blood by whites while horse trading. The killers had gone unpunished, and Peopeo Moxmox was convinced that his people would fare no better than his son had under American laws. "I know the value of your speech from having experienced the same in California, having seen treaties there." Peopeo Moxmox observed that Stevens had "spoken in a round about way." The Indians, he remarked, "have not seen in a true light the object of your speeches; as if there was a post set between us, as if my heart cried from what you have said; as if the Almighty came down upon us here this day; as if He would say, What are you saying?"[29]

Peopeo Moxmox asked Palmer and Stevens to "speak straight" so that he could know their hearts. "From what you have said," the chief remarked, "I think you intend to win our country, or how is it to be?" The whites, he said, had "Spoken in a manner partly tending to Evil." The Indian elder was perturbed about the governor's impatient, abrupt manner. "We require time to think," he remarked, "quietly, slowly." His request, made repeatedly during the council, fell on deaf ears. Stevens was anxious to conclude an agreement and to move across the Bitterroots to treat with the Flatheads and Blackfeet. Stevens's aggressiveness created dangerous feelings among the tribes. Ultimately, the Indians believed they were forced into making agreements which they did not have time to consider. In fact, the governor did not want the Indians to have time to weigh the benefits of the treaties, fearing they might not sign.

From the beginning Lawyer agreed to a treaty for the Nez Perces, and Peopeo Moxmox believed that Lawyer and William Craig, the interpreter (and later agent) for the Nez Perces, had made a prior agreement. It seemed to many "that the whole has been prearranged in the heart of the Indians [Nez Perces]." Peopeo Moxmox remarked: "I think my friend [Lawyer] has given his land." If this was the case, Lawyer was the only major leader who made such an early decision. The Palouses, Umatillas, Cayuses, Walla Wallas, and Wanapums opposed treaties that called for their removal to either the Yakima or Nez Perce Reservations. Originally, Stevens planned to establish two reservations, one in Nez Perce Country for the Walla Wallas, Cayuses, Umatillas, Spokanes, and Nez Perces and one in the Yakima Country for the Colvilles, Okanogans, Wenatchees, Klikatats, Yakimas, and Palouses. It is doubtful that Kahlotus, Kamiakin, or the handful of Palouses who were present fully understood this proposal. To have surrendered their land and moved constituted a sin — an act against God. Subsequent actions taken by the Palouses in violation of the Yakima Treaty and their participation in the subsequent war, verifies the fact that they would not leave their homelands without a fight.[30]

When Kamiakin spoke for the first time, he stated: "It is young men who have spoken." He remarked, "I have been afraid of the white men," because "their doings are different from ours." He was not certain about the validity of the Stevens-Palmer proposals, but he hoped that the white men would keep their promises. Tipyahlanah Kaoupu, the Eagle from the Light (Eagle of the Morning Light, or of the Dawn, or Eagle of Delight) shared Kamiakin's concerns, telling the governor that his people had been friendly to Lewis and Clark, but their kindness had been betrayed at the village of Palus. "A long time ago they hung my brother for no offense." Eagle from the Light spoke of Whitman and Spalding. He reminded everyone that his father, The Hat, and Chief Ellis had gone East but had died there. He concluded by saying: "We will come straight here — slowly — perhaps," he said, "but we will come straight."[31]

Stevens tried to allay these fears by explaining more fully the treaty terms. After outlining boundaries for the two proposed reservations, the governor stated that he wanted Indians to move onto reservations where they could farm, fish, gather roots, and graze their animals. "You will be allowed to pasture your animals on land not claimed or occupied by settlers, white men. You will be allowed to go on the roads, to take your things to market, your horses and cattle; you will be allowed to go to the usual fishing places and fish in common with the whites and to get roots and berries and to kill game on land not occupied by the whites; all this outside the Reservation."[32]

In addition, the governor promised to protect their property "from bad white men who cheat and steal from Indians." He explained his desire to appoint a "Head Chief" to represent all Indians on the reservations, a man who would be paid a salary of five hundred dollars a year for twenty years. Indians on each reservation would receive one hundred thousand dollars worth of goods — blankets, shirts, ploughs, and the like — the first year and two hundred and fifty thousand dollars worth of goods for the next twenty years.

Palmer proclaimed that whites wanted to build roads, a telegraph, and a railroad through the reservation. Palmer defined the operation of a railroad and telegraph, assuring the Indians that the transportation systems and new technologies would be advantageous to them. "You may not understand all the advantages of the propositions that have been made to you," Palmer asserted, "but they are for your benefits and those who come after you." He told them that he desired only to promote their interests, proclaiming that he would not deceive the Indians: "the Great Spirit who knows the heart of all men knows that I desire to promote your good." Some Indians were not convinced.

Stickus, a Cayuse chief, responded by first speaking earnestly through the interpreter, Andrew Pambrun. "My friends I wish to show you my mind, interpret right for me." His mind was troubled over the proposals, and he explained his position. "Had I two rivers I would be content to leave the one and live on the other."[33] He asked the government delegation to think of the earth as if it was their own mother. "If your mothers were here in this country who gave you birth, suckled you and while you were suckling some person came and took your mother and left you alone and sold your mother, how would you feel then?" The earth south of the Snake River had, since the beginning of time, belonged to the Cayuses, Walla Wallas, and Umatillas. The Indians could no more sell the land than Stevens or Palmer could sell their own mother. "This is our mother," Stickus proclaimed, "as if we drew our living from her." Stevens, Palmer, and the Indians were speechless for a time. Then Five Crows concluded the session, stating that the Indians required 'time to think." The Indians retired to their tipis to council among themselves.[34]

Indians leaders, as evidenced by their testimony during the council, were shocked by the proposals and angered by the arrogant and haughty manner in which they were presented. Many joined the malcontents after listening to the proposals, and "more hostile feelings towards the whites" developed. This growing feeling emerged among many headmen, except for Lawyer and those Nez Perces who supported him. But it must be remembered that under the terms of the treaty, the Nez Perces would retain a good portion of their traditional homelands. Other tribes — the Palouses, Wanapums, Wenatchees, Klikitats, Cayuses, and Walla Wallas — would lose most, if not all, of theirs.[35]

When the council reconvened on June 7, Lawyer presented a history lesson, ranging in topics from Columbus to Lewis and Clark. Lawyer then asked Stevens to "take care of us well." This upset Peopeo Moxmox who responded, "I think my friend has given his land, that is what I think from his words." The Walla Walla chief asked everyone to listen, saying this "is the way with your Chiefs, you white people. When you show us something then we think it is good, treating us as children." Peopeo Moxmox announced that he did not know what or who to believe, since he did "not see the offer you have made to the Indians." He asked Stevens and Palmer to adjourn the council and set another time to continue the discussion, so that there would be "no bad minds among the Indians." Peopeo Moxmox believed that the Indians could not come to decision on such weighty matters with just one meeting and with so many Indians absent. He told the whites that he would attend the session the next day but "towards evening I shall go home." Owhi was of a similar mind, arguing: "My people are far away they do not know your words, this is the reason why I cannot give you an answer now." Kamiakin also planned to leave the council, and the threat of the council adjourning without the signature of these chiefs worried Stevens considerably.

The Indian position was best presented by Young Chief and Owhi. Young Chief began by rebuking Lawyer. He stated that the "reason I do not know anything about this ground is I do not see the offer you have made." Sarcastically he stated: "If I had the money in my hand I would see." But Young Chief was no more concerned about money than the others. He was concerned about the earth, his ancestral land — his mother. His attitude toward the earth and its "chieftainship" was shared by the Palouses who approved of Young Chief's words.

> I wonder if this ground has anything to say: I wonder if the ground is listening to what is said. I wonder if the ground would come to life and what is on it; though I hear what this earth says, the earth says, God has placed me here. The Earth says, that God tells me to take care of the Indians on this earth; the Earth says to the Indians that stop on the Earth feed them right. God named the roots that he should feed the Indians on: The water speaks the same way: God says feed the Indians upon the earth: the grass says the same thing: feed the horses and cattle. The Earth and water and grass says God has given our names and we are told those names; neither the Indians or the Whites have a right to change those names: The Earth says, God has placed me here to produce all that grows upon me, the trees, fruit, etc. The same way the Earth says, it was from her man was made. God on placing them on the Earth desired them to take good care of the earth and do each other no harm.[36]

When Young Chief completed his oration, Palmer asked Kamiakin to speak. The Yakima replied wryly, "I have nothing to say." His uncle, Owhi, had something to say, however. In a profound, poetic manner, Owhi spoke of the earth and its relationship with the Creator. "God gave us day and night, the night to rest in, and the day to see, and that as long as the earth shall last, he gave us the morning with our breath; and so he takes care of us on this earth and here we have met under his care. Is the earth before the day or the day before the earth. God was before the earth, the heavens were clear and good and all things in the heavens were good. God looked one way then the other and names our lands for us to take care of." According to Owhi, God had charged the Indians to take care of and to use the lands forever. He then questioned the authority of the whites to meddle in God's law, since

God had "made this earth and it listens to him to know what he would decide. The Almighty made us and gave us breath; we are talking together and God hears all that we say today. God looks down upon his children today as if we were all in one body. He is going to make one body of us; we Indians present have listened to your talk as if it came from God."[37]

Thus, according to the religious beliefs of the Sahaptins, the earth could no more be sold than the wind, the rivers, or the sky. To have done so was considered a sin, and Owhi explained this to Stevens, saying "I am afraid of the laws of the Almighty, that is the reason I am afraid to speak of the land." Then looking about—at the white men and the Indians—Owhi asked: "Shall I steal this land and sell it?" And he asked, "Shall I give the lands that are part of my body and leave myself poor and destitute? Shall I say that I will give you my lands? I cannot . . . I am afraid of the Almighty." The Palouses concurred with these beliefs, and agreed that God had made their "bodies from the earth as if they were different from the whites." The physical bodies of the Palouses and the others were similar to the whites, but their hearts, minds, and spiritual being were worlds apart.[38]

Neither Stevens nor Palmer fully understood the words spoken about God and the earth, for many whites viewed the land not as a spiritual partner, but as a wilderness to be tamed and manipulated. Stevens and Palmer were unsympathetic to the Indian view of the earth, and both were angered by the presentations. Palmer became impatient, asking the Indians, "How long will these people remain blind. We can try to open their eyes, they refuse the light." Palmer explained that he had traveled a great distance to help them, but the Indians had refused the "light" and had listened to "bad council [sic]." He assured the Indians that he had not come to steal their land but was willing to pay for the "parched up plain." He asked them, "What is it worth to you or to us? Not one half of what we offered for it." Indian leaders wondered why white men wanted the land so badly, and Palmer had an answer: "It is because our Chief [the president] has told us to take care of his red people. We come to you with his messages to try and do you good. You throw his words behind you."

Before Palmer continued his tirade, Peopeo Moxmox patiently but urgently said, "Let us part and appoint another day." But the superintendent quickly responded: "Before that day would arrive we might have a great deal of trouble."[39] The talks had taken a bad turn, for Palmer and Stevens were so impatient that they cast aside the Indian request to proceed slowly in order to avoid difficulties. The superintendents urged the Indians to sign a treaty immediately to prevent problems, and they pressured them into a hasty act. Palmer argued that an agreement should be reached to avoid hostilities, pointing out that gold had been discovered near Fort Colvile and that white men, seasoned miners from the California diggings, "will come here by the hundreds." He maintained that among the miners "there will be some bad people, those bad people will steal your horses and cattle." If the Indians lived on reservations, Palmer proclaimed, the government would protect them. This was a shallow promise indeed, for neither superintendent was committed to protecting Indian rights, despite what they said, and the result of this broken promise would be war.[40]

The council session on June 7 was a stormy one, for the Indians were disturbed and divided. As Howlishwampum put it: "Your words since you

came here have been crooked." Peopeo Moxmox, fearing that the entire council might explode into hostilities, stated that the Indians and the whites had
"met as friends" and should "part . . . as friends." He asked everyone to "say
nothing that is bad" and to "act as friends and wise men." As for himself,
Peopeo Moxmox was so upset he said that he had been "blown away like
a feather."[41] Palmer and Stevens were not moved, and claimed again that
they simply wanted to open the Indians' eyes so that they might see the right
path. Stevens was blunt and chided Kamiakin and Owhi, asking them if they
were afraid to be leaders.[42]

The council reached a critical juncture, particularly after Stevens made
his remarks to the leaders. According to one white account: "The Nez Perces
through Lawyer, their Head Chief, unanimously agreed to the Treaty," but
the other tribes had not yet "seen the light." That evening the council ended
on a disturbing note, for the Indians were openly angered by the "bad talk."
Owhi was the last Indian to speak, and he told the whites: "We will settle
the matter among ourselves." Many of the Indians "were very much incensed
against the Nez Perces for agreeing to the terms of the treaty." This was particularly true of the Walla Wallas, Cayuses, and Umatillas who, under the
proposed agreement, would have been forced to move onto the Nez Perce
Reservation. That night, Indian leaders held a number of councils to determine their course of action, and "everything seemed to be in violent confusion." Factions occurred between pro-treaty and anti-treaty groups.[43]

The confusion caused the council to be delayed until late the next afternoon.[44] Hostility surfaced immediately as Young Chief told the Americans:
"Your marking of this country is the reason it troubles me so and has made
me sit here without saying anything." He could not see why he should surrender all of his land and asked, "where was I to go to, was I to be a wanderer
like a wolf." Young Chief said that he would not take his entire "country
and throw it to you." He would not make an agreement which forced him
to move from his native earth, and he told the whites to make another offer
so that he could "come to an agreement." He wished for a reservation in
"the land where my forefathers are buried."[45]

When Young Chief completed his statement, Palmer made a new proposal, calling for another reservation for the Cayuses, Walla Wallas, and
Umatillas. Although Young Chief had wanted to secure lands along the
Grande Ronde, the whites offered him the Umatilla Valley. Eventually he
agreed to move there. Like the other leaders of his region—Peopeo Moxmox, Stickus, and Five Crows—Young Chief would have desired more lands,
but he and others felt that this was the best deal that they could get. They
took it. The Nez Perces raised no major objections to their treaty until June
8, when word reached the council that Apash Wyakai, Old Looking Glass,
was on his way to the council.[46] Looking Glass made a dramatic entrance
into the American camp while the council was in session, riding proudly into
camp "painted and armed, singing a war song." From his horse he made a
"violent speech, . . . an expression of his indignation at their selling his country."[45] The seventy-year old chief looked defiantly down at Stevens and
Palmer before turning to the Indians and addressing them with gravity: "My
people, what have you done? While I was gone, you have sold my country.
I have come home, and there is not left [for] me a place on which to pitch
my lodge. Go home to your lodges. I will talk to you."[48]

The arrival of Looking Glass caused Stevens great concern since "a new explosive element dropped into the little political caldron." On the night of June 8 there was a great deal of discussion in the Indian camps, and many Indians prepared to leave the council. Owhi, Skloom, and Teias leaned toward making an agreement, while Kamiakin refused to concede one inch of his land. In order to avoid signing the treaty, Kamiakin decided to leave the council the next day.[49] As a courtesy he visited Stevens. The events associated with his audience are of monumental importance to the Palouses, for Stevens considered Kamiakin the head chief of many Indians, including the Palouses. The day before, Doty believed that Kamiakin was "in favor of some Treaty, but does not agree directly to the one proposed."[50] When Kamiakin visited Stevens the next day he said he "was tired of talking—tired of waiting, etc." and was prepared to ride home. Stevens demanded to know why Kamiakin, "the acknowledged Head Chief of the Yakimas did not speak his mind in Council as became a Great Chief, why he did not take a decided course for or against the Treaty." Stevens told Kamiakin that it was time for the chief to make "a Treaty of Peace and Friendship with the Whites, to endure forever." Stevens asked Kamiakin if he would leave the council "without doing anything."[51]

Kamiakin gave the governor's words a lot of thought before speaking, and following "considerable deliberation," Kamiakin allegedly said: "All say that I am the Head Chief of the Yakimas. They look to me to speak. Owhi and Skloom are Chiefs but they will not talk. They say let Kam-i-ah-kun speak. Well let it be so." According to Doty, Stevens's arguments carried the day, convincing Kamiakin to sign the treaty. The chief reportedly made a "list of the Tribes and lands over whom he had authority as Head Chief." This list included the Palouses, Yakimas, Wenatchees, Klickitats, and various tribes of the Columbia River. Kamiakin supposedly said that he was "head chief" of all of these people.[52]

Andrew Pambrun, an interpreter at the council, provided another account of the discussion between Stevens and Kamiakin. Pambrun briefly remarked that many "days were occupied in feasting and talking," but when little progress was made, Stevens said: "If you do not accept the terms offered and sign this paper (holding up the paper) you will walk in blood knee deep." This angered Kamiakin, but he signed the treaty nevertheless. According to Pambrun: "Kamiakin was the last, and as he turned to take his seat, the Priest [either Pandosy or Chirouse] hunched me and whispered, look at Kamiakin, we will all get killed, he was in such a rage that he bit his lips that they bled profusely." The priests in attendance thought that the governor's approach was a mistake, for Stevens had incited the Indians. "The Priest remarked that this is an error, he should not make such a threat." Doty made no record of this incident, stating only that there was "considerable deliberation."[53]

Kamiakin had openly opposed a treaty since meeting Doty on April 1, 1855. The Yakima chief had a reputation of standing aloof, refusing to have "much to do with the Whites," and throughout the Walla Walla Council, he had continually told them that he had "nothing to say." On the morning of June 9, when Kamiakin decided to leave the council, he probably believed that if he did not make an agreement, his lands would not be sold. After his meeting with Stevens, he made a complete turn-around, deciding not to leave, but to remain and sign an agreement.[54] Doty and Stevens maintained, and many historians have believed, that Kamiakin had assumed power over tribes he did not control, including the Palouses. The white men reported that Kamiakin had signed the treaty willingly; perhaps he did. Certainly a threat would not have been sufficient to have forced him to sign, but it is more likely that his relatives — Skloom, Owhi, and Teias — prevailed upon the chief. More important was the influence of Kamiakin's good friend, Peopeo Moxmox, who urged him to accept the treaty as an act of peace and friendship. Andrew Jackson Splawn, an authority who worked with the Indians for years, was "told by Chief Moses . . . that after the adjournment of June 7, Ka-mi-akin and Pe-peu-mox-mox met in the latter's lodge for a long consultation and that, on the following night, they held another conference. What argument Pe-peu-mox-mox used to induce the iron man of the Yakimas to sign, I never learned."[55]

It may never be known what caused Kamiakin to change his mind about the Yakima Treaty of 1855, but the fact that he did was of utmost importance to the Palouses. He was not the "head chief" of the Palouses or any other tribe; he never claimed to be. Doty wrote that Kamiakin listed the tribes over whom he had authority and that the list included the Palouse Indians "over whom he is of lineal descent the Chief." Kamiakin was a Palouse through his father, but Kamiakin never, under any circumstances, claimed to have been the "head chief" of these people. To have done so would have been unthinkable. Either the interpreter misquoted Kamiakin or Doty misinterpreted the events in his journal.[56]

Young Doty, like his boss, lumped several groups together under the leadership of Kamiakin, calling them a confederated tribe. This was done for the convenience of government officials, not the Indians. According to Stevens, the Indians had united under one leader "for the purpose of this treaty" and were "to be considered as one nation, under the name of "Yakima," with Kamiakin as its head chief, on behalf of and acting for said tribes and bands, and being duly authorized thereto by them."[57] This statement, directly from the Yakima Treaty of 1855, is clearly false. There is no evidence to suggest that Kamiakin was authorized to act on behalf of the Palouses or the others included in the treaty. He acted as a representative of his own band, and he signed the treaty as an act of peace and friendship. He did so to accommodate his friends and relatives. Kamiakin himself declared that he did "not speak this for myself it is my people's wish. Owhi and Teias and the chiefs. I, Kamiakin do not wish for goods myself. The forest knows me, he knows my heart, he knows I do not desire a great many goods . . . I have nothing to talk long about. I am tired, I am anxious to get back to my garden."[58]

During his speech, Kamiakin reportedly said that he wanted an agent who would "take care of us." He further said that he hoped that the Americans would "settle on the wagon route . . . so that the Indians may go and see them." His comments were meant as sarcasm against those Indians willing to sign the treaty which would admit whites into the Yakima Country. Kamiakin refused to accept any gifts during the council, and to his dying day, he took no presents from white men, fearing that if he received gifts, the *suyapo* would say that he had sold his lands.

Under the terms of the Yakima Treaty, the Palouses were to move from their homelands onto the Yakima Reservation. Stevens, Doty, and Palmer had employed an old trick of American Indian policy, one that had been used many times. They simply assigned one leader to be "head chief" and placed several tribes under his control. Kamiakin was a victim of a dishonest policy, and the Palouses suffered as a result. The Palouses were bound to the terms of the agreement, even though Kamiakin and Kahlotus could not and never intended to speak for them as a group. The Palouse Indians did not accept the terms of the Yakima Treaty, but most of them remained quiet until they were attacked. Indeed, Stevens had planted the seeds of conflict with his treaty signed at Walla Walla. The Pacific Northwest would reap the whirlwind when war between whites and Indians broke out.[59]

CHAPTER 6

THE YAKIMA WAR

We took common cause . . . to defend all together
our nationality and our country.
— Kamiakin

Governor Stevens left the Walla Walla Valley on June 16, 1855, making his way eastward across the Palouse Hills south of the Snake River. He found the land "a delightful rolling country, well grassed and arable," and he was convinced that the hills would make "a remarkably fine grazing and wheat country." The governor continued overland to the confluence of Alpowa Creek with the Snake River, where a Nez Perce named Red Wolf ferried Stevens across the great river. As the governor traveled north of the Snake toward the Coeur d'Alene Country, he met several bands of Indians digging camas roots, including twelve lodges of Palouses under a headman named Quillatose (Kahlotus). These Palouses had nothing to do with Stevens, or if they did, the governor made no mention of it.[1]

Two days later, Stevens met 137 Palouses digging camas with the Coeur d'Alenes. Slyotze, also known as Slowiarchy, the chief of this band of Palouses, visited the *suyapo* on the night of June 22, 1855. Slyotze was accompanied by twenty warriors who counseled with Stevens. "In conversation," Stevens wrote, "Slyotze expressed his own and his people's satisfaction with the treaty." Slyotze reportedly said that the Palouse Indians "regarded Kamiakin as the head chief of the Yakima nation, and the Peluses as a tribe of that nation." This comment certainly casts doubt on Stevens's honesty or that of his interpreter. Neither Slyotze nor any other Palouse chief would have claimed that Kamiakin was the head chief of the Palouse tribe or that the Palouses were a sub-tribe of the Yakimas. Stevens either misunderstood Slyotze or falsified his report to substantiate his declaration that all of the Indians, including the Palouses, were pleased with the Yakima Treaty.[2]

While Stevens journeyed across the Bitterroot Mountains to negotiate treaties with the Flatheads and Blackfeet, the various tribes on the Columbia Plateau returned home to ponder their own treaties. Little is known about Kahlotus or his reaction to the agreements, but there is a great deal known about how Kamiakin reacted. He was not pleased with the Yakima Treaty, and his feelings were shared by many Palouses. A slow-burning anger emerged among the Indians, as they remembered that Stevens had spoken to them as if they were children. They resented the governor's demand that Indians move off their homelands to the reservations. The Palouses would have agreed with Kamiakin that a reservation was "a place where people do not even have enough to eat." Under the terms of the Yakima Treaty, the Palouses were to move, but since most had not agreed to the treaty, they were unwilling to move. Many preferred to fight to preserve their country, sovereignty, and freedom.[3]

Whites as well as Indians felt that Stevens had made the treaties with too much haste. George Gibbs, a former secretary of Stevens, told a friend that the "greatest single blunder" committed by the governor "was in bringing together the Nez Perces, Walla Wallas, Yakamas [sic] and others into one council, and cramming a treaty down their throats in a hurry."[4] Kamiakin reacted to the council by organizing his allies for a possible war. The Yakima chief sent his emissaries to the various tribes on the coast, Plateau, and Bitterroot Valley. Like Pontiac, Little Turtle, and Tecumseh before him, he helped to organize a loose Indian confederacy in an attempt to act against the white invasion. Some Palouses joined the confederacy, and many visited Kamiakin's home to counsel with their relative. The missionaries at St. Joseph Mission on Ahtanum Creek reported seeing several "bands of Palous [sic] and Nez Perces passing the Mission going to his [Kamiakin's] camp to plot, to get ready." These visits increased after the treaties were signed.[5]

During the summer of 1855, the Palouses became alarmed for yet another reason. Gold had been discovered north of the Spokane River near Fort Colvile. After the treaties were signed, several whites rushed to the new diggings. The Palouses were aware of what had happened earlier to the tribes of California and Oregon during gold rushes and feared that they would suffer a similar fate. Miners were a hardy, ruthless lot who let nothing—heat, hardship, mountains, rivers, or Indians—stand between them and their gold. Many miners brought with them their prejudices and disregard of Indian rights and property.[6]

Some were as racist as their predecessors in California, while others acted in good faith, believing that the land was open to white exploitation. The Donation Land Act of 1850 offered them 180 acres anywhere in the vast Oregon Country, and Governor Stevens had opened the Northwest to the whites. But at Walla Walla, Stevens gave his solemn oath to keep whites out of the region and not force the Indians onto reservations for two or three years. He betrayed his promise even before leaving the Walla Walla Council, sending dispatches to the coastal newspapers announcing the opening of the interior. On June 23, 1855 the *Oregon Weekly Times* ran an article declaring that "the country embraced in these cessions and not included in the reservation is open to settlement." Many newspapers ran such articles, and the whites believed that a bargain had been struck and that the Indians had sold their lands. Gold, not farm land, was the primary motivation for the first substantial white invasion of the region. Catholic priests, close observers of the Indian community, feared that the gold strike and the opening of the interior Northwest to whites would cause war. In a prophetic statement, Father Ricard of Olympia said that "the mines of Colville will become a new cause of trouble." Certainly, he exclaimed, "there will be a lot more bloodshed." He was, unfortunately, correct.[7]

The events that followed were extremely significant to the Palouses. Regardless of the number of Palouses directly involved in the developing drama in the Yakima Country, the Palouses were ultimately drawn into the Plateau Indian War from 1855 to 1858. When white miners invaded the Yakima Country, some stole horses and raped Indian women. At least one white miner, Henri Mattice, was executed by Qualchin (son of Chief Owhi) for assaulting Qualchin's cousin, the daughter of Chief Teias. This was not an isolated incident, for Kamiakin reported that some of "the Americans who were going to the mines shot some Indians because they did not want to give them [the whites] their wives."[8] There were other attacks by miners, and the Indians retaliated. However, the conflict between Indians and miners did not impede the gold rush. In September 1855, Qualchin and six warriors wiped out six miners who were crossing the Yakima River. Other miners journeyed across Yakima lands, and some were killed by the younger men.

Charles H. Mason, acting governor of Washington Territory while Stevens counseled with the Flatheads and Blackfeet, called upon Major Gabriel Rains of the United States Army to investigate the report "that 3 American citizens have been murdered by Yakima Indians on the eastern side of the Cascades, while going to the Collvile mines."[9] Closer to the scene of the conflict, Andrew Jackson Bolon, Indian agent to the Yakimas, learned about the killings while traveling to the Spokane Country. East of The Dalles, Bolon met Spokan Garry who informed him of the recent events. Bolon, always brash and arrogant, investigated the report, proceeding alone to the Yakima Country. The Yakimas disliked Bolon, and Kamiakin openly despised the agent, characterizing the white man as a fool and liar. Bolon was a high-handed individual who attempted to turn the Indians against the Catholic priests. Father Louis J. D'Herbomez wrote that Bolon was a man of "little prudence and wisdom" and that many "Indians hated him for the manner in which he treated the Indians." Bolon misread the hostile climate in the Yakima Country and paid dearly for his error.[10]

As he rode to Toppenish Creek, where he visited Showaway, Kamiakin's brother, he was warned that the Indians were in an ugly mood and that his life was in danger. Bolon heeded the warning, turned his horse south, and rode toward The Dalles. But along the way, he fell in with a band of Yakimas riding to The Dalles to get salmon. Mosheel, the head of the party, knew and hated Bolon. Another member of the party, Suelel Lil, a young man of fourteen, later recalled that Mosheel and Wahpiwahpilah wanted to kill Bolon because the agent had hanged Mosheel's uncles and cousins. The Indians concealed their plans by speaking Yakima, and they treated Bolon cordially until that evening. Some of the Indians opposed the plan to murder the agent, but Mosheel had his way. Soon after they made camp, the Indians surprised Bolon, wrestled him to the ground, and slit his throat. Like the killings of Marcus and Narcissa Whitman, Bolon's murder became a watershed in Pacific Northwest history. Although Palouses had no direct involvement in the murders of either Whitman or Bolon, they felt the repercussions of these violent deeds. The Palouses were drawn into the Yakima War after events among other tribes triggered the conflict.[11]

Bolon's death was the most immediate cause of the northwestern Indian war fought intermittently between 1855 and 1858. After hostilities commenced, Palouse Indians fought alongside the Yakimas, Wenatchees, Walla Wallas, Umatillas, Cayuses, and others. News of Bolon's death spread quickly throughout the Northwest, receiving mixed reactions in the Indian villages. Some Indians were saddened and feared white reprisals. Others welcomed the news, believing that it was time for their people to stand against the whites. Destructive rumors circulated that whites intended to banish the Indians where the land was "never right with the sun and where consequently there is eternal night" or bind them "in chains and put [them] in prison in Steilacoom."

News of the impending trouble was received by the Palouses in a variety of ways, as some of the warriors rode off to join the Yakimas, while others remained in their homes.[12]

When Bolon did not return to The Dalles, Indian Agent Nathan Olney sent a delegation of DesChutes Indians to spy on the Yakimas. The DesChutes returned with the alarming news of Bolon's murder. Word of the agent's death spread. Whites believed that the Indians planned a war of extermination and that Kamiakin was single-handedly responsible. For many years following Bolon's death, whites contended that Kamiakin had directed Qualchin to murder the agent, but this was totally false. Nevertheless, the rumor evolved into "fact," eventually costing Kamiakin his reputation and Qualchin his life.[13]

Killing an agent of the United States government was unpardonable. Outraged by Bolon's death, whites invaded the inland Northwest to punish the Indians. Kamiakin, the only Indian at the time who left a written explanation of Bolon's death, stated that the agent had "strongly insulted us, threatened us with war and death." According to the chief, the Indians had let the agent "pass peacefully," for they originally had no intention of killing him. But because the agent had gone "on talking to us with much harshness and threatened us with soldiers" Mosheel and the others seized the red-haired agent and slit his throat. Kamiakin argued that Bolon had been executed as a defensive measure in order to prevent him from returning to The Dalles and ordering troops into the field.[14]

However, if this was the intent, the action had the opposite effect. Fearing that the Indians planned "to join in a general rising against the Americans," Acting Governor Mason and the territorial legislature demanded that the United States Army launch an expedition to "punish these Indians, and to check their murderous intentions."[15] They hoped that the punitive expedition would "prove sufficiently strong to inflict a severe punishment upon the Indians, and thus check the war at the outstart."[16] Major Gabriel Rains answered the public cry for protection by ordering Major Granville O. Haller to take one company of soldiers from Fort Dalles to investigate. Haller was supported by Lieutenant W. A. Slaughter and a force of fifty men from Fort Steilacoom. They were to march from Puget Sound over the Cascades and join Haller in the Yakima Country. In response to rapidly-developing events east of the Cascades, the military invasion of the inland Northwest commenced on October 2, 1855.[17]

One of Haller's objectives was "to prevent a combination of the various tribes."[18] Territorial officials, soldiers, and Indian agents feared that the Yakimas would "be joined by a large portion of the Walla Wallas, Palouses, and Conguses [Cayuses], all of whom are turbulent."[19] Whites believed that the Palouses were in league with the Yakimas, and no doubt some Palouses, particularly young men, sided with Kamiakin. However, most Palouses did not join the Yakimas despite the fact that they were sympathetic. The vast majority of Palouses embraced peace until their own lands were invaded and their people murdered. Then, and only then, did a significant number take "common cause . . . to defend altogether our nationality and our country." This is born out in the documents and the oral histories of Indians today who remember the stories related by their ancestors.[20]

While the Yakimas and their allies mobilized, Haller's soldiers traveled north from The Dalles, meeting the Indians in battle on October 5, 1855 near Toppenish Creek. Few men died on either side during the two-day fight, but the engagement proved significant, as the soldiers hastily retreated to The Dalles after burying their howitzer and destroying their supplies. Lieutenant Slaughter learned of Haller's defeat while he was crossing the Cascades, and he withdrew from the field before engaging the enemy. Some Palouses were pleased with the Indian victory, but some of them—the older and wiser people—whispered that the hostile leaders and the younger men had stirred up a hornet's nest.[21]

The military records are not clear about identifying all of the tribes involved in the conflict. Certainly some Yakimas, Cayuses, and Lower Palouses were involved but the exact numbers are not known. Regardless of the number of Palouses fighting, the tribe as a whole was to be greatly affected by the flow of events. While many Indians reveled in their victory, the army, territorial officials, and white citizenry prepared their retribution. News of Haller's defeat shocked the white settlers who quickly demanded severe punishment of the Indians. Kamiakin became the focus of their wrath. Owhi and Teias, jealous of their nephew, pointed to Kamiakin as the perpetrator of the war. Kamiakin's enemies quickly claimed that he was the source of their difficulties, because he had spoken out against whites, inciting the younger men. Kamiakin was also blamed for signing the Yakima Treaty.

Some Palouses blamed Kamiakin as well, and Quiltenenock, Quetalakin (Moses), and other leaders of the Salish-speaking tribes of the Columbia River, as well as some Chinooks, condemned Kamiakin for selling their lands. Kamiakin's role in the treaty and war are topics of discussion in Palouse homes today. Onto the shoulders of Kamiakin fell the frustrations, suspicions, and hostilities of the Indians and the whites, and the chief became the scapegoat among his own people and the whites.[22] The Palouse warriors who fought Haller's soldiers acted autonomously but were part of a loose-knit confederacy which Kamiakin had forged. Kamiakin did try to unite the interior Indians, but his efforts largely failed. After the war started his popularity waned, particularly when factions vied with one another over support for the war.[23]

Fear ran high in the white settlements west of the Cascades, for the "Indian problem" had exploded almost simultaneously in the Puget Sound, the Rogue River, and the Yakima Valley.[24] To combat the threat east of the mountains, Major Rains organized his forces at Fort Dalles, calling upon the territories of Oregon and Washington to recruit volunteers. Governor George L. Curry of Oregon and Acting Governor Mason of Washington requested the help of their constituents to defeat the Indians who had "appeared in arms to murder our citizens in defiance of the power of the United States." Volunteers were needed, the governors proclaimed, to protect "the lives of our citizens" and to "meet and subdue the foe." The response was overwhelming.[25] Young men of both territories enlisted to answer their "country's call to arms." While the Washington Volunteers remained west of the Cascades, the Oregon Volunteers, nearly five hundred men strong, assembled at The Dalles. Commanded by Colonel James W. Nesmith, not Major Rains, the volunteers operated independently of the United States forces. "Extermination of the Indians" soon became "the order of the day, and no efforts on the part of Territorial officers were made to check it."[26]

On October 31, Rains left Fort Dalles for the Yakima Country, joined soon after by Nesmith's volunteers. The total command numbered over five hundred strong. By November 8, the soldiers reached the Yakima River where they were engaged in skirmishing. Indecisive and sporadic fighting occurred

may. 1855. Walla Walla Council. Governor Stevens with Indians

The Walla Walla Council of 1855. *Yakima Nation Media Center.*

Arrival of the Nez Perces at the Walla Walla Council of 1855. Sketch by Gustavus Sohon. *Smithsonian Institution.*

Tamootsin, Timothy, a pro-government Nez Perce who served with Colonel Edward Steptoe. Sketched by Gustavus Sohon, June 7, 1855. *Washington State Historical Society.*

Hemene Ilppilp, Red Wolf, who operated a ferry on the Snake River, was headman of Alpowa near the upper Palouse Villages. Sketched by Gustavus Sohon, May 30, 1855. *Washington State Historical Society.*

Hallalhotsoot, Lawyer, Leader of the Christian, pro-treaty Nez Perces and signer of the Thief Treaty of 1863. Sketched by Gustavus Sohon, May 25, 1855. *Washington State Historical Society.*

In August 1858, Colonel George Wright and Captain E. D. Keyes erected a supply depot on the Snake River, naming it Fort Taylor in honor of one of the officers slain in the Steptoe Fight. This view is from a pencil sketch by Gustavus Sohon. *Manuscripts, Archives, and Special Collections, Washington State University Libraries.*

The place where the Palouse River flowed into the Snake became the site of a major village called Palus. This delineation of the location by John Mix Stanley appeared as a lithograph in Stevens's *Pacific Railroad Report. Private Collection.*

According to Isaac Stevens, Indians believed Palouse Falls was created by the Great Spirit to prevent the ascent of salmon upstream. Those who lived upstream, so the story went, had incurred the Great Spirit's wrath. This illustration, by John Mix Stanley, appeared in Stevens's *Pacific Railroad Report. Private collection.*

The Steptoe Battle of 1858. Sketched by Gustavus Sohon a few months after the fight. *Library of Congress.*

Smohalla (believed to be the man dressed in white and seated to the right in the front row) was a Wanapum religious teacher, who had many followers among the Palouses. *Relander Collection, Yakima Valley Regional Library.*

Chief Joseph, the famed Nez Perce exiled to the Indian
Territory. *Relander Collection, Yakima Valley Regional
Library.*

Isaac Ingals Stevens, first territorial governor of Washington and architect of Pacific Northwest Indian policy in the second half of the nineteenth century. Photograph by Matthew Brady. *Relander Collection, Yakima Valley Regional Library.*

Reverend James H. Wilbur, Yakima Indian Agent and Methodist Missionary. *Relander Collection, Yakima Valley Regional Library.*

Captain John Mullan, Road builder. *Relander Collection, Yakima Valley Regional Library.*

Andrew Pambrun, white interpreter for the proceedings at the Walla Walla Council in 1855. *Relander Collection, Yakima Valley Regional Library.*

Colonel George Wright, commander of the American forces during the 1858 Plateau Indian War. *Relander Collection, Yakima Valley Regional Library.*

General John Wool, commander of the Pacific forces during most of the Plateau Indian War. *Relander Collection, Yakima Valley Regional Library.*

Colonel Lawrence Kip, who provided eyewitness accounts of the Walla Walla Council and George Wright's campaign. *Relander Collection, Yakima Valley Regional Library.*

The Christian General, Oliver O. Howard, met the Nez Perces and Palouses at the Lapwai Councils. *Relander Collection, Yakima Valley Regional Library.*

The Battle of Spokane Plains, September 5, 1858, from a sketch by Gustavus Sohon. *Smithsonian Institution.*

Horse Slaughter Camp on the Washington-Idaho Border. *Library of Congress.*

Harlish Washomake, also known to whites as Wolf Necklace or Tilcoax the Younger, resisted government attempts to remove him to a reservation throughout the 1870s and 1880s. *Manuscripts, Archives, and Special Collections, Washington State University Libraries.*

Group of Palouse Indians photographed circa 1900. *Manuscripts, Archives, and Special Collections, Washington State University Libraries.*

Indians curing salmon on racks in front of their tipis. A sketch from *Northwest Magazine* 1894.

A delegation of Plateau Indians that visited Washington, D.C. in 1889. *Relander Collection, Yakima Valley Regional Library.*

Fathers Adrian Hoecken, a Dutch Jesuit, and Pierre Jean De Smet, a Belgian serving in the same religious order, brought Christianity to the interior tribes during the 1840s. Through his books and articles, Father De Smet did much to publicize Indian missions in the Pacific Northwest. *Crosby Library, Gonzaga University.*

Father Joseph Joset, a native of Switzerland, actively intervened as a peacemaker in the wars of 1858 and 1877. *Relander Collection, Yakima Valley Regional Library.*

Kamiakin's Daughter, Chamesupum. *Moorhouse Collection, Smithsonian Institution.*

Four of Kamiakin's sons: (*top to bottom, left to right*) Skolumlee Kamiakin, Tomeo Kamiakin, Tesh Palouse Kamiakin, Cleveland Kamiakin. *Manuscripts, Archives, and Special Collections, Washington State University Libraries.*

as the whites marched upriver through Union Gap, before heading west up Ahtanum Creek toward St. Joseph Mission. By the time the troops arrived at the mission, Father Charles Pandosy had fled with the Indians. The soldiers searched the mission grounds, discovering half a keg of gunpowder buried in the garden. They erroneously concluded that the priests had been arming the Indians and fomenting war. There had been a national bias against Catholics, particularly in the Northwest, where many believed that the missionaries conspired and incited the Indians to exterminate whites. When the gunpowder was discovered, bedlam resulted and "wild excitement ensued," wrote Lieutenant Philip H. Sheridan. The volunteers made a mad dash for the mission and Pandosy's home, setting the buildings on fire and burning them "to the ground before the officers in camp became aware of the disgraceful plundering in which their men were engaged."[27]

Before the mission was set aflame, Rains discovered a letter written by Father Pandosy and dictated by Kamiakin. The letter was most revealing, for it outlined the causes of the Yakima War and offered a sensible solution to the problems. "Write to the soldiers," Kamiakin had told Pandosy, and "tell them that we are quiet, friends to Americans." The Indians originally had no thought of warring against the Americans, Kamiakin declared, "but the way in which the governor spoke to us among the Cayuses has provoked us and made us determined upon a general war which will end with the complete destruction of all the Indians or all the Americans." Kamiakin maintained that had the war not started, the Indians would have willingly given the whites some of their land and "would have lived with all others [whites] as brothers."

The Indians had been prevented from pursuing such a course, Kamiakin asserted, because the governor had "taken us in numbers and thrown us out of our native country into a foreign land among a people who is our enemy, for, between us we are enemies." Not all of the Indians were friends, and they opposed the American policy of relocating several tribes onto one reservation. This was true of the Palouses, who were required to move onto Yakima lands as a result of Stevens's treaty.[28] "Now we know perfectly the heart of the Americans," Kamiakin declared, "for a long time they hanged us without knowing if we are right or wrong." He asserted that the Indians had "never killed or hanged one single American, though there is no place where an American has not killed Indians." Kamiakin was adamant, stating that the Americans considered the Indians "dogs" who owed their wealth in horses, cattle, and crops to the whites. He reasoned that whites had provided the Indians with these things so that the lands would be fully developed before whites arrived in the Northwest. All this, Kamiakin argued, was done to make the resettlement easier.[29]

The Palouses concurred with Kamiakin, believing that Stevens had pushed them into a hasty agreement which resulted in hostilities. According to this argument, Stevens "wanted war," by his demand that the Palouses should "go to such place [Yakima Reservation] and leave your land." This was the major grievance of Kamiakin, and as he saw it, the major cause of the war. The Palouses opposed Indian removal to reservations where the "people do not even have enough to eat." The Indians lamented the entire affair saying, "Our heart has been torn apart . . . our heart has been broken."[30] They claimed that the whites had "fired the first gun," forcing the Indians to unite in defense.

In his letter, Kamiakin offered the olive branch, stating that he did not want war. "If the soldiers and the Americans after having read this letter and taken notice of the motives which induce us to fight, want to retire and treat us in a friendly manner, we will consent to put down our arms and to grant them a piece of land in every tribe." All this he offered if the whites agreed not to "force us to be exiled from our native country." He realized that the Americans were stronger militarily, so he offered to negotiate and compromise. He also explained that the Indians were "resolved to be cut to pieces" rather than submit to the tyranny of the United States. Kamiakin was so against the removal and reservation policies that he vowed to fight to the end, saying "if we lose, the men who keep the camp in which are our wives and our children, will kill them rather than see them fall into the hands of the Americans and become playthings." He reminded the whites that the Indians had "hearts and respect ourselves."[31]

The chief concluded his letter, stating that he had over one thousand warriors ready to fight. "Some only will go to battle," he said, "but as soon as the war is started the news will spread among all our nations and in a few days we will be more than 10,000." This was, of course, wishful thinking, an expression of his dream of an Indian confederacy. Kamiakin hoped to negotiate, believing that "if peace is wanted, we will consent to it, but it must be in writing so we may know about it." Kamiakin realized that war was futile, and he hoped to end the conflict. The response he received was not the one for which he had hoped.[32]

Rains's reply was insulting and inflammatory, serving only to exacerbate the volatile situation. According to one historian, "In all the lurid literature of Indian-white warfare, no document . . . was ever more asinine than this one, nor—in light of the cause of the hostilities—more unjust."[33] The major told the Yakimas, Palouses, and others that the army came for war, not peace, "because your land has drunk the blood of the white man, and the Great Spirit requires it at your hands." Rains accused the Indians of starting the war: "You know that you murdered white men going to the mines who had done you no injury," Rains remarked, "and you murder all persons, though no white man had trespassed upon your lands." The eyes of the "Great Spirit" had witnessed the "foul deeds," and these same eyes had watched "Cain when he killed his brother Abel, and cursed him for it." He promised the Indians no rest on this earth, for he would "war forever, until not a Yakima breathes in the land he calls his own." Rains announced that the whites were "thirsting" for Indian blood and planned to feed the hungry crows with the bodies of dead Indians.[34] He promised to keep the Indians on the run, prevent them from hunting or fishing, and destroy their horses and cattle. Indeed, he promised to exterminate the Yakimas, Palouses, and others.[35]

Rains concluded his letter by threatening the Indians, saying that if there was an insufficient number of soldiers in the field, "a thousand for every one more will be sent to hunt you, and to kill you."[36] He advised the Indians to disperse among the friendly tribes, and he sent scouting parties to the Naches River to find the Indians. The lack of Indian "signs" and the abundance of snow in the Cascades convinced Rains to return to The Dalles. However, the Oregon volunteers under Colonel Nesmith turned east to set up camp in the Walla Walla Valley.[37] The volunteers became caught up in the "great excitement and alarm in Oregon and Washington" fearful that "all of the Indian tribes should combine and come down at once upon the settlements." They failed to accept the olive branch and surely antagonized the Indians.[38]

Rumors continued to circulate that the Indians planned to unite and kill all whites. But they were without foundation. Indians were far from forming a united confederation at the time Rains and Nesmith appeared on the Plateau. For example, most of the Palouses retreated hastily east of the Columbia River, taking refuge in the hills and valleys of the Palouse Country. The other tribes scattered to the east and north. Many openly blamed Kamiakin for their troubles, and this opinion spread to other tribes, particularly among selected bands of Wenatchees, Wanapums, Yakimas, Columbias, Klickitats, Wishrams, and even among the Palouses. Some Spokanes and Coeur d'Alenes feared that they too would be drawn into the conflict. Still some Palouses remained loyal to Kamiakin, retreating with him to the heart of the Palouse Country where most of his band eventually consisted of Palouses, not Yakimas. Indeed, after 1857, the Indians—Yakimas, Palouses, and their allies—considered Kamiakin a Palouse chief. Today his family resides on the Colville Reservation where they claim both their Palouse and Yakima heritage.[39]

Other Palouse bands stayed neutral and probably would have remained so if they had not been attacked by soldiers. The Oregon volunteers established a small post called Fort Henrietta near the banks of the Umatilla River. This force was augmented by Colonel James K. Kelly who took command of the volunteers and began operations south of Snake River. The Walla Wallas, Cayuses, Umatillas, and Palouses—Indians who had remained fairly uncommitted—were drawn into the war by Kelly's expedition.[40] The volunteers had failed to engage a large number of Indians in the Yakima Country, and they had failed to find Kamiakin. Now they turned against the friendly Peopeo Moxmox, "a chief of hardly less importance than Kamiakin." According to military reports, the Walla Walla chief had threatened whites living south of Snake River, endangered transportation through the Walla Walla Valley, and stolen property belonging to whites. The chief was also blamed for burning the Hudson's Bay post of Fort Walla Walla. The volunteers decided to punish the Walla Wallas, and at the same time redeem their honor. More Palouses, close allies of Peopeo Moxmox, were now drawn into this web of conflict.[41]

On the morning of December 5, 1855, Kelly divided his force into two groups, taking the main command himself to the Touchet River while sending Major M. A. Chinn up the Walla Walla River. In pursuit of Peopeo Moxmox, both hoped to "conquer, capture, and kill" the chief.[42] Kelly's main force found the chief's camp, but it had been abandoned. The volunteers marched up the Touchet River a short distance before encountering Peopeo Moxmox and about sixty armed warriors, including some Palouses. Accompanied by three headmen, Peopeo Moxmox rode forward to parley with the "evil-disposed persons, who would humble and reduce him to the condition of a slave to their caprices."[43] Peopeo Moxmox carried a white flag, offering to pay the whites in full for anything "his young men had done wrong." Kelly responded with hostility, telling the chief that "he had come up there for the purpose of fighting." He told Peopeo Moxmox either to surrender or face attack. The chief decided to surrender which gave his people an opportunity to gather their belongings and flee. He and the others were held prisoner while the soldiers progressed north toward the Palouse Country.

The Palouses, alarmed by the news that the soldiers had imprisoned Peopeo Moxmox, welcomed the Walla Wallas into their homes. The Palouses believed that the soldiers intended to fight, so they mobilized their forces on the rolling hills surrounding the Walla Walla River.[44]

On three occasions, Kelly sent out one of the Indian prisoners out to talk with the other Indians, demanding that they surrender. Each time the Palouses and Walla Wallas refused. The Indians warned Kelly to hand over their chiefs and end his march up the Walla Walla River. On December 7, 1855, the troops broke camp and moved up the Walla Walla River less than three-quarters of a mile when they were attacked. The volunteers foolishly fought a running battle with the Palouses and Walla Wallas for ten miles until their horses flagged. At this opportune time, a large number of Indians effectively challenged the soldiers and impeded their march.[45] A four-day battle ensued through the hollows and sagebrush along the Walla Walla River in which "the Indians poured a murderous fire from the brushwood and willows along the river . . . wounding a number of volunteers."[46]

Palouses, Walla Wallas, and Umatillas pinned down Kelly until the colonel ordered fifty mounted soldiers to charge. Kelly commented that "the enemy was steadily driven forward for two miles when they took possession of a farm house." From the farm the Indians fought back but were driven from the site after four rounds were fired at them from a howitzer. The fight resumed the next day when the Palouses and their allies "appeared with increased forces." The battle continued, but it was not decisive for either side. "As usual," Kelly asserted in his report, the Indians "were driven from their positions." He grudgingly admitted that the Indians had "fought with some bravery and skill." The fighting went back and forth indecisively for four days until, as Kelly put it, the Indians "fled in all directions to return to the battle field no more." Thus ended the "long contested fight" of "four trying days of battle."[47]

The battle may have ended for Kelly, but the controversy stirred by his unprovoked attack had just begun. The campaign caused a whirlwind of dispute, wrangling, and bickering in both white and Indian communities. General John E. Wool, Commander of the Department of the Pacific, was outraged by the excesses and expenses of the volunteers. He accurately perceived that the expedition served only "to unite all the tribes in that region against us."[48] Wool felt that the volunteers had acted unjustly against Indians who had not wanted to fight. The soldiers, Wool said, had attacked "without discriminating between enemies and friends." Stevens differed with Wool, supporting volunteers. This inaugurated a nasty feud fought out in the nation's newspapers. The situation, however tenuous for the politicians and their constituents, was catastrophic for the Palouses.[49]

Following the running fight on December 7, Kelly ordered his men to tie Peopeo Moxmox and the others, but as the soldiers reached to bind them, the prisoners reportedly bolted in an escape attempt. "One drew a butcher knife and stabbed a man in the arm," wrote Captain David Dayton, and Peopeo Moxmox allegedly reached for a gun held by another soldier. "Warfield struck him with such a blow upon the back of the head that knocked him to the ground." When the chief raised to his knees and tried to stand, Warfield hit him again, driving him to the ground. While Peopeo Moxmox laid unconscious, the volunteers gathered around him and fired their weapons point blank into his body. "All of the others were killed excepting one, who did not resist or show fight."[50] The volunteers murdered Peopeo Moxmox but defended their actions as justifiable because they felt that the chief was stalling for time to allow the Indians to mobilize their forces. Besides, the soldiers maintained that if released, the chief would rise up against the Americans.[51]

These actions were sufficient to elicit strong criticism from General Wool who wrote that "the Volunteers barbarously murdered Piu-Piu Mox-Mox whilst under the sacred protection of a flag of truce."[52] The incident was proof, Wool wrote, that "Extermination of the Indians was the order of the day, and no efforts on the part of the Territorial officers were made to check it."[53] Wool noted that the body of Peopeo Moxmox was dismembered by the volunteers. One volunteer confessed that "Peu-Peu-Mox-Mox has been taken up by Dr. Shaw [Benjamin Franklin Shaw] and his ears cut off and today he has been taken out and subject to further indignities." The volunteers flayed his skin, carved off his limbs, tore out his eyes from their sockets, and cut off his hands. All this was done to vent their anger and frustrations and to procure momentos of their foray. Friends and relatives of the volunteers received and displayed the souvenirs in Oregon.[54]

In the waning days of December 1855, Kelly resigned his command. The volunteers elected Thomas Cornelius their commander. The volunteers spent a miserable winter in the Walla Walla Valley without sufficient food or supplies, but the condition of the Palouses and their neighbors was no better. According to Father Eugene Chirouse, who lived with the Umatillas, the tribes suffered greatly from the abuses perpetrated by Cornelius's men. "The Volunteers without discipline, without orders, and similar to the madmen of the [French] revolution, menace us with death every day. They have already entirely despoiled of their provisions the inhabitants of the country, the Indians, who have so nobly followed the advice of Mr. Palmer to remain faithful friends of the Americans." The priest felt that the unjust actions of volunteers against the "friendly" Indians would push them into the hostile camp. Wool had said as much months before. This was the case for several Palouses who had remained neutral before Kelly's arrival. Some had engaged Kelly, but more joined the fighting after their homelands were invaded during the Cornelius campaign in the spring of 1856.[55]

Cornelius was ill-equipped to launch a campaign against the Palouse Indians. He lacked supplies and horses, but he set out on March 9 "to win a noble triumph over our common enemy."[56] Cornelius believed that Kamiakin and his Palouse allies had fled east of the Columbia River and resided somewhere in the Palouse Hills. For this reason he marched north to "cross snake river & give Camiackin a fight."[57] The first night out the command camped on the Touchet River where Cornelius learned from Lieutenant H. H. Wright that some Indians were herding cattle at the confluence of the Snake and Columbia Rivers. These were Palouses who were tending animals close to the village of Quosispah, and they were likely Palouses loyal to a prominent headman named Tilcoax. When Cornelius learned their whereabouts he prepared to attack.[58]

The volunteers traveled north, crossing the Snake River near the Palouse village of Tasawicks, twenty-five miles upstream from the mouth of the Snake. As the volunteers crossed the Snake, they spotted a few Indians, and Cornelius led an advance guard across the river to hunt them down. "I went in pursuit of the enemy," the colonel wrote, "who had fled in the direction

of the Columbia on observing our boats." The Palouses escaped down river
and in their haste left a number of packs filled with supplies and ammunition. The volunteers killed four Palouses, perhaps older individuals who could
not flee, and captured a small boy whom they named Thomas, after Cornelius. Some of the volunteers pursued the Palouses, and during the chase
overtook two women. Cornelius reported that the women were released and
not molested in any manner. In their oral histories, the Palouses remember
this raid and the kidnapping of the boy they called Thomash. The boy,
educated at a mission school, developed a contempt for his captors. Thomash
eventually returned to his people on the lower Snake River where he became
a respected religious leader and headman. The Palouse accounts of the incident coincide exactly with the official report, although the Indians argue that
the raid was severe and forced many Indians to chose between war or peace.
The Palouses scattered after the attack, some joining the hostile Indians east
of the Columbia River.[59]

From the village of Tasawiks, some of the volunteers "struck across the
country to the mouth of the Yakima" while the remainder of the troops under
Cornelius continued down the Snake through the lower Palouse Country.
Both groups of volunteers reunited about ten miles above the confluence of
the Snake and Columbia without engaging the enemy. "We failed to find
any considerable force of Indians," Cornelius reported, except for a few
Palouses who "were discovered, pursued and three or four were killed." The
Indians they had seen crossed the Columbia and made their escape. Seven
or eight Palouse Indians reportedly died during Cornelius's campaign. Many
Palouses responded by joining the hostile elements among the various Plateau
tribes.[60]

Not content with his march through the western end of Palouse Country, Cornelius ordered his men to ride east across the prairies to the Palouse
River. The volunteers traveled about seventy-five miles, finding no signs that
the hostiles had occupied the area. However, while one company made camp,
"they were fired upon by eight or ten Indians." A short fire fight ensued killing one Palouse. The Indians fought an intermittent engagement throughout
the night, sending an occasional bullet or arrow sailing into Cornelius's camp.
Private Harvey Robbins, the only casualty, was "slightly wounded in the thigh
with an arrow." The soldiers were not deterred by the skirmish, and Cornelius ordered a portion of his command up the Snake River toward Palus.
He marched upstream, camping two miles below the confluence of the Snake
and Palouse Rivers.[61]

As the volunteers traveled toward Palus, they "discovered no manifesta-
tion that the country had been occupied during the past winter by any large
body of Indians." Cornelius had believed that the Palouses and other Indians had fled east into the heart of Palouse Country to mobilize their forces.
His journeys overland proved this theory incorrect, but the volunteers hoped
to find their quarry living along the Palouse River. Cornelius camped two
miles below the Palouse before sending a detachment "forward to ascertain if
there was an encampment of the enemy at the mouth of the river." The soldiers
returned that evening reporting that they had found no Indians living at Palus.
Cornelius was disappointed, for he had no great victories to his credit. His
expedition was a failure, and his men were anxious to return home. The lack
of food and supplies caused Cornelius alarm, and he sent an emergency express to Walla Walla on St. Patrick's Day requesting provisions.[62]

On that same day, March 17, 1856, Cornelius ordered his command to scout for Indians up the Palouse River. The soldiers found no Indians, and few "signs" except for occasional "temporary camps of a few families." Some warriors watched the movement of the soldiers, but most fled the region to escape the volunteers and begin their seasonal rounds, traveling north toward Soap Lake and Badger Mountain to dig early roots. Their journey northwest accounts for the temporary camps and Indian signs found by Cornelius, as well as for their absence from their villages along the Snake. Segments of the volunteers traveled up the Palouse River past the great falls, overland on the Colville Trail, and westward to Priest Rapids. They found no hostiles and no animals, except for one horse which they quickly butchered and ate.[63]

Discouraged by the absence of Indians north of the Snake, Cornelius marched overland from the Palouse to the Columbia River, taking four days to complete the movement. His soldiers and horse "suffered severely for want of water and subsistence." With his horses broken down and his men grumbling about the lack of provisions, Cornelius considered ending his expedition. "Not an Indian was seen" as the volunteers traveled across the Palouse Country and not one was seen on the east side of the Columbia. At Priest Rapids Cornelius counseled with his men before ordering one detachment south of the Snake to destroy Fort Henrietta. Ultimately this detachment returned to The Dalles. The other command, under Cornelius, crossed the Columbia to the mouth of the Yakima River, traveling south to a site opposite Fort Walla Walla. After securing provisions, Cornelius entered the Yakima Country where Indians attacked a portion of his command near the confluence of the Yakima River with Cold Creek. One officer was killed during the five-hour skirmish, and an unknown number of Indians were killed or wounded before the main party withdrew.[64]

\ In early March 1856, Colonel George H. Wright, commander of Fort Vancouver, prepared his Yakima campaign, ordering troops up the Columbia toward The Dalles. As the soldiers moved upriver, the Indians — including some Palouses — attacked the white community called The Cascades. On the morning of March 26 a large party of Indians surprised the white settlers, sending the inhabitants fleeing into the mercantile store of Bradford & Co. The little steamboat, *Mary,* which had been moored at The Cascades, escaped down river to alert the troops. For two days the raiding party harassed the settlers with gunfire and laid siege to the store. On March 28 the tide turned against the Indians when forces under Lieutenant Philip Sheridan and Colonel Edward J. Steptoe arrived at the embattled town. Faced with a well-armed, superior force, the Indians withdrew and the battle ended.[64]\

Colonel Wright learned of the attack on the Cascades after he had set out from The Dalles on his expedition into the Yakima Valley. He received news about the Battle of The Cascades while camped at Five-Mile Creek and immediately ordered his men to return to the Columbia River. Wright remained on the Columbia until the Indians retreated and the area had been secured by the army. He stationed a contingent at The Dalles and The Cascades; then on April 28, he resumed his expedition, following the trail used by the ill-fated Haller. Wright hoped to surprise Kamiakin, but no great clashes occurred, only a few skirmishes. As the colonel rode forward, "the Indians appeared in large numbers on the crest of the long range of hills." They followed the soldiers, keeping their distance from the army and fleeing

pell mell when charged. Wright talked at length with some chiefs — something
Haller, Rains, Kelly, and Cornelius had failed to do.[66]

Unlike the volunteer leaders, Wright attempted to negotiate a peaceful
settlement, sending several messages indicating his desire to parley.[67] During the afternoon of May 7, Wright "received several messages from Kamiakin
and Skaloom [sic], expressing the greatest friendship for us, and a very great
desire for a permanent peace." These communications encouraged Wright
and provided him with the false hope that he would negotiate a permanent
peace.[68] Wright received several signs indicating that the Indians wanted
peace, and even Kamiakin sent two men to tell Wright that the "assembled
Chiefs had at last, all agreed to make peace." Wright believed that a settlement was close at hand and that the Indians "would come to my camp on
the next day."

Wright's hope of meeting Kamiakin was dashed when the chief and "a
large party was seen crossing the hills on the other side of the river, and moving off North toward the Wenass."[69] The Palouses left with Kamiakin before
negotiating with Wright, but the other chiefs — Owhi, Teias, Skloom,
Quiltenenock, Quetalakin — counseled with Wright, assuring him that they
wanted peace. Even Leschi, the Nisqually chief and cousin of Kamiakin, professed peace. These talks convinced Wright that he had brought peace to
the region. He gave the Indians "*five* days as the time to be allowed for the
Indians all to assemble here, prepared to surrender everything which has been
captured or stolen from the white people, and to comply with such other
demands as I may then make." A week passed, but the Indians refused to
surrender. Wright, who had been so jubilant, was angered and embarrassed.
He carried a grudge against the Indian leaders who had refused to surrender,
particularly against Kamiakin and the Palouses who had left. The colonel
never forgot.[70]

The Yakima campaign of 1856 did not end the conflict. George Gibbs
called Wright's expedition "a perfect farce."[71] But the period from the Battle of The Cascades to the end of Wright's expedition was significant for
several reasons. Initially, the war had gone well for the Indians, but their
early successes soon soured. The expeditions of Rains, Nesmith, Kelly, and
Cornelius put the Indians on the run, and several families lost their homes,
animals, and property. These campaigns and Wright's expedition caused conflict among the Indians who blamed each other for the war, especially
Kamiakin, Owhi, Showaway, and Teias. Owhi and Teias, always jealous of
Kamiakin, blamed their nephew for the war. Quiltenenock and Quetalakin
of the Columbias soon blamed Kamiakin as well. What had begun as a family
feud, developed into a conflict which cut across tribe, band, and family. Factions emerged among the Indians, playing into the hands of whites. Many
Palouses, but not all, sided with Kamiakin.[72]

Kamiakin realized the futility of the war. Yet, he did not trust the whites
and was afraid to surrender to Wright. Kamiakin's views were seconded by
the son of Peopeo Moxmox who joined with the Palouses, Yakimas, Columbias, and Wenatchees.[73] He reminded them of his father's fate, warning
"that they had been deceived before" and could not trust the *suyapo*. The
son of Peopeo Moxmox declared "that he was prepared for a general war"
against the whites, but at the same time he remarked "that he was on foot,"
owing to the fact that he had given away all of his horses. Kamiakin and
his Palouse band was not as bad off, but they too had suffered and could

not finance a war. Kamiakin crossed the Columbia River in May 1856 because he did not trust the colonel sufficiently to surrender. Furthermore, he was disgusted at his family and many Yakimas who blamed him for the war. He left the Yakima Country, not to prepare for further war, but to seek sanctuary among his father's people, the Palouses.[74] Owhi, Teias, Skloom, Quiltenenock, and Quetalakin also refused to surrender to Colonel Wright, fearing that they might be hanged or shot. Some Indians surrendered to Wright, but most fled north into the mountains and scablands.[75]

On July 2, 1856 Colonel Wright proclaimed that the war east of the Cascade Mountains had been concluded. But when events gave the lie to his proclamation, Wright became angry at the chiefs. Governor Stevens irritated him further by negotiating independently with the Indians. While Wright negotiated with representatives on the Naches River, another Indian delegation went to the Puget Sound to talk with Stevens. According to Wright, the Indians returned, warning that if they surrendered to Wright, they would be hanged. Wright was indignant, "exceedingly embarrassed" by the governor. The colonel believed that the war would be prolonged as a result, and he was right.

Wright determined to occupy and secure the inland Northwest with the regular troops, previously stationed only at The Dalles and The Cascades. During the summer of 1856, he ordered construction of two additional facilities, Fort Simcoe in the Yakima Valley and Fort Walla Walla in the Walla Walla Valley. In late August 1856, Colonel Edward J. Steptoe proceeded to the Walla Walla Valley with regular army troops to build the military post and secure the region from Washington volunteers under the command of Benjamin Franklin Shaw. But before this could be accomplished, Shaw ordered an attack, learning that a large group of Indians—Palouses, Walla Wallas, and Cayuses—had gathered on the Grande Ronde River.[76]

The Palouses and others camped in Oregon had fled the war, seeking refuge in the steep-sided valley. The camp, composed principally of old men, women, and children, included few warriors. Without provocation Shaw descended on the position on July 18. He first sent his Nez Perce scout, Captain John, to talk with the Indians. John rode out only a short distance before reeling his horse, galloping back, claiming that the Cayuse had ordered him shot. Shaw did not hesitate, crying out for his men to charge.[77]

The Palouses remember Shaw's attack as "the Massacre of the Grande Ronde," but Shaw recorded it as a great victory. It was a rout to be sure, as the Indians ran for their lives through the brush and trees, up the rocky ledges lining the Grande Ronde River. Some escaped across the water, while others scampered up the rocky canyons leading toward the Powder River. Many were gunned down, making it "impossible to state how many of the enemy were killed." At least twenty-seven men, women, and children were murdered on one side of the river "and many others we know to have fallen." The dead and wounded "were so scattered about that it was impossible to count them." The Indians who successfully swam the Grande Ronde were cut down. Shaw proudly proclaimed, "we may safely conclude that at least forty of the enemy were slain, and many went off wounded." Washington territorial officials were "delighted" over Shaw's "brilliant success at Grande Ronde." Three volunteers were killed and four were wounded, but Shaw had captured and destroyed a large supply of camas, dried meat, tipis, flour, coffee, sugar, and ammunition. "We took also about 200 horses," Shaw stated, "most of which were shot." But the volunteers' victory was not without a price.[78]

On the morning of August 28, over one hundred Palouses, Cayuses, and Walla Wallas ambushed a large pack train transporting thirty-three pack loads of supplies for the volunteers. A day-long battle ensued in which few people were hurt, but the entire pack train was lost. This event was a great humiliation to the soldiers, especially because the fight occurred within sight of the volunteer headquarters. The Indians were elated at their prize of nearly one hundred horses and several packs of provisions. The loss of the pack train was also seen as a setback for Governor Stevens who was then in the region to negotiate more treaties and to reaffirm his "peaceful" intentions among the friendly Indians. "Great mortification" was felt as a result of the attack, and the incident did not bode well for the second council Stevens wished to have in the Walla Walla Country.[79]

The Palouses "in arms against the Whites" were invited to meet again with Stevens in the Walla Walla Valley. They were told to surrender unconditionally and hand over the "murderers and instigators" of the war. On August 28 Stevens convened his second council, but the Indians did not attend the first meeting. The Indians refused to convene until September 11, 1856. "Assembled for the opening session at 11 A.M., were representatives of the Nez Perce, Cayuse, Walla Walla, Des Chute, John Day's, and Palouse tribes." Stevens spent the first day talking, not listening, telling the Indians that he was their friend, interested in doing them good. All of the Indians had heard this before, and Tumneh Howlish, a Cayuse, spoke for many when he asked Stevens, "Why are you talking to us? I have a head to think, a heart to feel, and breath in my body; I am equal to you. For that reason, as we are equal, I do not know why you are to tell me what to do."[80]

These words were a prelude to overt hostility toward the governor. Stevens was alarmed at what he heard, shocked by the hatred expressed by the Indians. He rightfully feared for his life and asked Colonel Steptoe, stationed at Fort Walla Walla, for help. The colonel reluctantly came to Stevens's aid, but on September 18, the council ended in failure. The next day Palouses and others attacked Stevens, burning the prairie around Fort Walla Walla. Nearly three hundred Indians then surrounded Stevens and harassed Steptoe, but they made no concerted effort to kill the whites. They were content to flex their muscles as an expression of their contempt for the Americans.[81]

Steptoe withdrew to the Umatilla River, allowing tempers to cool. Colonel Wright visited the Walla Walla Valley soon after, and in a series of interviews with the Indians, became convinced that the major cause of the Indian war was Stevens and his treaties. The Palouses, Walla Wallas, Cayuses, and other Indians would have agreed, but they disagreed with Wright's contention that the War Department was better suited than either the Interior Department or the territorial governments to handle Indian affairs. Virtually all of the Indian leaders believed that they alone should control their own destiny.[82]

By the winter of 1856, Colonel Wright, writing from Fort Dalles, said that the Palouses and their neighbors had ended their fight.[83] Steptoe, commander of Fort Walla Walla, was not so certain, declaring: 'I am not at all satisfied as to the peace status at present existing between us & the Indians." Palouse leaders, like Tilcoax, "continue to harangue & will not suffer the minds of the better disposed to be at rest." The Palouses were like many other tribes. Some of them wanted no part of continued warfare while others wanted to continue the conflict. The Palouse war faction moved north of the Snake River to join the Yakimas, Spokanes, Columbias, Wenatchees, Coeur d'Alenes, and others. Some Palouses pledged to renew the fight if the army invaded north of the Snake or east of the Columbia. They waited in the heart of the Palouse Country to see what the army planned to do.[84]

CHAPTER 7

THE STEPTOE AND WRIGHT CAMPAIGNS

I will hang them all, men, women, and children.
— George B. Wright

In the spring of 1857, Isaac Stevens won election to the Congress of the United States as Washington's territorial delegate. And during that summer, General John Wool, one of the most ardent supporters of Indian rights, was relieved of his command of the Pacific Department and replaced by General Newman S. Clarke. As delegate to congress, Stevens supported the use of volunteer forces against the Indians and advocated the construction of the first transcontinental railroad across a northern route bordering Canada. Stevens also championed the cause of white settlement of the Northwest, but he believed that the major obstacle to this development was the so-called "Indian barrier." General Clarke did not necessarily share these views nor did he agree with Stevens's solutions to the "Indian problem." Nonetheless, Clarke soon figured prominently in the prosecution of a military campaign that would cripple the Palouses and other tribes who stood in opposition to white expansionism east of the Cascades.[1]

The establishment of Fort Walla Walla by the United States Army was a bad omen for the Palouses. Composed primarily of log buildings arranged in a row, the outpost was not an imposing sight. It was, however, an American foothold in the heart of Indian country. Not long after the fort was built, Palouse warriors swept down into the Walla Walla Valley, making a successful night raid on the government herd. On April 12, 1858, between fifteen to twenty Palouses rode off with nearly two dozen head of cattle. Walter Davis, a civilian employed to oversee the army's animals, lost all of his own cattle as well as the government's herd. Outraged by the bold attack, Steptoe ordered a detachment of men to pursue the Palouses. The soldiers followed a trail north for seventy miles but gave up the chase upon reaching the Snake River.[2]

News of the raid was published in several coastal newspapers, with blame falling squarely on Kamiakin. This Palouse adventure was heralded as the first stage of renewed warfare. But it was Chief Tilcoax of the lower Snake, not Kamiakin, who likely instigated the attack.[3]

Shortly after the raid, two miners, probably French Canadians, were killed while traveling through Palouse Country near present-day Colfax, Washington. Tilcoax and Kamiakin were again implicated, although they later claimed that two other Palouse Indians, Mahkeetahkat and Slowiarchy the Younger, were the culprits. The raid and killings spread fear among both the Indians and the whites. Miners at the town of Colville, Washington, for example, believed that the Indians planned to attack all white men. Forty miners signed a petition requesting military aid from the army. As a result, Steptoe organized an expedition to march from Walla Walla through Palouse Country to Colville in an effort to awe the Indians into submission. The colonel anticipated little resistance, although he hoped to engage a few Palouse warriors. Steptoe expected to defeat the Palouses without difficulty, and he expected no trouble from the Spokanes, Coeur d'Alenes, or their neighbors. The Indians had warned the soldiers not to cross north of the Snake River: 'Tell Steptoe to come," the Palouses and others had boasted, "we dare Steptoe to come." Nevertheless, Steptoe prepared to cross the Snake and invade the Palouse Country in a defiant demonstration of force.[4]

On May 6, 1858, Steptoe left Fort Walla Walla in command of five officers, 152 men, and a few civilians. A graduate of West Point and a veteran of the Mexican War, he had all the makings of a great military leader. A handsome man with dark features, jet black hair, and a full, well-groomed mustache, Steptoe had a pleasing face and a personable countenance, reflecting a strong inner confidence. Before leaving Fort Walla Walla, he outfitted men for a skirmish, not for a major engagement. Further, the command was "destitute of ammunition," since the colonel had issued only forty rounds per man. Worse yet, over half of his soldiers were armed with the short, widemouthed musketoons, accurate only to fifty yards. Clearly, Steptoe "did not expect to fight," so he ordered his men to leave their sabers at the fort, believing there would be no hand-to-hand combat. Steptoe took two mountain howitzers which were of no use, unable to out-distance the smoothbore Hudson's Bay muskets used by the Indians. As Father Joseph Joset put it, Steptoe's command was "miserably armed" and suffered as a result.[5]

The party traveled northeast, bypassing the well-traveled route north to the Spokane River. As he snaked his way through the expansive, rolling hills north of Fort Walla Walla, the colonel hoped to find hostile Palouses. The march proved uneventful until the command neared the Snake River, where the scouts saw thirty Palouse riders. The Indians sat quietly but alertly on their horses for a moment before turning their mounts and riding off. Steptoe did not pursue them even though he knew that they would warn their friends and neighbors. He moved on to the Snake River, where he crossed with the help of an enterprising Nez Perce named Tammutsa, known to the whites as Chief Timothy. At the confluence of Alpowa Creek with the Snake, Timothy operated a ferry which he used to cross Steptoe's soldiers, mounts, and baggage. When the troops reached the river, John McBean, Steptoe's scout who was married to one of Timothy's daughters, refused to cross the Snake. He had learned that the Palouses and their allies intended to attack, but he had no influence on Steptoe who refused to heed the warning.

The soldiers crossed the river safely. On the far side of the Snake, Timothy, Levi (Timothy's brother), and thirteen other Nez Perces offered to accompany the command as scouts. According to Father Joset, Timothy and Tilcoax had a personal feud, the origins of which the priest did not know.[6] Timothy volunteered to scout for Steptoe, in part because of this feud, and he rode north with Steptoe out of the deep, basalt canyon by way of a major ravine cut by a small stream through the rocky canyon walls. Brush and trees lined the stream, but the soldiers followed an Indian trail out of the steep canyon until they reached the plateau above. Stretching in front of the soldiers were the Palouse Hills, not unlike those south of the Snake. Most of the soldiers with Steptoe were raw recruits who hoped to pass through Palouse

Country with no resistance. On May 15, Steptoe wrote that "the Palouse are in front of us—we expect to come up to them today." Now he expected the Palouses to fight but was confident that his young soldiers would "be able to give them a good drubbing." The colonel believed that only one tribe had joined the Palouses, stating that "if my information is correct, quite a number of the Spokanes are found with the Palouses." Steptoe was correct, but many others had joined the Palouses, forming the largest force ever assembled by the hostile Plateau Indians.[7]

Tilcoax, whose "influence rivaled that of the great Kamiakin," had been actively advocating war for months before Steptoe crossed the Snake River. Father Joset, the Jesuit ministering to the Coeur d'Alenes, believed that Tilcoax, not Kamiakin, had fomented hostilities among the Sahaptin- and Salish-speaking Indians. He further believed that the Palouses "had bribed the Spokanes, and some Kalispels to continue hostilities." Tilcoax reportedly had chided the Coeur d'Alenes into joining the hostiles, saying that they were "very brave in words" but acted "like cowards and women."[8]

Tilcoax had hated whites since the days of the Cayuse War, when he was chased from his homeland and forced to establish a new residence on the Snake River. He vehemently supported Palouse involvement in the so-called Yakima War after Cornelius's march through lands claimed by Tilcoax. Like Kamiakin, Tilcoax had worked for an Indian confederacy, and his cause was greatly strengthened after Steptoe's troops invaded north of the Snake. The actions of Chief Timothy, an adversary of Tilcoax and the principal guide for Steptoe, further played into the hands of the Palouse chief. As the soldiers moved slowly through the Palouse Hills, bordering the present-day border of Washington and Idaho, Timothy sent his Nez Perce envoys to tell Tilcoax that soon the Palouses would lose their women and their horses. Similar messages reached the Coeur d'Alenes and other Indians gathering to the north. The Nez Perce scouts knew that the Palouses and their allies had gathered in large numbers, but did not share this intelligence with Steptoe. Timothy spoiled for a fight with Tilcoax, and he probably directed his Nez Perces to remain silent.[9]

Steptoe had hoped to engage a few Palouses, but never had he expected to encounter a united Indian front, well-armed and eager to fight. The actions of Timothy and Steptoe played into the hands of Tilcoax, facilitating the first major conflict of 1858. The night before Steptoe encountered the Indians, over one thousand warriors congregated in several different camps to counsel, plan, and boast. Through their war songs, prayers, and speeches, they prepared to meet their enemy.[10]

The Indians met Steptoe's command on Sunday morning, May 16, 1858, all "painted and dressed in the most fantastic and savage style." One soldier reported that the Indians made an "awesome sight to the inexperienced command." Steptoe himself said that the army was surprised when "we found ourselves suddenly in the presence of ten or twelve hundred Indians of various tribes—Spokanes, Palouses, Coeur d'Alenes, Yakimas, and some others—all armed, painted, and defiant." Steptoe halted his command briefly before ordering his men to turn west toward a small lake. The Indians sat on their colorful mounts momentarily watching Steptoe's men. Some of the warriors rode forward in two large bands, awaiting the army's reaction. Steptoe ordered his men not to fire and continue moving.[11] The Indians dogged Steptoe's command as it moved along a small ravine. They taunted the soldiers, "yelling, whooping, shaking scalps, and such things over their heads, looking like so many fiends."

The Indians followed the soldiers to the lake and kept up their unmerciful challenges. Not a shot was fired, however, and the Indians retreated after a three-hour barrage of verbal insults. The soldiers accused the Palouses of initiating this action, but they had not fired at the soldiers. Tilcoax, unsure of his confederacy, was afraid that his allies might withdraw their support if he sprang on his prey without cause. Also, the Christian Indians refused to fight on the Sabbath. Chief Vincent of the Coeur d'Alenes and Chief Sgalgalt of the Spokanes urged their people to return to their homeland without drawing blood, and Father Joset worked among the Coeur d'Alenes, urging them to do the same. Divisions emerged among the various tribes regarding their course of action, for the Indians were not truly united. All of this caused a delay in the battle, but the war chiefs eventually had their way.[12]

While his men rested beside the lake, Steptoe parleyed with several Indian delegations. The colonel camped beside the lake and spent a sleepless night in the Palouse Hills surrounded by angry Indians. Before daybreak he prepared to retreat and was apparently on the trail before the Indians noticed his "retrograde movement." Father Joset, who had spent Sunday evening trying to convince the Coeur d'Alenes that a war would be disastrous, set out at dawn on May 17 to counsel with Steptoe. The priest was escorted by several Indians as he rode south to overtake Steptoe's forces. The Indian escorts fell behind, while Joset rode pell mell to meet the colonel. Steptoe and Joset talked as they moved south, and during the conversation Steptoe assured the priest that his troops were simply traveling to Colville, that they were not looking for a fight, and that they had had no previous warning that the Indians would not permit them to cross to the Spokane River. All of Steptoe's assertions were lies, and Joset suspected as much. But the priest urged the colonel to reassure the Indians that the soldiers had no ill intentions.[13]

Steptoe refused to stop his command but agreed to parley with the Indians while his troops moved south. Joset rode off to gather some of the primary leaders, but he succeeded only in rounding up Chief Vincent. Minor Indian leaders may have been included in the small delegation, but none of the important hostile leaders were present. The Palouses under Tilcoax did not support Joset's quest for peace. Apparently some leaders believed that Joset was in league with the soldiers, and one Coeur d'Alene reportedly "heard a Pelus who told the great chief [Steptoe], that the Black gown has arrived to the Coeur d'Alenes with a horse load of Ammunition." Many Indians, wary of Joset, refused to accompany him and Vincent on their peace mission.[14]

Vincent and Joset met with Steptoe and talked of the differences between Indians and whites. A congenial meeting ensued, and for a time it appeared as though the two men would reach unanimity. Joset reported that the two men were "fully satisfied" with one another, and he believed that the parley would bring about a peaceful settlement. Just at that moment, a heated argument arose between Levi, one of the Nez Perce scouts, and Vincent. While the chief and the colonel engaged in conversation, Levi struck Vincent on the shoulders with a whip and cried out to the Coeur d'Alene leader, "Proud man, why do you not fire?" Levi "accused one of the Coeur d'Alenes who had followed Vincent of having wished to fire upon a soldier." Vincent glared at Levi, saying "hereafter you will be ashamed of having struck" another Indian. Vincent's uncle raced forward on horseback to warn that the Palouses were about to open fire. Joset relayed this message to Steptoe before reeling his horse and riding off to quiet the Coeur d'Alenes and Spokanes.[15]

Despite the warning, the Palouses did not attack. According to Father Joset, a few Coeur d'Alenes began the battle after some elders admonished Melkapsi for fighting with another Coeur d'Alene named Victor. "What do you do?" the elders asked. "You maltreat your own people! If you wish to fight, behold your enemies." The first wave of the attack on Colonel Steptoe came from a handful of young Coeur d'Alenes, no more than twelve in number, who rushed forward on horseback exclaiming: 'Oh, well, let us go and die." Paschal Stellam led the attack, followed close behind by Hilary Peenchi, Melkapsi, and other young Coeur d'Alenes. The soldiers held their fire for several minutes after the Indians had commenced shooting, but when pressured by an increasing number of warriors, Steptoe opened fire. The soldiers immediately shot three important Coeur d'Alenes, including James Nehlukteltshiye, Zachary Natatkem, and Victor Smena. When the smoke cleared and the Indians saw that these Coeur d'Alenes had been shot, a number of Indians rushed forward to engage the bluecoats. At this point, Palouses joined in the fight.[16]

Indians rode off the Palouse Hills at breakneck speed, firing guns and shooting arrows. In small lightning waves, they raced forward, retreated, regrouped, and dashed out again in a most unorganized and haphazard manner. The Palouses fought in an individualistic fashion, led by warriors known for their prowess in war. The Indians had no war plan except to drive the *suyapo* south of the Snake River. The Palouses wished to strike a blow at the soldiers, but they had no desire to annihilate Steptoe's command. Such was not the nature of Indian warfare on the Columbia Plateau, and such was not the Palouse intent.[17]

As the battle unfolded, more Indians appeared on the hillsides surrounding the ravine through which Steptoe traveled. A running battle developed, as Steptoe's men rode toward Pine Creek. The Palouses had decorated themselves and their mounts in brilliant colors and were armed with guns, painted shields, lances, bows, and arrows. Some wore feathered headdresses, like those of the Plains tribes, while others wore headpieces and helmets of buffalo horns, eagle feathers, and the dried bodies of birds and animals. Some Palouses carried medicine bundles filled with earth, stones, hair, feathers, furs, and skins, items which had special meaning and power to the individual who took them into battle. The Palouses and their allies outnumbered the soldiers who fled across an unfamiliar terrain.

During the battle, "the firing became continuous." The soldiers and Indians launched a series of charges and counter-charges, and the experience of Lieutenant David Gregg was typical. "Seeing that we must fight, and that the action must become general, I was ordered to move forward and occupy a hill that the Indians were making for, and upon which they would have a close fire upon the head of the column." Gregg galloped up one hill while Indians took another overlooking the one Gregg had taken. Seeing that the Indians could fire down upon his men, the lieutenant left "a few men to defend the first hill, and deploying my men, I charged the second and drove them off."[18]

The first phase of the fight found the soldiers "warmly engaged with 500 Indians." Three major companies, led by Lieutenant Gregg, Lieutenant William Gaston, and Captain Oliver Hazard Perry Taylor, fought several skirmishes much like the one described by Gregg. At one point a large number of Indians moved in between the companies of Gregg and Gaston, and the two men worked together, squeezing the Indians and pushing them away. The two companies succeeded in their task and reportedly killed twelve Indians before continuing their retreat south. "After getting together, we kept up the fight for half an hour," Gregg wrote, "and again started to reach water, moving half a mile under a constant and raking fire." As the troops reunited and made their way toward Pine Creek, Gaston and Taylor were given "the difficult and dangerous duty of flanking the column." During this movement, Gaston and Taylor fell.

Gaston, a young officer who had graduated from West Point just a year before, carelessly exposed himself to the Indians' fire. His men believed that he had needlessly rushed forward to die fighting. He had developed a cancerous tumor on his neck and had often told his comrades that he did not want to die from the lingering disease. Gaston was shot through the body, the first of Steptoe's officers to die in combat. Captain Taylor, who had been ordered to protect Steptoe's right, was shot through the neck shortly afterwards. The Kentucky-born West Pointer was not killed immediately, but fell from his horse and was rescued by the soldiers after some fierce hand-to-hand combat. Taylor died, but his effort and that of Gaston enabled Steptoe's command to reach a long ridge which sloped west toward Pine Creek. It was there on the high ground overlooking Pine Creek that Steptoe made his "last stand."[19]

From the gradual valley along Pine Creek, the hillside which Steptoe defended looked like an eyebrow protruding out from the face of the hills. The slope was covered with bunchgrass, interrupted occasionally by a few pine trees. In the middle of the hill, the soldiers, according to one account, "dismounted and picketed our horses close together on the centre of the flat inclined summit, and posted our men around the crest, making them lie flat on the ground, as the Indians were so close and so daring as to attempt to charge the hill." Steptoe deployed the two mountain howitzers to the north edge of the brow and to the south side of the same ridge overlooking the creek. The soldiers stationed themselves on top of the ridge and all around the horses and baggage. The Palouses took up position along Pine Creek, fighting from the south and west of the soldiers. The Spokanes and Coeur d'Alenes stationed themselves to the north and east. The other Indians — Yakimas, Pend Oreilles, Flatheads, Columbias, and others — positioned themselves all around the soldiers. Each group fought independently of the other.

From these locations, the fighting continued "with unabated activity" as the Indians occupied "neighboring heights . . . working themselves along to pick off our men." As the ammunition dwindled and the number of wounded increased, Steptoe feared "the most serious consequences." The colonel reported that "twice the enemy gave unmistakable evidence of a design to carry our position by assault." Steptoe worried, writing "that the loss of their officers and comrades began to tell upon the spirit of the soldiers; that they were becoming discouraged, and not to be relied upon with confidence." He worried for good reason. His men, inexperienced recruits, found their musketoons and howitzers useless, and "most alarming," their ammunition was nearly exhausted.[20]

By nightfall, May 17, Steptoe's situation was dangerous and desperate. The soldiers, "suffering so much from thirst and fatigue required all our attention to keep them up." The men had not slept the night before, and they had exhausted themselves during the day-long battle. Pinned down, Steptoe's men were forced to crawl about on hands and knees to move from point to point. All around the soldiers was "the howling of Indians, the groans of the dying, and the whistling of balls and arrows." Steptoe and his men doubted that they would survive the night, and if they did, they were confident "that on the morrow we must "go under," and that not one of us would escape." Cut off from Fort Walla Walla and reinforcements, Steptoe's position was desperate. Apparently he considered making a stand to the finish on the lonely hill not far from present-day Rosalia, Washington, but he determined instead "to run the gauntlet, so that if possible some might escape."[21] Colonel Steptoe consulted his officers and "not an officer of the command doubted that we would be overwhelmed . . . in the morning." For this reason, Steptoe decided to run for the Snake River.[22]

The soldiers, "with deep pain," buried the howitzers. They strapped their wounded to the horses, discarded unneeded baggage, and slipped off the hill. At ten o'clock at night they moved off the ridge into the bottomlands of Pine Creek, passing the site once held by the Palouses and Spokanes. According to Father Joset, who was not at the battle ground, the Spokanes left "to return the next day with fresh animals."[23] Some historians have suggested that Timothy arranged the escape, but no evidence exists to support this assertion which is doubtful given the feud between Tilcoax and Timothy. Father Joset thought that Steptoe's escape was a miracle, executed by a man of intelligence and ability. "It is not," Joset wrote, "the first officer you will meet who could have drawn himself out from so bad a situation." The priest believed that Steptoe had "deceived the vigilance of his enemies, and throwing them his provision, as an inducement to delay, he defeated their plan." Thus, he argued, "the Indians on the one hand had let him take the advance, and on the other tempted by the booty advanced the pursuit."[24]

Regardless of how he did it, Steptoe and his men made a successful escape from the battlefield. According to most white accounts, Steptoe emerged the hero who duped the Indians by quietly riding from the scene and leaving his baggage as spoils of war. Eight hundred to a thousand fighting men surrounded Steptoe. It seems strange indeed that not one of these Indians heard the soldiers — over 150 in number — bury their howitzers, scrap their baggage, mount their horses, and ride off the hills. Stranger still that the Indian war parties were more interested in pillaging Steptoe's baggage than chasing down the enemy. By leaving the hill, Steptoe exposed himself. The Indians knew he was vulnerable, and with fresh mounts, the Indians could have pursued. They chose not to do so on the night of May 17 or the next morning. Most historians believe that this was due to Steptoe's capable handling of the situation and the lure of booty, but at least one account claims that the Indians waited to attack by the morning light so they could see the blood flow. None of these interpretations are adequate; all ignore the nature of Plateau Indian warfare. The Palouses never intended to annihilate Steptoe's soldiers. Some warriors undoubtedly harbored a desire to destroy the command, but the elders, older men and women, advised moderation. The Palouses and their allies were not out-maneuvered; they were not too busy dividing the loot; they allowed Steptoe to escape.[25]

Afterward, they celebrated their victory, dividing horses, mules, saddles, blankets, and other baggage captured in the battle. Feelings of pride and excitement swept the Indian camps. The Palouses and their allies had defeated the soldiers, and were confident that they could do it again if the soldiers returned. Words of caution, spoken by men and women—wise in years and experience—fell on deaf ears. Chief Vincent, a Christian and friend of Father Joset, proclaimed that "all the fault is on our side." He believed that the battle would bring more war, more sorrow, and more bloodshed. The Indians had won a victory, but they would lose the war. "What will be the consequences?" he asked. "Fools that we are, we always doubt the truth of what the Father told us." Vincent prophesied that the Indians who lived through the next war would say with regret, "our people are dead."[26]

While the Palouses celebrated their victory, Steptoe galloped south to the Snake River where he was greeted by Nez Perces living near Alpowa Creek. With Timothy's aid, the soldiers once again ferried across the Snake at Red Wolf's Crossing, before turning southwest toward Fort Walla Walla. News of the "Steptoe Disaster" spread across the Northwest with the force of a Chinook wind. Exaggerated rumors about the battle circulated in official reports and the newspapers, and the story grew with each telling. Some accounts reported that half of Steptoe's command had been wiped out by the "Spokane, Palouse and Coeur d'Alene Indians, mustering some 1500 men."[27] The whites accused Kamiakin of leading the Indians. If he was present at all, he certainly arrived late and did not play a major role in the conflict. The Palouses and their key figure, Tilcoax, were also singled out as culprits and killers. When the soldiers returned to avenge the death of their comrades, they particularly hoped to strike a resounding blow against them.[28]

A great deal of racial hatred emerged in the aftermath of the defeat. The Palouses were depicted as fiends who had murdered innocent soldiers "without cause." Some newspapers blamed General Wool and the army for its "soft" policies in handling the "Indian problem." One editor argued that the government had "been feeding, clothing, and feasting the Indians" and in general had "protected and sympathized with the Indians, in place of whites." The harvest of this policy, the editor asserted, was "murder, rapine, and destruction." This, the editor declared, was also due to the "natural instincts and designs" of the Indians. "It is far cheaper to whip them at once and bring them into subjection" than it was to pamper them any longer.[29] Fear of a large Indian uprising spread across the Pacific Northwest, overlapping into Canada, where bloody outbreaks surfaced between Indians and miners. The cry went out from every corner of the Northwest to punish the Indians for their insolence.[30]

In response, General Newman S. Clarke, who replaced Wool, pursued two parallel policies toward the Palouses and their allies. This became apparent in June 1858, when Clarke, headquartered in Benecia, California, visited Father Joset at Fort Vancouver. The general asked the priest to tell the Indians to live in peace with whites and to surrender unconditionally to the army. Joset carried these demands to the Indians and urged them to lay down their arms. At the same time, Clarke prepared for war.

He met Wright, Steptoe, and other officers at Fort Vancouver; unfortunately, no one kept minutes of these meetings. In light of subsequent events,

Clarke laid out his course of action, giving Wright a free hand to deal severely with the Palouses and their allies.[31] The Indians refused Clarke's proposal of an unconditional surrender. Confident in their ability to defeat the whites, the Palouses ignored these peace proposals. He also believed that if they surrendered they would be hanged. In the aftermath of the Cayuse War, the whites had hanged Cayuses who had surrendered. More recently, the whites had hanged Kamiakin's cousin, Leschi, and other Indians in the Puget Sound. Chief Polatkin of the Spokanes represented the views of many when he said that he was willing to negotiate but would "not deliver my neighbors."[32] The Palouses would not surrender but would fight if their land were invaded again.[33]

General Clarke placed greater emphasis on his preparations for war than on his overtures of peace. While Joset rode into the interior, Clarke increased the number of soldiers in the Northwest. He ordered over six hundred men into the region from such far-off outposts as Fort Yuma and San Diego.[34] These soldiers may not have relished the idea of participating in an Indian war, but the business community looked forward to the impending conflict, and the Northwestern economy flourished because of the increased demand for supplies.[35] In addition to buying goods from local civilians, the army acquired new arms. The soldiers who marched with Wright against the Palouses carried three different rifles, including those produced at Harper's Ferry and Springfield, with ranges of a thousand yards, and the new Sharp's rifles. The soldiers also were equipped with Colt pistols, musketoons, and six mountain howitzers. The Indians were not as well armed but willing, nevertheless, to engage the army.[36]

The strategy used against the Indians called for Major Robert Garnett, commander of Fort Simcoe, to take three hundred men north to the confluence of the Columbia with the Okanogan River. Garnett aimed to punish the Indians who had harassed miners, and at the same time flush out the hostiles, pushing them eastward into the face of another force under Colonel Wright. While Garnett marched north from the Yakima Valley, Wright planned to ride north from Fort Walla Walla, across the Snake River, and through the Palouse Country to the Spokane River. Throughout the summer of 1858, troops and supplies moved up the Columbia River and through The Dalles to Forts Walla Walla and Simcoe. During the last week of July, Wright arrived at Fort Walla Walla where he inspected and drilled his soldiers. Before setting out on his expedition, Wright sent "expressmen to all the friendly Nez Perce's [sic], with instruction to meet him in council at the fort." On August 4 several Nez Perce leaders met with the white-haired colonel to pledge their peaceful intentions. The Nez Perces not only professed friendship, but "some thirty of these Indians volunteered to accompany the command against the hostile Indians." The Nez Perce scouts were invaluable allies to the command, just as they had been in May when some of Timothy's people had joined Steptoe.[37]

On the morning of August 7, the first detachment of soldiers left Fort Walla Walla for the Snake River. The patrol was led by Captain E. D. Keyes who selected a crossing on the Snake, constructed a supply depot, and kept communications open with the post. On the second day out, Captain Keyes learned by courier "that the night before a party of Indians had driven off thirty-six oxen from Walla Walla." The captain sent some of his men to pursue the Palouses, and Lieutenant Gregg, who had been with Steptoe, led the party. They chased the Indians but never caught them. The Palouses forded the Snake and rode off into the hills with their booty. Several "parties of Indians" hovered around the soldiers, reported Lieutenant Lawrence Kip, an officer attached to Keyes' patrol.[38]

The Indians and the troops soon exchanged insults and gunfire, and according to Kip, the Indians proved "exceedingly bold and insulting." The lieutenant learned that the Indians had rejected Joset's peace offering with a comment "that the whites were always talking of war, and the first to propose peace; that the Indians were ready for war and did not wish peace, but a war of extermination." The Indians had reportedly threatened the whites, warning that if they crossed Snake River, "we shall none of us live to cross back." The Indians may have issued this challenge, for they were in a surly mood, confident that Wright would meet the same fate as Steptoe. Circumstances had changed, however, and not to the advantage of the Palouses. Colonel Wright led a much larger army than Steptoe, and he was better prepared for combat. His expedition numbered 570 officers and men, 30 Nez Perce scouts, and 100 packers, wranglers, and mule skinners. With a combined command of approximately 700, including artillery, infantry, and dragoons, Wright left Fort Walla Walla quite confident that he could whip the Indians if they would stand and fight in large groups. But if the Indians scattered and fought in guerrilla fashion, Wright feared that his expedition would fail.[39]

The command made its way toward the Snake River over the rolling prairie which had been burnt by the Indians, presenting "an appearance of sad desolation." Wright joined Captain Keyes at the supply depot, named Fort Taylor, in honor of one of the officers slain during the Steptoe fight. A storm raged until August 25, when the command crossed the Snake. The soldiers, animals, and baggage were ferried across the Snake "without loss or incident." The colonel camped on the banks of the river a few days before moving downstream in search of a suitable trail to take out of the canyon. Wright's command worked its way out of the deep and rocky Snake River Canyon, emerging onto a mesa where they "had a fine panoramic view of the country, which to our front and right was a swelling prairie, while that near and along the Palouse and Snake rivers was barren and rugged." The troops edged their way through the scablands of the central Palouse Country, passed several dramatic basalt columns, and moved through the rolling hills, laying out before them like a sea of unending waves.[40]

The Prairie had been "burnt over" by the Palouses, and although grass, wood, and water were scarce, the army found enough to make their way northward into Spokane Country. Wright marched across a broad, beautiful prairie, through a brush-covered scabland, and onto a plateau dotted with ponderosa pines. On August 30, his troops camped at a small lake south of the Spokane River, where "two friendly Indians rode in, informing us of the presence of the hostiles in the timber above us." Some scouts from the Indian camps had located the soldiers and had fired on the guards. *"Boots and Saddles* is sounded," wrote Lieutenant John Mullan, "and a squadron of dragoons . . . and the foot troops . . . moved forward to the attack." Wright pursued the Indians "for four miles over a very broken country, and then returned to camp at sunset." The Indians returned to their camps to inform the others that the soldiers had arrived.[41]

Wright's command had marched into the heart of the hostile encampments, and on the morning of August 31, several bands of Indians watched the soldiers march toward the Spokane River. That morning a few Indians rushed the pack train "but were handsomely dispersed and driven off by the rear guard." The Indians made no further show of force but gathered on the hills in front of the soldiers to impede their journey. The next morning's light brought the first dramatic clash between the army and the Indians. Observing that the Indians had collected "on the summit of a high hill, about two miles distant," Colonel Wright ordered his men to prepare for battle. The Palouses and their allies congregated en masse on top of the hill, and Wright ordered Captain Keyes to drive them away. At the same time, Wright told Major W. N. Grier to move his dragoons to the left side of the hill and Lieutenant Mullan to the right side. Keyes and his soldiers charged up the hill, spread a heated fire on the Indians, and drove them from their position. The Palouses and others regrouped "in the pine on the edge of the lakes, in the ravines and gullies, on the opposite hillsides." There they waited in a defensive manner to meet the soldiers.[42]

Lieutenant Kip rode with Keyes up the hill, and from his position he looked out over a "splendid panorama." Four lakes dominated the broken landscape, and before him, Spokane Plain stretched out "terminated by bare grassy hills, one succeeding another as far as the eye could reach." Along the horizon, Kip saw "a line of mountains covered with the black pine." The Indians, not the landscape, captured his attention as four to five hundred warriors swarmed over the plain on horseback. The Indians rode "back and forth, brandishing their weapons, shouting their war cries, and keeping up a song of defiance." The Indians made a magnificent scene: "They were in all the bravery of their war array, brightly painted and decorated with their wild trappings. Their plumes fluttered above them, while below skins and trinkets and all kinds of fantastic embellishments flaunted in the sunshine." The Palouses had decorated their horses in "glaring finery," and some warriors had painted their mounts with "fantastic figures." In addition, "Beads and fringes of gaudy colors were hanging from their bridles, while the plumes of eagles' feathers, interwoven with the mane and tail, fluttered as the breeze swept over them, and completed their wild and fantastic appearance."[43]

From the crest of a hill, Wright "saw at once that the Indians were determined to measure their strength with us, showing no disposition to avoid combat, and firmly maintaining their position at the base of the hill."[44] The artillery and infantry advanced down the hill "with all the precision of a parade," and when the soldiers came within six hundred yards of the Indians, they opened fire. The Indians charged, then retreated before being shot. "But minnie balls and long range rifles were things with which now for the first time they were to be made acquainted!" The new weapons and ammunition were effective, and some of the Indians fell during the heated engagement. The soldiers continued their advance, and "as the line drew nearer, the fire became too heavy, and the whole array broke and fled towards the plain."[45] At the same time, Captain F. T. Dent, Lieutenant J. L. White, and Lieutenant Robert O. Tyler "were hotly engaged with the Indians in the pine forest, constantly increasing by fugitives from the left." The Palouses and their allies were no match for the soldiers, but they fought gallantly in the trees and on the plains. They were thrown into confusion minutes after they were forced onto the plain, and the results were disastrous.[46]

Major Grier and his dragoons had remained behind Keyes during the advance down the hills, but once the Indians moved onto the plain, Grier's men went into action. "At a signal," Wright wrote the day after the battle, "they mount, they rush with lightning speed through the intervals of skirmishes, and charge the Indians on the plains, overwhelm them entirely, kill many, defeat and disperse them all."[47] When the dragoons mounted up, Lieutenant Kip heard Grier cry out: "Charge the rascals!" Kip wrote that "Taylor's and Gaston's companies were there, burning for revenge," and they rushed headlong into the Indians with their swords drawn and their pistols loaded. "We saw the flash of their sabres as they cut them down." Many of the Indians were overrun, shot down, or clubbed. "It was a race for life, as the flying warriors streamed out of the glens and ravines and over the open plain, and took refuge in the clumps of woods or on the rising groups." They sought refuge in the trees and ravines, and did not regroup or challenge the soldiers again that day. The recall was sounded, for "not a hostile Indian was to be seen on the plain."[48]

The days following the Battle of Four Lakes were quiet ones for the soldiers, but the Palouses spent these days in councils with the other tribes, discussing losses and their future course of action. For three days the soldiers remained at their camp before setting out for the Spokane River on September 5. Wright's men marched a few miles north across the Spokane Plain, when they suddenly "saw the enemy collecting in large bodies on our right." The Indians rode parallel to the command's line of march, increasing in numbers the farther north they rode. As the soldiers "emerged from the rough broken country and entered on a prairie," the Indians gathered in large numbers in a woods to the right. Some of them moved in small bands out of the pines and onto the plain, where they set fire to the dry bunchgrass. Within a few seconds, the wind, which was whipping down from the north, blew the fire high and wide into the face of the whites. Wright deployed skirmishers to the right of the command while artillerymen with the howitzers moved in front and to the left of the main body. While the flames enveloped the soldiers, the Indians took up positions in front and on the flanks of Wright's army. Wright remembered that the "firing now became brisk on both sides" and the Indians, positioned in a horseshoe around the soldiers, prepared to pin down or repulse the United States Army. The Battle of Spokane Plain had thus begun.[49]

As the conflict developed, more Indians arrived. Many dashed "down a hill five hundred feet high and with a slope of forty-five degrees, at the most headlong speed." They rushed forward to join their brethren just as Wright ordered his mounted men through the flames into the face of the attackers. "The men, flushed with their last victory, dashed through the flames, charged and drove the enemy before them." The Palouses were driven from their positions and many returned to the woods for cover. The soldiers pushed forward and the soldiers fired the howitzers into the pines where the Indians sought refuge. The shells burst into the pines, spewing debris in every direction. One of the shells nearly killed Kamiakin who was knocked from his horse after a shell hit a tree tearing off a limb. He was on the right flank of Wright's command at the time of his injury, accompanied by his youngest wife, Colestah, who was known as a medicine woman, psychic, and "warrior-woman." Armed with a stone war club, Colestah had vowed to fight to the death by her husband's side. For this reason she went into battle wearing her finest buckskin dress with her hair tightly braided around her head. When Kamiakin was wounded, Colestah carried him off and used her skill as an Indian doctor to nurse him back to health. Driven from the pine trees by the howitzer shells, she and others sought protection "behind the trees and rocks, and through the ravines and canons." Wright soon employed his infantry to flush the Indians from the woods.[50]

Some of the Palouses regrouped in the woods, where they joined forces with warriors of other tribes. The fighting soon turned to the woods, where Wright ordered his infantry to charge and drive the Indians back onto the plain. Lieutenant Robert O. Tyler, Captain E. O. C. Ord, and Lieutenant H. G. Gibson drove the Indians from their natural fortress and forced them back. "Skirmishing continued all the way," wrote Kip, as the command advanced toward the Spokane River. Every now and then Lieutenant White ordered the howitzers loaded and fired at bands of Indians who had collected in large numbers. Then the infantry charged the Indians, dispersing them in many different directions. Wright reported that the Indians remained in front of his command as he marched forward for fourteen miles, but after the initial stages of combat, the Indians posed no threat. The soldiers camped on the southern bank of the Spokane where they rested and refreshed themselves with the clear waters of the river. There, the soldiers reflected on the battle.[51]

"The enemy was braver and bolder than Indian enemies usually are," Wright wrote in the aftermath, "and left the field from the most dire necessity." The Indians had been driven from the field and had suffered a great loss. "How many were killed and wounded we cannot tell," wrote one soldier, because the Indians carried off their dead and wounded "before the troops could cross the ravines to get at them."[52] Few Indians were killed or wounded in the two battles: "Almost no one had been hurt by this battle," writes one historian, "though the bullets fell thick as rain." The Battles of Four Lakes and Spokane Plains "had been all flags and sabers, foam-flecked horses and a confusion of musketry: the game of war with an illusion of danger, an illusion of dedication. The Colonel was at the end of his tether, on short supplies and with winter in the offing." According to this historian, Wright had actually lost the war. This may have been true in terms of numbers killed, but Wright had counted coup by destroying the Indian spirit and their unity.[53]

The two battles took a toll on the Indians. An old enemy returned to plague them following the Battles of Four Lakes and Spokane Plain. Factionalism spread in the camps, pitting Palouses against Kettles, Spokanes against Columbias, and Coeur d'Alenes against Pend d'Oreilles. Some favored peace, while others urged war. They blamed each other for their unenviable predicament. Wright's campaign destroyed the confederacy Tilcoax and Kamiakin had worked so diligently to form, and it negated the effects of the Steptoe Battle. The Wright campaign demoralized the Indians and was, in fact, a victory for the colonel.[54]

On September 7 the army broke camp and marched east along the Spokane River. The soldiers met no resistance and some had time to enjoy Spokane Falls. "It is a high, narrow, basaltic canõn where the whole river passes over an inclined ledge of rocks, with a fall of between forty and fifty feet." The soldiers saw salmon "in great abundance," and they absorbed the scenery which was "exceedingly picturesque."[55] As the soldiers passed Spokane Falls, they saw a few riders across the river. Spokan Garry, one of the

Indians, "expressed a wish to have a "talk" with Colonel Wright."[56] Two miles above the falls, Spokan Garry crossed the river. He talked to Wright, expressing his dismay over the recent conflict and his desire for peace. Wright's reply "was very plain, but by no means pleasing."[57] He told Garry that the Indians had been "badly whipped" and that before a peace agreement could be made, the Indians had to "come to me with your arms, with your women and children, and everything you have, and lay them at my feet; you must put your faith in me and trust to my mercy. If you do this, I shall then dictate the terms upon which I will grant you peace."[58]

Wright dictated his Indian policy in no uncertain terms, telling Garry to return to the Indians and relay his message. The colonel finished his oration by telling the Spokane chief that he must do as the white men wished or "war will be made on you this year and next, and until your nation shall be exterminated." Garry returned and his interview with Wright encouraged others to sue for peace. Chief Polatkin and nine warriors visited Wright, but the colonel held Polatkin and a Palouse Indian captive. The Palouse, "who was strongly suspected of having been engaged in the murder of the two miners in April" was taken prisoner. Ultimately, Wright hanged him on suspicion of being party to the Colfax killings. "I investigated the case of the Indian prisoner suspected of having been engaged in the murder of the two miners," wrote Colonel Wright. Without a trial or testimony from others, Wright sentenced the Palouse to death: "the fact of his guilt was established beyond doubt, and he was hung at sunset." Wright spared Polatkin but forced him to proceed with the soldiers.[59]

The command traveled toward the Coeur d'Alenes, and as the bluecoats moved along saw huge clouds of dust rising to the east of them. Dragoons and Nez Perce scouts rode forward to investigate, and they soon found a huge horse herd belonging to the Palouses. The soldiers overtook the Palouses, engaging them in a fire fight. The soldiers drove the Indians into the hills, forcing the Indians to abandon the herd of approximately nine hundred horses. Army officials believed that Tilcoax, the well-known Palouse chief and "a notorious freebooter," owned the horses. However, Indians maintain that most of the animals belonged to two Palouse leaders from Wawawai, Poyahkin and Penockahlowyun (The Whistling Bird). Wright reported "that this large band of horses composed the entire wealth of the Pelouse chief Til-co-ax." The horses slowed Wright's advance because he could not handle such a huge herd and conduct a war at the same time. On the morning of September 9, Wright convened a meeting with his officers to discuss the horses. "They decided that one hundred and thirty should be selected for our use, and the rest shot."[60] Wright "deeply regretted killing these poor creatures," but he said that "a dire necessity drove me to it." Near the present-day border of Washington and Idaho the soldiers made a rope corral and began their grisly business at the "Horse Slaughter Camp."[61] Kip reported that 270 horses were "lassoed and dragged out, and dispatched by a single shot" while the "colts were led out and knocked in the head." All night the soldiers heard the "cries of the brood mares whose young had thus been taken from them." To expedite the process, the soldiers moved about the corral shooting a series of volleys killing the horses.[62]

The horse killings had a significant impact on the Indians. One officer suggested that "Nothing can more effectually cripple the Indians than to

deprive them of their animals."[63] This was true, but the horse shootings left
an unforgettable impression upon the Indians. What nature of mankind, they
asked, could kill horses—stallions, geldings, mares, and colts—in such a cold-
blooded manner? They never forgot the horse slaughter. The Palouses told
their children and grandchildren, who in turn told their children and grandchildren. The event is remembered today through historical sources—written
and oral.[64]

Wright's command journeyed into the Coeur d'Alene Country with no
difficulty, but a rumor circulated that "a war party of the Pelouzes were
following." If that were the case, the Palouses never attacked. Near the
Catholic mission Wright met a delegation of Coeur d'Alenes, and in the hills
southeast of the mission, he held another council with the Spokanes. At both
meetings Wright delivered the same ultimatum, telling the Indians to end
their fighting, return stolen property, and surrender hostages to accompany
Wright to Fort Walla Walla. The Coeur d'Alenes and Spokanes consented,
signing peace agreements with the colonel.[65]

The army next moved south, meeting several Indians who sued for peace.
On September 21, a party of ten Palouse warriors rode into Wright's camp,
indicating that since "peace had been granted to the Coeur d'Alenes, they
wished it extended to them."[66] The next day Wright reported that "Kamiaken
and Til-co-ax, are not far off, but it is doubtful whether they will voluntarily come in."[67] He instructed Spokan Garry and Big Star to find the two
leaders and encourage them to surrender. Wright circulated the word among
the Indians that if Kamiakin came in voluntarily "he should not be harmed;
but if he did not surrender himself, he [the colonel] would hunt him down
until he captured him, and then put him to death." Kamiakin was considered
"the most powerful chief among all these tribes, and at the same time the
most relentless enemy of the whites." The soldiers recognized that Kamiakin
had a great deal of influence among the tribes of the interior, and one soldier
felt that he occupied "the same position with them that Tecumpsah [sic]
formerly did with our north-western tribes." The great Yakima-Palouse chief,
the single most important Indian leader in the Pacific Northwest, would have
made quite a prize for Wright to have captured.[68]

Kamiakin and Tilcoax wisely kept their distance. They never surrendered
or met with Wright. Spokan Garry rode in and out of Wright's camp without
difficulty, but he was not considered a dangerous man or one who had favored
war. Some whites considered Owhi and his son, Qualchin, "the worst Indians this side of the Rocky Mountains." Wright wanted them, nearly as much
as he wanted Kamiakin. At sunset on the night of September 23, Owhi visited
Wright "to make peace." He was "taken off by the guard and put in irons,"
and Wright sent a message to Qualchin about Owhi's capture. Wright used
Owhi as bait, but before Qualchin received the note, he also rode into Wright's
camp to negotiate peace.[69]

Accompanied by his wife and two warriors, Qualchin rode directly to
Wright's tent. He dismounted as the colonel stepped through the tent flaps.
When Qualchin learned that his father was held captive, he called out to him.
Sensing his predicament, Qualchin moved toward his horse, but a guard
grabbed and disarmed him. His wife and fellow warriors rode off. Six soldiers
tied Qualchin and dragged him to a tree. He was thrown onto his back and
a noose was placed around his neck. The soldiers had no interest in killing
Qualchin quickly. They preferred a slow death by strangulation. He was "run

up" the tree, kicking and jerking at the end of the rope. Wright put it succinctly, saying: "Qual-chian came to me at 9 o'clock this morning and at 9¼ a.m. he was hung."[70]

Wright held Owhi hostage while the command traveled toward the Snake River. After crossing the Snake, Owhi finally attempted an escape. To do so, he beat Lieutenant Michael R. Morgan with a whip and rode off to freedom. Morgan recovered and galloped off in pursuit. During the chase, Morgan shot three rounds from his pistol which found their mark in Owhi's body. The Yakima chief, wounded as he was, rode on but was soon hemmed in between the rest of the command and Lieutenant Morgan. When he realized that escape was impossible, he reeled his horse and sat quietly. Morgan rode near Owhi, ordering Sergeant Edward Ball, a veteran of the Steptoe fight, to shoot the chief. With pistol drawn, Ball pointed the barrel at Owhi's head and fired. Owhi fell to the ground, lived until dusk, and died.[71]

Following the Battles of Four Lakes and Spokane Plain, many Palouses "scattered and fled to the mountains," but some followed the soldiers south from the Coeur d'Alene Country. Still others visited Wright to counsel for peace. "We were met on our road today by Schly-ot-se [Slow-i-archy]," wrote Lieutenant Mullan, "a chief of a band of friendly Pelouse Indians, who, with two of his men, accompanied us to camp." Mullan disliked the Palouses, believing them "a tribe formed of the renegades of each and every tribe." He maintained that the Palouses enjoyed "a most unenviable reputation for lying and thieving — their best of traits."[72] Kip commented that the Palouses were "a worthless set" who did not deserve "the consideration shown to the other Indian tribes." Colonel Wright informed the Palouses that "they had no business to fight against the soldiers, and he was going to punish them." He ordered his men to "put the chief and two others in irons, and told the rest to go and bring in their people, and if they did not deliver themselves up before he crossed the Snake river, he would hang these three."[73]

On September 25 ten Palouses visited Wright, desiring peace. "The whole party were at once taken to the guard-house and ironed." That evening, Wright judged them guilty of "various atrocities." Without fanfare, the colonel hanged six Palouses for their alleged crimes.[74] Two days later Wright "was met by the Pelouse chief, Slow-i-archy" who the colonel considered a "good Indian." Slowiarchy professed his friendship with the Americans, but explained "that some of his young men had, contrary to his advice, engaged in the war, but that they were all now assembled and begging for peace." Wright requested an audience with the Palouses. Slowiarchy obliged, sending out scouts to gather his Palouse band.[75]

The last day of September, 1858, found a number of Palouses in Wright's camp on the Palouse River. In Wright's own words, he reported having "addressed them in severe language, enumerating their murders, thefts, and war against the United States troops." He demanded to know who had murdered the two miners the previous spring. One of the Palouse warriors came forward, apparently admitting that he had been party to the murders. He was taken out with three others who were identified as "notorious marauders" and "were marched by the guard to a tree several hundred yards distant, and there hung."[76] The soldiers parked a wagon under a tree and forced the Indians to stand on the bed of the vehicle. The soldiers slipped nooses over their heads, but before the wagon moved out from under them, a few of the Indians jumped off the wagon, intending to snap their own necks. Following the executions, Wright selected five Palouse men and their families to accompany him to Fort Walla Walla. They were taken hostage to ensure the "future good behavior" of the tribe.[77]

While the soldiers hanged the four Indians, Wright conducted his Palouse council, telling the Indians that he would not make a separate peace with them as he had with the Coeur d'Alenes and Spokanes. He characterized them as "rascals" who all deserved to be hanged. He warned that Palouses caught south of the Snake or in the Coeur d'Alene villages would be hanged. If he heard of any disturbances, Wright promised to spare no one but to "annihilate the whole tribe." However, if the Palouses behaved "themselves and do all that I direct, I will make a written treaty with them next spring." If they refused American rule, Wright promised "to make war on them" and "hang them all, men, women, and children."[78] Wright had "treated the Indians severely," believing that "they justly deserve it." Whether they did or not, Wright's campaign had a tremendous impact on the Palouses. They had been defeated militarily and driven from their homes. Some remained in exile, while others drifted back to their homes. Regardless of the path they chose, their lives changed forever as a result of the treaties, wars, and reservations. "They will remember it," Wright recorded after the campaign, and indeed it has become a part of their rich oral tradition.[79]

CHAPTER 8

DIVIDING THE SPOILS

This land is your land and you are being robbed of it.
—George Harvey

The traditional life of the Palouse Indians was altered repeatedly after the Lewis and Clark Expedition, but the rate of cultural change accelerated after the war of 1858. The Palouses had once roamed over "an immense tract of splendid country" but after Wright's campaign whites began to settle in their homelands. Men like Meriwether Lewis, Isaac Stevens, and George Wright had recognized the value of the Palouse Country, speculating about the day when the land would be cultivated. Such was the essence of America's philosophy of Manifest Destiny, to expand from shore to shore, to spread the cultural elements of white America. The Battles of Four Lakes and Spokane Plains put an end to Indian rule and spawned a new era of white control in the Palouse Hills. The war also ushered in an era of tragic upheaval for the Palouses. Some tribal leaders had been executed, while others escaped into exile. Most Palouses returned to their villages along the Snake River to live, but their lives would never be the same.[1]

In 1858 Lieutenant Kip wrote prophetically that "the time is not far distant when settlers will begin to occupy it [the Palouse Country], and the farmer will discover that he can reap his harvest . . . without danger from their former savage foes."[2] Still, a few years passed before whites moved north of the Snake River to farm. During this period, most of the Palouse bands returned to their homelands to begin life anew, digging roots, fishing salmon, and hunting game. White agents did not converge on them, ordering them to move immediately to the reservation. That would come later after the American Civil War, when the new wave of settlers began claiming the rich lands of the Palouse Country. In 1858, while most Palouses returned home, those with Kamiakin and Tilcoax fled into northern Idaho. Tilcoax continued on to the Great Plains, while Kamiakin moved north toward Canada. In late September his band of Palouses arrived in the Pend d'Oreille Country, but the Pend d'Oreilles refused to help them, fearing they would be punished for harboring hostiles.[3] The Pend d'Oreilles refused to receive the weary and wounded Kamiakin, ordering the chief and his Palouses to leave. They remained despite the cold reception until some Indians stole one of their horses. The Palouses then moved on to the land of the Kutenai Indians living near the Canadian border. The Kutenais were equally cool to the exiles, refusing to allow them to settle in their country. Lacking horses, shelter, and food, the Palouses were "in a very hungry situation."

Some Palouses went to join Tilcoax on the buffalo plains of Montana, where they hunted and lived with friendly Plains tribes. Others remained with

Kamiakin, his four wives and children, and his brother, Skloom. From the Kutenai Country they traveled into Canada before moving nearly two hundred miles to St. Ignatius Mission in Montana. At the mission, the Palouses met Father Adrian Hoecken and Chief Alexander of the Kalispels, both of whom turned their backs on the destitute band. Hoecken knew of the hostilities on the Plateau and feared that the anti-Catholic sentiment west of the Bitterroots might extend to his mission. Neither he nor Chief Alexander wanted anything to do with Kamiakin, and they ordered the Palouses to "move out of the country." The Palouses next moved onto the lands of Chief Victor, a Flathead and friend who gave them sanctuary for a short time. However, none of the mountain tribes embraced the Palouses with great friendship, because they feared reprisals by whites. Kamiakin and his Palouses were outcasts, people without a home. While they resided in Montana, they lived in fear of their lives. But in February 1859, their spirits rose after a visit from Father Pierre J. DeSmet.[4]

Following the war, Father DeSmet had accepted an assignment by General William S. Harney to find Kamiakin and offer him the olive branch. DeSmet had been in the saddle nearly five months tracking Kamiakin, and during those months on the trail, he had encountered several other Palouses who had received the priest with "much kindness."[5] DeSmet received the same hospitality from all Indians as he traveled across the Palouse Hills, through the Coeur d'Alene Country, and into the Bitterroot Valley. Kamiakin and the exiled Palouses gave DeSmet a warm welcome, receiving the priest in friendship. Appalled by the miserable condition of the Palouses in Montana, DeSmet reported that they were destitute of food, clothing, and shelter. Many were sick and dying from starvation. Others suffered from exposure. DeSmet was moved to tears at the sight. About Kamiakin, he wrote, once the possessor of "thousands of horses and a large number of cattle—he [Kamiakin] has lost all, and is now reduced to the most abject poverty." Nevertheless, the Indians acted in a dignified manner, offering to counsel with the priest.[6]

Between February and April 1859, DeSmet met with the Palouses many times. They listened "with attention and respect" but were divided over whether or not to return to their homeland. Kamiakin declared that he "never was a murderer, and, whenever he could, he restrained his people against all violent attacks on whites passing through the country."[7] Kamiakin conveyed to DeSmet that the Indians wanted "the path of peace," convincing the priest that if "allowed to return . . . to his country, it will have the happiest and most salutary effect among the Indian tribes." After months of discussion among themselves and DeSmet, Kamiakin agreed to return to their homeland and meet with government agents. With horses supplied by Spokan Garry, and in the company of DeSmet, they traveled across the Bitterroot Mountains, reaching Fort Walla Walla on May 13, 1859. After arriving at the fort, DeSmet rode forward to meet with General Harney at Fort Vancouver. The Indians, who were camped at Fort Walla Walla, soon heard rumors that the whites planned to hang Kamiakin. He did not remain at the fort to test the validity of the rumors but slipped quietly away.[8]

Kamiakin rejoined his band in Montana, camping first on the Clark Fork River before moving north toward the Canadian border. They feared that an army might pursue them, so they moved to remote regions of the Canadian borderlands. Still suffering from the lack of food and shelter, the Palouses hunted buffalo on the Great Plains, drying the meat into jerky and tanning the hides for tipis, clothing, and moccasins.[9] They lived in Montana for a time, and by the summer of 1860, returned to live in the eastern part of Spokane Country. During that year in exile, Kamiakin's band was not bothered by the army or volunteers. No expeditions pursued them, so they gradually drifted westward to live nearer their friends and relatives, not far from their own homeland. Kamiakin was not in contact with any representative of the United States government until the early summer of 1860, when he met Dr. Richard H. Landsdale, Indian agent on the Yakima Reservation. Landsdale sought out Kamiakin to ask him to assume the position of "Head Chief," as stipulated by the Yakima Treaty of 1855. Kamiakin flatly refused, informing Landsdale that his band of Palouses and Yakimas did not recognize the treaty. Landsdale returned to the reservation disappointed.[10]

Landsdale had assured the Palouses that the government wanted peace. Kamiakin had received the same assurance from Father DeSmet, Spokan Garry, and Seltice. The Palouses also heard that General Harney wanted peace as well. Buoyed by these messages, Kamiakin returned to the land of his father to raise his family and to live in peace. Typically, the Palouses would have established themselves along the Snake River, but they choose to settle elsewhere because of increased steamboat traffic. Also, Kamiakin's people disliked Slowiarchy, a pro-government chief who resided at Palus. For these reasons, Kamiakin selected a campsite on the north side of the Palouse River near present-day Endicott, Washington. In the sparsely timbered river valley, later dubbed "Kamiak's Crossing," the men built dwellings and corrals while the women dug roots and made clothing. Kamiakin chose a lovely spot in the heart of Palouse Country, one that was well watered and blessed with fertile soil. He had developed a love for gardening before the war and found great pleasure raising crops at his new home. Here, he and his followers planted gardens, fished, hunted, collected wood, and tended their horses. Slowly, they returned to their old ways and a relative state of peace.[11]

The Palouse Indians under Kamiakin prospered while living on the Palouse River, for their lives stabilized after years of war, turmoil, and exile. In 1864 Kamiakin and his youngest wife, Colestah, had a son whom they called Tomomolow. The birth of this boy caused great rejoicing in Kamiakin's camp, the infant was the chief's son by Colestah. In the months that followed, Tomomolow grew in strength, but his mother's health failed. Revered as a medicine woman and healer, Colestah was powerless to cure herself. Kamiakin's favorite wife, a woman who had fought alongside him in the Battles of Four Lakes and Spokane Plain, died and was buried in an unmarked grave in the Palouse Country.[12] Kamiakin grieved for months, withdrawing into himself and refusing to eat or talk. Only Kamiakin's daughter, Chamesupum, could comfort him during this difficult time. Kamiakin's older sons encouraged their father to move their village north to Rock Lake, where they hoped that everyone could escape the troublesome memories associated with their camp on the Palouse River. At the same time, the Indians wanted to remove themselves from the increasing number of whites entering the region. In the spring of 1865, Kamiakin consented to move the Palouse village to a large tract of land on the south side of Rock Lake.[13]

Their first years at the lake were pleasant, except for the concern about white settlement north of the Snake. They gathered roots, hunted game, and raised vegetables in newly-cultivated fields. They planted corn, beans, and potatoes and maintained a small herd of beef cattle and milk cows. The men fished Rock Lake, a body of water known to the Spokanes as *Encushchelux-om* (Never Freezing Water) and to the Palouses as *Tahklite.* All believed that a giant serpent lived in the lake and had once devoured a canoe carrying three Indian women. The legend of Rock Lake was one of many stories Kamiakin shared with his family and friends. Many Indians visited the venerated chief, asking advice and counsel. Spokan Garry and Andrew Seltice often came to the Palouse village at Rock Lake, and a host of others consulted Kamiakin about marriages, thefts, alcoholism, and commerce.[14]

The Palouses traditionally traveled a great deal, and from Rock Lake they ventured to root grounds in the Coeur d'Alene Country, where Kamiakin and his followers camped among the towering pines two miles southeast of present-day Latah, Idaho. In the spring of 1870, the Palouses joined the Spokanes, Coeur d'Alenes, and several other tribes at this spot to discuss their mutual problems stemming from white expansion and farming. Traders had sold bad liquor to Indians, and rustlers stole Indian horses and cattle. White ranchers pre-empted the choicest grazing lands and watering holes and denied Indians the right to use them. Finally, the government had reneged on most of its promises, particularly the guarantee to survey reservation lands and prevent whites from encroaching on Indian land. Outraged by these events, the younger men and women advocated war. Tribal elders, veterans of Wright's campaign, opposed outright hostilities and frequently wept when the younger people spoke of war. The Palouse elders advised against conflict, and the Indians followed this course.[15]

Shortly after the council near Latah, the Indians met with George Harvey of the Colville Indian Agency. Harvey had summoned the Indians ostensibly to hear their concerns, but in truth, to tender their favor. When they met Harvey at *Tceliyutum* (Place Where the Woodpeckers Are Found), the agent denounced William Park Winans, the "Industrial Instructor" at Colville. During the council, Harvey asked the Indian leaders to sign a petition asking Superintendent of Indian Affairs Samuel Ross to appoint Harvey the sole agent at Colville. According to Winans' report, Harvey told the Indians: "The Whites have been abusing you. They will drive you to the mountain tops. They will make slaves of you, use you like horses and cattle, make you pull your own plows. This land is your land, and you are being robbed of it."

Harvey's fiery oratory moved some of the Indians to sign his petition, but the Palouses refused. Some of the non-treaty Indians tried to use the situation to their advantage and were "anxious to negotiate a treaty," establishing a separate reserve for them. Chiefs Seltice, Tonasket, and Garry all signed Harvey's petition hoping to secure their own separate reservation through Harvey's influence. But Kamiakin and the Palouses refused to sign. They chose to avoid becoming embroiled in an internal administrative fight within the Office of Indian Affairs. The Palouses asked for no separate reservation; they had never wanted one and were content to live near Rock Lake, away from governmental control.[16]

Harvey's attempts to rally the Indian community to his support failed to win him the agent's position at the Colville Reservation. On January 1, 1871, Winans was selected agent. Upon receiving his appointment, he set out to "Make a tour of observation" among the Indians. Harvey's council among the Indians had born bitter fruit, for the Indians received the new agent with indifference. During one of his councils, the Indians refused to recognize Winans, and the agent became "annoyed and hindered in every possible way." He found the chiefs insolent, except for Kamiakin. While in the Palouse Country, Winans learned that Kamiakin had recently lost his son, Tomomolow, in a drowning accident in Latah Creek. The boy had been entrusted to Oskallapam, one of Kamiakin's wives, who had taken the boy swimming. While playing in the water, Tomomolow's sister pushed him into the swift stream, and the boy drowned. Winans learned that Kamiakin had banished his wife, not knowing that Oskallapam was carrying Kamiakin's last child, Peopeo Kah Ownot (Bird Talking All Night). Despite Kamiakin's personal loss of his six-year-old son by Colestah, the chief received the agent warmly.[17]

As a gift for the Palouses, Winans brought a wagon load of six hundred blankets and other supplies to distribute. Kamiakin was hospitable to Winans, but he refused to accept any gifts, fearing that government agents might claim that the chief had sold his lands in the Yakima Country. A proud man, Kamiakin told Winans: "I do not want to hurt the superintendent's feelings but I cannot receive them. When all the Indians around here, Palouses, Spokanes, and Coeur d'Alenes receive presents and should there be any left, I will think about receiving them." Winans tried to reason with the chief after witnessing the impoverished conditions in which he and the others lived. He replied that since Kamiakin had been named head chief of the Yakimas, he was entitled to such gifts. The chief was unyielding. He lifted his arms to show his ragged sleeves and proclaimed: "I am a poor man but I would rather have the government indebted to me than to be indebted to the government." He and the agent parted friends. The agent left Rock Lake impressed with the strength and spirit of the Palouse people.[18] Winans sincerely wanted to aid the Palouses living at Rock Lake. Other agents of the government shared Winans's concern, as did some ranchers and farmers in the area.

White settlement in the Palouse Country did not begin until 1862 when George Pangburn squatted on unsurveyed land on lower Union Flat Creek.[19] Pangburn was soon followed by Joseph "Kentuck" Ruark and his Indian wife who settled on the same creek. The Palouse Indians and these whites lived in peace with one another. Many Indians and whites lived peacefully near one another because of mutual respect. This was the case with Joseph DeLong who settled on Union Flat Creek before moving to Kamiak's Crossing in 1867, two years after the Palouses moved to Rock Lake. Kamiakin maintained cordial relations with DeLong and other whites, including John D. Eaton and Bayless Thorp. Indeed, the Palouses enjoyed good relations with all of these early white settlers, in large part because the whites wanted to live in peace with the Indians. Their experiences taught them the wisdom of being friendly, and they often hunted, traded, and counseled with each other. Initially, the white population treated the Palouses with respect, but relations deteriorated. With a larger number of whites living in the region, it was inevitable that some newcomers would dislike or fear Indians, particularly non-reservation Palouses.[20]

White settlement of the region was greatly stimulated by the growth of transportation systems in the inland Northwest. Before 1858 whites followed Indian trails, but after the Yakima War, Lieutenant John Mullan surveyed a road for the United States Army, linking Fort Walla Walla with Fort Benton, Montana, on the Missouri River. Some of the Palouses attempted to "retard" and "obstruct" the expeditions, while others, namely those led by Chief Slowiarchy, guided the survey parties.[21] Slowiarchy personally guided and interpreted for Gustavus Sohon when the first party surveyed the Palouse Country eastward to the Bitterroots along the plateau running north of the Snake River. When he reached the mountains, called *Tat-huh-nah* (the Moscow Mountains of Idaho) by the Palouses, Sohon turned north to the Coeur d'Alene Country.[22]

While Sohon surveyed the Indian trail north, paralleling the Bitterroot Mountains to the east, another survey party under P. M. Engle, one of the topographical engineers, surveyed the Snake River Valley. Traveling upstream on the south side of the river, Engle moved from Fort Taylor, located opposite the village of Palus, to the lands of the Upper Palouses. He was surprised to find that the Palouses and Nez Perces in this region cultivated seven large farms "amounting to from 300 to 400 acres." The Palouses farmed the river banks as well as some of the islands in the river. "Besides wheat and corn," Engle noted, "they raise vegetables of different kinds, and gain sufficient crops to encourage them in their labors." Although Engle judged the soil in the valley to be gravelly and sandy, he astutely recorded that "the plateaus on both banks produce fine grass, offering magnificent pasture grounds."[23]

The main survey party under Mullan moved north of Walla Walla to the Snake River. One man was lost during the crossing of the Snake, but the party continued its march through the Palouse Hills. Mullan's men met no Indians until they crossed the Spokane Trail in the northern part of the Palouse Country. However, the Palouse Indians knew that soldiers had crossed their lands and that whites planned to open a road. Still, the surveyors encountered no difficulty from them. Both Sohon and Engle remarked in their reports that the soil of the Palouse Country was rich and fertile. The rolling bunchgrass hills, once grazed by hundreds of Indian horses, was viewed as a potential farming region. Mullan recorded that "the soil is mostly a black loam and will doubtless produce cereals and vegetables." The lieutenant predicted that it was "not at all improbable that the grazier and agriculturalist will find at no distant day tracts of land that will amply repay their reclamation." News of the lush earth attracted other whites who resettled Indian lands and gradually pushed nearly all of the Palouses onto a reservation.[24]

Shortly after the Mullan Road was completed, gold was discovered in Idaho and Montana. As a result, numerous fortune hunters passed through the Palouse Country.[25] Whites established several ferries on the Snake River to accommodate the miners and built roadhouses to serve travelers.[26] Many whites who passed through the region recognized its potential, and some travelers returned to the Palouse Hills to settle. The Homestead Act of 1862 offered "free land" to those who settled on the public domain. Adult citizens could claim 160 acres, although whites could not legally claim lands that had been "improved" by Indians. Under the terms of the Walla Walla treaties of 1855, Indians did not have to go to the reservations until the government paid them for their improvements, and since the government had not compensated the Palouses, they were not legally bound to move.[27] Many Palouse Indians remained on their lands, refusing to go to the reservations until the 1870s and 1880s. During the last quarter of the nineteenth century, white settlement of the Palouse Country accelerated rapidly as families and individuals from America, Asia, and Europe moved to the region. As on other

American frontiers, whites replaced the Indian population and demanded the removal of the Indians to the reservations. In other words, the growth and development of white settlement had catastrophic effects on the Palouses.[28]

Many whites sadly "found all the land taken up in the Willamette Valley" but many "heard there was still plenty of good land in the Palouse Country." As early as 1872, Washington's territorial surveyor general, L. P. Beach, recorded that "During the last two years the Palouse country has been rapidly settling up, and those who first located in that section, for the purpose of grazing stock, have found that the soil produces abundance of all grains and vegetables."[29] In October 1870, James Perkins, Hezekiah Hollingworth, and Dan Anderson Cox established the first sawmill in the Palouse Country, and the new enterprise stimulated further settlement. The white population increased, and farms soon dotted the region. In 1872 whites raised over sixty thousand bushels of wheat in Whitman County, Washington. The Portland *Oregonian* lamented that "this amount will not any more than supply the settlers with seed for this year and yet, strange to relate, they have no thriving mill between the Snake and Spokane Rivers."

Whitman County had become "dotted all over with the improvement of energetic farmers and some of the land was already in a high state of cultivation." In 1873 Joseph W. Davenport arrived from the Willamette Valley to construct a flour mill in Colfax, Washington, and local farmers responded warmly by pledging to process five thousand bushels of wheat. More farmers moved to the Palouse Country to claim the land, turn the sod, and raise the wheat. Soon they needed a transportation system to carry wheat and other produce to markets. White farmers demanded a trans-continental railroad.[30]

Henry Villard, a rotund, moustached Bavarian, transformed Isaac Stevens's dream of a northern trans-continental railroad into a reality. He journeyed from Germany to the United States in April 1874, as the representative of several prominent European banking firms that had invested heavily in Ben Holladay's waning Oregon and California Railroad. After reaching Portland in July, Villard became enamored with the region's beauty and its agricultural potential. Within seven years Villard rose to the presidency of the Northern Pacific Railroad. The company had long held plans to exploit the valuable lands of the Pacific Northwest, and he devoted special attention to the development of the Palouse Country. A Northern Pacific subsidiary, the Oregon Improvement Company, was organized largely to develop its 150,000 acre land grant in the Palouse Hills.

Through a congressional grant of 1864, the railroad received all odd-numbered sections within a forty-mile right-of-way along its route, except for sections within Indian reservations. The railroad cut a wide path across the Palouse and Spokane Countries, without regard for non-reservation Indians like the Palouses. The forty-mile swath covered every township in the Spokane Country and all those in the Palouse region northwest of Colfax. As early as 1872, Agent John A. Simms had tried to explain the advantages of the Northern Pacific Railroad to the Palouses. Simms told the Indians to relocate to reservations or face eviction. Whites intended to purchase the land for $2.50 per acre and settle Palouse Country. To white farmers from Colfax to Spokane, the railroads meant financial profits, new markets, and communication with the outside world. The Palouse Indians stood in the way of "progress," and whites demanded their removal.[31]

Rumors that the Northern Pacific Railroad would be built stimulated white settlement in the Palouse Country. Whites cultivated more acres each year, and enterprising businessmen soon expanded farming by beginning the steam navigation of the Snake River. One factor retarding the economic development of the region was the relative isolation of Palouse area farmers from markets. The names of former Palouse villages on the Snake took on new meanings after the Oregon Steam Navigation Company established landings near Indian villages. In 1876 businessmen built shipping facilities for grain, fruit, and freight, enabling farmers in the Palouse Country to export nearly ten thousand bushels of wheat to Portland while "four threshers, three sulky plows, three reapers, three headers, fifteen wagons and 100 tons of produce were unloaded there." The following year, officials constructed other shipping warehouses at the Palouse villages of Wawawai and Penawawa. The volume of river traffic increased significantly in 1877 as Henry Spalding (son of Reverend Henry H. Spalding) reported that farmers had shipped one thousand tons of produce from the port at Almota. The Palouse Country, once synonymous with bunchgrass and wild horses, became a haven for prospering farmers and orchardists. In the mid-1870s whites settled in large numbers along the Snake River where the Palouse Indians clung to a tiny sliver of their former domain.[32]

Increased white migration and settlement inevitably led to problems. The newspapers recorded several conflicts between whites and Palouses, as stockmen and farmers filled up "the country between the Snake and Spokane Rivers."[33] One well-documented case involved William Henderson who homesteaded on the grass-covered prairie near Rock Lake. Unlike other whites, like Eaton and Thorp, Henderson and his four sons disliked Indians. Trouble arose over the use of Rock Lake. Bound by massive cliffs along its edges, stockmen had difficulty watering their animals along its shore. The south side provided the best access, but Kamiakin had located his village at this end of the lake. The Palouses willingly shared their water rights with Henderson, but they refused to move their lodges away from the lake or permit Henderson's cattle to trample their gardens. As a result, resentment began to build into open conflict.[34]

In August 1872, Henderson and his sons attacked the Palouse village, pillaged their grain fields, and threatened to shoot the Indians if they refused to move. Kamiakin avoided bloodshed by resettling his people on a rocky flat not far away. At the same time the old chief sent one of his sons to find Agent Winans at Colville to ask for help. Preoccupied with agency matters and harvest, Winans sent an assistant, S. F. Sherwood, to investigate. Sherwood learned that the Palouses had cause for concern and that the Hendersons planned to file claim on lands occupied by the Indians. Henderson reasoned that the Indians had no legal right to lands off the reservation, and he wanted them removed.

Winans reported the problems to Robert H. Milroy, superintendent of Indian affairs, who responded that the Indians had surrendered their tribal claims, lived on the lands for over five years, and therefore had filed a *de facto* claim to the land. The former general used his position as superintendent "to protect Kamiakin and his sons" since "civil power . . . [was] not sufficient." Milroy directed John A. Simms, the new agent at Colville, to tell Kamiakin that his claim would be recognized by the government. Henderson and his boys were ordered to leave Rock Lake which they reluctantly consented to do.[35] Despite a resolution of their difficulties with Henderson, Kamiakin and his band had problems with other whites who reflected "the general dislike to Indians that is felt to some extent all over the west."[36]

Kamiakin and his people were not the only Palouses to encounter trouble with white settlers. In May 1873, farmers in Paradise Valley armed themselves against a band of Palouses who frequented a root ground on the border between Washington and Idaho. During the previous spring the Indians had journeyed "into the valley with their stock and entered . . . fields for the purpose of digging camas. When ordered out they refused, and pistols were drawn by the Indians and shooting seemed imminent. But the timely arrival of settlers with rifles held them in check." The editor of the Lewiston *Idaho Signal* wrote that it was "high time that the settlers should know whether they have any rights that are not subject to the arrogance of these Indians."[37]

The whites considered the Indians "trespassers" who should be prevented from entering lands inhabited by the newcomers. Chief Hahtalekin and Upper Palouses living along the Snake River east of Palus village often frequented these root grounds. Increasing numbers of whites in the region plowed over the roots. In 1873, when the Palouses decided not to dig roots in Paradise Valley, whites feared that they plotted an uprising. A minor hysteria gripped the region when the Indians failed to appear. A militia mobilized and a blockhouse was built. Whites sent several petitions to the governor asking for arms and ammunition. Agent Sherwood, dispatched to the eastern Palouse Country, assured whites there that the Indians had no hostile intentions but were digging camas. Sherwood's assurances allayed fears and prevented a full-scale hysteria.[38]

During the late summer of 1876, white farmers harvested a bumper crop which made them more determined to remain in the Palouse Country. That same summer, Kamiakin became ill at his home at Rock Lake, his health rapidly deteriorating during the fall and winter. John Eaton gave Kamiakin kidney medicine and periodically looked after his old friend. Kamiakin's condition stabilized for a short time, but he could not leave his bed for months. His wives kept him isolated from his children until April 1877, when his condition worsened. According to Kamiakin's granddaughter, the chief awoke one day, telling his family, "I always have dreamed and seen things and could read people's minds. Now I know there is a heaven. I can see it." Kamiakin summoned his family, asking them to bring a priest from the new Coeur d'Alene mission, near present-day DeSmet, Idaho. The family member recalled that a priest returned and baptized the dying chief, giving him the name Matthew. The following day, Kamiakin died. Dressed in his finest buckskin and placed in a simple wood coffin made by John Eaton and Thomas May, the family prepared for Kamiakin's burial. Eaton, May, and Jack McElroy accompanied the family to the top of a rocky hill overlooking the southern end of Rock Lake. There they buried the great chief in the heart of Palouse Country. Dying in obscurity, the passing of one of the Northwest's great chiefs went unheralded by the general public or the Indian office. Recorded by the Indian community, the death of the once-powerful warrior-statesman is remembered to this day in the oral traditions of the Palouse Indians.[39]

Following the Yakima War and their exile in Montana, Kamiakin's Palouse band attempted to live in accommodation with white settlers. Kamiakin had once expressed his philosophy, saying "There is no more war. I wish to live in peace until the Great Spirit calls me to take the long trail.

I have lived to see Wa-tum-nah's words fulfilled." According to Andrew Jackson Splawn, who recorded these events over a half century after they had occurred, the chief's final words referred to a prophecy delivered to Kamiakin's father by an aged Yakima medicine man who predicted that Kamiakin's Palouse father would marry a Yakima woman, a daughter of Weowicht. The medicine man had prophesied that their first-born son would lead the people in a valiant but futile effort against white people. The prophecy had come true, but no one could have envisioned the final indignity against this great leader.[40]

Approximately one year after Kamiakin's death, his grave was desecrated by white men. In April 1878, while on a fossil-hunting tour of the inland Northwest, Professor Charles H. Sternberg met the Henderson family and learned where the famous chief was buried. Sternberg was on the staff of Dr. E. D. Cope, a prominent paleontologist in Philadelphia. Accompanied by two other white men, Sternberg disinterred the body and tore off Kamiakin's head, placing it in a sack and taking it away reportedly to "make certain measurements."[41] The Indians did not learn of the ghoulish deed for another year, when members of the family returned to the grave to reclothe and rewrap the remains, a custom among some Plateau tribes. When the family opened the grave, they found that the body had been disturbed. Some Indians wanted to retaliate against the white settlers, but Eaton calmed them, explaining that he and other whites deplored such acts. The Palouses had a holy man supervise the reinterrment of Kamiakin's remains across Rock Lake near an orchard belonging to Henry Babcock. Whites and Indians reburied Kamiakin's body in the bosom of his mother in the Palouse Country.[42]

Kamiakin's death marked the end of an era for the Palouse Indians of his band. Some members of his band remained at Rock Lake, while others joined relatives along the Snake River. Kamiakin's sons—Tesh Palouse, Tomeo, Locos, and Cleveland—stayed at Rock Lake with their mothers and sisters. Kamiakin's other sons, Weetkwal Tsicken (known as Young Kamiakin), and his half-brother, Siyiyah, moved to the village of Palus. Weeatkay Tsicken died in an accident a few years later, and his family ultimately moved to the Coeur d'Alene Country. Another son, Skolumkee (known as Snake River Kamiakin), sought solitude in the canyons and coulees of the western Palouse Country, where he ranged part of the family's herd from Rock Lake to the Snake River. Members of Kamiakin's band went their separate directions, despite their best efforts, they all finally settled on one of the reservations. There were, however, some Palouses who refused to move onto the reservations without a fight, including many Upper Palouses. In the 1870s the lives of these Indians meshed with the non-treaty Nez Perces. In the same year that Kamiakin died, the Upper Palouses became involved in a tragic conflict that ended in the exile of two bands to the Indian Territory—present-day Oklahoma.[43]

CHAPTER 9

THE PALOUSE IN THE NEZ PERCE WAR

I will fight no more forever.
—Hinmahtooyahlatkekht

By the 1870s, many Indian lands in the trans-Mississippi West were overrun by white miners, most of whom disregarded Indian rights. The mining frontier in the Pacific Northwest affected native peoples as well, and the Palouse Indians had felt its impact in 1855 when Indians killed white miners in the Yakima and Palouse Countries. War had resulted. The Upper Palouses and their neighbors, the Nez Perces, were not directly affected by miners until the 1860s when gold was discovered east of the Palouse Country on the Nez Perce Reservation. This discovery had disastrous implications for the Palouses and Nez Perces. It led to the final military conquest of bands within both tribes.

As early as 1856 rumors circulated that gold had been discovered on the South Fork of the Clearwater River in present-day Idaho. A year later a trapper named Jack Lassier reportedly found color along the banks of Orofino Creek in northern Idaho. Fear of Indian reprisals kept whites from investigating the rumors, including Ellias D. Pierce who claimed to have found gold in the Bitterroot Mountains in 1852. He left the region for California and British Columbia, but in 1858 he returned to the inland Northwest, ostensibly to trade with the Nez Perces. In February 1858, Pierce and his partner, Seth Ferrell, found gold on the Clearwater River. Nez Perce Agent A. J. Cain kept the miners at bay a short time but could not hold back the gold rush which followed. In August 1860—without the consent of the Nez Perces or their agent—Pierce and ten miners made a rich gold discovery on Canal Gulch, a tributary of the Clearwater River. News of the discovery near present-day Pierce, Idaho, soon spread among the whites.[1] The Nez Perce Treaty of 1855, signed into law in 1859, prohibited white intrusion onto the reservation without tribal permission. Lacking military support, Cain could not prevent encroachment by miners. Prospectors also asserted that gold was found east of the reservation, but this was false. Cain wrote Edward R. Geary, superintendent of Indian affairs for Oregon and Washington, for instructions. The superintendent met with George Wright who recommended that the Indian Bureau renegotiate the Nez Perce Treaty, permitting miners to dig for gold on the reservation.[2]

Communities of miners sprang up on the Nez Perce Reservation, including Lewiston, Elk City, and Florence. The Palouses watched a never-ending stream of merchants, miners, prostitutes, traders, gamblers, and whiskey peddlers make their way to the "new El Dorado." They came in steamboats and in wagons, on horseback and on foot. Whites anxiously awaited news that the government would revise the Nez Perce Treaty; many put pressure on lawmakers to do so. On May 14, 1862, the Senate appropriated $50,000 to renegotiate a smaller reservation for the Nez Perces, and less than a year later the government created the Territory of Idaho, encompassing present-day Idaho, Montana, and most of Wyoming. Two months later, Superintendent of Indian Affairs Calvin H. Hale and two commissioners, Charles Hutchinson and S. D. Howe, traveled to Fort Lapwai to make "a new treaty, whereby the reserve was reduced . . . excluding the Wallowa, Salmon River."[3]

Some Palouses attended the Lapwai Council of 1863 to observe the proceedings. Superintendent Hale and the commissioners were wary of them, particularly after a few Palouses insulted the government agents. Colonel Justus Steinberger told the Palouses to leave Lapwai, but the Indians ignored his order, camping with Big Thunder, a Nez Perce chief. No doubt, the Palouses shared their ideas with the other Indians, discussed the direction of the council, and speculated about the future. On May 25, the first day of the council, Superintendent Hale bluntly informed the Indians that he wanted them to consent to a smaller reservation. Before the arrival of many Nez Perce leaders—including Joseph, White Bird, Eagle From the Light, and Koolkool Snehee—the Indians flatly refused to surrender their lands. Chief Lawyer, long-time friend of whites in the region, reminded Hale of the Nez Perce Treaty of 1855, arguing that the Indians would not sell any lands.[4]

Superintendent Hale assured the Indians that the government wished to reduce the Nez Perce Reservation for the good of the Indians, reasoning that a smaller reservation would make it easier for the army to protect them. His arguments failed and the council recessed. Meanwhile, Hale met separately with Indians who arrived late, but fared no better with them. Hale talked individually with the Nez Perce leader, but found Lawyer's faction of the tribe the only one willing to renegotiate the treaty. On June 9, 1863, Lawyer and fifty-one Nez Perces signed a treaty ceding 6,932,270 acres of land for less than eight cents an acre. None of the Palouses signed the Nez Perce Treaty of 1863. Eventually the Office of Indian Affairs and the army ordered them to abide by the Lapwai agreement, treating the Palouses as if they were bands of Nez Perces.[5] Chief Lawyer and the other signers of the "Thief Treaty of 1863," as the document became known, sold lands that did not belong to them, but not one of the "non-treaty" chiefs, whose lands were lost, signed the document. The Palouses were totally against the treaty, and many eventually sided with Joseph, White Bird, and Toohoolhoolzote. Most Palouses no doubt agreed with Chief Joseph's assessment that if the Indians "ever owned the land we own it still, for we never sold it."[6] The Palouses were not considered "official parties" to the the 1863 Thief Treaty but were simply grouped with the non-treaty Nez Perces and considered as part of that tribe. The Yakima Treaty of 1855 had called for removal of all Palouse Indians to the Yakima Reservation, but at that time most refused to move. During the three decades following the Walla Walla Council, most tried to live on their ancestral lands. But white settlement of the Palouse Country did cause a schism within the Palouse communities, for a few Indians, remembering the fate of their friends and relatives who had fought Colonel Wright, moved from the Snake and its tributaries to settle on one of the reservations east of the Cascades. They moved to the Yakima, Colville, Warm Springs, Nez Perce, and Umatilla Reservations. Most, however, remained on their lands to live as their fathers and mothers before them.[7]

Between 1863 and 1876, miners, merchants, stockmen, and farmers resettled lands that were once the sole domain of the Palouses. With the growth of the white population came demand by settlers that the non-reservation Indians be forced onto the reservations. The settlers made their wishes known to legislators, military leaders, and bureau officials. To counter this action, Indians organized a loose-knit inter-tribal confederacy based on the Washani religion. To some degree, all of the non-treaty Indians — Palouses and Nez Perce — were influenced by the Wanapum Prophet, Smohalla, and the confederacy was based on a common belief in the sacredness of the earth. Agents and soldiers alike worried about the "new-fangled religious delusion," labeling the religious leaders "wizards" and "magicians" who fomented trouble within the Indian communities. Among other motives, government officials wanted to place non-Christian Palouses and Nez Perces onto a reservation where they could be watched and Christianized.[8]

Plans to remove the non-treaty Indians accelerated after the government decided to force Chief Joseph out of the beautiful Wallowa Valley of northeastern Oregon. Officials determined to move all of the non-treaties at the same time, and to this end, the Secretary of the Interior appointed a board of commissioners to settle the Palouse and Nez Perce question. Ignoring the suggestions made by Nez Perce Agent John B. Monteith and General Oliver O. Howard, the secretary selected as commissioners David H. Jerome, A. C. Barstow, William Stickney, Major H. Clay Wood, and General Howard. The commissioners arrived at the Nez Perce agency on November 7, 1876 with instructions to "lose no time in sending for the non-treaty Nez Perce Indians, and especially for Joseph." Six days after their arrival, they met with Chief Joseph, the great leader of the Wallowa band known to his people as Hinmahtooyahlatkekht (Thunder Traveling to Loftier Mountain Heights). The first Lapwai Council convened on November 13, 1876, and its outcome greatly altered the lives of the Palouse Indians.[9]

Several Upper Palouses attended the council where Chief Joseph was asked to give up the Wallowa Valley and move onto the Nez Perce Reservation. Joseph explained his position in terms of his religion. "The Creative Power, when he made the earth," Joseph stated, "made no marks, no lines of division or separation on it." The Indians were "of the earth," and the earth was "too sacred to be valued by or sold for silver or gold." The Indians told Howard that they could not give up their lands and would not move to the reservation. Angered by this response, Howard asserted that the Indians had "denied the jurisdiction of the United States over them."[10] Joseph reflected the sentiment of all of the non-reservation Indians: "We will not sell the land. We will not give up the land. We love the land; it is our home." Upset by these words, the whites closed the council which ended unsatisfactorily for everyone.[11]

The commissioners left disappointed that the Indians "firmly declined" to surrender their lands.[12] Howard and the others blamed their failure on the Indian spiritual leaders, or *tooats,* who counseled the others not to sign treaties, surrender lands, or live on reservations — all of which the *tooats* considered acts against God. Husishusis Kute of the Palouses and Toohoolhoolzote of the Nez Perces were the two great holy men among these Indians. The commissioners labeled them "Dreamers," a derogatory term used in reference to all non-Christian spiritual leaders. Commissioners considered them "fanatics" who undermined the work of the government. General

Howard and Agent Monteith loathed both *tooats* and the traditional religious beliefs of the Indians, which proved to be great obstacles to their mission. This view appeared in the annual report of the commissioner of Indian affairs. "The dreamers, among other pernicious doctrines, teach that the earth being created by God complete, should not be disturbed by man, and that any cultivation of the soil or other improvements to interfere with its natural productions, any voluntary submission to the control of the government, and improvement in the way of schools, churches, etc., are crimes from which they shrink."[13]

Because of their fear of the Washani leaders, the commissioners recommended that the *tooats* "be required to return to the agencies . . . and in case of refusal that they be removed from further contact with the roaming Indians by immediate transportation to the Indian Territory." The commissioners further requested the military occupation of the Wallowa Valley by Howard's troops and resettlement of the non-treaty Palouses and Nez Perces on to the reservation. The Palouses and Nez Perces were to be given "a reasonable time" to move onto the reservation, but if they refused, the commissioners wanted "sufficient force to bring them into subjection, and to place them upon the Nez Perce Reservation." As the commissioners put it: "The Indian Agent at Lapwai, Agent Monteith should be fully instructed to carry into execution these suggestions, relying at all times upon the department commander [General Howard] for aid when necessary."[14]

In January 1877, while the Palouses wintered along the Snake River, Agent Monteith received word to move the Upper Palouses and non-reservation Nez Perces onto the reservation in "a reasonable time." Monteith asked Howard to station his soldiers in the Wallowa Valley. Monteith wanted all of the non-treaty Indians on the reservation by April 1, an unreasonable demand due to the unpredictability of the weather and spring flooding. The agent placed a burden on the Indian leaders to convince their people that they had to move in order to prevent bloodshed. Palouse leaders would have concurred with Chief Joseph's assessment of the situation. "The country they claim belonged to my father, and when he died it was given to me and my people, and I will not leave it until I am compelled to."[15] Joseph and his brother, Ollokot, asked Monteith and Howard for another meeting. They agreed, and the second Lapwai Council commenced on May 3, 1877.[16]

Two Palouse bands attended the council, but Howard opened the meeting before they arrived. The Indians warned Perrin Whitman, the nephew of Marcus, to interpret correctly, because the council would be of importance to "coming generations, the children and the children's children, both whites and Indians." Pent-up anger surfaced when one of the holy men spoke in "a cross and querulous manner," arguing that, "We want to talk a long time, many days, about the earth, about our land." Howard answered that "Mr. Monteith and I wish to hear what you have to say, whatever time it may take; but you may as well know at the outset that in any event the Indians must obey the orders of the government of the United States."[17]

During the next few days, two Palouse leaders from the village of Wawawai, located fifteen miles below Lewiston, Idaho, arrived at the council. One of them, Husishusis Kute, was described by General Howard as "the oily, wily, bright-eyed young chief." He arrived at the Lapwai Council on May 7, "with a number of followers." Husishusis Kute, aged thirty-seven years, was a holy man of the Washani faith who to some extent was influenced by the teachings of Smohalla.[18] According to a Nez Perce named Peopeo Moxmox (Yellow Bird), Husishusis Kute practiced "a religion unlike some of the others." He was one of the "new religious people" who used "a drum to beat in his worship."[19] He had learned his religion first from his father "who was an outstanding Dreamer Prophet, and spiritual man." Smohalla influenced his faith by stressing the abhorrence of reservations and control by the Bureau of Indian Affairs. Husishusis Kute "inherited both the name and mantle of his father," who had fought in the Cayuse War and had been chosen "chief of the Paloos band after the war."[20]

Husishusis Kute was not a war chief, but he had seen battle. He had been wounded by a cannon ball during Wright's Campaign. As a result of a head wound, the young warrior lost his hair, "and he told his warriors that he was going to take the name of Husishusis Kute," meaning Bald Head. Known for his sound judgment and wisdom, the Palouses selected Husishusis Kute to speak for them at the Lapwai Council. When he arrived at Lapwai, he was disposed toward peace.[21] The other Palouse leader from Wawawai was Hahtalekin (sometimes spelled Nahtalekin), civil chief of the village. Known to the Palouses as Taktsoukt Ilppilp (Red Echo), Hahtalekin was a tribal elder from the distinguished "buffalo-hunter" class, and reckoned a "brave, discreet warrior."[22] The Palouse band "constituted the smallest of the 'non-treaty' groups at the Lapwai councils, where Husis-husis Kute was their spokesman." Indeed, Husishusis Kute "was held in highest esteem by all the Dreamer tribesmen" and was selected to be the second orator during the Lapwai Council after the old Nez Perce spiritual leader, Toohoolhoolzote.[23] However, Husishusis Kute was never given an opportunity to speak because of a quarrel that developed between Howard and Toohoolhoolzote. But had he spoken, Husishusis Kute would have agreed with the precepts enunciated by the Nez Perce *tooat*. Early in the council, Toohoolhoolzote's disagreement with General Howard set the tone and established a level of tension that characterized the entire proceedings.[24]

Ollokot was the first to wrangle with General Howard, however, when he said that Indians had "respect for the whites; but they treat me as a dog, and I sometimes think my friends are different from what I had supposed. There should be one law for all." Toohoolhoolzote next attacked the white man's law; in so doing, he angered Howard. The general described Toohoolhoolzote as "broad-shouldered, deep-chested, thick-necked, five feet ten in height, had a heavy guttural voice, and betrayed in every word a strong and settled hatred of all Caucasians." In no uncertain terms, Toohoolhoolzote told Howard that he had "heard of a bargain, a trade between some of these Indians [referring to the treaty Nez Perces] and the white men concerning their land; but I belong to the land out of which I came." Howard was perturbed by the "cross-grained growler" who became "crosser and more impudent in his abruptness of manner." He explained that a "majority" of the Nez Perces had signed away part of the original reservation and that "the non-treaty Indians being in the minority [a false assertion] in their opposition, were bound by that agreement, and must abide by it." The non-treaty Palouses and Nez Perces disagreed, believing that no man could order them to abide by a treaty which they had not signed.[25]

In every meeting Toohoolhoolzote spoke of the "chieftainship of the earth" and explained that Indian "law" came from God and revolved around a reverency of Mother Earth. Howard became so irritated with Toohoolhoolzote's redundant statements that he told the Nez Perce, "Twenty times over you repeat that the earth is your mother, and about the chieftainship from the earth. Let us hear it no more, but come to business at once." Toohoolhoolzote announced, "You white people get together, measure the earth, and then divide it; so I want you to talk directly what you mean!" Howard explained again that the treaty Indians had sold the land, that the law came from Washington, and that the Indians had to move onto the reservation. Toohoolhoolzote again spoke, "Part of the Indians gave up their land. I never did. The earth is part of my body, and I never gave up the earth." The general replied "that the government has set apart a reservation, and that the Indians must go upon it." Toohoolhoolzote looked fiercely at Howard and asked, "What person pretends to divide the land, and put me on it?" Howard exclaimed, "I am that man. I stand here for the President, and there is no spirit good or bad that will hinder me. My orders are plain, and will be executed." Toohoolhoolzote wished to be left alone, warning Howard that the white men were "trifling with the law of the earth." Toohoolhoolzote concluded, announcing that, "The Indians may do what they like, but I am not going on the reservation." Howard instructed Captain David Perry to hold Toohoolhoolzote, at which point the leader responded by asking, "Do you want to scare me with reference to my body?" Perry escorted the headman to jail.[26]

The council was tense, but Howard asked Husishusis Kute, Hahtalekin, Joseph, White Bird, and others if they would go "peaceably on the reservation," or if they wanted him "to put them there by force?" None of the Palouses or Nez Perces, except Toohoolhoolzote, favored war which the Indians felt resulted in disaster. One by one, they consented to move to the Nez Perce Reservation, including Husishusis Kute and Hahtalekin. Chief Joseph assessed their situation: "We were like deer. They were like grizzly bears."[27] The Palouses and Nez Perces agreed to move, and to this end Husishusis Kute, Hahtalekin, and the Nez Perce chiefs toured the Nez Perce Reservation, selecting lands onto which they would move. Howard wrote that "Hush-hush-cute will go to the land along the Clearwater, just above the agency."[28] For religious reasons, some of the non-treaty Nez Perces wanted to be located next to Husishusis Kute where "no body will interfere with our worship."[29] Chief Hahtalekin chose lands nearby the other Palouses. Howard told the Palouses to relocate on the Clearwater within thirty-five days, an unreasonably short time for the Palouse leaders to convince their people to move, gather their belongings, round up their herds, and move to Lapwai. Howard and Monteith feared that Husishusis Kute would use his position as a *tooat* to rally the Indians and incite violence.[30]

Howard told the Palouses that if they "let the time run over one day, the soldiers will be there to drive you on the reservation, and all your cattle and horses outside of the reservation at that time will fall into the hands of the white men."[31] This added insult to injury, but neither the Palouses nor the Nez Perces could stand against the United States Army. At the end of the meeting on May 14, Howard handed each Indian leader a "protection paper," assuring them safe passage from their homelands to the reservation. When Howard handed the protection paper to Husishusis Kute, the Palouse refused it "with a curt explanation." He told Howard, "I do not want it! I might get it dirty!" Husishusis Kute made this remark because "the proud Paloos Chieftain" was "incensed at the penury of the time limit for their removal."[32] Howard and Monteith considered Husishusis Kute's remarks an insult, so the general withdrew the paper, explaining later that Husishusis Kute "was the only Indian who, at this time, betrayed any symptoms of treachery. His protection papers were withheld on account of it, and given to the agent to be presented to him when the agent should be satisfied of his good intentions." Husishusis Kute upstaged the general, and the non-treaty Indians laughed at his remark.[33]

Husishusis Kute and Hahtalekin returned to the Snake River to tell their people of the Lapwai Council and the decisions made there, news which made their "hearts sink to the ground."[34] Because of the nature of Palouse society, each family and band decided for themselves whether they would move onto the reservation or remain in their homeland. In order to avoid bloodshed, Hahtalekin chose to move onto the reservation. Some Palouses went to another reservation to live with relatives, while others defied the government altogether. A few Palouses prepared to move onto the Nez Perce Reservation immediately, joining a large gathering of non-treaty Nez Perces on the Camas Prairie. In west-central Idaho, the Indians met to gather roots, race horses, and visit friends and relatives.[35] While most of the Upper Palouses prepared to move onto the banks of the Clearwater River, Howard convened a meeting with some of the Lower Palouses living on the Snake River between Palus and Qosispah.

Among the Lower Palouses, Thomash commanded great respect as a Washani holy man. He lived at the village of Sumuya (near Fishhook Bend on the Snake River) with fifty followers, including his brothers and relatives of Tilcoax. In May 1877 Howard summoned Thomash to a meeting. The Lower Palouse chief did not trust white men, and since his youth, he had boasted that because of his *somesh* (spirit power), no shackles or jails could hold him and no bullet could penetrate his body. In 1856 the Palouse headman had been captured by volunteer troops under Colonel Thomas Cornelius, and as a young man, Thomash had learned the ways of the whites.[36] Howard convened a council among the Lower Palouses, Cayuses, Walla Wallas, and others. After some consideration, Thomash attended the council and joined Young Chief of the Cayuses, Homli of the Walla Wallas, and Smohalla of the Wanapums. Over three hundred Indians "freshly bedecked with paint and feathers" met Howard near the decaying walls of old Fort Walla Walla. Howard characterized Thomash as "a refractory chief" whose people "wanted peace, but they desired much more to roam at large whenever and wherever they pleased."

The general believed that before the Lower Palouses moved to any reservation, they would observe the Upper Palouse and Nez Perce situation, knowing that "should they alone [the Lower Palouses] precipitate war . . . they would soon be annihilated." During the council, Howard and Umatilla Agent W. A. Connoyer explained the benefits of reservation life. The Indians convinced Howard and Connoyer that most of the Indians, except for the Palouses, had come to the council "with apparent good feelings." Howard reported that Thomash "was wild and fierce to the last," and he later recalled that Thomash "wanted to know why I had been sending troops to Wallowa, and denounced the action and wishes of the United States government in unmeasured terms." The chief and his people stormed out of the parley, returned up the Snake River "making better time than the steamboat."[37]

Andrew Pambrun served as Howard's interpreter, and when Thomash spoke out and bolted the council, Pambrun offered to "tame him a little" by incarcerating the boastful leader. Given the volatile situation, Howard refused and instead convened another meeting at Fort Simcoe on June 8. This council was attended by "all the Indians far and near, north of the Columbia River." Thomash, Moses, Smohalla, and the Yakima, Calwash, attended. After formal introductions, Howard delivered a brief address striking at the heart of the issue: "The government requires that you shall all come on this [the Yakima] or some other of its reservations." He announced that "the commander of the military forces will enforce this requirement." On Monday, June 10, Moses and Smohalla agreed to move to a reservation. Finally Thomash, "a spare, tall man afflicted with a nervous trembling," arose to say that he would "go to the Umatilla reservation by the first of September." When the chiefs agreed to relocate to a reservation, Howard left the council for Fort Lapwai to supervise the Nez Perce relocation, arriving at the post as a messenger entered the garrison with news of great importance.[38]

While Thomash met Howard, a few Upper Palouses and several Nez Perces gathered at Tolo Lake, located six miles east of Grangeville, Idaho. The purple flowers of the camas covered the prairie like the nap of a carpet, and the people dug spring roots to dry before moving onto the reservation. While the men and women prepared to move, the young people fretted over their own fate and that of future generations. Depressed over the situation, some drank to excess. One young man, Wahlitits, rode about camp in a rage, permitting his horse to trample roots that had been laid out to dry. A man and a woman who had gathered the roots rushed out, scolding Wahlitits and telling him that if he thought himself a great warrior, then he should avenge the death of his father, Eagle Robe. The previous year, a white settler named Larry Ott had murdered Eagle Robe. Angered by the rebuke, the young man accepted the challenge, deciding to kill his father's murderer.

Wahlitits, along with two friends, Wetyetmas (Swan Necklace), and Sarpsis Llppilp (Red Moccasin Tops) raided white settlements along the Salmon River, killing three white men and wounding another. They did not find Ott but had tasted revenge. Word of their deeds quickly spread among the whites and Indians, and the next day other Indians joined Wahlitits. The small force swept down on the Salmon River settlements again, triggering a tragic conflict known as the Nez Perce War. Young Palouses probably did not join this war party, but the group's actions influenced the course of Palouse history.[39]

The raids caused great anxiety in both white and Indian communities. Joseph moved his people off the Camas Prairie into White Bird Canyon, while Husishusis Kute elicited support among the interior tribes on behalf of the non-treaty Indians. At the outbreak of the Nez Perce War, several bands of Palouses camped with hundreds of other Indians on a camas meadow near the Coeur d'Alene Mission. The Coeur d'Alenes had no agent, and many Indians rendezvoused to dig roots, race horses, and discuss recent events. The Catholic missionaries and Christian Indians living near the mission were "much bothered" by the "unruly" followers of the Washani faith. The Jesuits labeled them "pagan Dreamers" and feared that these unwanted elements would cause violence. For this reason, Seltice—a Christian and Coeur d'Alene leader—prohibited all drinking and gambling. The prohibition upset many Indians, but they reached a compromise after three Spokane

Chiefs suggested that all who did not wish to abide by the restrictions should move west to Elposen, located nine miles off the reservation near present-day Tekoa, Washington.[40]

News of the Salmon River raids reached the Palouses as they resettled at Elposen. Many Palouses were sympathetic to the Nez Perce cause, and some advocated active support of their neighbors. Seltice stood firmly against joining, saying that the Coeur d'Alenes "were friends of the whites, and we will have nothing to do with the murderers." Some of the younger men among the Palouse bands immediately rode off to engage white settlers in the Palouse Country, but found most cabins empty. When whites learned of the Salmon River raids, they sought refuge in small frontier towns. Farmers east of Colfax, Washington, heard about events when a rider from Lewiston rode into a camp meeting on Saturday, June 16, near present-day Elberton. The assembly was "thrown into a fervor by the news that the Indians were assuming hostile positions in the district east of us toward Lewiston." The messenger reported that one family near Lapwai had just been massacred and that "others had been murdered without mercy." Cooler heads prevailed, and the attending preacher offered prayers of comfort to the assembled families. Although this initial report "did not have much effect" on the congregation, they left for their homes with anxious feelings.[41]

Unsubstantiated rumors about hostile Indians floated about like ominous storm clouds. From Lewiston, Idaho, to Dayton, Washington, white settlers sounded the alarm that the interior Indians had launched a general uprising. A Lewiston newspaper reported that the Nez Perces and Upper Palouses were to be joined by "several hundred fighting men from the different bands who have hitherto been considered friendly."[42] The citizens of Colfax received word that "400 Indians, more or less, traveling in a body had killed 80 persons on the Clearwater, and were coming toward Colfax, sweeping all before them."[43] White settlers rushed to the nearest town, as rumors circulated and "terror ruled supreme." Volunteer troops organized; towns readied for full-scale attacks; women and children sequestered in schoolhouses, mercantile stores, and saloons. Sixty wagons of panic-stricken people fled their farms and stock to seek refuge in a Colfax schoolhouse. While women and children prepared for a siege, the men dug fire pits and gathered guns and ammunition. Citizens Frank Bowman, Carl Floyd, and George Sutherland acted as guards on the south side of Colfax, but neither these guards nor those on the north end of town saw any Palouses. However, one sentry fired a round at a phantom Indian. White settlers feared all of the Indians of the region, believing that Joseph had sent runners to the "Palouse, Spokane, Columbia River and Umatilla Tribes." Some believed that all of the interior Indians would soon join the Nez Perces and Upper Palouses "and that they would capture the whole country."[44]

At Palouse City the citizens cut 480 wagonloads of pine and fir poles, using them to build a sturdy stockade around the Ragsdale Store. The blockhouse measured 125 feet in circumference and housed 200 people. Women and children took up residence on the second floor of the store, while the men camped in tents outside, but inside the walls of their fort. Local residents organized a volunteer company under the banner of the "Palouse Rangers," and they elected Captain J. M. Greenstreet their commander. At the same time that the citizens of Colfax and Palouse City prepared for an attack, residents of Pine Creek (Farmington), Leichville, Spangle, and Four

Mile Creek (near Moscow, Idaho) made similar fortifications and formed local militias. Whites living in the present-day Orecho District along the Snake River learned from local Palouse Indians of potential danger. Many whites had gathered at Penawawa to ship their bales of wool on a steamboat of the Oregon Steam Navigation Company, and while they waited for the boat, they constructed a fort out of the wool bales, complete with gun portals and corner standouts. The herders remained there a few weeks, but the impending attack never materialized.[45]

Every community in the Palouse Country received conflicting reports and exaggerated rumors of hostile Indians. David Bowman and James Tipton of Colfax scouted the Washington and Idaho border, returning to report "that the Indians [Palouses and Nez Perces] had not crossed the Clearwater but were going toward the mountains." Another scouting party led by James Perkins returned to Colfax with similar news about the hostile Palouses and Nez Perces. While citizens breathed a sigh of relief after learning that the hostiles had headed east over the Bitterroot Mountains, they worried over a report from Bowman and Tipton that "the Coeur d'Alenes were going to break out the next day, kill all the people at Mr. Howard's stockade [located on the Idaho border], and send a detachment to Colfax to massacre all the people there." The whites feared this rumor since Bowman and Tipton had received this intelligence from an Indian who had recently been at the Coeur d'Alene Mission. Settlers at Pine Creek had heard similar reports from James M. Graden and Melville Choate who had visited the mission and found the Indians "in a high state of excitement." They learned no other substantive information and returned to Pine Creek. On their journey across the Palouse Hills, they saw two Indians armed with rifles, but the Indians simply rode off.[46]

Father Joseph Cataldo of the Coeur d'Alene Mission worked to prevent peaceful Palouses, Spokanes, and Coeur d'Alenes from being drawn into a needless and bloody conflict. For this reason, he penned a letter to the *Lewiston Teller* informing whites that "the Indians are all quiet up on Hangman Creek, although a good many of the Nez Perces and Palouses are there." The same day, the *Walla Walla Union* reported five hundred Indians on Hangman Creek but that there were "no hostilities there yet." After conferring with the Indians in the northern Palouse Country, Cataldo became concerned, because they feared a possible attack by white settlers. The Indians had good reason for concern, since the whites had mobilized their forces in reaction to "the harrowing, horrible details of the . . . Indians." According to the editor of the *Walla Walla Union,* "No live Indian can be trusted," since "ninety-nine hundreths of the people of this country" favored the extermination of all Indians. Before another war broke out, Cataldo sought to quiet the dangerous direction of events on the Plateau.[47]

The Jesuit told Bowman and Tipton of his concerns after they arrived at the mission on another scout of the region. The citizens of Colfax, Bowman and Tipton told Cataldo, remained in near hysteria, fearing attacks from Palouses, Nez Perces, Coeur d'Alenes, and others. Cataldo introduced Bowman and Tipton to Chief Seltice and two Palouse chiefs, Ususpa Euin and John Fla. Ususpa Euin, a Palouse headman from Almota, and John Fla, a leader from the Snake River, explained their peaceful dispositions. Both men wished to return to the Snake, but both feared being attacked by the white settlers. Ususpa Euin, an imposing figure six feet tall with heavy brows and long black hair, told Bowman and Tipton that the Palouses had "come up here to run horse races and our women are out digging camas. By and by they will all come in and we will go home. We don't want war for many reasons and you don't want any war." The Palouse headman assured the two white men that his Palouses wanted "to live together [with white people] and be friends."[48]

Following a brief speech by Fla, Chief Seltice spoke, asking "why the white people had all gone to Colfax and were building big houses." It appeared to the Coeur d'Alene that whites wanted war. When Bowman and Tipton assured the chiefs that the whites did not want war, the Indians asked them to tell the settlers to return to their homes. At the urging of Father Cataldo, the chiefs dictated letters, sending them to towns explaining that their bands wanted peace. Ususpa Euin wrote that his Palouses had no intention of giving "trouble to any white." He prophetically stated that "If Joseph and his friends make war against the whites, that war will finish them." Fla confirmed that his "heart is always good, and the whites have nothing to fear from me, or my people." The letters helped quiet the region. Bowman and Tipton returned to Colfax where the local newspaper reported that the "Indian scare" had actually turned out to be "the grand Palouse humbug."[49]

Nevertheless, trouble stirred among the Coeur d'Alenes and Palouses. Agents of Husishusis Kute had moved among the Indians, attempting to rally support for the war. Some Palouses still wished to return to their homes on the Snake, while others thought it wiser to move north to the Spokane Country. To reassure the whites that the Palouses and Coeur d'Alenes wanted no trouble, Seltice wrote General Howard informing him that "the Palouse Indians were quiet here amongst us digging camash as of old; now a report came of late, telling them to run away from amongst us, because the soldiers would come and drive all Catholic Indians away." Seltice said that while he put no faith in these rumors, his friend, "Chief Ususkein wanted to move off" as did the Nez Perce chief, Three Feathers. The priest blamed these stories on a campaign designed by Husishusis Kute, to "turn the good feelings of our Catholic Indians" against the whites and join the warring factions.

Husishusis Kute had tried to unite the non-committed Indians of the region. He believed that they had been enticed by the "American religion," and he sought their return to the traditional way of the Washani and his peculiar brand of the religion. Father Joset reported that "Skwelkeel or his brother" had visited the Indian camps near the mission carrying Husishusis Kute's message.[50] Unlike some of the Palouse and Nez Perce leaders, Husishusis Kute viewed the outbreak of hostilities as a pretext to unify the tribes in a violent crusade against all whites and their religion. His efforts failed to elicit the kind of response for which he hoped. The Palouse bands under Ususpa Euin and Fla either returned to their river homes or fled to the Spokane Country where another group of Palouses under Chief So-ie camped far from harm's way. Emissaries from the disparate bands prompted the influential Spokane chief, Sgalgalt, to write General Howard, reassuring him that the Spokanes would not join the fighting. He assured Howard that the Spokanes and Palouses would not loot the deserted homes of surrounding settlers who had fled to Spokane Falls or the nearest frontier town.[51]

In mid-June 1877, Chief Thomash of the Lower Palouses arrived in Waitsburg, Washington, with five Palouses from their Snake River home of Sumuya. General Howard had feared that Thomash might be drawn into

into war if the Nez Perce took the initiative, but the headman opposed war. Dozens of curious whites watched as the six Palouses rode into the town and listened as Thomash assured everyone that "all the Indians with the exception of a portion of the Nez Perce tribe, are peaceable disposed, and anxious to maintain friendly relations with the whites." Smohalla remained cordial, but he and other Indians remained "alarmed for fear the whites would turn against them." A local correspondent for the *Walla Walla Union* urged everyone to "act sensible and prudent, and deal justly with the Indians."[52]

With Husishusis Kute's envoys spurned by leaders of virtually all the interior tribes, some hostiles developed a more direct method to embroil the tribes in the crisis. By June 22, individuals and families who had gathered in the Pine Creek area during the "Indian scare" returned to their homes. One of the settlers, John Ritchie, rode horseback to his cabin near Elposen on Hangman Creek. The day after returning, two Palouse warriors rode into the Elposen Indian camp announcing that they had killed two whites. According to their version, they had been accosted and had defended themselves in a gunfight. Fathers Cataldo and Joset identified the young Indians as sons of a respected Palouse Indian named Etelschen whose people belonged to a "small band of Indians on the Snake River." After creating a sensation at Elposen, the two brothers rode southeast about ten miles to the camp of Coeur d'Alene Chief Konmoss where their father had camped.[53]

Upon hearing the report, both Chief Konmoss and Etelschen condemned the act, informing the priests that the Indians did not want a repeat of the tragic events that followed the killing of two miners near Colfax nearly two decades earlier. On the evening of June 23, Chief Konmoss dictated a letter to Father Joseph Giorda, informing the white settlers that "two Indians from between Palouse and Nez Perces River came to his camp telling that they have attacked and shot at two white men." The Jesuit believed that one of the whites had been killed. The Indian leaders realized that the killing might trigger a war, and Father Giorda reasoned that such an act in Coeur d'Alene territory would constitute what "in Indian policy would be an act of hostility on their part against the whites; had the Coeur d'Alenes looked upon it indifferently it would have been taken as a sign that they were at heart with the rebels."[54] Moreover, the deed would give credence to articles circulating in the Walla Walla papers "that the Coeur d'Alene Indians had joined Joseph's band of outlaws, that they numbered several hundred warriors; and that they were marching down from Hangman's Creek, killing and destroying as they came."[55]

Chief Seltice confiscated the horse brought in by the two young Palouses, returning it to the whites with a letter stating that it had been taken by "an Indian of the Snake River: and that the owner was robbed and killed; the thief says he murdered the white man."[56] The news created a sensation among the farmers at Pine Creek, where whites recognized Ritchie's horse. Two white men and an Indian rode to Ritchie's place and found that the settler had been struck in the forehead with an axe and shot in the breast with "the ball ranging downward." It appeared as though Ritchie had been murdered, and news of this finding had an immediate impact in both the white and Indian communities. The whites scrambled back to their sanctuaries, and the Indians followed suit. As for the Palouses, they feared both the whites and the Coeur d'Alenes.[57]

Once again whites living in the Palouse Country feared all Indians, believing that hostiles had camped "a short distance from us" and had "taken up arms and have murdered Men, Women and Children in cold blood." The whites wanted retribution for the Ritchie killing, stating that "in the present condition of the Public Mind many Innocent persons may suffer and much property may be destroyed."[58] Although outraged by the killing, the whites did not attack any of the Indian camps, and a calm again settled on the Palouse Country. Some Palouses who had fled northward professed their friendship with the whites, while others proved hostile. Some of the younger men, swayed by the arguments presented by the messengers of Husishusis Kute, joined the Palouses who had moved off the Snake River and onto the Clearwater. Husishusis Kute had favored hostilities with the whites since the early stages of the Nez Perce War, but no evidence exists suggesting that Hahtalekin wanted war. Indeed, after the raids on the Salmon River, Hahtalekin returned to the Snake River and later moved his people onto the reservation. Yet, Hahtalekin soon joined forces with the hostiles in response to an unprovoked attack on Looking Glass's village.[59]

When news of the Salmon River raids reached the Nez Perce camp on the Camas Prairie, the Indians feared that war would result. Anticipating the movement of troops against them, Joseph and Ollikot directed their people into White Bird Canyon. Full scale war commenced on June 17, 1877, when troops under Captain David Perry engaged the Indians in the Battle of White Bird Canyon. The army suffered heavy losses and were driven from the field. Shortly afterward, General Howard assumed field command, and the war commenced in earnest. While the Nez Perces engaged the soldiers north of Salmon River, some Palouses and Nez Perces sought refuge on the Clearwater. Nez Perces conducted nearly all of the early fighting, although some Palouses did fight with Joseph's band. One such Palouse, Kosooyeen (Going Alone), "was reputed by his compatriots to be a brave warrior and adroit scout." A favorite among the Indians, Kosooyeen belonged to Hahtalekin's band. He fought with the Nez Perces along the Salmon River and had spied on the soldiers for Chief Joseph.[60] According to Yellow Wolf, a Nez Perce warrior and nephew of Joseph, Hahtalekin "did not want war." But the Palouse chief joined the fight after Captain Stephen G. Whipple attacked the camp of Looking Glass. Some Palouses, including Hahtalekin, were likely related to the Looking Glass family. When word reached Hahtalekin that his friends and relatives had been attacked, his band joined the conflict.[61]

Most Palouse warriors who joined forces with the Nez Perces arrived in mid-July 1877, when the various Indian bands met on Weippe Prairie. The chiefs held council to determine what course of action to take. Looking Glass, Hahtalekin, Five Crows, Rainbow, Toohoolhoolzote, and Five Wounds favored crossing the Bitterroot Mountains and living with the Crows in Montana. Reluctant to leave the Wallowa for Montana, Joseph and Ollicot decided to do so after learning that most chiefs favored the move. Looking Glass, the strongest advocate of the move to the Crow Country, led the Indians. Hahtalekin and Husishusis Kute deferred to Looking Glass, believing as many did, that aside from Toohoolhoolzote and White Bird — the older statesmen of the non-treaty Nez Perces — Looking Glass had the greatest war experience. Looking Glass led the Indians from Idaho to Montana across the Lolo Pass, believing that once they left Idaho, they would no longer be harassed by soldiers.[62] The Palouses and Nez Perces encountered little trouble from the soldiers, traveling across the Bitterroot Mountains before turning south through the Bitterroot Valley. They continued to the basin of the Big Hole River where they fished, hunted, and cut lodge poles. Tired from their arduous journey, the Indians rested for the first time in many weeks, dancing and singing in celebration of their escape.[63]

Some Indians objected to remaining at the Big Hole, particularly after Wootolen, a man of "strong powers," dreamed that soldiers were near. Some Indians wanted to backtrack through the Bitterroot Valley, but Looking Glass spoke against the plan. Angry at the lack of support for the scouting party, Five Wounds remarked pointedly: "All right, Looking Glass. You are one of the Chiefs! I have no wife, no children to be placed fronting the danger that I feel coming to us. Whatever the gains, whatever the loss, it is yours."[64] On August 9, 1877, the dream of Wootolen came true, when soldiers under Colonel John Gibbon, commander of the Montana District, attacked at the Big Hole. Gibbon surprised the Indians, and his soldiers crawled close to the Indian camp in the pre-dawn hours of that summer morning.[65] As the Palouse leader, Hahtalekin, went out to check on the horse herd, he was shot after a brief exchange with the soldiers. Before he fell, Hahtalekin sounded a warning. The women and children rushed out of their tipis in the face of fierce fighting.[66] Wounded Head said it best: "Hand to hand, club to club. All mixed up, warriors and soldiers fought. It was a bloody battle." Bullets showered down on the Indians like hail, and bullets ripped "the tepee walls, pattering like raindrops."[67]

In the heat of the Battle of the Big Hole, a number of warriors fell, including several Palouses. Chief Hahtalekin died after sounding the alarm, and so did his son, Pahka Pahtahank (Five Fogs). According to Yellow Wolf, Pahka Pahtahank fought alone on the banks of the Big Hole River wearing a white King George blanket. "Aged about thirty snows, he was of an old-time mind. He did not understand the gun. He was good with the bow, but had only a hunting bow." Yellow Wolf thought to himself, "If he [Pahka Pahtahank] had good rifle, he could bring death to the soldiers."[68] The young Palouse warrior died protecting the camp, and Yellow Wolf recorded the event. "He was just in front of his own tepee. Soldiers were this side, not far from him. He stood there shooting arrows at the enemies." The soldiers fired repeatedly at the Palouse warrior who dodged the bullets by stepping "about a little," but all the time continuing to fire arrows at the soldiers. "Three times those soldiers fired and missed him. The fourth round killed him."[69]

Twenty minutes after the battle commenced, Gibbon took the Indian camp. The Nez Perces and Palouses had been cut to pieces, but White Bird and Looking Glass rallied the warriors and counter-attacked, showering the soldiers with bullets and driving them from camp. The Indians captured a mountain howitzer and a mule loaded with two thousand rounds of Springfield rifle ammunition. The warriors kept the soldiers at bay until the women, children, and elders escaped the Big Hole during the night of August 10. Approximately fifty-four women and children died in the battle, while thirty-three men perished. Joseph and Ollikot lost their wives during the fight, and several noted warriors died, including Hahtalekin, Pahka Pahtahank, Rainbow, Wahlitits, and Sarpsis Llppilp. Looking Glass survived, but much of his power dissolved after the Big Hole disaster. Lean Elk emerged as the major chief, and he and others led the people on a trying journey through western Montana, eastern Idaho, and the Yellowstone National Park of northwestern Wyoming.

In their escape to the open plains of central Montana, the Indians skirmished with Howard's troops at Camas Meadows and eluded the command of Colonel Samuel D. Sturgis, assigned to surprise the Indians along the Clark Fork River. Under orders from Howard, Colonel Sturgis engaged the warriors at Canyon Creek, but the Indians escaped. Looking Glass had bragged of his friendship with the Crows, claiming that they would aid the people, but when the chief contacted them, he was given an insulting rebuff. The summer before the Crows had scouted for Colonel George Armstrong Custer, and they wanted nothing to do with the Nez Perce War. When the Palouse and Nez Perce headmen learned that the Crows would not help them, the leaders decided to escape to Canada. Some thought that Sitting Bull might provide support, but their hopes were dashed when the exiled Sioux never arrived.[70]

Following the Battle of Canyon Creek, Sturgis sent a rider to Tongue River Cantonment with a message from Howard to Nelson A. Miles, asking the colonel to cut off the Indians from the east. Miles longed for such an opportunity and moved quickly to act on Howard's request. With a combined force of approximately four hundred men, including thirty Sioux and Cheyenne warriors, Miles crossed the Missouri River, racing northward toward the Canadian border to intercept the fleeing Nez Perces and Palouses. Of this the Palouses and Nez Perces knew nothing, believing that the only soldiers following them were those under General Howard. With the army far behind, Looking Glass rode about the tired and wounded Indians urging them to slow down. The Grand Mother Country—Canada—was not far off, he argued. The Indians had ample time to escape. After leaving the Missouri River, they camped early each day to rest. On the afternoon of September 29 they reached the valley of a small tributary of Milk River called Snake Creek. The creek laid between Bear Paw and the Little Rocky Mountains, approximately forty miles from the Canadian border—forty-eight hours from freedom. There they rested for two nights while the soldiers under Miles closed in on the unsuspecting band.[71]

In a cold rain and a pea soup fog, Sioux and Cheyenne scouts found the Palouse-Nez Perce camp. Shortly afterwards, Miles charged and a bloody battle ensued. The soldiers and warriors fought at close quarters, and some of the women and children fought with digging sticks and butcher knives. Miles lost many men and officers because of the deadly marksmanship of the hostile warriors. For this reason the colonel laid siege to the Indian position with Hotchkiss and Napoleon guns. Some Indians, including Yellow Wolf, White Bird, and the twelve-year old daughter of Chief Joseph, left the battlefield for Canada. Most took cover from the gunfire and miserable weather that dumped five inches of snow on them. On October 1, Miles raised a white flag in his camp and called out to Joseph requesting a parley. The Indians met in council to discuss a cease-fire, but missing from the gathering were Ollikot, Toohoolhoolzote, and Lean Elk, all of whom had been killed during the first day of fighting. Looking Glass and White Bird feared that if the Indians surrendered, Howard would hang them, just as Colonel Wright had done in 1858. Tom Hills, a Nez Perce interpreter, visited Miles and received an assurance that Joseph would not be harmed. As a result, Joseph met Miles halfway between the two camps.[72]

The two men talked of surrender, and Miles demanded that the Indians lay down their arms. Joseph suggested that half of the firearms would be kept and used for hunting. Miles refused to allow the Indians to keep any weapons, whereupon the talk ended. Before Joseph had reached his camp, Miles seized and took him prisoner. The Indians retaliated, detaining Lieutenant Lovell H. Jerome until Joseph was released. Meanwhile, General Howard arrived at the Bear Paws on October 4 but did not assume command or direct the peace negotiations. Instead, Miles finished "the work he had so well begun."[73] On October 5 two treaty Nez Perces negotiated a peace. Meopkowit (Old George) and Jokais (Captain John) served the army as scouts, and they rode into the Indian camp to tell the warriors that Miles and Howard wanted "no more war!"[74] This news provided the Indians an honorable way to end hostilities without surrendering. As Yellow Wolf put it, "We were not captured. It was a draw battle." The Indians believed that the army had agreed to a conditional surrender, whereby the warriors would not be punished but allowed to return to the reservation in Idaho. Joseph reported that Miles had said, "If you will come and give up your arms, I will spare your lives and send you back to the reservation." If the Nez Perces and Palouses had not believed Miles "they never would have surrendered."[75]

Some Indians escaped to Canada, joining the Sioux under Sitting Bull. But most, however, too old, tired, or sick to escape, surrendered. Husishusis Kute, now head of all Palouses, capitulated with the Nez Perces. Toward evening on the night of October 5, 1877, Joseph rode out to surrender. The chief rode forward with his rifle across the pommel of his saddle, and he halted his horse a few steps in front of Howard and Miles. Joseph dismounted, walked toward Howard, and offered his weapon to the general. "Howard waved him to Miles. He then walked to Miles and handed him the rifle."[76] Whether or not Joseph presented the elegant speech generally attributed to him cannot be documented. The chief was in fact sick and tired of fighting and greatly concerned about the wounded, ill, and dying people who had fought with him. When he handed his rifle to Miles, he knew in his heart that he would "fight no more forever."[77]

Over 400 Indians surrendered that cold October day in the Bear Paws, including Husishusis Kute and Palouse men, women, and children. The Palouses had suffered their last military defeat but not their final indignity. Like the Nez Perces, they anticipated a return to the Idaho Reservation. Instead, the soldiers sent them to Fort Keogh before loading them on boats to be sent down the Yellowstone and Missouri Rivers. General William Tecumseh Sherman, commander of the United States army, ordered the Palouses and Nez Perces sent first to Fort Leavenworth, Kansas, and then to the Quapaw Agency in the Indian Territory.[78]

The Indians arrived at Fort Leavenworth on November 27, 1877, remaining there until July 21, 1878. Depression, death, and disease characterized their captivity at Fort Leavenworth, and during their eight months' stay, twenty-one people died. One observer reported the deplorable condition of the Palouses and Nez Perces at Fort Leavenworth. "The 400 miserable, helpless, emaciated specimens of humanity, subject for months to the malarial atmosphere of the river bottoms, presented a picture which brought to my mind the horrors of Andersonville." Over half of the Palouses and Nez Perces, "principally women and children," were sick, and all of the Indians suffered from the "poisonous maleria."[79]

The condition of the Palouses and Nez Perces at Fort Leavenworth was so dreadful that one individual stated that the Indians "had better be moved soon or their removal to the burial ground will be completed."[80] In July 1878, the soldiers escorted the Palouses and Nez Perces to their new home on the Quapaw Agency in the Indian Territory. They remained there for a year, before the Bureau of Indian Affairs transferred them to the Ponca Agency in present-day north central Oklahoma near the town of Tonkawa. The land upon which the Indians resettled had been chosen the previous October by Husishusis Kute and Joseph who found the lands located west of the Ponca Agency, near the junction of the Chikaskia and Salt Fork Rivers, more to their liking but unacceptable.[81] At the Ponca Agency, the Palouses suffered the same problems as the Nez Perces. They died of malnutrition, disease, and despair. Indeed, starvation, sickness, and death characterized the entire exile in what they called *Eekish Pah,* the Hot Place. Ponca Agent William H. Whiteman was ill-prepared to handle the Palouses and Nez Perces, and he candidly explained to the Indians that he "was utterly ignorant of the plans of the Department [of Indian Affairs]" to move them to his agency. Consequently, they received little food, clothing, shelter, or hope. Worse yet, Whiteman had no quinine or medicine of any sort.[82] The Indians made the best of their situation, and in the years following their removal to the Ponca Agency, they farmed, ranched, built homes, and attended mission schools. Yet, they clung to the hope that one day they would return to their beloved Northwest. During their years of exile the Indians looked to Husishusis Kute as their spiritual leader. He led them in singing, dancing, and praying in the old Washani faith, and through their *tooat,* the Indians asked for deliverance.[83]

The Indian leaders — Husishusis Kute, Joseph, and Yellow Bull — did not sit idly, praying for deliverance from a land described by Joseph as a "poor man; it amounts to nothing." The Indians fully cooperated with investigations by a Board of Indian Commissioners and Commissioner of Indian Affairs Ezra A. Hayt. The various inquiries provided white interest in the Nez Perce-Palouse situation, but did little to boost their spirits.[84] In January 1879, Joseph and Yellow Bull traveled to Washington, D.C., where they spoke to politicians and newspaper reporters, who gave them an enthusiastic reception. Joseph said his "heart was sad when I think of my home, which the Great Spirit gave my fathers."[85] The Indians met congressmen, senators, and the Commissioner of Indian Affairs, but to no avail. Resentment against the Palouses and Nez Perces remained intense in the Northwest, and the government refused to permit them to return to their homeland. But they did not give up hope.[86]

In March 1879, Joseph returned once again to Washington, D.C., to plead his case, and once again he received a grand reception. He gave an interview to the popular *North American Review* that appeared in the April issue under the title, "An Indian's View of Indian Affairs."[87] Joseph outlined the history of his people and explained his view of their problems, stating that he did "not believe that the Great Spirit Chief gave one kind of a man the right to tell another . . . what to do." According to his beliefs and those of the Indians he represented, "no man owned any part of the earth, and a man could not sell what he did not own." Joseph appealed to the American sense of democracy and equality: "All men were made by the Great Spirit Chief. They are all brothers. The earth is the mother of all people, and all people should have equal rights upon it." Chief Joseph expressed his opinions and his philosophy, and the essay won him personal acclaim while providing the Nez Perces and Palouses with nationwide recognition of their plight.[88]

Joseph's efforts provided few immediate results, however, and the Indians became increasingly sick in soul as well as body. When former Superintendent of Indian Affairs for Oregon A. B. Meacham visited the Indians in the fall of 1879, he reported that Chief Joseph said: "You come to see me as you would a man upon his death-bed. The Great Spirit above has left me and my people to our fate." Joseph believed that his people had been forgotten, saying that "death comes almost every day for some of my people. He will soon come for all of us." Joseph prophesied that the Palouses and Nez Perces were "a doomed people" who would soon "be in the ground."[89] As the Indians grew more depressed, the white community became more aware of the Nez Perce-Palouse situation. As early as April 1879, Indian Inspector John McNeil wrote to Commissioner Hayt stating that a "great wrong has been done this people." According to the inspector, "No other tribe moved to this territory has better claim to be returned to its homeland."[90] McNeil was not alone, as individuals and institutions petitioned congressmen and senators in support of the Indians. The pressure placed on the Indian bureau and the congress resulted in a decision to return thirty-three women and children to the Nez Perce Reservation of Idaho. James Reuben, a Christian Nez Perce assigned to guide the first Indians back to their homeland, stated that word could not "express our joy when we remember that our feet will soon tread again on our native land, and our eyes behold the scenes of our childhood. The undying love for home, which we have cherished in our hearts so long, has caused our tears to flow for years, but now we are but one step from that home, and how great is our joy."[91]

The public pressure on American Indian policymakers continued. Petitions, letters, and telegrams poured into Washington, D.C., from religious organizations, the Indian Rights Association, and congressmen and senators who championed the Nez Perce-Palouse cause. The movement gained impetus on Independence Day, 1884, when Senator Henry L. Dawes secured passage of a bill empowering the Secretary of Interior to decide the fate of the Indians. After nearly a year, on April 29, 1885, Commissioner of Indian Affairs John D. Atkins ordered the return of the Nez Perces and Palouses to the Pacific Northwest. The commissioner assigned Dr. W. H. Faulkner special agent to oversee the transfer. Because of indictments against Joseph and others, the government divided the Indians into two groups. Agents appointed Husishusis Kute to accompany 118 people to the Nez Perce Reservation in Idaho Territory, while Joseph and Yellow Bull took the remaining 150 Indians to the Colville Reservation in Washington Territory. Of the original 431 Palouses and Nez Perces who arrived at Fort Leavenworth in 1877, only 268 left the Indian Territory on the morning of May 22, 1885.[92]

Before departing, Husishusis Kute, Joseph, and Yellow Bull willingly signed a document forfeiting their claim to any land in the territory. Tears of sorrow fell with tears of joy, as they boarded the train. Memories of their exile in the Hot Country filled their minds, as did their grief for the children and loved ones they left behind. The Palouses and Nez Perces traveled together by rail until they reached Wallula Junction on the Columbia River, Washington Territory. Husishusis Kute took the Indians assigned to him to the Nez Perce Reservation, while Joseph and Yellow Bull traveled northward to the Colville Reservation.[93] Most Palouses went to the Colville Reservation with Joseph, but some settled on the Nez Perce Reservation with their friends and families. When Husishusis Kute arrived at Lapwai on May 27, he reported to Agent Monteith, but the Washani headman did not remain there. Husishusis Kute joined Joseph and Yellow Bull on the Colville Reservation, living out his life among the non-Christian Palouses and Nez Perces. The Upper Palouses had returned to the Northwest but no longer were they free to live along the rivers, to hunt, or to gather camas root from prairies of their native Palouse Country.

CHAPTER 10

PALOUSE INDIAN HOMESTEADS

I wish to stay where I have always lived.
— Quetalakin

When the Palouses returned from the Indian Territory, they found that much had changed. The Northern Pacific Railroad had been completed, and several spur lines snaked across the inland Northwest, carrying produce to far-off markets. Farming enterprises had been extended from the bottom lands to the Palouse Hills, since whites had discovered that "the hill lands prove to be the best for all kinds of grain."[1] Some settlers filed homesteads while others purchased lands from the railroad which had been granted thousands of acres in the Palouse Country. Land speculators had also invested in the region, buying up large tracts and selling smaller parcels to individuals. White farmers viewed the remaining Palouse Indians, who either lived on the lands claimed by whites or used the lands to obtain their livelihood, as obstacles in the way of civilization and progress.

Many settlers wanted the few remaining Indians removed to the reservations, and their demand for removal increased each year in proportion to the growth of the white population. White constituents in the Washington Territory had the ear of territorial and national politicians. These people supported Indian removal. Congressmen, senators, and members of the cabinet pressured the Interior Department to remove the Indians, and agents on the Nez Perce and Yakima Reservations pressured their superiors to force the Palouses onto a reservation. Thus, political forces at the grassroots and national levels of government pushed for Palouse Indian removal. The pressure persisted throughout the 1880s and ultimately led to the removal of most of the Palouses to one of the regional reservations.[2]

The close of the Nez Perce War marked the beginning of major settlement of the Palouse Country. For many years white observers had proclaimed that the soil in the region was fertile, and as the farmers turned the sod in the Palouse Hills, they confirmed this. Word of the rich soil moved out the area like spokes from a hub, as some whites asserted that the inland Northwest possessed "a soil richer than any other portion of the Pacific Coast."[3] Such stories spawned an array of colorful promotional brochures and booster literature, which attracted thousands of immigrants to the Palouse Country. In 1879 whites cultivated 17,964 acres in Whitman County, Washington; in that same year, the district land office at Colfax received more land claims than in any other district office in the entire United States. In one month alone, the district office received claims for 711 farms, totaling 144,207 acres. Within ten years that figure increased fivefold, and by the end of the 1880s, whites owned virtually all the farmland in the Palouse Country. At the dawn of that decade, about 350 Palouses lived in the region, while the white population in Whitman County alone numbered over 7,000 people. The Northern Pacific Railroad owned about 175,000 acres in Whitman County and sold parcels to prospective colonists from Europe and the United States. Clearly, the Palouse Indians witnessed considerable change in their social, economic, and cultural lives as whites settled the Palouse Country.[4]

The "Indian hysteria" that had characterized the beginning of the Nez Perce War did not end with the capture of the Indians at Bear Paws. The Paiute-Bannock War of 1878 caused another Indian scare in the Palouse Country. The newspapers in the region, including the *Palouse Gazette*—the first newspaper north of the Snake River—reflected the white view concerning Indians. C. B. Hopkins, editor of the tabloid, wrote that the settlers generally feared that "the Indians are going to prevent this country from a speedy settlement." Reflecting the sentiment of his readers, Hopkins argued that the "feeble remnant of a savage race" was going to come to the inevitable "realization that their race is fast withering from the land. Right or wrong, such is the logic of events."[5] Whites had a genuine reason for concern. The remaining Palouses still resented the invasion of their land; some even advocated fighting rather than "withering" from the land. More important, white settlers worried about the possibility of an Indian war in the Palouse Country. Their fear of the "Indian problem" brought an increased demand for the government to remove the Palouse remnant and other non-reservation Indians.[6]

When the Bannock-Paiute War spread from southern Idaho to northern Oregon, whites in the Palouse Country believed that the Palouses would rise, once again, in a general war.[7] In early July 1878, rumors of an impending war threatened to create another Indian-white panic. Joe McGee, a farmer on the Touchet River, reported that Indians stole his stock, and because of the Indian scare, a Colfax newspaper warned that "farmers cannot be too careful of their stock now." Another report suggested that a new hysteria would drive people "from their homes, causing individual loss of property and a damage to our prosperous young country." During the summer, settlers gathered for mutual protection at Wallula, Umatilla, Walla Walla, and Pendleton. Whites also responded by launching two armed steamboats on the Columbia to patrol the shores of the great river.[8]

The gunboats churned up and down the Columbia from The Dalles to Wallula looking for signs of Indian hostilities. No evidence has surfaced that the Palouses and others living along the river planned war, but the whites believed war was likely. On one excursion, the two steamboats opened fire on a number of small Indian camps. And as one group of Indians crossed the Columbia below Wallula, Lieutenant M. C. Wilkinson, commander of the gunboat, *Spokane,* ordered his men to open fire. Armed with Gatling guns and muskets, Wilkinson's men pulled up alongside the Indians and shot point-blank at the men, women, and children. When some of the Indians reached the northern bank of the Columbia, they opened fire on the *Spokane,* riddling the pilot house with bullets. The boats continued along the river until the soldiers found another Indian camp. Again Wilkinson ordered his men to fire upon the Indians, who had no warning that the boats intended trouble.

Andrew Pambrun provided an eye-witness account of the attack. "The squaws were busy washing the Salmon . . . and the little children happy in their innocence, played along the beach, some stopped to gaze at the

approaching steamer, when suddenly the destructive missiles came scream-
ing in like hail, laying waste to everything that came within their range, men,
women, and children." As Pambrun surveyed the bloody scene, he reported
that "a few escaped and made for the hills" but the corpses of "men, women,
and children lay in every direction." Following the massacre, some white men
picked over the remains, taking trophies, curios, and everything of "value."
Not long after the attack, white soldiers in Portland and Vancouver proudly
displayed many of the buckskin shirts and dresses formerly worn by the dead.[9]

Over one hundred Indians, including Palouses who whites labeled
"desperate renegades," fled the Columbia River seeking refuge among their
neighbors to the north. One Umatilla warrior, Waughaskie (later known as
Old Bones), escaped to Palus where he told Chief Big Thunder the gunboat
story.[10] According to Juklous (Sam Fisher), Waughaskie "was in some kind
of trouble with the government involving the Bannock War," and so Big
Thunder gave the Umatilla sanctuary among the Palouses.[11] Waughaskie remained at Palus and became a prominent member of the community. Enraged
by Waughaskie's story of the Columbia River killings, several young men
advocated war, but the elders restrained them. However, a group of Umatilla
warriors avenged the deaths of friends and relatives by capturing a young
couple, Lorenzo and Blanche Perkins, who were riding to Yakima City.
Wiahnecat and Tamahhoptowne opened fire on the couple and successfully
drove off Lorenzo. At a rugged ravine, Blanche's horse threw her to the
ground where she laid stunned. When she could not get up, Wiahnecat drew
his pistols and shot her to death.[12]

In the tense atmosphere of southeastern Washington, the Indians felt the
impact of the "Perkins Murder." Settlers from the Yakima Valley to the
Palouse Country rushed to town and country fort to await an all-out attack.
Stories circulated of new alliances between the Palouses, Columbias,
Wanapums, Bannocks, and Paiutes. Upon hearing of the death of Blanche
Perkins, James Ewart summoned the Colfax militia to report immediately
so that each soldier could "know where the guns are, and have them ready
for use in case of emergency."[13] During the middle of July 1878, white settlers near the Palouse villages of Almota and Wawawai formed a "Home
Guard" under Captain James Kuifong. The Home Guard planned to construct another stockade, more formidable than the wool bale structure they
had previously erected. The volunteer soldiers in Colfax and Almota heard
that a "well-armed" and "united force of the hostile bands" had traveled north
toward the Snake River. The Palouses reportedly watched the situation with
the intent of "making a general strike." Farmers near Colfax recorded "the
mysterious disappearance and movements of Indians," saying that the Indians they met acted "saucy and sullen."[14]

The Indian scare spread to other areas of the Palouse Country as well.
John M. Harper, a prominent rancher north of the Snake, held a meeting
of whites living near "Union Flat, Wawawai, Penawawa and vicinity." On
July 20, 1878, the settlers gathered at the farm of D. R. Summers to discuss
the Indian problem. Harper, an outspoken opponent of the Palouses, charged
the Indians with "frequently making hostile demonstrations . . . brandishing
knives at any attempt to restrain such conduct, shooting at individuals while
looking after stock, and committing various other saucy acts." Harper stated
he did not intend "to agitate Indian excitement," but he found little reason
to rejoice at the temporary calm in the area since "past experience has proved

that when we least suspect danger, there may be a dark cloud of trouble near at hand." He therefore recommended that a militia be formed to protect the white communities. Fifty men answered the call, forming another volunteer company. Many members of the company, like Robert and William McNeilly, were among the region's first settlers. They elected Harper captain of the regiment which pledged itself to mutual protection "against the outrages and devastations of our common enemy, the Indian."[15]

About the same time, whites living near Four Lakes formed two companies of militia, totaling over one hundred fifty men commanded by Captain James H. Kennedy. He expressed a firm resolve to set up an independent force, if the territorial governor denied his request for arms. Reflecting the general suspicion of the Palouses, Kennedy claimed he had "plenty of men to stand by the country until the last red devil is put on a reservation."[16] The much-anticipated Indian offensive in the Palouse Country never materialized, as most of the Indians remained near their villages during the summer and fall. The massacre near Wallula demonstrated to the Palouses that whites did not distinguish between peaceful and hostile bands. In response, peaceful Palouses decided not to visit their favorite root grounds located near white homesteads and towns, a distinct change in their life cycle which revolved around the gathering of roots. Their inability to procure roots also upset a religious life that was tied to the gathering, preparation, and consumption of these plants. The Palouses could not hold their annual root feasts, ceremonies conducted in thanksgiving to the Creator for providing this food. Thus the Indian scare restricted more than the movement of Indians across the Plateau; it upset social and cultural elements of their world, destroying the fragile balance between the plants, animals, and the Palouse Indians.[17]

The settlers in the Palouse Country remained sequestered in their towns and makeshift forts until August 1878, when many returned to their farms and ranches. At this time, the *Palouse Gazette* headlined an article, "The Indian Excitement Over" and told its readers to "resume their usual vocations without fear of Indian trouble." However, the piece carried the ominous prediction that, due to a general dissatisfaction among the tribes over white encroachment and Indian removal, an outbreak would be forthcoming the next spring. To prevent an Indian war, the editor advocated either the establishment of a strong military force in the heart of Palouse Country or the removal of non-reservation Indians.[18] The newspaper report did not ease tensions between whites and Indians. The "Indian scare" stirred up greater public demand to displace the Indians. The economic motive for placing these Indians on reservations was certainly a consideration of some settlers, but equally important, farmers and ranchers genuinely feared hostile acts. For example, white settlers near the lower Snake River expressed particular concern about Thomash. Brash and defiant, Thomash and his Palouse band adhered to the Washani religion, openly refusing to abide by his agreement to move to the Umatilla Reservation. Whites demanded that he and the other "Dreamers" be sent to the reservation.[19]

At the Fort Simcoe Council in 1878, Thomash had agreed to move to the Umatilla Reservation. When he did not follow through, Andrew Pambrun made an arrangement with the commander at Fort Walla Walla whereby the chief would be lured into the post and incarcerated. Thomash visited the fort under false pretenses, and when he entered the post, Pambrun detained and questioned him. Asked why he had not taken his people to the reservation, Thomash replied that the matter had been considered and that the Lower Palouses had decided to remain on their ancestral lands where they could practice their traditional religion. The Palouses, he maintained, feared that if they moved onto the reservation, particularly the Yakima or Nez Perce where the agents were Christian zealots, they would be denied their religious rights. Thomash explained that the Indians would never give up their religion. Such defiant talk angered Pambrun who told the chief, "Thomash, you got a big head."[20]

Pambrun told the soldiers to shackle Thomash and throw him into jail. He blamed Thomash and Smohalla for "harboring all the renegades and disaffected of all the surrounding tribes . . . as they themselves resisted all inducements offered by the government to settle on some reservation."[21] Though the incident succeeded in humiliating Thomash, Pambrun failed to discredit the chief or scare the Indians into submission. Actually, the event strengthened Thomash's resolve to remain on the Snake River. When the chief refused to relent, Pambrun confined him to a cell for several days. Besides upsetting the Indian community, the incarceration also turned some white sentiment in favor of the Indian. Through his non-violent resistance, Thomash won the admiration and help of whites throughout the region who openly protested Pambrun's actions. Ultimately, Pambrun released Thomash, whereupon some of the chief's supporters encouraged him to file a "legal" claim for his lands along the lower Snake River. Thomash returned to his home where he shared his experiences with his brother, Choawatyet, his sister, Toyut, and his people. Moreover, Thomash shared his information regarding land claims with members of the powerful Tilcoax family.[22]

Through his grandfather, Thomash was related to Tilcoax, whose family had returned to the lower Snake after the Yakima War. The three sons of Tilcoax—Harlish Washomake, Sheplakhaween, and Whokokawhyken—had built the family's horse herd and maintained a prosperous business during the 1870s and 1880s. The prime mover in this enterprise was the eldest son, the proud Harlish Washomake (Wolf Necklace), known to whites as Tilcoax the Younger or Peter Wolf. Thomash was related to Wolf, and these Palouse leaders worked together to deal with the white problem.[23] The Palouses feared white encroachment into their country, and the growing white demand to remove them to a reservation. While the Indians considered their situation, white agents on the Yakima and Nez Perce Reservations pressured their superiors for the removal of all non-reservation Indians east of the Cascades. The small bands of Palouse Indians were of particular interest to the agents, who viewed them as heathens who would benefit from the Christian influences found on the reservation.[24]

In February 1880, George Hunter, a white rancher living along Snake River and advocate for the Palouses, composed a letter to Secretary of Interior Carl Shurz asking him to intervene on behalf of the tribe. White settlers had encroached on Indian lands, and the Palouses asked for the government's help. The secretary referred the matter to Acting Commissioner of Indian Affairs E. J. Brooks, instructing him to resolve the question. Such action, rare in the Bureau of Indian Affairs, developed as a result of Hunter's letter which had created a minor furor within the Indian office. When Commissioner Brooks checked his office records regarding the Palouse Indians, he found a dearth of information on the tribe. Brooks learned little about the

Palouses, except that they had been parties to the Yakima Treaty of 1855.

Hunter had stated in his letter that the Palouses did not want "to be put on any reservation" and that they had "never sold any lands or drawn any annuities." Brooks's records indicated that the Palouses belonged on the Yakima Reservation and that the Indians had received an annuity a decade before. The Palouses living off the reservation never received an annuity, and most would not have accepted one if it had been offered. Brooks was less concerned with the issue of the annuities than he was with resolving the Palouse Indian question. For this reason, the commissioner wrote Yakima Agent James H. Wilbur, asking him to "Furnish this office with all necessary information as to the condition of the Palouse Indians, how long and for what reasons they have been away from the reservation and your view generally." Brooks indicated that he could find "no special mention" of Palouse Indians in any of Wilbur's reports which greatly disturbed the commissioner. The Yakima agent wrote the commissioner voicing his contempt for the Palouses and their neighbors, the Wanapums, who also practiced the Washani religion and refused to move onto the reservation.[25]

On April 6, 1880, Wilbur composed a lengthy letter to Brooks expressing his views on the Palouse Indians. He pointed out that under the terms of the Yakima Treaty, the Palouses could remain on their lands until their improvements had "been paid for, at a fair valuation to be fixed in a manner specified in the treaty." According to the agent, the Palouses "had made improvements of considerable value" because the Indians had been cultivating small tracts of land. Since these lands "had never been purchased or any steps taken to ascertain their value, they have occupied them continuously since." Wilbur recommended that the Indians be paid for their improvements and then removed to the reservation "where they belong." Wilbur stated that "quite a number of Indians . . . have been induced by the advice of White people to avail themselves of the provisions of the [Indian Homestead] law giving them the privilege of locating homesteads on Public Lands.'

Wilbur referred to the Indian Homestead Act and its revisions which permitted non-reservation Indians to file claim on the public domain, lands which had long belonged to the Indians but which had been ceded to the United States by various treaties. In order to file a claim, Indians had to relinquish their tribal status, although they retained their right to a share of tribal funds. Reform-minded whites viewed the Indian Homestead Act as a means through which the Indians could be quickly "civilized" since whites considered private ownership of the land a significant element of white civilization. Wilbur informed the commissioner that whites had told the Palouses "that the proper way to become prosperous like the whites is, like them, to locate on a homestead and go to work!" Wilbur lamented this development because many Indians, he argued, had "abandoned their tribal relations, left their reservations and located a claim!" According to Wilbur, the result of this trend was most "misfortunate," for the Indians who filed claims had become poor and had the "least promise for the future."[26]

Concerned over non-reservation Palouses, Wilbur wrote that the Indians were far removed from "the oversight and supervision of the agent" which caused the Indians to become "the prize of designing men, who take advantage of his ignorance of the law." He claimed that the Palouse Indians often became easy marks for whites who took advantage of them by stealing their property, "till discouraged with the unequal struggle, he [the Palouse] ceases all efforts at improvements, and gradually drifts back to his old, idle dissolute ways."[27] The Yakima agent strongly opposed the Indian Homestead Act and concluded his letter by damning the legislation. "I do not say this is always the case, but . . . till the generation of Indian children now at school are grown up and take upon themselves the management of affairs, I am unalterably opposed to removing the Indians from the watchful care and over-sight of the government."[28]

The commissioner's inquiry fired Wilbur's desire in "returning fugitive bands of Indians to the reservation." He shared his view with Special Indian Agent H. Clay Wood, arguing that over one thousand Indians "belonging to this reservation" were "widely scattered from the Palouse River to White Salmon and the Lewis [Snake] River."[29] Wilbur urged Colonel Wood to force the Palouse Indians onto the reservation. When the special agent made no effort to remove them, Wilbur became dismayed but not discouraged. He continued his one-man mission to force Palouse removal. In his annual report of 1881 to the commissioner of Indian affairs, Wilbur remarked that the Palouse Indians "still occupy their original country." Although he admitted that they lived in peace with the whites and were in fact "quiet, industrious and worthy," the agent advised the commissioner that "the trifling sum re-quired to purchase their improvements should be paid according to the treaty, and they should be brought to the reservation." Despite Wilbur's efforts, the commissioner failed to order the expenditure of funds to pay for Palouse improvement or to remove the Indians to the Yakima Reservation. Wilbur continued his crusade to remove the Palouses, and was joined by the agent on the Nez Perce Reservation.[30]

Nez Perce Agent John B. Monteith was as eager as Wilbur to move the Palouses to a reservation. Not all of the Upper Palouses had joined the Nez Perces during the war. Some had remained on their traditional lands, despite General Howard's demand to relocate on a reservation. When the Nez Perce War commenced, Howard pursued the hostiles and forgot the non-reservation Palouses. The Upper Palouses claimed correctly that they were not party to the Nez Perce Treaty of 1863 and not required to move. Monteith, a Chris-tian who despised the Washani faith, also believed the Palouses to be heathens who would benefit from Christian instruction and white civilization. He re-mained convinced that non-reservation Palouses belonged on his reservation where they could be watched and influenced by Christian Indians.

Monteith also believed that the Palouses would be a source of future trouble if they continued to live near white society, since many settlers had moved onto the Palouse Hills near present-day Uniontown and Colton in southeastern Washington. The farmers from this region, most of whom were of German descent, disliked Indians and believed that the Palouses threatened the safety of their families. These immigrants complained vehemently to Monteith that the Palouses traveled through their farmlands, as they moved to root and hunting grounds. Monteith responded, writing the commissioner that the government should pay the Palouses for their improvements which, the agent maintained, were "meagre and of little value and are not sufficient to hold such lands." Echoing Wilbur's sentiments, Monteith called for the forced removal of the Palouses to the reservation.[31]

The Monteith-Wilbur view about the non-reservation Palouses were shared by R. H. Milroy, Wilbur's replacement as Yakima agent. He stood firmly against the Indian Homestead Act and the followers of the Washani faith, condemning the "wild anti-civilization Indians" like the Palouses whom he described as "drummers, dreamers, or pumpummers who have a wild superstitious belief . . . that renders them unalterably opposed to the white man's ways."[32] Milroy thought that the Palouse followers of the Washani religion had associated with the followers of Wovoka, the Paiute Prophet who had revitalized what whites called the "Ghost Dance Religion." Although the Palouse Indians followed the teachings of Smohalla, they did not accept the teachings of the Paiute holy man. Still, Milroy feared that the Palouses believed that "the Great Spirit will in the near future suddenly bring to life all Indians who have died for the last thousand years or more, and will enable the Indians to at once to expel or exterminate all the whites and have the whole country to themselves." This was not, however, a precept of the Washani. Milroy believed that Indian religion was a great impediment to his mission on the reservation, for the believers in the Washani refused to send their children to reservation schools, which sought to destroy their "savage" ways.[33]

Milroy opposed the homesteading of Indians near whites, arguing that it created cultural conflicts which resulted in problems outside the jurisdiction of his agency. Milroy felt that whites, not Palouses, should homestead land. He outlined his beliefs in an annual report to the commissioner of Indian affairs published in 1884, stating that the Palouses were "obtaining homesteads, or rather occasional stopping places, among the white settlers, to whom they become 'nuisances and constant sources of annoyance.' " Milroy wrote that the Palouses caused further problem because their horses grazed on ranges belonging to whites, and Indian dogs fed on the sheep, pigs, and chickens of the white settlers. Since the Palouses traveled "about on horseback much of the time, they are opposed to having their way obstructed or to being turned aside by the white man's fence, and will take the trouble to throw down but never to put up fences in their way." The agent mirrored the views of many whites when he characterized the typical Palouse as a "trespasser." Like other agents, Milroy called for their removal to the reservation and for an end to the Indian Homestead Act.[34]

Not all government officials agreed with the policies enunciated by these Indian agents. General Howard supported the Indian Homestead Act, and a number of white men actively worked with the Palouse to help them file claim on the public domain. One such man, George Hunter, not only championed the Palouse Indian cause, but he worked with General Howard to register land claims on behalf of Indians. Hunter had served as a volunteer soldier under Colonel Kelly during the Yakima War and had led a group of Washington volunteers during the Nez Perce War. With his wife and son, he had made his home in Grange City, Washington, along the Snake River, where he became a close friend of the Indians living near Palus. At the outbreak of the Bannock-Paiute War, General Howard held a council with Chief Big Thunder and the Palus villagers. Since Hunter was "well acquainted" with the Palouses and a personal friend of Big Thunder, Howard invited him to serve as interpreter. During the council, Big Thunder told Howard that "none of his people had ever promised to go onto a reservation; but they wished to remain where they were" and take up lands in severalty. Howard replied, "it is right to do so, and that was just what the great father in Washington wanted all Indians to do; and by so doing they would never

be molested by the soldiers." Since the Palouses had no agent, Howard asked
Hunter to assist the Indians in filing land claims and to provide information
"necessary in conforming to the land laws."[35]

The day after the meeting at Palus, Big Thunder and fifty Palouses visited
Grange City. At first the appearance of fifty Palouses riding pell-mell into
Grange City alarmed white residents, but the Indians assured them that their
intentions were peaceful. They asked to speak with Hunter who learned from
Big Thunder that following their meeting with Howard, they had decided
to grant Hunter an honorary position in the tribe. They believed that this
would allow them both the protection and privilege of the white man's law.
Hunter was flattered by his new status, and he lived up to the honor. Soon
after, Hunter intervened on behalf of two Palouses falsely accused of stealing wool blankets. Hunter provided evidence substantiating the innocence
of the Indians, and a white jury acquitted the Indians. The action enhanced
the band's confidence in Hunter and provided the Indians with a worthy ally
within the white community. Oddly enough, the Palouse Indians who remained off the reservation during the Nez Perce War, but who refused to
join the Nez Perces, found a good friend in General Howard.[36]

In late August 1878, Howard toured the inland Northwest in an attempt
"to secure a permanent settlement of difficulties that keep that region in hot
water."[37] No large number of Palouses met Howard, but he concluded an
agreement with other Indians which had a long-term significance to them.
Howard made a formal agreement with Indians living north of the Spokane
River which became the basis of an Executive Order creating the Colville
Reservation, and some Palouses ultimately relocated there. Of more immediate importance to the Palouses, Howard became convinced that non-
reservation Indians like the Palouses should file claim on their lands and live
like white homesteaders. In this manner, he believed the Palouses could learn
to farm and reap the economic and social benefits of private ownership.
Howard's view received the support of other military officials who remained in the Northwest.[38]

Big Thunder's band of Palouses obtained direct help in filing claims from
others. Some of them traveled to Fort Vancouver where they complained
to General Nelson A. Miles who had been appointed commander of the
Pacific post. Miles, the recent adversary of hostile Palouses, treated the Indians with respect and hospitality. Knowing that the Indians could not read
or write English and did not understand the process of filing, Miles commissioned Major J. W. MacMurray to assist them. Miles instructed him to investigate the Palouse problem and locate unclaimed lands on the public domain upon which the Indians could enter their claims. Accompanied by an
interpreter, driver, and engineer, MacMurray set out from Fort Vancouver
in June 1884, traveling in a four-mule team wagon filled with supplies, maps,
and survey equipment.[39]

MacMurray traveled throughout the inland Northwest working with non-
reservation Indians like the Palouses who were interested in filing land claims.
He believed in private Indian ownership of the land and felt that individual
ownership would give them a stake in the new territory, aiding in their
development toward "civilization." MacMurray spent months explaining the
homestead law to various Indians, using a checkerboard to demonstrate the
white man's process of dividing up the land into equal parcels. Such a concept, so deeply engrained in the minds of Euro-Americans, was foreign to

the Indians. Although individual land ownership ran contrary to the teachings of their Washani religion, they had to reconcile their religious beliefs with the realities of the new era. If the Palouses wished to remain off the reservations, they had to accept the white man's concept of private ownership, despite the fact it was in violation of God's law. They could either accept individual ownership of the land or move onto the reservation. Despite their religious beliefs, many Palouses filed homestead claims.[40]

As MacMurray moved among the Indians, the major learned that Smohalla, the Wanapum Prophet, continued to oppose private ownership. During his travels along the Columbia River, MacMurray met Smohalla at the prophet's village of Pna near Priest Rapids. Within a short time, the major learned about the religion practiced by the Palouses, Wanapums, and other interior tribes.[41] He witnessed "a grand ceremonial service" in the log and rush matted longhouse that stretched seventy-five feet in length. In the dimly lighted, smoke-filled interior, MacMurray watched as Smohalla, clad in a white shirt, directed the rhythm of prayers, drums, and songs made by the worshipers who knelt in carefully arranged rows. As the "excitement and persistent repetition" intensified, some of the participants fell in deep trances. The ceremony concluded after Smohalla fell into such a trance until he became virtually lifeless while the "Saghalee Tyee [would] send his soul back to earth to reoccupy his body." After Smohalla's soul had traveled, the prophet related wisdom he had gained from the "Spirit World." One of the prophet's most fundamental beliefs, one that had the support of the spirit world, was that the Indians should never take lands in severalty or move onto the reservations. To consent to either violated God's teachings.[42]

While on his tour of the Snake and Columbia Rivers, MacMurray met another spiritual leader named Kotaiaquan.[43] Originally from the village of Pakiut at Union Gap on the Yakima Reservation, Kotaiaquan often lived near Smohalla at Priest Rapids. Kotaiaquan represented the view of many when he told MacMurray that he favored "limited progress" which would allow Indians to live with "fixed homes and agriculture." However, Kotaiaquan felt strongly that the Indians should not leave their villages or "abandon their religious faith." During the 1880s and 1890s, many Lower Palouses resided with Kotaiaquan's band rather than move onto the Yakima Reservation. MacMurray encouraged Palouses on and off the reservations to file land claims. The Indians responded to MacMurray, much to the chagrin of Agent Milroy.[44]

In late July 1884, MacMurray traveled from the Columbia River to the Yakima Reservation to counsel with the reservation Indians about the Indian Homestead Act. The people residing on the Yakima Reservation had learned of MacMurray's activities among the non-reservation Palouses and others, and some reservation people viewed the major as a minor deliverer. Large numbers of Indians gathered to hear MacMurray's thoughts on Indian homesteads. Agent Milroy knew nothing of the council until MacMurray left, but when he learned of the mission, he reacted with hostility, writing a blistering complaint to the Commissioner of Indian Affairs. Milroy stated that "no officer of the War Department has any legal right to hear complaints of Indians of this agency." Milroy's remonstrations underscored the long-standing feud between the Interior and War Departments, but Milroy's denunciation came too late to affect MacMurray's work. By not informing Milroy or white settlers of his mission, MacMurray succeeded in registering land claims for many Indians, and he informed numerous others of the opportunities available under the Indian Homestead Act.[45]

Other whites equalled MacMurray's efforts on behalf of the Palouses. Such men as Daniel Lyons, Jack Pettyjohn, and George Hunter helped numerous Palouses register claims along the Snake River. As a result, the people held land along the Snake from Almota to Quosispah. Maps in the general land office reflected the successful efforts of the military and civilians to use the Indian Homestead Act. Hunter was, however, most active in his efforts to file land claims for the Indians, and he kept his Palouse friends apprised of changes in the homestead laws. When congress revised the Indian Homestead Act permitting Indians to file claims without paying entry fees and making their land claims inalienable for twenty-five years, Hunter told the Palouses. And since the Palouses could not read English, Hunter's communications proved critical. All along the Snake River white farmers had planted extensive orchards of soft fruit, and many demanded the removal of the Palouses. Hunter kept the Indians informed of their rights, however, and he stood beside them as others attempted to force the Indians from the river's banks.[46]

The Palouses had a high regard for Hunter, consulting him about land policies. Big Thunder often asked the white man "to go with him and others of the [Palouse] tribe to find the 'corner' and 'lines' and generally assist them in locating and entering their lands in severalty at the local land office in Colfax." Hunter traveled with Big Thunder and Bones to Colfax and helped them file claims on their ancestral lands. Lyons and Pettyjohn also joined Hunter as unofficial guardians of the Palouse Indians. They helped them retain their native lands, actions which made them unpopular with many whites. With the help of these three white men, Husishusis Moxmox (Yellow Hair), Hiyouwath (Peter Bones), Yosyostulekasen (Something Covered With Blue), members of the Kamiakin family, and other Palouses filed Indian homesites.[47] By carefully arranging their entries on unsettled lands, Pettyjohn, Lyons, and Hunter helped the Palouses claim quarter-sections along the entire course of the Palouse River, from its mouth to Palouse Falls.

Unfortunately, some of the Palouse claims conflicted with titles granted by congress in 1870 to the Northern Pacific Railroad. For example, Sam Fisher, grandson of Husishusis Kute, and five other Palouses were permitted by the General Land Office to file on property in section seventeen on land also claimed by the railroad. In 1886 officials of the Northern Pacific appealed to the Secretary of the Interior to reverse this decision, contending the Indian Homestead Act was not passed until five years after the government had granted the railroad its land. Railroad officials believed that prior to 1875, any Indian claimant "was as much an alien as though he were a citizen of a foreign Country, and with no better right to the law." They also pointed out that as recently as 1881 the district land office in Colfax had denied a request by an Indian named Quinnemosee to enter a homestead application on railroad land. The Secretary of the Interior, however, ruled in favor of the Palouses. The government honored Fisher's application and that made by the other Indian homesteaders. This enabled the Palouses to acquire an immense tract of over 1,500 acres which, though semi-arid and rocky, gave them complete control of the lower Palouse River Canyon.[48]

Hunter, Lyons, and Pettyjohn helped members of the prominent Kamiakin family and other Palouses file claims. They aided Lower Palouses register land claims near the villages of Sumuya, Tasawiks, and Qosispah. Thomash and his brother, Chowatyet, registered claims near Sumuyah, while Big Sunday entered his claim for lands near Tasawiks. Wolf Necklace filed on land between Tasawiks and Qosispah, and he managed a huge horse herd, fished the rivers, and gathered roots in relative peace with whites.[49]

The registration of land claims by Palouses did not guarantee that the Indians would remain on their homesteads. Indians drifted on and off the reservations, visiting relatives and traveling to favorite root and hunting grounds. The son of Tilcoax, Wolf Necklace, frequently visited the Umatilla Reservation where he had several friends and relatives. Wolf became a friend to Lee Moorehouse, a former officer in the United States Army, who in 1889 became the Umatilla Indian agent. As agent, Moorehouse received numerous complaints from the Indians regarding transgressions against them by whites. Moorehouse organized a delegation of chiefs to take their protests directly to the Commissioner of Indian Affairs. The only Palouse chief to visit Washington, D.C., Wolf Necklace traveled with Homli of the Walla Wallas, Peo of the Umatillas, and Showaway and Young Chief of the Cayuses. The immense structures in the nation's capitol awed Wolf, but he was not favorably impressed with the commissioner who listened politely but promised nothing. Wolf returned to the Pacific Northwest empty-handed, except for a bronze medallion bearing a likeness of President Benjamin Harrison. The chief went home to the Snake River where he resumed his ranching enterprise and pondered his recent trip to Washington.[50]

With great business prowess, Wolf had become a wealthy man. After the Yakima War, he restored his father's fortune in horses, which by 1893 numbered over two thousand. The horses of Tilcoax had carried the "Flying U" brand which Wolf replaced with the "Box Brand." He sold fine horses locally, but he shipped his best stock by rail to distant markets. Through his financial skills, Wolf made a considerable amount of money. His business acumen enabled him to build a spacious home and a large barn. His house, located seven miles up the Snake from its confluence with the Columbia, also served as his business headquarters. Indeed, Wolf managed one of the largest ranches in the Northwest, grazing his herd on hundreds of square miles between the Snake and Moses Lake in central Washington Territory. His ranges encompassed a vast, remote region covered with sand, sagebrush, and black basalt rock. Wolf only owned a quarter section of land, but he used hundreds of acres on the public domain. He often worried that he did not own sufficient land to support his vast herds, so he decided to purchase land from the government to add to his homestead. To make such a purchase, Wolf traveled to Washington, D.C., in 1893 to ask the commissioner for help.[51]

Tall and strong, the stately fifty-year old chief traveled to Washington in the company of Charley Ike, who was hired as Wolf's interpreter. The Palouse purchased two train tickets to the District of Columbia, where Wolf visited officials of the Indian office. Wolf's directness and his requests for American citizenship and the right to buy land parcels puzzled the government officials who told the chief that the matter of buying additional land would be "held in status quo until the department could perfect a necessary inquiry into the case." Wolf remained in Washington, believing that the commissioner would make a decision within a short time. Wolf waited until his money ran out, and then he wired his son for three hundred dollars. His son was illiterate, so a white man read the message for Wolf's son. Rumors had long circulated that Wolf had over twenty thousand dollars hidden in various caches on his homestead, so the white man followed Wolf's son. Learning where the money was hidden, the white man stole some cash, making a successful escape. Wolf had no better luck in Washington, D.C., than his son did in Washington Territory. He never heard from the commissioner, and he eventually returned home where more trouble awaited him.[52]

The tax assessor of Franklin County, Washington Territory, claimed that the county could tax Wolf and other non-reservation Indians, despite the fact that the Indians were not citizens of the county, territory, or country. The Indian office had been of no help to Wolf in resolving this question, and the agents lacked the power to award citizenship to Indians or to rule on county issues. The assessor ordered the county sheriff to collect a tax from Wolf in the form of horses. The sheriff executed this order, despite the protests. Wolf could not contest the sheriff's actions. Adding to his predicament, Wolf's interpreter, Charlie Ike, demanded two hundred and fifty dollars for his services and won a judgment against Wolf. The court ordered the sheriff to take two hundred and fifty more horses from Wolf, and again the chief could do nothing to prevent this action.

Wolf had attempted to live like a white man, managing a large herd and maintaining a substantial business. He had abandoned his mat lodge and had saved his money in order to progress financially like whites. Wolf had even tried to become a citizen of the United States and live in peace with whites. All of this meant nothing to those who were jealous of a successful Indian who "belonged" on a reservation. In despair and disillusioned by the many changes in his life, Wolf sold his stock, closing his mammoth enterprise. His nephew, Harry Jim, and thirty-four riders guided Wolf's remaining herd of three thousand horses to Ephrata, Washington, where Wolf sold them for ten to fifteen dollars a head. Wolf retired to the Umatilla Reservation where he lived out his life. He died on November 12, 1914 and was buried in an unmarked grave where ghouls could not locate and desecrate his remains.[53]

By the last decade of the nineteenth century, the Palouses still remaining in their homelands began moving onto the reservations. Surrounded by a sea of white settlers, most of whom favored Indian removal, the Palouses became strangers in their own land. Kamiakin's band at Rock Lake lacked some of the resources enjoyed by the Palouses living along the Snake. The salmon did not run into Rock Lake, and the root grounds had been plowed by white farmers. The game had disappeared, and the Indians had lost their food sources. About 1885 Tesh Palouse, Tomeo Kamiakin, Peopeo Kah Ownot, and their sisters made the long trek from Rock Lake to the Colville Reservation where they joined the Palouses of Hahtalekin's and Husishusis Kute's band, settling at Nespelem, Washington.[54] The Palouses who removed to the Colville Reservation had relatives on most of the other reservations in the inland Northwest, and slowly the non-reservation people drifted onto one of these reserves. Wolf and Husishusis Moxmox moved to the Umatilla Reservation where several Indians from Palus joined them. Palouse descendants still reside on the Nez Perce, Colville, Umatilla, and Warm Springs Reservations.

A smallpox epidemic in 1890 drove some Palouses to the reservation. The disease spread among the Indians after some Palouse women washed clothing belonging to white citizens of Dayton, Washington, who had smallpox. Some Palouses fled to the reservations where they could receive medical attention. Tuberculosis, influenza, and other diseases also forced many to relocate onto reservations. Hunger drove others to the reservation where the Indian bureau provided some foods. By 1897 only seventy-five Indians lived at Palus, including the remnants of bands once led by Hahtalekin, Big Thunder, and Husishusis Moxmox. These Palouses continued "to cling tenaciously to this barren spot where their children were born and their mothers and fathers have died." Events had moved rapidly in their lives, but they had "not changed their minds" about the land. Even these "long hairs," these "traditionalists" could not stop the wind from blowing or the sun from shining. Even they could not stop the removal policies of the United States.[55]

Yakima Agent Lewis T. Irwin visited Palus in April 1897, to survey the land and the condition of the Indians. He reported that the Indians cultivated ten acres but lived primarily from their fishing. Their root grounds had been destroyed by the plow, and the Indians had difficulty eking out a living fishing due to the intense salmon harvests at the mouth of the Columbia. The agent wrote about the Palouses with respect, but he recommended to the commissioner "that they be forcibly removed to either the Nez Perce, Umatilla, or Yakima Reservations."[56] Indian agents and white settlers alike agreed with Irwin's suggestion to remove them. Eight years later, the Indian bureau acted upon this recommendation.

In the spring of 1905, a steamboat arrived at Palus loaded with American soldiers who ordered the Indians to gather their belongings and get aboard. The Indians complied, and after boarding, they congregated at the stern of the boat where they looked at their homes and the graves of their loved ones. From the rear of the boat they watched Standing Rock pass from their view. Standing Rock — the petrified heart of the giant beaver slain long ago by two Palouse warriors — symbolized the strength of the Palouse people. The Indians stood quietly until they lost sight of their village. One Palouse Indian, a small boy at the time, recalled the entire scene which appeared in his mind "like a vision of the way things were." Andrew George remembered the removal of his family like a dream or an event which occurred outside the confines of his mind. When Andrew grew older, he asked tribal elders about that spring but found that "they never wanted to talk about it much." The memory of their removal was too painful for them to discuss. Andrew said that when the elders spoke about the event, the men and women grew silent and often wept. A few Palouses remained on the Snake and Palouse Rivers, but as the years passed nearly all of them moved to one of the reservations.[57]

CHAPTER 11

PALOUSE REMNANTS

They say we are extinct, but we are not.
—Karie Jim Nightwalker

In the fall of 1914 the five remaining residents of Palus village gathered at the river's edge to witness a dramatic event. For eleven months construction crews of the Union Pacific Railroad had built the largest bridge along the entire transcontinental route. Since the center span stretched 236 feet without support, the Indians feared that the bridge would collapse under the weight of the massive black locomotive. But in the afternoon shadows of the steel crossbeams, the five Palouses watched the engine cross the bridge without incident. The Indians returned to their simple homes, once the site of the tribe's largest village, riotous horse races, and historic meetings. The village had dwindled to a mere camp consisting of two tipis, a canvas-tule mat lodge, and several wooden shacks. The eighty-seven year old Waughaskie, commonly known as Old Bones, led the small band. Blind in his old age, Waughaskie lived with his wife, Meyatat, their children, Hiyouwath (Peter Bones), Me-a-tu-kin-ma, and an elderly couple. The survivors of great cultural changes, these few Palouses continued living at their ancestral village.[1]

The only other remnant of the Palouse tribe residing on the river was the small group led by Chowatyet, known to the whites as Fishhook Jim. Chowatyet, the brother of Chief Thomash, headed the village of Sumuya on the lower Snake River. Each fall Chowatyet's four children and their families journeyed upstream to supply their relative at Palus with corn, dried salmon, and firewood. Together, the two bands traveled to the Blue Mountains to gather berries and hunt game. Often they moved eastward to the Nez Perce Country where they hunted along the Clearwater River, visiting friends and relatives along the way. Returning from their fall hunt in 1916, the Lower Palouse band learned that the venerated Waughaskie had died in October and had been buried at Palus in his star-spangled velvet shirt, a gift to his father from Marcus Whitman. A solitary gray headstone marked his grave, in a cemetery situated on a knoll and fenced with driftwood. Over 250 Palouses had been laid to rest in the same cemetery, and Waughaskie became one of the last of his people to be buried there. However, he was not the last Indian to live at the village of Palus. Remnants of the tribe inhabited Palus periodically until the mid-twentieth century.[2]

Sam Fisher, grandson of the famed Washani leader, Husishusis Kute, lived at Palus long into the twentieth century. Known to his people as Yosyostulekasen (Something Covered With Blue), Fisher adhered to the old Washani faith, keeping his braids long. He had been among the first Palouses to file for a homestead under the terms of the 1884 Revised Indian Homestead

Act, and in 1886 he had successfully thwarted an attempt by the Northern Pacific Railroad to deny him official entry on his land. In 1895 he homesteaded additional land adjacent to his earlier claim, using a wide strip of land totaling 160 acres along the east bank of the Palouse River. The Palouse Indian homesteads along the Palouse River provided a vast open rangeland for the horse herds maintained by Fisher, the Kamiakin brothers, and others. Fisher loved spotted Appaloosa horses and bred them using "a powerful medicine." Three times he would mark "the pregnant mare with a special kind of paint, mixed by a secret formula and applied [it] at the critical moment." Fisher and other Palouses tended their horse herds along a two-mile strip beside the Palouse River until the early 1900s when most of them, including Sam Fisher, moved to the Colville Reservation and resided at Nespelem with remnants of other Palouse bands. These Palouses remained on the reservation only a short time, however, before they returned to their homelands along the Palouse and Snake Rivers.[3]

During the late nineteenth and early twentieth centuries, whites often created problems for the Palouses, encroaching on their land and demanding their removal. Other whites — Hunter, Lyons, and Pettyjohn — served as advocates for the Indians. In 1883 two new white men entered the region; their family would later help the Palouses retain title to their land. They were the McGregor brothers, Archie and Peter, Scottish immigrants from Canada. In the fall of 1883, they explored the Palouse Country for ranching possibilities adjacent to those lands homesteaded by the Palouse Indians. That same year, both men filed claim on Alkali Flat near present-day Dusty, Washington, and in order to earn extra money with which to establish their own enterprise, the McGregors herded sheep along the Snake River for other ranchers. Two years later they acquired their own stock and prospered. Their brothers, John and William, soon joined them. Together the McGregors forged one of the largest ranches in the region, and much of their land, an area seventeen miles wide and twenty-one miles long, bordered the Palouse Indian homesteads on the southwest.[4]

The McGregors maintained peaceful relations with their Palouse neighbors, respecting the Indians right to the land. Indeed, the McGregors helped Sam Fisher re-establish himself on his old homestead after the Palouses decided to return to the Snake River. Around the turn of the century, Fisher, George, Kamiakin, and other Palouse families had been forced to move onto one of the interior reservations. While agents took the George family and others to the Nez Perce Reservation, government officials forced the Fishers and Kamiakins onto the Colville Reservation. Like so many Indians, Sam Fisher despised reservation life, but it was there he met and married Helen, a Nez Perce woman and participated in the war of 1877. Since Fisher still held title to his land near Palus, he and Helen moved to the homestead. Fisher encouraged others owning Indian homesteads to do the same, but most, including members of Kamiakin's family, stayed on the Colville Reservation.[5]

Fisher's plans to return to his homeland ended in 1920, when officials of the General Land Office informed him that the government had revoked his homestead because he had received an allotment on the Colville Reservation. Other Palouses who had received allotments on the Yakima, Nez Perce, and Umatilla Reservations also lost their homesteads. According to D. K. Parrott, a government spokesman, the Palouses who had received reservation allotments had forfeited their legal status as Palouse Indians and thus had lost both their former claims and their right to file future claims on the public domain. Fisher refused to accept this ruling, and in 1922 he reapplied for lands along the Palouse River. His nephews, Carter Slouthier and Peter Bones, joined him, applying for an additional 1,100 acres.

When officials of the General Land Office received the applications, they suspended them and investigated the case. The General Land Office referred the matter to the Commissioner of Indian Affairs who reaffirmed the earlier decision, denying the applications on the grounds that Fisher, Bones, and Slouthier had received reservation allotments. However, the commissioner agreed to "take up the question of the elimination of the lands applied for under the act" if the Palouses would surrender their allotments on the reservation. When Fisher learned of this decision, he determined to relinquish his reservation allotment which was unpatented. He felt that by forfeiting his reservation allotment and returning to his home, he could regain his status as a Palouse Indian and qualify for his homestead. Accordingly, in 1924, Sam, Helen, Peter, and Carter returned to the Snake River where they took up residency at Palus. They fished, hunted, farmed in their ancestral lands, and leased some of their grazing lands to the McGregor family.[6]

A year after returning to Palus, the Indians learned that a farmer named Charles Harrison had applied for a homestead on lands claimed by Carter Slouthier. When the Palouses inquired about Harrison's claim at the federal land office in Spokane, they learned that the land office had erred in allowing the white man to file on lands that had been set aside in 1907 specifically for the Palouse Indians. In checking Harrison's land claims, the land office confirmed that the white man's application had been denied but that Fisher's claim for a homestead had also been denied. Fisher was infuriated when he learned that his application for a homestead in 1922 had been denied. Since all of the Palouses who had once held homesteads on the Palouse River either had received allotments on a reservation or had died, the land office seized the opportunity to open all lands that had been withdrawn for Palouse Indian homesteads. The land office promptly recognized Harrison's claim and on January 26, 1927, opened all Palouse homesteads. Numerous whites rushed to file claims on the 2,650-acre cession. Harrison filed on lands that had long been claimed by Fisher, while Harrison's brother, Edward, filed on lands claimed by Peter Bones. Because the Palouses spoke limited English and could not write, they were late filing their land claims. Fisher finished his application in May 1927, only to learn a few months later that the government denied his application in lieu of Harrison's claim. Fisher had long held the land that Harrison claimed, and the Palouse appealed to the land office for redress. When Fisher's efforts failed, he asked the McGregor family for help.[7]

Peter McGregor, upon learning what had happened to his old friend, contacted his attorney who composed an affidavit supporting Fisher's claim to the land based on his family's residency on the property "as far back as the Indians have any knowledge." The document detailed Fisher's use of the land, his many improvements on the property, and his repeated attempts to file a legal land claim. The affidavit also explained the similar circumstances surrounding the land claims of Bones and Slouthier. The McGregors supported the Indians' right to their ancestral homes. When the land office received the document, officials called a hearing to consider the statements it contained. On July 10, 1928, at a meeting in Spokane, Peter McGregor played an important role in defending these Palouse rights. On the issues of occupancy and improvements, McGregor's testimony and that of the Harrison brothers conflicted "in the extreme." The registrar of federal land claims in Spokane listened carefully to the testimony and made an independent investigation of the case, traveling to the disputed land to inspect the property. On August 3, 1928, he reversed the earlier decision of the land office, awarding Fisher his prior homestead. Harrison appealed to the General Land Office and to the Secretary of the Interior, but they denied his appeals.[8]

Sam Fisher returned to his home with his wife and nephews, and they finally lived peacefully on their land. They raised horses, fished, hunted, and gathered food, scratching out a living as best they could. Peter Bones divided his time between his homestead and the Umatilla Reservation where he helped his relatives raise a large horse herd. Both Bones and Fisher fenced the burial ground at Palus and carefully tended the graves at the sacred site. Moreover, they preserved many of their oral traditions by sharing their history with Maurice, the son of Peter McGregor. Fascinated by Palouse Indian history, Maurice spent hours with Sam Fisher listening to legends and stories relating the the Palouse people. Fisher spent his last years sharing his stories with Maurice and traveling to Starbuck and Hooper, Washington, where he related his colorful tales to his many friends. By horseback Fisher often traveled to Hooper, a company town of the McGregor enterprise, where he purchased supplies and swapped stories with the ranch hands. Indeed, the elder Palouse Indian enjoyed riding his horses through the canyons and coulees of his beloved homeland, and he did so until his late eighties when he was thrown from a horse and severely injured. He lived out the rest of his life at Palus where he died in 1944. Sam Fisher, the last Palouse Indian laid to rest in the village cemetery, was not the last Palouse to reside there. Between 1944 and 1954, Peter Bones tended the burial ground at Palus and enjoyed living periodically at his old home on the Snake River. On one such visit to Palus in 1954, Bones suffered a stroke. He was taken to Dayton, Washington, for medical attention but died there on August 13. Much of the land homesteaded by Fisher, Bones, and others, remains under Indian title, but most of it has been flooded by the reservoirs behind Ice Harbor and Lower Monumental Dams. Slowly, the last Indians vanished from Palus, but some of the Lower Palouses remained at Sumuya on the lower Snake River.[9]

Not long after the death of Waughaskie, in October, 1916, Chowatyet, the brother of Thomash, died at Sumuya. His family wrapped the body in buckskin, placing it in a long dugout canoe. The Palouses buried him on an island in the Snake River known as Ychemak (Big Island). In the 1960s the island's graves were desecrated when artifact collectors looted the site despite Indian protestations. Such outrages against Indian burials were common throughout the nineteenth and twentieth centuries, despite frequent appeals by Indians and non-Indians to prevent the looting of bodies and skeletons. In May 1911, Chief Big Sunday led a delegation of Palouses to Walla Walla to appeal to a superior court, "begging for a paper to stop the vandalism by whites, who, he declared, are pillaging the graves for curios to sell in eastern markets." Pleading his case "with tear-wet cheeks and countenance plainly showing his anguish, the old Indian delivered an eloquent oration." His efforts failed, however, for the judge ruled against the Palouse chief.[10]

Although a follower of the Washani religion, Chowatyet had chosen to homestead 116 acres on the north side of the Snake River, and his heirs remained on the river until 1959 when "the law" told them to move. The Army Corps of Engineers had condemned the land to make way for the construction of Ice Harbor Dam. For over a half-century, Chowatyet's granddaughter, Mary Jim, had clung tenaciously to this last outpost of Palouse Indian culture, remaining on her people's lands along the Snake River. Indeed, Mary Jim and other descendants of Fishhook Jim held onto their land despite the declining fish runs, the assault on Indian fishing rights, threats by governmental officials, and dealings of land speculators. Mary Jim stubbornly refused to sell her land or move to the reservation. Instead, she relied on the earth to provide for her, to sustain her body and soul. In the early 1960s, however, "the law" expelled Mary Jim from her land, forcing her to comply with a state regulation requiring her children to attend school. To avoid prosecution, she moved to the Yakima Reservation. When the school year ended, Mary Jim and her children returned to the Snake River only to find that the waters of Lake Sacajawea had flooded her lands and the graves of her loved ones. With her lands flooded and her home destroyed, she went back to the Yakima Reservation, ultimately taking up residence in a small wooden house in the middle of a fruit orchard. Neither the house nor the land upon which it stands belongs to her. She is not troubled by this, but she mourns the loss of her home on the Snake River, and she cries when she remembers that her mother's grave—and those of so many Palouses—are buried beneath the waters of a man-made lake. She often recalls that her river once "played music to my people," but that the river "is silent today." She laments her removal to the reservation, a fate she shared with all Palouses.[11]

Like Mary Jim, whites forced all of the Lower Palouses from their homes and placed them on reservations. Some of them moved to the Yakima Reservation while others drifted to the Warm Springs, Umatilla, and Nez Perce Reservations. Still others moved to the Colville Reservation in north-central Washington, where the Palouses formed a small enclave composed of descendants of Husishusis Kute, Hahtalekin, and Kamiakin. Over the years the Palouses intermarried with other bands on the reservation, but they maintained their identity as a distinct people. Some Palouse families on the Colville Reservation—the Felix, Pahween, and Kamiakin—became prominent leaders. Most of these families lived north of the agency headquarters on Nespelem Creek where they shared a common area with the Nez Perce band of Chief Joseph. Included in the Palouse band were the surviving sons of Chief Kamiakin, including Tesh Palouse, Tomeo, Cleveland, and Skolumkee. The lives of the Kamiakins and other Palouses meshed with the other Indians on the Colville Reservation, where they lived out their lives far from the winding rivers and rolling hills of the Palouse Country. Tesh Palouse died on the reservation in 1932, while his brother, Skolumkee, spent days on end roaming the Palouse Country where his family had once grazed huge horse herds. Tomeo and Cleveland became chiefs, and they preserved the traditions of their people. Both men were respected elders who spoke Sahaptin and imparted their rich oral traditions to the younger people. Reservation leaders often consulted Tomeo and Cleveland regarding cultural, spiritual, political, and economic matters. The Indians at Colville liked the Kamiakins who shared their wisdom, knowledge, and history with Indians and non-

Indians alike. The Indians considered Tomeo and Cleveland Keepers of the Traditions, preserving Palouse history for future generations.[12]

In the fall of 1928, Tomeo accompanied William C. Brown, an attorney, judge, and historian, on a tour through the Palouse Country. The Indians trusted Brown and shared much of their past with this white man. At the age of seventy-three, Tomeo returned to his father's country and recounted to Brown the joys and tragedies of his family. His stories and those of his contemporaries formed the basis of much of what is known about Chief Kamiakin. Brown took meticulous notes of his conversations with Tomeo and others, and some of what Brown learned appeared in his book, *The Indian Side of the Story.* He returned to the Colville Reservation, and much of the cultural heritage preserved today emerged from the teachings of Tomeo and Cleveland Kamiakin. Their legacy is honored by Palouse descendants of the Colville Confederated Tribes.[13]

Tomeo died in 1935 and Skolumkee Kamiakin died in 1949, leaving their brother, Cleveland, to head the Palouses living near Nespelem. Thus, Kamiakin's youngest son became the last direct link to the great patriot chief, and he shared the mantle of leadership with Charley Williams whose family had been removed from Palus around 1888. At the age of nine Williams had moved to Nespelem Creek where he spent the rest of his life among the Palouses and Nez Perces. Cleveland Kamiakin and Charley Williams grew up together and formed a lifetime friendship. Both men, born in the Palouse Country, spent most of their adult lives on the reservations. Nevertheless, Cleveland and Charley had a strong, spiritual attachment to the land of their birth, the original home of the Palouses. Like the tribal leaders before them, they hoped one day to secure for their people a portion of their former holdings. None of the Indian leaders from the Colville Reservation — Joseph, Moses, Tomeo Kamiakin, and others — had been able to secure their former homelands, and it seemed unlikely that the Palouse leaders would succeed where others had failed. Still, Cleveland and Charley were encouraged in 1946 when they learned from government agents that a bill had been enacted allowing Indian tribes to file claims against the United States government.[14]

On August 13, 1946 Congress passed the Indian Claims Commission Act empowered to decide the validity of claims by Indians against the government. Most of the tribes in the inland Northwest filed such documents, including the Palouses on the Yakima and Colville Reservations. The Palouses had been party to the Yakima Treaty of 1855, one of eleven affected by the agreement. Under the terms of the treaty, the various tribes ceded to the government 8,176,000 acres of land for a paltry consideration of $593,000 — a little over seven cents per acre. Many Palouse Indians had denied being party to the treaty, but the Yakima Tribe claimed that the Palouse leadership had agreed to the document and that the claim was legitimate. Many Indians argued that they had held lands outside those described in the Yakima Treaty and that they should be compensated for those lands. Others sought redress for the "theft" of their lands through the Indian Claims Commission, as did other bands and tribes on the Yakima Reservation. On July 20, 1948, the Yakima Tribe hired Paul M. Niebell, an attorney in Washington, D.C., to represent their claims against the government on behalf of the displaced tribes who, with the Palouses on the Yakima Reservation, claimed that 10,828,000 acres had been illegally expropriated by the United States. Sixteen months later, the Colville Confederated Tribes hired the legal firm of I. S. Weissbrodt,

James E. Curry, and Lyle Keith to represent their claims, including Indian bands also named in the Yakima claim.[15]

To simplify the trial process, the Indian Claims Commission consolidated the claims of the Palouse Indians of the Yakima and Colville Tribes. After an exhaustive examination of the evidence, the commission reported on July 28, 1959 that both the Yakima and Colville Tribes "contain members or descendants comprising the Yakima Nation and are, therefore, entitled to present claims." At this point the Colvilles filed a formal claim on behalf of their Palouse band under Docket 222 in the names of Cleveland Kamiakin and Charley Williams. Since the Palouse case involved lands already under consideration in Dockets 161 and 224 of the Yakima Tribe, the commissioners combined these two cases with Docket 222 filed by the Colvilles.[16] In 1960 Chief Commissioner Arthur V. Watkins convened a hearing into the Palouse Indian claims case. Verne F. Ray, the eminent anthropologist who had spent his academic career studying northwestern Indians, served as the expert witness for the Palouses. Stuart A. Chalfant, an ethnologist, testified on behalf of the government, presenting testimony and documentation against the Palouse claims. The testimony and deliberations took months, as the petitioners and the government presented their cases and as the commissioners examined the evidence. On July 29, 1963 Commissioner William M. Holt delivered the initial opinion of the commission to the representatives of the Colville and Yakima Tribes. He maintained that both tribes had members who were Palouse Indians and that both tribes had legitimate claims. Furthermore, Holt argued that awards would be made "to the tribal entity" and "not to individual descendants." Holt then ordered the case to proceed to determine "the acreage of the lands involved; the market value thereof as of March 8, 1859 [the date when the Yakima Treaty was ratified]; and the consideration paid."[17]

On April 5, 1965, the commissioners reached final judgment, stating "that the consideration totaling $593,000 paid by the defendant the United States government to the Yakima Nation for the cession of lands having a fair market value of $4,088,000 was so grossly inadequate as to make the consideration unconscionable." The Yakima and Colville Tribes received $3,446,700 on behalf of the Palouses. The government did not appeal the case, and the two tribes accepted and divided the award. The judgment meant the end of a long struggle by tribal leaders to attain an equitable compensation for the lands forfeited over a century earlier. The settlement created the foundation for building new opportunities on the reservations, and tribal elders, who still maintained a keen sense of loss of the ancestral lands, received some consolation for their persistent efforts to gain redress. But most of the Palouse Indians did not celebrate a victory when they learned the outcome of the Indian claims case, for the Indians had won money, not the return of their lands. The few remaining elders lamented the loss of their lands, remembering well the words of their parents and grandparents regarding the sacredness of the earth, the site where so many of their ancestors were buried. Thus victory was a hollow one for individual Palouse descendants, for they did not receive the return of their lands.[18]

Cleveland Kamiakin did not live to see the results of the Indian claims case involving the Palouse Indians. He died on September 3, 1959 at his home in Nespelem. Hundreds of Indians from throughout the Pacific Northwest traveled to the small reservation town to pay their respects to Cleveland,

Kamiakin's last son. They buried their respected elder two days later in the windswept cemetery north of Nespelem, a short distance from the grave of Chief Joseph. Ten years later Charley Williams, a plaintiff with Cleveland in the Palouse claims case, died and was buried at Nespelem. With their passing and that of Cleveland Kamiakin's widow, Alalumti, in 1977, the Palouse band on the Colville Reservation lost the last of its members who had lived "in the old way" in the Palouse Country. Their former homeland had become an artistic patchwork of grain fields and rangelands controlled by the heirs of the first *suyapo*. But the Palouse Indians have not forgotten their heritage.[19]

In the spring of 1980, as in the spring of every other year, numerous Palouses and Wanapums met on the Lower Snake River at a Washington State Park named for the Palouse headman, Fishhook Jim. There, they prepared an extensive feast of native foods, including a wide variety of roots, fish, eel, berries, and game. They cooked salmon over an open fire, and the sweet aroma of smoke swirled throughout the Indian gathering. Children scurried about laughing, racing between the legs of their elders. The Palouses and Wanapums served dinner in a fashion resembling a Thanksgiving celebration, and after everyone was served, they offered praise and thanks to the Almighty. At the conclusion of the feast, the tribal elders rose to deliver short orations in the Sahaptin language. The elders spoke from their hearts, each in their own way asking the Creator to bless the earth, the rivers, the plants, and the animals. They offered prayers to God, asking to be returned one day to the canyons, rivers, and hills of the Palouse Country.

The last address was made by Mary Jim, who rose to remind everyone that the land upon which they stood was hallowed ground, a land where her people had lived and died. Without bitterness, she spoke of the past, telling of her own life and speaking of her mother, grandmother, and great-uncle— Thomash. Tears filled her eyes, and she choked as she prayed that her grandchildren and their children might one day know the joys of life in the Palouse Country. She spoke of a time long ago, when as a young girl, she had ridden bareback across the vast Plateau and rolling hills. To some, those days of freedom belonged entirely to the past. But for Mary Jim and Palouses like her, it is a dream for which they still struggle and pray.[20]

ABBREVIATIONS

AG	Adjutant General
CIA	Commissioner of Indian Affairs
Cong.	Congress
Doc.	Document
DS	Archives of the Diocese of Seattle
HED	House Executive Document
LR	Letters Received
MHS	Maryland Historical Society
NA	National Archives
No.	Number
OHS	Oregon Historical Society
OS	Oregon Superintendency of Indian Affairs
RCA	Records of the Commands of the United States Army
RG	Record Group
ROIA	Records of the Office of Indian Affairs
SED	Senate Executive Document
Sess.	Session
SMD	Senate Miscellaneous Document
SS	Serial Set
SW	Secretary of War
UW	University of Washington
WS	Washington Superintendency of Indian Affairs
WSL	Washington State Library
WSU	Washington State University

NOTES

INTRODUCTION

[1] For detailed discussions of the geographical features of the region, see William D. Thornbury, *Regional Geomorphology of the United States,* pp. 442-59; J. Harlan Bretz, "The Channeled Scablands of the Columbia Plateau," *Journal of Geology* 31 (1923): 617-49; Otis W. Freeman, J. D. Forrester, and R. L. Lupher, "Physiographic Divisions of the Columbia Intermontane Province," *Annals of the Association of American Geographics* 35 (1945): 53-75; D. W. Meinig, *The Great Columbia Plain,* pp. 5, 11.

[2] There are many variations of the spelling of Palouse and there has been much confusion over the origin of the word since Lewis and Clark labeled a band of Indians "Pelloatpallah." For discussions about the word, see Albert W. Thompson, "The Early History of the Palouse River and Its Names," *Pacific Northwest Quarterly* 62 (1971): 69-71; Roderick Sprague, "The Meaning of Palouse," *Idaho Yesterdays* 12 (1968): 22-27; C. C. Todd, "Origin and Meaning of the Geographic Name Palouse," *Washington Historical Quarterly* 24 (1933): 192; John R. Swanton, *Indian Tribes of North America,* p. 433; Ruth Kirk, *The Oldest Man in America;* Roderick Sprague, "Palus," Unpublished manuscript in Sprague Files, Department of Anthropology, University of Idaho, Moscow; hereafter cited as Sprague Ms. Besides Sprague's essay, that of Deward Walker, Jr., will appear in a forthcoming volume on the Plateau in the *Handbook of North American Indians* to be released by the Smithsonian Institution.

[3] There is a wealth of information describing the political and economic configuration of the Palouses and other Plateau tribes. The best materials are found in Verne Ray, "Palus Tribal Territory" and "Economic Use of the Tribal Territory of the Palus Tribe," United States Indian Claims Commission, Dockets 222 and 161, National Archives, Record Group 279; hereafter cited as "Economic Use of the Tribal Territory," Indian Claims, Docs. 222 and 161, NA, RG 279; Verne Ray, "Cultural Relations in the Plateau of Northwestern America," pp. 14-24; Verne Ray, "Native Villages and Groupings of the Columbia Basin," *Pacific Northwest Quarterly* 27 (1936): 115-17; and Roderick Sprague, "Aboriginal Burial Practices in the Plateau Region of North America."

[4] A lengthy discussion of the Lewis and Clark expedition through the Palouse Country is provided in Chapter 1 of this volume. The explorers identified the Indians living along the Snake River as Choppunish.

[5] A recent work, James P. Ronda, *Lewis and Clark Among the Indians,* pp. 163-68, deals with the Corps of Discovery as it passed through the Palouse Country. Ronda identifies the Indians living along the Snake as Nez Perces and those residing at the confluence of the Columbia and Snake as Wanapums.

[6] "Testimony of Verne L. Ray," Indian Claims, Docs. 222 and 161, NA, RG 279, p. 735, 738-39, 741-42; Ray, "Native Villages and Groupings," pp. 107-12; Ray, "Cultural Relations," pp. 14-24; Richard Scheuerman, "Kinship and Marriage Among the Palouse," and "Kamiakin Family History," unpublished manuscript and chart, Department of American Indian Studies, San Diego State University; oral interviews by authors with Mary Jim, November 9-10, 1979 and April 25, 1980.

[7] "Testimony of Verne L. Ray," Indian Claims, Docs. 222 and 161, NA, RG 279, pp. 735, 738-39, 741-42, 755; Ray, "Native Villages and Groupings," pp. 107-12.

[8] The first comprehensive map of Palouse villages appeared as "Evidence in Support of Proposed Findings of Fact of Petitioners in Docket Nos. 222 and 161," Indian Claims, NA, RG 279. Our evidence (see map in this volume) indicates that there were forty or more villages from Alpowa, which was inhabited by Upper Palouses and Nez Perces, to Quosispah at the junction of the Snake and Columbia Rivers. For evidence specifically regarding the village at Steptoe Butte, see Ray's

Testimony, Indian Claims, Doc. 222 and 161, NA, RG 279, p. 788; also, Ibid, pp. 750-52, 755.

[9]George Gibbs, "Report on the Indian Tribes of Washington," *Secretary of War Reports of Exploration* 1 (1854): 400-49.

[10]"Opinions of the Commission, Dockets Nos. 161, 222 and 224, April 5, 1965," Indian Claims Commission Decision 15, pp. 227, 231b.

[11]Palouse Indians reside on many northwestern reservations, including the Yakima, Colville, Nez Perce, Umatilla, and Warm Springs. These individuals know that they are of Palouse Indian ancestry and some still speak the Palouse language, despite the fact that they are enrolled on a reservation which is not their own.

[12]Reader's Report from the University of Oklahoma Press to the authors, Department of American Indian Studies, San Diego State University.

[13]Clifford E. Trafzer, "The Earth, Animals, and Academics," in Donald Fixico, ed., *Native Views of Indian-White Relations,* forthcoming from the University of Utah Press.

[14]Clifford E. Trafzer and Margery Beach, "Smohalla, the Washani, and Religion as a Factor in Northwestern Indian History," in Clifford E. Trafzer, guest ed., "American Indian Prophets and Revitalization Movements," *American Indian Quarterly* 9 (1985): 309-24.

[15]The authors wish to thank Andrew George, Mary Jim, Karie Jim Nightwalker, Emily Peone, and the other Palouses who shared their culture and heritage with us. Some of their oral interviews are cited herein.

CHAPTER 1

[1]The Sahaptin-speaking Indians of the Plateau labeled whites *suyapo,* meaning crowned heads due to the crowned rims of the hats worn by them. The best published sources on the expedition are found in Reuben Gold Thwaites, ed., *Original Journals of the Lewis and Clark Expedition, 1804-1806* 3 and 4. Volume 8 of the edition provides several helpful facsimile reproductions of maps made on the expedition. Hereafter cited as *Journals of Lewis and Clark.* Under the direction of Gary Moulton, the University of Nebraska Press is reprinting a revised edition of the *Journals.* The updated work was not available to the authors at the time of this publication. Other useful sources on the Corps of Discovery includes Donald Jackson, ed., *Letters of the Lewis and Clark Expedition, With Related Documents, 1783-1854;* Ernest S. Osgood, *The Field Notes of Captain William Clark;* and John Bakeless, *Lewis and Clark.* A few sources analyze the significance of the expedition to Native Americans, see L. V. McWhorter, *Hear Me, My Chiefs!,* pp. 4-21, 78, 498; "Testimony of Verne L. Ray," pp. 766-782; and "Evidence in Support of Proposed Finding of Fact of Petitioners in Docket No. 222 on Issues of Liability," Indian Claims, Docs. 222 and 161, NA, RG 279; Stuart A. Chalfant, "Palus Indians," *Interior Salish and Eastern Washington Indians,* (1974): 5-8.

[2]*Journals of Lewis and Clark* 3, pp. 108, 111, 113. *Journals of Lewis and Clark* are filled with misspellings. Therefore, the authors of this book have chosen not to designate each misspelled word with [sic] in order to provide readers with the original spellings of the entries. Protection of grave sites was an important element of Palouse Indian culture and demonstrated a religious affinity to their ancestors and to the land which held the bones. All of our Palouse Indian consultants refer to the sacredness of the land which holds the bones of their ancestors, and their feelings are shared by other Indians of the Inland Northwest. On his deathbed, Old Joseph admonished his son never to sell the land that held the bones of his father. Understanding the relationship of the Indians to their hallowed ground is paramount in understanding the course of Northwest Indian history. "Testimony of Verne L. Ray," Indian Claims, Docs. 222 and 161, NA, RG 279, p. 735, 738-39, 741-42; oral interviews by authors with Mary Jim, May 1, 1977, April 2, November

10, 11, 17, 1979, and April 25, 1980; also, oral interview by authors with Andrew George, November 15, 1980; *Lewiston Morning Tribune,* May 3, 1936; Stuart A. Chalfant, "Ethno-Historical Report on Aboriginal Land Occupancy and Utilization by the Palus Indians," *American Indian Ethnohistory,* pp. 30-47; Ray, "Cultural Relations," pp. 14-16; Ray, "Economic Use of Tribal Territory," Indian Claims, Docs. 222 and 161, NA, RG 279; Stuart A. Chalfant, *Interior Salish and Eastern Washington Indians* 1, pp. 81-85; Sprague, "Aboriginal Burial Practices," pp. 10-12.

³*Journals of Lewis and Clark* 3, p. 110; Leslie Spier, "The Prophet Dance of the Northwest and Its Derivatives: The Source of the Ghost Dance," *General Series in Anthropology;* Mooney, "Ghost-Dance Religion," Chapter VII: Clifford E. Trafzer and Margery Beach, "Smohalla, the Washani, and Religion as a Factor in Northwestern Indian History," Clifford E. Trafzer, ed., *American Indian Prophets.*

⁴Materials on the village of Palus include "Testimony of Verne L. Ray," Indian Claims, Docs. 222 and 161, NA, RG 279, pp. 737-41; Verne Ray, "The Palus Tribe," Indian Claims, Docs. 222 and 161, NA, RG 279; Ray, "Palus Tribal Territory," Indian Claims, Docs. 222 and 161, NA, RG 279; "Evidence in Support of Proposed Findings of Fact of Petitioners in Docket No. 222 on Issues of Liability," Indian Claims, Docs. 222 and 161, NA, RG 279; *Indian Claims Commission Decisions* 12 pt., A, pp. 304-306; Sprague, "Aboriginal Burial Practices," pp. 8-9, 12-23.

⁵An interesting biography on the man for whom the explorers named the Palouse River is M. O. Skarsten, *George Drouillard: Hunter and Interpreter for Lewis and Clark.* For details of the journey down the Snake River, see *Journals of Lewis and Clark,* 3, pp. 112-13; Ella E. Clark, *Indian Legends of the Pacific Northwest,* pp. 117-18; Click Relander, *Drummers and Dreamers,* pp. 94-95; Paul Kane, *Wanderings of an Artist among the Indians of North America,* p. 274; Thompson, "The Early History of the Palouse River," pp. 69-70; Ella E. Clark, "The Mythology of the Indians in the Northwest," *Oregon Historical Quarterly* 54 (1953): 164; Sprague, "The Meaning of Palouse," pp. 22-27; Herbert J. Spinden, "Myths of the Nez Perce Indians," *Journal of American Folk-Lore* 21 (1908): 14-15; and Franz Boas, ed., *Folk-Tales of Salishan and Sahaptin Tribes,* pp. 148-51.

⁶*Journals of Lewis and Clark* 3, p. 115, 120-22, 126-27; "Testimony of Verne L. Ray," Indian Claims, Docs. 222 and 161, NA, RG 279, pp. 735, 739-40, 755.

⁷Ray, "Economic Use of Tribal Territory," Indian Claims, Docs. 222 and 161, NA, RG 279; Herbert J. Spinden, "The Nez Perce Indians," *American Anthropological Association Memoirs* 2 (1908): 205-11; "Testimony of Verne L. Ray," Indian Claims, Docs. 222 and 161, NA, RG 279, p. 744; oral interview by authors with Mary Jim, November 9-10, 1979 and April 25, 1980; Relander, *Drummers and Dreamers,* pp. 76-77; *Uncommon Controversy,* pp. 3-5.

⁸Oral interview by authors with Mary Jim, November 9-10, 1979; Ray, "Economic Use of the Tribal Territory," Indian Claims, Docs. 222 and 161, NA, RG 279.

⁹*Journals of Lewis and Clark* 3, p. 115

¹⁰Ibid., pp. 116-17.

¹¹Ibid., pp. 117-19.

¹²Quosispah, the western-most village of the Palouse Indians, was located at the confluence of the Snake and Columbia Rivers at the present-day site of Pasco, Washington. Steward Chalfant, "Ethno-historical Report on Aboriginal Land Occupancy and Utilization by the Palus Indians," Defense Exhibit 69, Indian Claims, Docs. 222 and 161, NA, RG 279, pp. 5-8. The Palouses who resided along the Snake River often referred to themselves as *Nahahum.* Oral interview by authors with Mary Jim, May 1, 1977.

¹³*Journals of Lewis and Clark* 3, p. 120.

¹⁴Ibid. The explorers gave out medals of varying sizes. One of the medals was unearthed in 1964, when archaeologists excavated the village site of Palus. The small medal is now the property of the Nez Perce Tribe of Idaho. For an enlightening study of Lewis and Clark medals and many other medals, see Francis Paul Prucha, *Indian Peace Medals in American History.*

[15] *Journals of Lewis and Clark* 3, pp. 120-22. For more information on the Wanapums, see Relander, *Drummers and Dreamers.* The Relander Collection of the Yakima Valley Regional Library in Yakima, Washington, contains extensive notes, documents, and manuscripts on the Wanapums. Two of these, "Palouse Notes" and "Yakima Notes," contain important information regarding the relationship of the Wanapums to other tribes, including the Palouses.

[16] Journals of Lewis and Clark 3, pp. 125-26. In future chapters of this volume, it will be shown that white observers, particularly fur trappers and traders, often mistook Palouses for Nez Perces.

[17] Ibid., pp. 123-24; oral interview by authors with Mary Jim, November 9-10, 1979.

[18] *Journals of Lewis and Clark* 3, pp. 124-25.

[19] Ibid.

[20] Ibid., p. 128 and volume 4, p. 321.

[21] *Journals of Lewis and Clark* 4, p. 323; Meinig, *The Great Columbia Plain,* p. 16. The scientific name for the principal of bunchgrass is *Agropyron spicatum,* but there were other species. Some sources on horses include Haines, "Where Did the Plains Indians Get Their Horses?," *American Anthropologist* 40 (1938), and "The Northward Spread of Horses Among the Plains Indians," *American Anthropologist* 40 (1938); Robert M. Denhardt, *The Horse of the Americas;* Frank G. Roe, *The Indian and the Horse;* Josephy, *The Nez Perce,* pp. 32-34, 41-48, 70-76; see also these two volumes by John C. Ewers, *The Horse in Blackfeet Culture and The Blackfeet.* Most of the tribes of the inland Northwest, including the Palouses, journeyed over the Bitterroot Mountains into the buffalo country before the horse, but traveling was greatly facilitated by the acquisition of the horse. Oral interview by authors with Mary Jim, April 25, 1980. There is a controversy regarding the horse labeled the Appaloosa. It has been argued by some authorities that the Nez Perces, Palouses, Walla Wallas, and other Sahaptins bred horses for color alone. For this view see Francis Haines, George B. Hatley, and Robert Peckinpah, *The Appaloosa Horse,* and Haines, *The Nez Perces.* Others have challenged this interpretation, arguing that "they bred their horses for swiftness and intelligence, not for color." Oral histories taken by the authors with Palouse, Wanapum, Umatilla, Yakima, and Nez Perce informants seem to support this view, although a few Palouses favored spotted horses. See Grace Bartlett, "The Appaloosa," unpublished manuscript, Grace Bartlett files, Joseph, Oregon. The best article to examine both of these interpretations is Alvin Josephy, Jr., "Nez Perces and the Appaloosa Horse . . . False History?," *The Westerners New York Posse Brand Book* 14 (1967): 73-75, 81-82, 87; also in the same volume, see H. E. Bartlett, "The Appaloosa Was Not the Nez Perce War Horse," pp. 88-89.

[22] Meinig, *The Great Columbia Plain,* p. 16.

[23] *Journals of Lewis and Clark* 4, pp. 323, 341. According to editor Thwaites, the root described here was *Lomatium macrocarcum.*

[24] Ibid., pp. 354-55. There are many references to the plants used by Palouses in the various exhibits and testimonies, Indian Claims, Docs. 222 and 161, NA, RG 279. For an informative article on camas, see J. E. Konlande and J. R. K. Robson, "The Nutritive Value of Cooked Camas and Consumed by Flathead Indians," *Ecology of Food and Nutrition* 2 (1972): 193-95. There are some informative studies regarding the medicinal aspects of the expedition, but the most important is E.G. Chuinard, *Only One Man Died: The Medical Aspects of the Lewis and Clark Expedition.*

[25] "Testimony of Verne L. Ray," Indian Claims, Docs. 222 and 161, NA, RG 279, pp. 739, 741, 749-53; Ray, "Economic Use of the Tribal Territory," Ibid.; see also William N. Bischoff, "The Coeur d'Alene Country, 1805-1892," *Interior Salish and Eastern Washington Indians,* pp. 82, 97-98.

[26] Oral interview by authors with Mary Jim, November 17, 1979, and April 25, 1980.

[27] Ibid.

[28] Ray, "Economic Use of the Tribal Territory," Indian Claims, Docs. 222 and 161, NA, RG 279.

[29]Oral interview by authors with Mary Jim, April 25, 1980.

[30]Steven J. Gill, an ethnobotanist at Washington State University, has been most helpful in identifying native plants used by Palouse Indians and assessing the nutritive value of edible plants. Gill's "Field Notes" are filled with data on the topic and are found at the Department of Botany, Washington State University. Also, see Helen H. Horton and Steven J. Gill, "The Ethnobotanical Imperative: A Consideration of Obligations, Implications, and Methodology," *Northwest Anthropological Research Notes* 15 (1981): 117-34; Jerry Galm, Glen Hartmann, Ruth Masten, and Garry Stephenson, "A Cultural Resource Overview of the Bonneville Power Administration's Mid-Columbia Project," Central Washington University *Management Report* 1 (1981); "Nutritive Values of Native Foods of Washington State Indians," Oregon University Extension Service *Circular 809* (1972); M. Lee, R. Roburn, and A. Carrow, "Nutritional Studies of British Columbian Indians," *Canadian Journal of Public Health* 62 (1971): 285-96; D. H. Calloway, R. D. Giauque, and F. M. Costa, "The Superior Mineral Content of Some American Indian Foods," *Ecology of Food and Nutrition* 3 (1974): 203-11; and three articles by the same authors, Pat Kelley, Eugene Hunn, Charles Martinsen, and Helen Norton, "Composition of Northwest Native Fruits," "Composition of Northwest Native Root Foods," and "Ascorbic Acid Content of Northwest Native Plant Foods," *Journal of the American Dietetic Association,* in press.

[31]Gill's "Field Notes."

[32]L. V. McWhorter Collection, Document 213 B/84, Manuscripts and Archives, Washington State University Library, Pullman. Hereafter cited as Manuscripts and Archives, WSU.

[33]*Journals of Lewis and Clark* 4, p. 354. Forthcoming chapters of this volume will illuminate this common theme of Manifest Destiny and Mission.

[34]Ibid.; also, volume 5, p. 11.

[35]*Journals of Lewis and Clark* are the best sources on the subject, but numerous scholarly studies, far too many to cite here, have analyzed the Corps of Discovery. Some of these include Harold P. Howard, *SacaJawea;* Blanche Schroer, "Boat-Pusher or Bird-Woman? Sacagawea or Sacajawea?," *Annuals of Wyoming* 52 (1980); Jerome O. Steffen, *William Clark: Jeffersonian Man on the Frontier;* Charles G. Clarke, *The Men of the Lewis and Clark Expedition;* Richard Dillon, *Meriwether Lewis: A Biography;* Donald Jackson, ed., *Letters of the Lewis and Clark Expedition, With Related Documents, 1783-1854;* Roy E. Appleman, *Lewis and Clark: Historic Places Associated with the Transcontinental Exploration, 1804-06.*

CHAPTER 2

[1]"Kootenae House, Kullyspell House, Saleesh House, and Spokane House" were respectively established in 1807, 1808, 1809, and 1810. For sources dealing with the North West Company and early trade in the inland Northwest, see Elliott Coues, ed., *New Light on Early History of the Greater Northwest: The Manuscript Journals of Alexander Henry and David Thompson;* J. B. Tyrrell, ed., *David Thompson's Narrative of His Explorations in Western America, 1784-1812;* T. C. Elliott, ed., "Journal of David Thompson," *Oregon Historical Quarterly* 15 (1914); and M. Catherine White, ed., *David Thompson's Journals Relating to Montana and Adjacent Regions, 1808-1812.* For an overview of trade items, see Arthur Woodward, *Indian Trade Goods.*

[2]*American State Papers: Documents, Legislative and Executive* 2, p. 201; Coues, *New Light* 2, p. 712; *The American Heritage Book of Indians,* pp. 324-25; Josephy, The Nez Perce, pp. 41-43; and Elliott, "Journal of David Thompson," pp. 43, 48, 49, 57.

[3]Ibid.

[4]Elliott, "Journal of David Thompson," p. 57, 63; Tyrrell, "Thompson's Narrative," pp. 495-98.

[5]See two articles edited by T. C. Elliott, "The Journal of David Thompson," p. 58 and "The Discovery of the Source of the Columbia River," *Oregon Historical Quarterly* 26 (1925): 43. For excellent published accounts of Thompson, see Robert Ruby and John Brown, *The Cayuse Indians: Imperial Tribesmen of Old Oregon,* pp. 23-25; Meinig, *The Great Columbia Plain,* pp. 36-39; and Josephy, *The Nez Perce,* pp. 43-44, 654-57.

[6]Elliott, "The Journal of David Thompson," p. 58.

[7]There are numerous accounts of the Astorians. The sources include Alexander Ross, *Adventures of the First Settlers on the Oregon and Columbia Rivers;* Gabriel Franchere, *Narrative of a Voyage to the Northwest Coast of America in the Years 1811, 1812, 1813, and 1814;* J. Neilson Barry, "Archibald Pelton, The First Follower of Lewis and Clark," *Washington Historical Quarterly* 19 (1928); J. Neilson Barry, "Madame Dorion of the Astorians," *Oregon Historical Quarterly* 30 (1929); Robert Stuart's "Narratives," Wilson Price Hunt's "Diary," and "An Account of the Tonquin's Voyage" in Philip Ashton Rollins, ed., *The Discovery of the Oregon Trail;* J. Neilson Barry, "The Trail of the Astorians," *Oregon Historical Quarterly* 13 (1912); Constance L. Skinner, *Adverturers of Oregon;* Miles Cannon, "Snake River in History," *Oregon Historical Quarterly* 20 (1919); and B. C. Payette, ed., *The Oregon Country Under Union Jack.*

[8]Elliott, "Journal of David Thompson," pp. 118-19.

[9]Ibid.

[10]Ibid.

[11]Ibid., pp. 120-21.

[12]Ibid., p. 122.

[13]Ross, *Adventures of the First Settlers,* p. 137.

[14]Ibid., pp. 136-37. Also see Melville Jacobs, "Historic Perspective in Indian Languages of Oregon and Washington," *Pacific Northwest Quarterly* 28 (1937): 55-74.

[15]Ross, *Adventures of the First Settlers,* p. 138-39.

[16]Ibid.

[17]Ibid., pp. 139-40. Several references were made by trappers and traders regarding the strategic importance of the region surrounding Quosispah. For discussion, see Meinig, *The Great Columbia Plain,* pp. 44-45; Rollins, *The Discovery of the Oregon Trail,* pp. 281-328; Washington Irving, *Astoria,* chapters 13-27; Hiram M. Chittenden, *The American Fur Trade of the Far West* 1, chapter 10; and Hubert H. Bancroft, *Northwest Coast* 2, chapter 8.

[18]Ross, *Advertures of the First Settlers,* pp. 140-41.

[19]Ibid.

[20]Ibid., pp. 115, 140-41, 194-209, 214; Ross Cox, *The Columbia River,* pp. 84-92.

[21]Cox, *The Columbia River,* pp. 88-90.

[22]Ibid.

[23]Ibid., pp. 90-91; Ross, *Adventures of the First Settlers,* pp. 208-09.

[24]Ross, *Adventures of the First Settlers,* pp. 214-15; for an excellent analysis of the Nez Perce reaction to the trappers, see Josephy, *The Nez Perce,* pp. 47-48.

[25]Ross, *Adventures of the First Settlers,* p. 216.

[26]Ibid., pp. 216-21; Josephy, *The Nez Perce,* pp. 48-49.

[27]Ibid.

[28]Ibid.; Cox, *The Columbia River,* pp. 117-19.

[29]Ross, *Adventures of the First Settlers,* pp. 212-13; Cox, *The Columbia River,* pp. 118-19.

[30]Ibid.

[31]Ibid. There is some debate over whether the person hanged was an "outlaw" from another tribe, possibly a Nez Perce, or a Palouse. Whether he was a Palouse Indian or not matters little. The significance of the event was that it altered the attitudes of and the relationship between the whites and Palouses. The two parties viewed each other with suspicion and hostility, and their image of each other changed from that day forward.

[32]Ross, *Adventures of the First Settlers,* p. 221.

[33]Ibid., pp. 195, 221-22.

[34]Ibid.; Josephy, *The Nez Perce,* pp. 50-54.

[35]Ross, *Adventures of the First Settlers,* pp. 221-22.

[36]Oral interview by the authors with Andrew George, November 15, 1980.

[37]Cox, *The Columbia River,* p. 128.

[38]Ibid., pp. 128-29.

[39]Alexander Ross, *The Fur Hunters of the Far West,* edited by Kenneth A. Spaulding, pp. 22-27.

[40]Cox, *The Columbia River,* pp. 195-96.

[41]Ibid., pp. 196-97.

[42]Ibid., p. 203.

[43]Ross, *Fur Hunters,* pp. 138-54; Cecil W. MacKenzie, *Donald MacKenzie, King of the Northwest,* pp. 110-14; Josephy, *The Nez Perce,* p. 55; Meinig, *The Great Columbia Plain,* pp. 61-65, 86.

[44]Ross, *Fur Hunters,* p. 119.

[45]Ibid.

[46]Ibid., p. 118.

[47]Ibid., pp. 120-21.

[48]Ibid., pp. 122-23; see also Josephy, *The Nez Perce,* pp. 62-68.

[49]Ibid.

[50]E. E. Rich, ed., *Part of a Dispatch from George Simpson Esqr., Governor of Ruperts Land, to the Governor & Committee of the Hudson's Bay Company, London, March 1, 1829. Continued and Completed March 24 and June 5, 1829,* p. 51; E. E. Rich, ed., *The Letters of John McKoughlin: First Series, 1825-38,* p. 196; Frederick Merk, ed., *Fur Trade and Empire: George Simpson's Journal, 1824-1825,* p. 287; and Burt B. Baker, ed., *Letters of Dr. John McLoughlin Written at Fort Vancouver 1829-32,* p. 254.

[51]Rich, *Simpson Dispatch,* p. 51.

[52]Merk, *Fur Trade and Empire,* pp. 54-57, 126-28.

[53]T. C. Elliott, ed., "Journal of John Work, Covering Snake Country Expedition of 1830-31," *Oregon Historical Quarterly* 13 (1912): 363-71; 14 (1913): 280-314.

[54]Rich, *The Letters of John McLoughlin,* p. 26.

[55]Ross, *Fur Hunters,* p. 200.

[56]Oral interviews by authors with Mary Jim, November 9-10, 1979. For sources regarding the interaction of the Plateau Indians with American trappers, see Dale L. Morgan, *The West of William H. Ashley;* Merk, *Fur Trade and Empire;* J. Cecil Alter, ed., *Life in the Rocky Mountains, 1830-1835;* Chittenden, *A History of the American Fur Trade in the Far West;* Washington Irving, *The Adventures of Captain Bonneville;* John B. Wyeth, "Oregon: A Short History of a Long Journey," in Reuben Gold Thwaites, ed., *Early Western Travels, 1748-1846;* and "The Correspondence and Journals of Captain Nathanial J. Wyeth, 1831-1836," in F. B. Young, ed., *Sources of the History of Oregon* 1.

CHAPTER 3

[1]Andrew Colville to George Simpson, March 11, 1924, quoted from Frederick Merk, *Fur Trade and Empire: George Simpson's Journal,* p. 205. Also see, William N. Bischoff, *Jesuits in Old Oregon,* pp. 9-12, 17-22; Robert I. Burns, *The Jesuits and the Indian Wars of the Northwest,* pp. 36-48; and Lawrence B. Palladino, *Indian and White in the Northwest,* p. 8.

[2]Merk, *Fur Trade and Empire,* pp. 135-38; J. O. Oliphant, "George Simpson and Oregon Missions," *Pacific Historical Review* 6 (1937): 234-39. Further materials on the boys who were sent to the Red River Mission can be found in the Oliphant Collection, Manuscripts and Archives, WSU; Clifford M. Drury, "Oregon Indians

in the Red River School," *Pacific Historical Review* 7 (1938): 52-54; Thomas E. Jesset, *Chief Spokan Garry, 1811-1892*, pp. 22-38, 41-46. For an excellent survey of the issues involved regarding the Christianization of the Salish boys, see Josephy, *The Nez Perce*, pp. 84-88.

[3]Warren A. Ferris, *Life in the Rocky Mountains, 1830-1835*, pp. 75-80; Hubert Howe Bancroft, *History of Oregon* 1, pp. 54-55; Clifford M. Drury, *Henry Harmon Spalding*, pp. 72-90; McWhorter, *Hear Me*, pp. 29-30; George Catlin, *Letters and Notes on the Manners, Customs, and Conditions of the North American Indians* 2, pp. 108-09; Chittenden, *The American Fur Trade of the Far West* 2, pp. 640-47. See also in this volume the various letters regarding the Nez Perce delegation in Appendix D, pp. 912-25. The four Nez Perces who traveled to St. Louis were Tipyahlahah (Eagle), Hiyutstohenin (Rabbit Skin Leggings), Tawis Geejumnin (No Horns On His Head), and Kaoupu (Man of the Morning).

[4]"Diary of Reverend Jason Lee," *Oregon Historical Quarterly* 17 (1916): 138- 29, 264. Lee established his church in the Willamette Valley, ten miles northwest of present-day Salem, Oregon. For a survey of Lee's endeavor, see Bancroft, *History of Oregon* 1, pp. 56-68, 104-34 and Josephy, *The Nez Perces*, pp. 121-29; Samuel Parker, *Journal of an Exploring Tour Beyond the Rocky Mountains*, pp. 3, 25, 28, 82, 125-29, 134, 264-66, 287-89, 297, 307. Parker's *Journal* was published originally in 1838 and received immediate recognition by the public. The third edition of 1842 has been used here.

[5]The most detailed studies of the Protestant missionaries are presented by the sympathetic historian, Clifford M. Drury. In addition to his volumes, *Henry Spalding* and *Marcus Whitman, M.D.: Pioneer and Martyr*, see Drury (ed.), *Letters of Henry H. Spalding and Asa Bowmen Smith Relating to the Nez Perce Mission 1838-1842; First White Women over the Rockies*, 2 Vols.; *Elkanah and Mary Walker;* and *Tepee in His Front Yard;* and for the views of Narcissa and Eliza, see Drury, *First White Women*, pp. 80-85. For the best presentation of early missionary activities on the Plateau, see chapter seven of Drury, *Marcus Whitman*, and chapters six and seven in his *Henry H. Spalding*.

[6]These views are apparent in the writings of the missionaries. See Drury, *First White Women; Henry H. Spalding; Marcus Whitman; Diaries of Spalding and Smith;* and "Gray's Journal of 1838," *Pacific Northwest Quarterly* 29 (1938): 277-82. A survey of the missionary system of the Protestants is presented in Bancroft, *History of Oregon* 2, pp. 328-48. It was a common belief among many Plateau people that one day they would be visited by a "new" people who would destroy the world. They also believed that those Indians who defied the "new" ones and adhered to the old Indian ways would be resurrected into an eternal life. See Leslie Spier, "The Prophet Dance of the Northwest and its Derivatives: The Source of the Ghost Dance," *General Series in Anthropology* (1953): 17-18, 21.

[7]The religious philosophy of the Palouses and their Sahaptin brothers has not been thoroughly examined in one comprehensive study. For a general overview of the religious beliefs of the Palouses and others see the following: Spier, "The Prophet Dance"; Relander, *Drummers and dancers;* Cora DuBois, "The Feather Cult of the Middle Columbia," *General Series in Anthropology* (1938); Chapter VII of James Mooney, "The Ghost Dance Religion," *Fourteenth Annual Report of the Bureau of Ethnology* (1896); J. W. MacMurray, "The 'Dreamers' of the Columbia River Valley in Washington Territory," *Transactions of the Albany Institute* 2 (1887); E. L. Huggins, "Smohalla, The Prophet of Priest Rapids," *Overland Monthly* 17 (1891). Most of the primary sources regarding Sahaptin religion used in this study were derived from the McWhorter Collection, Manuscripts and Archives, WSU, Folder 149 D, H, and M; Folder 520 A; and McWhorter to Hedge, Mad Moon, 6, 1935, Folder 149 A. Also see the following documents in the Relander Collection, Yakima Valley Regional Library: G. B. Kuykendall, "Smohallah," unpublished ms., Box 55, Folder 16; "Smohalla Services at Yakima Village," Box 60, Folder 10; "Frank Buck's Speech, June 2, 1962," Box 55, Folder 6; "Yakima Notes," Box

18, Folder 2. Margery Ann Beach has written recently on the Washani, including "Smohalla, the Washani, and Religion as a Factor in Northwestern Indian History," with Clifford E. Trafzer, *American Indian Quarterly* 9 (1985): 309-24, and "The Wanapums of the Priest Rapids Dam: Fulfillment of an Indian Prophecy," forthcoming in the *Pacific Northwest Quarterly*. Robert Ruby and John Brown are also completing a book on Northwestern Indian religions.

[8]Spier, "The Prophet Dance," p. 46; Mooney, "The Ghost Dance Religion," pp. 716-19; Kuykendall, "Smohallah," Relander Collection, Box 55, Folder 16.

[9]Mooney, "The Ghost Dance Religion," pp. 716-19; Huggins, "Smohalla," p. 212; and MacMurray, "The 'Dreamers' of the Columbia River Valley," p. 244. Also see the accounts of Major J. W. MacMurray in "Reports of August 26 and September 19, 1884, to the Acting Assistant Adjutant General, Department of the Columbia," National Archives, RG 94, also published in Mooney, "The Ghost Dance Religion."

[10]Relander, *Drummers and Dreamers,* pp. 27, 79; Spier, "The Prophet Dance," 17-21, 41, 46; DuBois, "The Feather Cult," p. 5; Sharkey, "The Wanapums," pp. 5-6.

[11]Relander, *Drummers and Dreamers,* pp. 84-85.

[12]The various works of Drury detail the expansion of the Protestant mission system. For the role of Catholics, see Bischoff, *The Jesuits in Old Oregon;* Hiram M. Chittenden and Alfred T. Richardson, *Life, Letters and Travels of Father Pierre-Jean DeSmet, S.J., 1801-1873;* and Francis N. Blanchet, *Historical Sketches of the Catholic Church in Oregon.* For information regarding white immigration and Indian reaction to it, see Relander, *Drummers and Dreamers,* pp. 83, 139; Dorothy O. Johansen and Charles M. Gates, *Empire of the Columbia,* pp. 191-94, 212; Bancroft, *History of Oregon* 1, chapters 15, 17, 19, and 20.

[13]Drury, *First White Women* 1, p. 123; Smith to Greene, September 2, 1840, Correspondence of the American Board of Foreign Missions, Oregon Historical Society, quoted from Drury, *Henry H. Spalding,* p. 216; Josephy, *The Nez Perce,* pp. 434-36; oral interview by authors with Patricia Jones, August 25, 1980.

[14]Drury, *Diaries of Spalding and Smith,* pp. 194-97; Bancroft, *History of Oregon* 1, pp. 642-44, 647-52, 657-58.

[15]Robert I. Burns, *The Jesuits and the Indian Wars of the Northwest,* pp. 13, 647-50, 652-53, 656-58; William H. Gray, *A History of Oregon,* pp. 462-64; Drury, *Marcus Whitman,* pp. 276, 390; Drury, *Henry H. Spalding,* p. 332; Drury, *Marcus and Narcissa Whitman and the Opening of Oregon,* pp. 86, 104, 121-23, 182-83, 206-07, 225, 264, and 338; Drury, *Diaries of Spalding and Smith,* pp. 237, 342. Archaeologists at Washington State University and the University of Idaho have excavated Palouse burial sites over the past two decades and have reportedly studied Indian remains for information regarding diseases. However, the authors were unable to secure from the archaeologists evidence (e.g., forensic reports) regarding the influence of diseases in bringing about the extirpation of the Palouses. Also, see Roderick Sprague, "Aboriginal Burial Practices in the Plateau Region of North America," p. 20. A forthcoming dissertation, "A Skeletal Biological Study of the Nez Perce" may deal with disease and other factors learned from a study of bones found at a Palouse burial site. Oral interview, William Willard with Walter Birkley (forensic expert at the Palouse burial site), August 25, 1980. See also Roderick Sprague, "The Descriptive Archaeology of the Palus Burial Site, Lyon's Ferry, Washington," *Washington State University, Report of Investigations* 32 (1965).

[16]McWhorter Collection, Manuscripts and Archives, WSU, Folder 162.

[17]Ibid., Folders 520 A, 88, 213 A. Also, see J. Ross Browne, "The Report of J. Ross Browne on the Late Indian War in Oregon and Washington Territories," *Senate Executive Document (SED)* 35th Cong., 1st Sess., No. 40, Vol. 12, SS 929. For a concise discussion of events leading to the Whitman killings, see Ruby and Brown, *The Cayuse Indians,* pp. 84-112, and Josephy, *The Nez Perce,* pp. 201-52.

[18]Ruby and Brown, *The Cayuse Indians,* pp. 109-12; Josephy, *The Nez Perce,* pp.

250-52, 256; Bancroft, *History of Oregon* 1, pp. 658-61; Drury, *Marcus and Narcissa Whitman,* chapter 22.

[19]Bancroft, *History of Oregon* 1, pp. 669, 680-82, 685-90; Ruby and Brown, *The Cayuse Indians,* pp. 119-21. Kamiakin chose neutrality and condemned the Cayuses responsible for the Whitman murders.

[20]Bancroft, *History of Oregon* 1, pp. 669-72, 675-76, 682-84, 700-14; Ruby and Brown, *The Cayuse Indians,* pp. 115-16, 188, 130-43; Drury, *Marcus Whitman,* pp. 390-411. For an eyewitness account, see Dorothy O. Johansen, ed., *Robert Newell's Memoranda,* pp. 81-115, 127-39. The Oregon newspapers followed the war, sometimes accurately and unbiasedly but more often not. See the *Oregon Spectator,* February 10 and 24, March 23, April 6 and 20, June 15, and July 13, 1848.

[21]Johansen, *Robert Newell's Memoranda,* p. 111; Clifford M. Drury, *Nine Years with the Spokane Indians: The Diary, 1838-1848, of Elkanah Walker,* p. 472.

[22]Bancroft, *History of Oregon* 1, pp. 722-23.

[23]Ibid., pp. 723-24; Josephy, *The Nez Perce,* p. 276-76.

[24]Ibid.

[25]Ibid.

[26]See chapter 7 of Francis Fuller Victor, *The Early Indian Wars of Oregon.*

[27]Ibid., pp. 248-51; Ruby and Brown, *The Cayuse Indians,* pp. 162-71; Josephy, *The Nez Perce,* pp. 220, 226-40, 283-84; Bancroft, *History of Oregon* 1, pp. 268-91; A. J. Allen, *Ten Years in Oregon,* pp. 181-205; Drury, *Marcus Whitman,* p. 287

CHAPTER 4

[1]Some of the best sources which deal with American Indian policy include Lyman Tyler, *A History of Indian Policy;* Felix S. Cohen, *Handbook of Federal Indian Law;* Charles J. Kappler, *Indian Affairs, Laws and Treaties;* Alban Hoopes, *Indian Affairs and Their Administration;* J. A. James, *English Institutions and the American Indian;* Walter H. Mohr, *Federal Indian Relations, 1774-1778;* Francis P. Prucha, *American Indian Policy in the Formative Years* and *Indian Policy in the United States.* For the best sources on general Northwestern Indian policy, see Herman J. Deutsch, "Indian and White in the Inland Empire: The Contest for the Land, 1880-1912," *Pacific Northwest Quarterly* 47 (1956): 44-51; C. F. Coan, "The First Stage of the Federal Indian Policy in the Pacific Northwest, 1849-1852," *Oregon Historical Quarterly* 22 (1921): 46-82.

[2]Kent D. Richards, *Isaac I. Stevens: Young Man in a Hurry,* pp. 98-99. Richards presents a different view of Stevens in an earlier article, "Isaac I. Stevens and Federal Military Power in Washington Territory," *Pacific Northwest Quarterly* 63 (1972): 81-86. Other works on Stevens include his son's two volumes, Hazard Stevens, *Life of Isaac Ingalls Stevens;* Joseph T. Hazard, *Companion of Adventure;* John S. Richards, ed., "Letters of Governor Isaac I. Stevens, 1853-54," *Pacific Northwest Quarterly* 30 (1939): 301-37; and J. Ronald Todd, ed., "Letters of Governor Isaac I. Stevens, 1857-58," *Pacific Northwest Quarterly* 31 (1940): 403-59. Manuscript collections on Stevens are found at the Beinike Library, Yale University; Washington State Library, Olympia; the Washington State Historical Society, Tacoma; and the University of Washington Library, Seattle.

[3]Dorothy O. Johansen and Charles M. Gates, *Empire of the Columbia: A History of the Pacific Northwest,* pp. 231, 234, 246-47.

[4]Ibid.

[5]General Report of Captain George B. McClellan, Corps of Engineers, USA, in Command of the Western Division, February 25, 1853, p. 188 in "Reports of Explorations and Surveys to Ascertain the Most Practicable and Economical Route for a Railroad from the Mississippi River to the Pacific Ocean," *House Executive Document (HED),* 33d Cong., 2d Sess., No. 91, Vol. 1, SS 791; hereafter cited as Railroad Reports.

[6]Ibid.; also, see A. J. Splawn, *Ka-mi-akin: Last Hero of the Yakimas,* p. 19; Ricard to Stevens, March 2, 1855 and Shaw to Stevens, February 10, 1856, Records of the Washington Superintendency of Indian Affairs, 1853-74, National Archives, Record Group 75, Letters Received; hereafter cited as WS, NA, RG 75, LR. Also, see William Norbert Bischoff, "The Yakima Indian War: 1855-1856," p. 56.

[7]Railroad Reports 12, pp. 107-08; William C. Brown, *The Indian Side of the Story,* pp. 60-80; and Splawn, *Ka-mi-akin,* pp. 17-21. For numerous oral histories describing Kamiakin's family history see the Brown Collection, Manuscripts and Archives, WSU. Kamiakin's family geneaology is found herein.

[8]Ibid. Kamiakin's father, Tsiyiak, is sometimes spelled Kiyiyah. For the names of Kamiakin's wives, see Kamiakin's genealogy.

[9]The quotes are from Theodore Winthrop, *Canoe and Saddle,* p. 178 and Splawn, *Ka-mi-akin,* p. 15. Also, see Brown, *The Indian Side,* pp. 60-80. Kamiakin's first wife, Sunkhaye, was his first cousin.

[10]*Railroad Reports* 12, p. 107; Splawn, *Ka-mi-akin,* pp. 15-21; Robert I. Burns, *Jesuits and the Indian Wars of the Northwest,* pp. 52, 54, 74, 126, 363-64.

[11]"McClellan Journal," August 9, 1853, Papers of George B. McClellan, Library of Congress. Also, *Railroad Reports* 1, p. 190.

[12]*Railroad Reports* 1, p. 191.

[13]Ibid. 12, pp. 139-41; Splawn, *Ka-mi-akin,* pp. 19-20. Quiltenenock was the brother of Quetalakin or Chief Moses. For the best source on this family of Columbias, see Robert H. Ruby and John A. Brown, *Half-Sun on the Columbia: A Biography of Chief Moses.*

[14]*Railroad Reports* 12, pp. 140-41; Splawn, *Ka-mi-akin,* p. 21-30.

[15]*Railroad Reports* 1, p. 253.

[16]Ibid., p. 254.

[17]Ibid., p. 255.

[18]Ibid.

[19]Ibid.

[20]Ibid.

[21]Ibid., p. 256. According to Saxton the Palouses told him that Spaniards had once warned the Indians that Americans would invade the Indian country. Saxton threatened to hang the "Spaniard" responsible for the rumor.

[22]Ibid. 12, pp. 139-41.

[23]Ibid., p. 134.

[24]Ibid., p. 146.

[25]Ibid., p. 146-50.

[26]Ibid, p. 150.

[27]Ibid.

[28]Ibid., pp. 154-55. Stevens was outraged because of McClellan's failure to cross the mountains.

[29]Ibid., pp. 163-67.

[30]Ibid., p. 155.

[31]Ibid., p. 155; Hubert H. Bancroft, *History of Washington, Idaho, and Montana, 1845-1889,* pp. 65-98; Stevens, *The Life* 2, pp. 25-26.

[32]Tyler, *A History of Indian Policy,* pp. 54-86; Jennings, *The Invasion of America,* pp. 19-20, 61-69; Arrell M. Gibson, *The American Indians: Prehistory to the Present,* chapter 14.

[33]Richards, *Isaac I. Stevens,* pp. 170-72, 181-93.

[34]Ibid.; Tyler, *A History of Indian Policy,* pp. 54-86; Gibson, *The American Indian,* chapter 16. For general studies on Indian policy, see Elsie M. Rushmore, *The Indian Policy During Grant's Administration;* Francis P. Prucha, *American Indian Policy in Crisis;* and Richard N. Ellis, *General Pope and U.S. Indian Policy.*

[35]Splawn, *Ka-mi-akin,* pp. 20-21, 24-26; Brown, *The Indian Side,* pp. 85-90; Josephy, *The Nez Perce,* pp. 312-13; Stevens, *The Life* 2, pp. 25-36.

[36]Splawn, *Ka-mi-akin,* p. 22; Brown, *The Indian Side,* pp. 85-104; Bischoff, "The

Yakima War," chapters 1, 2.

[37]Splawn, *Ka-mi-akin*, pp. 22-24; Bancroft, *History of Washington,* p. 109.

[38]*Railroad Surveys* 1, p. 179.

[39]Ibid.

[40]Ibid., p. 408.

[41]Alfred W. Crosby, Jr., *The Columbian Exchange: Biological and Cultural Consequences of 1492,* p. 37.

[42]Ibid., p. 56.

[43]The most scholarly study of the treaties surrounding the Puget Sound and Stevens' negotiations with the Coastal Indians were done by Carole Seeman and are published in Clifford E. Trafzer, ed., *Indians, Superintendents, and Councils: Northwestern Indian Policy, 1850-1855,* pp. 19-67. Also, see Stevens, *The Life* 1, p. 454; B. F. Shaw, "Medicine Creek Treaty," *Proceedings of the Oregon Historical Reminiscences of Puget Sound: The Tragedy of Leschi,* pp. 207, 234-35, 240-45; James Wickersham, "The Indian Side of the Puget Sound Indian War," (1893): 5-6, in Relander Collection. For the minutes of the council proceedings, see Documents Relating to Negotiations of Ratified and Unratified Treaties, NA, RG 75, Microfilm T494, Reel 5; hereafter cited as Council Proceedings. The Council Proceedings of the Northwest were published in Office of Indian Affairs, *Report on Sources, Nature and Extent of the Fishing, Hunting and Miscellaneous Related Rights of Certain Tribes in Washington and Oregon,* pp. 324-49; hereafter cited as Treaty Proceedings.

[44]Treaty Proceedings, pp. 239-40; Meeker, *Pioneer Reminiscences,* pp. 234-35; Wickersham, "The Indian Side," pp. 5-6. According to these sources, Leschi listened to Stevens during the council at Medicine Creek, then he "stood up before the Governor and said that if he could not get his home, he would fight." When Stevens informed him that the treaties would not be changed, "Leschi then took the paper out of his pocket that the Governor had given him to be subchief, and tore it up before the Governor's eyes." After ripping it apart, Leschi "stamped on the pieces, and left the treaty ground, and never came back." Stevens was very "nervous and uneasy" about Leschi's departure because the governor wanted the chief's signature on the treaty. According to L. F. Thompson, a pioneer of the Puget Sound area who witnessed and proceedings, Agent Michael T. Simmons "told Leschi that if he did not sign . . . he would sign . . . for him." The marks of Leschi, his brother Quiemuth, and others appeared on the treaty, despite the fact that they had left the council ground. Their names were forged on the treaty, and the Indians resented it deeply and still do. Seeman, "The Treaties of Puget Sound," in Trafzer, ed., *Indians, Superintendents, and Councils,* pp. 24-25.

[45]Doty to Stevens, May 22, 1855 in Edward J. Kowrach, ed., *Journal of Operations.* There are several copies of Doty's Journal, and Kowrach worked through them all in order to produce his edited volume. For the original, see Doty's Journal of Operations in Council Proceedings, 1855.

[46]Ibid.

[47]Ibid.

[48]Brown, *The Indian Side,* pp. 90-91.

[49]Doty's Journal.

[50]Ibid.

[51]Ibid.

[52]Ibid.; Brown, *The Indian Side,* pp. 86-91; Splawn, *Ka-mi-akin,* pp. 24-26; Stevens, *The Life* 2, pp. 28-36.

CHAPTER 5

[1]For accounts specifically dealing with the Indian policy of Stevens and Palmer, see Stevens, *The Life;* Richards, *Isaac I. Stevens;* Bruce Wendt, "A History of the Warm Springs Indian Reservation"; and Stanley J. Spaid, "Joel Palmer and Indian Affairs in Oregon."

[2]Doty's Journal.

[3]Stevens, *The Life* 2, p. 31.

[4]Doty's Journal.

[5]Stevens to Doty, May 20, 1855, Records of the Bureau of Indian Affairs, Washington Superintendency of Indian Affairs, NA, RG 75, Letters Sent (LS); hereafter cited as WS.

[6]Annual Report of the Commissioner of Indian Affairs, 1855, Department of Interior, Office of Indian Affairs, p. 12; hereafter cited as Annual Report, CIA, 1855. Copies of the Annual Reports were used from the Microcard Editions, Washington, D.C., 1968.

[7]Ibid.; Stevens to Mannypenny, May 28, and June 13, 1855, Council Proceedings, 1855.

[8]Doty's Journal.

[9]Brown, *The Indian Side,* p. 95.

[10]Doty's Journal.

[11]Stevens, *The Life* 2, p. 34; Lawrence Kip, "The Indian Council at Walla Walla, May and June, 1855," in *Source of the History of Oregon* 1 (1897); hereafter cited as Kip's Journal.

[12]Stevens, *The Life* 2, pp. 34-35.

[13]Ibid., p. 37.

[14]Doty's Journal.

[15]Stevens, *The Life* 2, pp. 37-38.

[16]Stevens to Doty, May 20, 1855, WS, NA, RG 75, LS.

[17]Doty's Journal; Stevens, *The Life* 2, pp. 40-41.

[18]Council Proceedings, 1855; Stevens, *The Life* 2, pp. 40-41.

[19]Stevens, *The Life* 2, pp. 40-42.

[20]Josephy, *The Nez Perce,* pp. 313-18.

[21]Council Proceedings, 1855.

[22]Ibid. Many times the Indians stated that they were unsure what was being said, and they were continually concerned that the whites "interpret right" for the Indians.

[23]Ibid. Throughout the council Stevens addressed the Indians as "my children," which was a condescending approach recognized by the Indian leaders.

[24]Ibid. For an excellent study of John Ross and his position on removal, see Gary Moulton, *John Ross: Cherokee Chief.*

[25]Council Proceedings, 1855.

[26]Ibid.

[27]Ibid.

[28]Ibid.; Brown, *The Indian Side,* pp. 49-50. In addition to being a Cayuse chief and half-brother to Joseph, Five Crows was also known as Hezekiah by Spalding and other whites. After the Whitman killings, Five Crows had taken a female prisoner to the Umatilla River. He was wounded during the Cayuse War, and he was distrustful of all whites.

[29]Ibid.

[30]Ibid. For the religious beliefs of the Palouse, see Relander, *Drummers and Dreamers;* Spier, "The Prophet Dance"; DeBois, "The Feather Cult"; and Mooney, "The Ghost Dance Religion"; and Trafzer and Sharkey, "Smohalla, the Washani, and Religion as a Factor in Northwestern Indian History.'

[31]Ibid. For information on The Hat and Ellis, see Josephy, *The Nez Perce,* pp. 165-82, 228-46, 280-77, 292, 323.

[32]Council Proceedings, 1855. Josephy provides an excellent discussion of the boundaries outlined by Stevens during the council in *The Nez Perce,* p. 324.

[33]Ibid. Chapter 1 of this volume provides a discussion of Indian religion on the Columbia Plateau.

[34]Ibid.

[35]Ibid.; Kip's Journal, p. 18.

[36]Council Proceedings, 1855.

37Ibid.

38Ibid.

39Ibid.

40Ibid. After war broke out in the Fall of 1855, Kamiakin wrote a letter to the soldiers presenting the causes of the conflict. Kamiakin stated that the Indians had not conspired for war but joined the conflict because of "the way in which the governor . . . talked to us at the Cayuses." The chief told Stevens, "It is you, governor, who has wanted war." The Indians blamed the war largely on Stevens and the way he conducted the council at Walla Walla. Some of the whites blamed the war on Stevens as well, and evidence of the fact is seen throughout the newspapers of the region. Kamiakin's letter is found at the archives at the Diocese of Seattle and a translation of the letter is found in the Relander Collection. Edward J. Kowrach refined the translation. The two best newspapers to consult regarding Stevens and the *Walla Pioneer and Democrat,* April 21; June 29; August, 3, 10, 21; September 7, 14, 21, 28; October 5, 12, 19, 26; November 9, 16, 23, 1855; *Puget Sound Courier* September 7, October 19, and November 23, 1855.

41Kip's Journal, p. 20.

42Council Proceedings, 1855.

43Ibid.

44Doty's Journal.

45Council Proceedings, 1855.

46Ibid.; Doty's Journal.

47Kip's Journal, p. 23.

48Ibid.; Doty's Journal.

49Kip's Journal, p. 23.

50Doty's Journal.

51Ibid.

52Ibid.; Council Proceedings, 1855.

53Andrew D. Pambrun, *Sixty Years on the Frontier in the Pacific Northwest,* ed. Edward J. Kowrach, p. 95. The details of Kamiakin's decision may be exposed in an edited work of Pandosy's letters presently being translated by Edward J. Kowrach.

54Doty's Journal.

55Splawn, *Ka-mi-akin,* pp. 32-33.

56Ibid.; Doty's Journal; Pambrun, *Sixty Years,* pp. 94-96; Brown, *The Indian Side,* pp. 85-130; Splawn, *Ka-mi-akin,* pp. 27-35; Richards, *Stevens,* pp. 215-26. Hazard Stevens' account of the Walla Walla Council is very biased, presenting the meeting in the very best light for his father and the other white negotiators. He made no attempt to present Indian views of the council. Stevens' account is criticized by Richards in his book, *Isaac I. Stevens.* Richards claims to be objective in his account of Kamiakin and the Walla Walla Council, and this author openly criticized Hazard Stevens' volume. However, Richards' account is based almost totally on records left by Stevens, Doty, Landsdale, and Kip. He fails to use the few available Indian accounts, and his study does not fully analyze the council in terms of Indian religion, kinships, and political structure. Richards accepts the position stated by Doty and Stevens regarding Kamiakin's decision to sign the treaty. Richards fails to use Kamiakin's letter and accounts by Splawn, Brown, and Pambrun.

57For the Yakima Treaty, see Kappler, *Indian Affairs* 2, pp. 694-705.

58Council Proceedings, 1855.

59The notion that Kamiakin proclaimed himself Head Chief over various Sahaptin-, Chinook-, and Salish-speaking peoples is ludicrous in the Plateau Indian world view. Doty and Stevens knew that their accounts of the council would be preserved, and they composed their reports very carefully, believing that one day their accounts — whether published or not — would be read and used by others. Kamiakin's decision to sign the Yakima Treaty is a matter of great controversy today in the Indian world, as he is damned by many for selling lands over which he had no control.

CHAPTER 6

[1]*Railroad Reports* 12, pp. 199-200.

[2]Ibid.

[3]Kappler, *Indian Affairs* 2, pp. 698-702.

[4]Gibbs to Swan, January 8, 1857 in James G. Swan, *The Northwest Coast: or, Three Year's Residence in Washington Territory,* p. 428.

[5]Durier a Ricard, note, April 12, 1855 in Bischoff, "The Yakima Indian War," p. 61.

[6]Josephy, *The Nez Perce,* p. 345; Brown, *The Indian Side,* pp. 131-35; Splawn, *Kami-akin,* pp. 37-41.

[7]*Oregon Weekly Times,* June 23, 1855; Ricard to Monsieur, March 26, 1856, Relander Collection.

[8]Kamiakin to the Soldiers, October 7,1855, Archives of the Diocese of Seattle; hereafter cited as DS. Mason to Rains, September 26, 1855, Archives of the Washington State Library, Olympia; hereafter cited as WSL. Also, see Granville O. Haller, "The Indian War of 1855-6 in Washington and Oregon," Manuscript Collections, University of Washington Library (UWL); and Haller's "Kamiakin—In History: Memoir of the War, in the Yakima Valley, 1855-1856," Manuscript A128, H. H. Bancroft Collection, University of California, Berkeley. The miners included men named Jamison, Cummings, Huffman, Fanjoy, and Walker.

[9]Mason to Maloney, September 24, 1855, NA, Records of the Commands of the United States Army (RCA), RG 393, LR.

[10]For an Indian account of Bolon's death, see L. V. McWhorter, *Tragedy of the Wahk-shum: Prelude to the Yakima Indian War, 1855-56,* pp. 4-5. See also D'Herbonez to Brouillet, August 28, 1854, DS; and Gaston Carriere, "The Yakima War: An Episode in the History of the Oregon Missions, Refutation of a False Accusation," *Vie Oblate Life* 34 (1975): 153-63.

[11]Ibid.; Brown, *The Indian Side,* p. 133.

[12]Ricard to Stevens, March 2, 1855, Relander Collection.

[13]Palmer to Stevens and Cain to Mannypenny, October 6, 1855 and Mason to Stevens, October 3, 1855, NA, WS, RG 75, LR; Rains to Mason, September 29, 1855, WSL; Haller to Townsend, October 1, 1855, NA, RCA, RG 393, LR.

[14]Kamiakin to the Soldiers, October 7, 1855, DS.

[15]Mactavish to Smith, October 10, 1855 and Palmer to Cain, October 3, 1855, Department of Cultural Affairs and Historical Resources, Hudson's Bay Company (HBC), Winnipeg, Manitoba; the second quote is from Wool to Thomas, October 19, 1855, *HED* 34th Cong., 1st Sess., No. 93, SS 858.

[16]Cain to Mannypenny, October 6, 1855, NA, WS, LR.

[17]Wool to Thomas, October 19, 1855, *HED,* 34th Cong., 1st Sess, No. 93, SS 858; Frances Fuller Victor, *Early Indian Wars of Oregon,* pp. 425-28.

[18]Palmer to Cain, October 3, 1855, Annual Report, CIA, 1855.

[19]Cain to Palmer, October 6, 1855, Annual Report, CIA, 1855.

[20]Kamiakin to the Soldiers, October 7, 1855, DS.

[21]Brown, *The Indian Side,* p. 138. Five soldiers were killed and seventeen wounded while the Indians lost three.

[22]Ibid., pp. 131-55.

[23]Ibid.

[24]The Indian war in the Puget Sound is beyond the scope of this study, but for a sound overview of the war, see Robert H. Ruby and John A. Brown, *Indians of the Pacific Northwest,* pp. 150-54.

[25]Rains to Curry, October 9, 1855 and Order No. 17, 1855, NA, RCA, RG 393, LS.

[26]Wool to Davis, May 15, 1856, *HED,* 34th Cong., 1st Sess., No. 118, SS 859.

[27]Philip H. Sheridan, *Personal Memoirs* 1, pp. 63-64.

[28]Kamiakin to the Soldiers, October 7, 1855, DS.

[29]Ibid. Some of the text of the letter reads: 'They tell us that our ancestors had no horses nor cattle, nor crops nor instruments to garden, that we have received everything of these riches from the Americans, that the country was already full

of us at the same time they chase us from our native lands, as if they were telling us: I have sent you all these things so that you cultivate them until my people arrive, as soon as they will be on the place they will find something to eat."

30Ibid.

31Ibid.

32Ibid.; Carriere, "The Yakima War," pp. 162-65.

33Josephy, *The Nez Perce,* p. 357.

34For Rains' letter to the Indians, see Victor, *Early Indian Wars,* pp. 430-31.

35Ibid. Some of the text of Rains' letter includes: 'Your men we have killed; your horses and your cattle do not afford them enough to eat. Your people shall not catch salmon hereafter for you, for I will send soldiers to occupy your fisheries, and fire up upon you. Your cattle and your horses, which you got from the white man, we will hunt up, and kill and take them from you. The earth which drank the blood of the white man, shed by your hands, shall grow no more wheat nor roots for you, for we shall destroy it. When the cloth that makes your clothing, your guns, and your powder are gone, the white man will make you no more."

36Ibid.

37Ibid., pp. 431-32. After reaching The Dalles, Rains traveled to Fort Vancouver to meet with General John Wool.

38Wool to Thomas, December 13, 1855, *HED,* 34th Cong., 1st Sess., No. 93, SS 858.

39Ibid.; Brown, *The Indian Side,* pp. 182-83.

40There are numerous documents relating to the early military engagements of the war in *HED,* 34th Cong., 1st Sess., No. 93, SS 858; *HED,* 34th Cong., 1st Sess., No. 118, SS 859; *SED,* 34th Cong., 1st Sess., No. 26, SS 819; *SED,* 34th Cong., 1st Sess., No. 66, SS 822.

41Shaw to Stevens, February 10, 1856, NA, WS, RG 75, LR.

42Bischoff, "The Yakima War," p. 219.

43See Palmer's Report, November 21, 1855, *HED,* 34th Cong., 1st Sess., No. 93, SS 858.

44Kelly to Adjutant General (AG), March 1, 1856, NA, RCA, RG 393, LR.

45Kelly to Farra, December 14, 1855 in the *Portland Oregonian,* January 5, 1856; Layton to Farrar, June 18, 1856, Layton Papers, Oregon Historical Society (OHS), Portland. This letter is also found in NA, RCA, RG 393, LR.

46Kelly to AG, March 1, 1856, NA, RCA, RG 393, LR.

47Ibid. Accounts of the Washington Territorial volunteers are deposited at the Washington State Library, Olympia. There are letters relating to the Washington and Oregon volunteers at the Huntington Library, Spokane Public Library, Oregon Historical Society, and the Oregon State Archives, Salem.

48Wool to Thomas, December 25, 1855, *HED,* 34th Cong., 1st Sess., No. 93, SS 858.

49Wool to Stevens, February 2, 1856, *HED,* 34th Cong., 1st Sess., No. 93, SS 858.

50Layton to Farrar, June 18, 1856; Wilson to Farrar, June 15, 1856; Pillow to Farrar, June 18, 1856; and Raymond to Farrar, November 14, 1856 in NA, RCA, RG 393, LR. Also, see Wool to Thomas, May 15, 1856, *HED,* 34th Cong., 1st Sess., No. 118, SS 859.

51The primary documents on the death of Peopeo Moxmox are numerous, including Layton to Farrar, June 18, 1856; Kelly to Curry, January 15, 1855; Bates to Farrar, June 19, 1856; Kelly to AG, March 1, 1856; Curry to Davis, January 19 and April 12, 1856; Pillow to Farrar, August 20, 1856; Wilson to Farrar, June 15, 1856 in NA, RCA, RG 393, LR; Wool to Wright, January 20, 1856, NA, RCA, RG 393, LS. The secondary literature on the killing includes T. C. Elliott, "The Murder of Peu-Peu-Mox-Mox," *Oregon Historical Quarterly* 16 (1915): 123-30; Clarence L. Andrews, "Warfield's Story of Peo-Peo-Mox-Mox," *Washington Historical Quarterly* 25 (1934): 182-84; J. F. Santee, "The Slaying of Pio-Pio-Mox-Mox," *Washington Historical Quarterly* 25 (1934): 128-32.

52Wool to Palmer, February 7, 1856 and Bonnycastle to Palmer, January 12, 1856, NA, Oregon Superintendency of Indian Affairs, RG 75, LR; hereafter cited as OS.

⁵³Wool to Thomas, May 15, 1856, 34th Cong., 1st Sess., No. 118, SS 859.

⁵⁴K. B. Mercer Diary, December 14, 1855, William Robertson Coe Collection, Yale University Library; hereafter cited as Mercer Diary. Also, see McDonald to Stevens, January 27, 1856, NA, WS, RG 75, LR.

⁵⁵Chirouse to Mespile, January 15, 1856 in Bischoff, "The Yakima War," p. 226.

⁵⁶Ibid., p. 234.

⁵⁷Cornelius to wife, February 6, 1856, Cornelius Collection, Huntington Library.

⁵⁸Cornelius to Curry, April 2, 1856, NA, RCA, RG 393, LR.

⁵⁹Ibid.; oral interview by authors with Mary Jim, April 25, 1980.

⁶⁰Cornelius to Curry, April 2, 1856, NA, RCA, RG 393, LR.

⁶¹Ibid.

⁶²Ibid.

⁶³Ibid.

⁶⁴Cornelius to Wool, June 13, 1856, NA, RCA, RG 393, LR; also see the excellent discussion of the volunteer campaign to Bischoff, "The Yakima War," Chapter 7.

⁶⁵Hubert H. Bancroft, *History of Washington, Idaho, and Montana,* pp.145-56; Victor, *Early Indian Wars,* pp. 458-70; Haller, "Kamiakin in History," UWL; *Pioneer and Democrat,* April 25, 1856.

⁶⁶Wright to Jones, May 6 and 8, 1856, NA, RCA, RG 393, LR; William N. Bischoff, "The Yakima Campaign of 1856," *Mid-America* 31 (1949): 174-75; Mactavish to Smith, April 5, 1856, UWL; F. M. Sebring, "The Indian Raid on the Cascades," *Washington Historical Quarterly* 19 (1928): 98-100; Coe to Bradford, April 6, 1856, in *Oregon Native Son* (1899): 497.

⁶⁷Archer to Sister, January 5, 1856; Archer to Mother, March 30, 1856 and June 8, 1856, Maryland Historical Society (MHS), Baltimore. This collection contains numerous letters by Archer to his family pertinent to the Yakima War. Copies of some letters are also found in the Relander Collection.

⁶⁸Wright to Jones, May 8, 1856, NA, RCA, RG 393, LR.

⁶⁹Wright to Jones, May 9-11, 15, 1856, NA, RCA, RG 393, LR; Archer to Mother, June 8, 1856, MHS; Bischoff, "The Yakima Campaign," pp. 181-97.

⁷⁰Wright to Jones, June 11 and July 1, 1856, NA, RCA, RG 393, LR.

⁷¹Gibbs to Swan, January 7, 1857, in Swan, *The Northwest Coast,* p. 428.

⁷²Brown, *The Indian Side,* pp. 166-77, 181-84; Splawn, *Ka-mi-akin,* pp. 69-81.

⁷³Bancroft, *History of Washington,* p. 141. According to Bancroft, the soldiers flayed Peopeo Moxmox: "They skinned him from head to foot, and made razor straps of his skin."

⁷⁴Wright to Jones, May 9, June 11, 1856, NA, RCA, RG 393. Bischoff, "The Yakima Campaign," p. 178.

⁷⁵Wright to Jones, June 11, 1856, NA, RCA, RG 393.

⁷⁶Stevens to Shaw, May 20 and 22, 1856; Wright to Shaw, May 27, 1856, WSL.

⁷⁷Shaw to Tilton, July 24, 1856 in *Message of the Governor of Washington Territory,* p. 42. This document is a defense of Governor Stevens, and for Wool's side of the controversy over the war, see the many letters in *SED,* 34th Cong., 1st Sess., No. 66, SS 822; Josephy, *The Nez Perce,* pp. 369-70. Josephy suggests that Shaw's "Official Report" was edited and should be used with caution. For the original report, see "Stevens Correspondence, 1848-57," Yale University Library.

⁷⁸The Powder River referred to here flows east of the Blue Mountains of Oregon for approximately 150 miles before entering the Snake River. The quotes are respectively from Shaw to Tilton, July 24, 1856, *Message of the Governor,* p. 46; Tilton to Shaw, August 3, 1856, WSL.

⁷⁹Gates to Shaw, August 31 and Tilton to Stevens, September 8, 1856, WSL; Stevens to Steptoe, August 31, 1856, NA, RCA, RG 393, LR.

⁸⁰Stevens to Mannypenny, August 18, 1856, and "Official Proceedings of a Council held in the Walla Walla Valley," September 11-17, 1856 in NA, Records of the Office of Indian Affairs, Treaty Talks and Treaties; hereafter cited as ROIA.

[81]Stevens to Steptoe, September 18 and 19, and Steptoe to Wright, September 18, 1856, *HED,* 34th Cong., 3rd Sess., No. 5, SS 876.

[82]Wright to Mackall, October 30 and 31, 1856, NA, RCA, RG 393, LR.

[83]Wright to Mackall, December 4, 1856, NA, RCA, RG 393, LR.

[84]Steptoe to Wright, December 5, 1856, NA, RCA, RG 393, LR.

CHAPTER 7

[1]There are numerous works which trace this period, including some accounts by participants. See Waman C. Hembree, "Yakima Indian War Diary," *Washington Historical Quarterly* 16 (1925): 273-83; Plympton J. Kelly, *We Were Not Summer Soldiers: The Indian War Diary of Plympton J. Kelly, 1855-56;* Jerome Peltier and B. C. Payette, *Warbonnets and Epaulets;* Thomas W. Prosch, "The Indian War in Washington Territory," *Oregon Historical Quarterly* 16 (1915): 1-23; Benjamin F. Manring, *Conquest of the Coeur d'Alenes, Spokanes and Palouses;* Burns, *The Jesuits and the Indian Wars;* and Josephy, *The Nez Perce.*

[2]Steptoe to Mackall, April 17, 1858, *SED,* 35th Cong., 2d Sess., No. 1, SS 975. This document contains numerous letters, reports, and accounts of the Steptoe and Wright campaigns.

[3]Ibid. Chief Tilcoax was a rich man owning thousands of horses. While coastal newspapers blamed Kamiakin for the raid on Fort Walla Walla, sources closer to the scene of events, including Colonel Steptoe, believed Tilcoax was responsible.

[4]Owen to Nesmith, July 16, 1858, Annual Report, CIA, 1858, pp. 269-71; Jack Dozier, "The Coeur d'Alene Indians in the War of 1858," *Idaho Yesterdays* 5 (1961): p. 23; Brown, *The Indian Side,* pp. 317-18.

[5]Steptoe to Mackall, May 23, 1858, *SED,* 35th Cong., 2d Sess., No. 32, SS 984; hereafter cited as Steptoe's Report. In the same *SED,* see Joset to Congiato, June 27,1858; hereafter cited as Joset's Narrative. Also, see Lawrence Kip, *Army Life on the Pacific,* p. 9.

[6]Robert I. Burns, "Pere Joset's Account of the Indian War of 1858," *Pacific Northwest Quarterly* 38 (1947): 294-95; Brown, *The Indian Side,* p. 193.

[7]Steptoe to Grier, May 15, 1858 and Grier to Mackall, May 16, 1858, NA, RCA, RG 393, LR.

[8]Steptoe to Mackall, April 17, 1858, *SED,* 35th Cong., 2d Sess., No. 1, SS 975; Burns, "Pere Joset's Account," pp. 293, 295, 301.

[9]Burns, "Pere Joset's Account," pp. 294-95; Joset's Narrative.

[10]Ibid.; *Weekly Oregonian,* May 29, 1858; Burns, *The Jesuits and the Indian Wars,* pp. 204-05. According to a variety of accounts, some of the Indians represented at the Steptoe Battle include the Kalispel, Pend Oreille, Palouse, Coeur d'Alene, Spokane, Nez Perce, Walla Walla, Thompson, Lake, Kutenai, Okanogan, and Flathead Indians.

[11]Steptoe's Report.

[12]Ibid.; I. Ridgeway Trible, ed., "Captain C. S. Winder's Account of a Battle with the Indians," *Maryland Historical Magazine* 35 (1940): 57; John O'Neil, "Recollections of a Soldier," in E. F. Tannatt, ed., *Indian Battles in the Inland Empire,* pp. 6-7; Burns, *The Jesuits and the Indian Wars,* p. 212.

[13]Steptoe's Report.

[14]Ibid.; Burns, "Pere Joset's Account," p. 295; Manring, *Conquest,* p. 150. The Palouses, particularly Tilcoax, spread the rumor that Joset was in league with the Americans, supplying the *suyapo* with intelligence. Burns defends Joset in *The Jesuits and the Indian Wars,* p. 218, stating: "It has been suggested that because Joset brought a Coeur d'Alene delegation to Steptoe, he was not speaking for all the chiefs. But Joset had talked last night with the chiefs of the several tribes. He is explicit that "all the other chiefs as well Coeur d'Alenes as Spokanes," with the exception of the Palouses, were not united behind him for peace. In a moment

he would return to both the Spokane and Coeur d'Alene chiefs. This is understandable. During the several peace efforts subsequent to the battle, as during the 1856 troubles, the Jesuits did not work for the mission tribes alone. Colonel Wright could therefore later condemn the attack by the various tribes on Steptoe as "contrary to the orders of their chiefs.'"

[15]H. M. Chittenden and A. T. Richardson, eds., *Life, Letters and Travels of Father Pierre Jean DeSmet, S.J., 1801-1873, Missionary Labors and Adventures Among the Wild Tribes of the North American Indians, Embracing Minute Descriptions of their Manners, Customs, Modes of Warfare and Torture* . . . 2, p. 752.

[16]Joset's Narrative; Manring, *Conquest*, p. 97; Burns, *The Jesuits and the Indian Wars*, p. 221; W. E. Rosebush, *Frontier Steel, The Men and Their Weapons*, p. 326.

[17]Burns, *The Jesuits and the Indian Wars*, pp. 220-30.

[18]Gregg to Vancouver friend, n.d., *SED*, 35th Cong., 2d Sess., No. 32, SS 984. This letter also appeared in the *Weekly Oregonian*, May 29, 1858; hereafter cited as Gregg's Letter.

[19]Ibid.; Steptoe's Report; Trimble, "Winder's Account," p. 46; Manring, *Conquest*, p. 103.

[20]Gregg's Letter; Steptoe's Report.

[21]Ibid.

[22]Steptoe's Report

[23]Joset to Hoecken, June 17, 1858, *SED*, 35th Cong., 2d Sess., No. 1, SS 975.

[24]Ibid.; Joset's Narrative.

[25]*The Spokesman-Review*, August 30, 1931. Section 5 of this edition is devoted to the "pioneer days" of Spokane's history and was printed as part of that city's fiftieth anniversary celebration.

[26]Joset's Narrative.

[27]Jordon to Ingalls, May 22, 1858, NA, RCA, RG 393, LR; *Weekly Oregonian*, May 29, 1958; *Oregonian*, June 6, 1858; *Alta California*, June 9, 10, and 13, 1858.

[28]Brown, *The Indian Side*, pp. 189-90. General accounts of the Steptoe Battle are found in Victor, *Early Indian Wars;* Bancroft, *History of Washington;* Thomas B. Beall, "Pioneer Reminiscences," *Washington Historical Quarterly* 8 (1917): 83-90; S. J. Chadwick, "Colonel Steptoe's Battle," *Washington Historical Quarterly* 2 (1908): 333-43; and T. C. Elliott, "Steptoe Butte and Steptoe Battlefield," *Washington Historical Quarterly* 18 (1927): 243-53. For evidence of Kamiakin's lack of participation in the Steptoe Battle, see William C. Brown, "Trip with Tomio Kamiakin in 1928," Manuscripts and Archives, WSU.

[29]*Oregonian*, June 6, 1858.

[30]Burns, *The Jesuits and the Indian Wars*, p. 241.

[31]Ibid.; Clarke to AG, July 23, 1858, Clarke to Joset, June 25, 1858, and Wright to AG, May 26, 1858, *SED*, 35th Cong., 2d Sess., No. 1, SS 975.

[32]Congiato to Clarke, August 3, 1858, *SED*, 35th Cong., 2d Sess., No. 1, SS 975. For an interesting study of Leschi, see Della G. Emmons, *Leschi of the Nisqualies*.

[33]Burns, *The Jesuits and the Indian Wars*, pp. 266-68. It is impossible to determine the number of Palouses involved, and authors who purport to know are simply guessing.

[34]Kip, *Army Life*, p. 12. For an eyewitness account of the war and the subsequent hangings see G. B. Dandy's Reminiscences (1907) in the Brown Collection, Manuscripts and Archives, WSU.

[35]Chittenden and Richardson, *Life, Letters, and Travels* 2, p. 749.

[36]Burns, *The Jesuits and the Indian Wars*, pp. 271-74.

[37]John Mullan, "Topographical memoir and Map of Colonel Wright's Late Campaign Against the Indians of Oregon and Washington Territories," p. 11, *SED*, 35th Cong., 2d Sess., No. 32, SS 984; hereafter cited as Mullan, "Topographical Memoir."

[38]Ibid.; Kip, *Army Life*, p. 39. Kip had previously attended the Walla Walla Council and recorded his observations.

[39]Ibid., p. 12.

[40]Wright to Mackall, August 31, 1858, *SED,* 35th Cong., 2d Sess., No. 32, SS 984.

[41]Ibid.; Mullan, "Topographical Memoir," pp. 13-14; Cain's Report, *SED,* 36th Cong., 1st Sess., No. 2, SS 1024.

[42]Wright to Mackall, September 2, 1858, *SED,* 35th Cong., 2d Sess., No. 32, SS 984; Kip, *Army Life,* p. 55.

[43]Kip, *Army Life,* p. 55-57.

[44]Wright to Mackall, September 1, 1858, *SED,* 35th Cong., 2d Sess., No. 32, SS 984.

[45]Kip, *Army Life,* pp. 56-57.

[46]Wright to Mackall, September 2, 1858, *SED,* 35th Cong., 2d Sess., No. 32, SS 984.

[47]Ibid.

[48]Wright to Mackall, September 1, 1858, *SED,* 35th Cong., 2d Sess., No. 32, SS 984; Kip, *Army Life,* pp. 57-59.

[49]Wright to Mackall, September 6, 1858, *SED,* 35th Cong., 2d Sess., No. 32, SS 984; Kip, *Army Life,* p. 63. The details about Colestah were provided by Emily Peone, oral interviews by authors with Emily Peone, January-June, 1981.

[50]Ibid.,; Kip, *Army Life,* pp. 63-66.

[51]Ibid.

[52]*Weekly Oregonian,* September 18, 1858; Kip, *Army Life,* p. 66.

[53]Burns, *The Jesuit and the Indian Wars,* p. 297.

[54]Brown, *The Indian Side,* pp. 294, 310, 339-42.

[55]Kip, *Army Life,* p. 66.

[56]Ibid., p. 67; Wright to Mackall, September 9, 1858, *SED,* 35th Cong., 2d Sess., No. 32, SS 984.

[57]Kip, *Army Life,* p. 67.

[58]Wright to Mackall, September 9, 1858, *SED,* 35th Cong., 2d Sess., No. 32, SS 984.

[59]Ibid.

[60]Kip, *Army Life,* pp. 69-71; Brown, *The Indian Side,* pp. 252-56.

[61]Ibid., p. 71; Wright to Mackall, September 10, 1858, *SED,* 35th Cong., 2d Sess., No. 32, SS 984.

[62]Kip, *Army Life,* p. 71.

[63]Ibid.

[64]Statement of Mary Moses, daughter of Owhi and sister of Qualchin, n.d., Brown Collection, Manuscripts and Archives, WSU; oral interview by authors with Mary Jim, November 10, 1979.

[65]Kip, *Army Life,* pp. 83-85, 93-95.

[66]Ibid., p. 88.

[67]Ibid., p. 91; Wright to Mackall, September 15, 1858, *SED,* 35th Cong., 2d Sess., No. 32, SS 984.

[68]Kip, *Army Life,* p. 91.

[69]Ibid., pp. 67, 99-102; Wright to Mackall, September 24, 1858, *SED,* 35th Cong., 2d Sess., No. 32, SS 984.

[70]Kip, *Army Life,* pp. 104-05; Wright to Mackall, September 4, 1858, *SED,* 35th Cong., 2d Sess., No. 32, SS 984.

[71]Kip, *Army Life,* p. 104; Manring, *Conquest,* pp. 244-45.

[72]Mullan, "Topographical Memoir," pp. 40, 70.

[73]Kip, *Army Life,* p. 110.

[74]Ibid.; Mullan, "Topographical Memoir," p. 54.

[75]Wright to Mackall, September 30, 1858, *SED,* 35th Cong., 2d Sess., No. 32, SS 984.

[76]Kip, *Army Life,* p. 117.

[77]Mullan, "Topographical Memoir," p. 75; Wright to Mackall, September 30, 1858, *SED,* 35th Cong., 2d Sess., No. 32, SS 984.

[78]Kip, *Army Life,* pp. 117-18.

[79]Wright to Mackall, September 30, 1858, *SED,* 35th Cong., 2d Sess., No. 32, SS 984.

CHAPTER 8

[1] The events that unfolded in the lives of the various Palouse Indian groups were not uncommon among the Indian population as a whole in the United States. The military conquest of the Indian was often followed by the white settlement of Indian lands by Euro-Americans who perceived that they had a natural right to the soil. Indians were viewed as obstacles, and once hostilities subsided, whites expanded to lands formerly claimed. It was an old pattern in American history, but a very destructive one for the Palouse Indians.

[2] Kip, *Army Life,* p. 128; for a discussion of the concept of just wars and right of conquest, see Jennings, *The Invasion of America,* pp. 406, 44-45, 60-61, 125, 128; Francis Paul Prucha, *American Indian Policy in the Formative Years,* p. 40; Gary B. Nash, "The Image of the Indian in the Southern Colonial Mind." *William and Mary Quarterly* 29 (1972): 192-230.

[3] The Palouses had long recognized Kamiakin as an important Indian leader, but he was considered a Yakima chief until the beginning of the Yakima War of 1855 when many Palouses looked to him as their chief. Once Kamiakin movced to the Palouse Country, his band was composed of Palouses and Yakimas alike, if not other tribes as well. From the mid-1850s forward Kamiakin was recognized in the Indian community as a Palouse chief, but not the "Head Chief" of all Palouses.

[3] Hoekin to DeSmet, February 3, 1859 in Burns, *The Jesuits and the Indian Wars,* p. 314; DeSmet, *Life, Letters and Travels* 2, pp. 745-46.

[5] Ibid.

[6] Pierre DeSmet, *Life, Letters and Travels* 3, p. 967; DeSmet to Pleasanton, May 25, 1859, *HED,* 36th Cong., 1st Sess., No. 65, SS 1051.

[7] Ibid.

[8] Harney to Owen, March 28, 1859 and Harney to Scott, June 1, 1859, *HED,* 36th Cong., 1st Sess., No. 65, SS 1051; *Morning Oregonian,* June 4, 1859.

[9] Oral interviews by authors with Emily Peone, January through June, 1981; Meinig, *The Great Columbia Plain, p. 201; Josephy, The Nez Perce, p. 385.*

[10] Landsdale to Geary, April 27 and July 9, 1860, NA, WS, RG 75, LR.

[11] Oral interview by William C. Brown with Hay-Hay-Tah, July 21, 1932, in Brown's *Journal, 1931-38,* Brown Collection, Manuscripts and Archives, WSU; Brown, *The Indian Side,* pp. 181-83; oral interviews by authors with Emily Peone, January-June, 1981.

[12] Oral interview by Click Relander with Sophie Williams, no date, in Relander, "Colville and Palouse Note," pp. 46-47, Relander Collection; oral interviews by authors with Emily Peone, January-June, 1980.

[13] Thomas B. Beal, "Pioneer Reminiscences," *Washington Historical Quarterly* 8, (1917): 83-90; Splawn, *Ka-mi-akin,* pp. 8-9, 121-23; *Walla Walla Statesman,* June 2, 1865.

[16] Oral interviews by authors with Emily Peone, January-June, 1981; Winans to McKenny, February 5, 1871, NA, WS, RG 75, LR.

[15] Ibid.

[16] Winans to McKenny, March 6, 1871 and Harvey to Ross, May 26, 1870, Winans Collection, Manuscripts and Archives, WSU.

[18] Winans to Partee, November 18, 1870 in Winans' Reports, W 34, Box 147-4, Winans Collection, Manuscripts and Archives, WSU; Harvey to Ross, May 26, 1870, NA, WS, RG 75, LR.

[19] Washington Territorial Census, 1871, National Archives Microfilm 276, Reel 8.

[20] Oral interview by authors with Ray DeLong, July 19, 1980; J. B. Holt, "List of Pioneer Residents of Whitman County (1871)," *Spokesman Review,* January 15, 1922; *Morning Oregonian,* September 12, 1869; W. H. Lever, *An Illustrated History of Whitman County,* p. 360; Harry Painter, "New Light on Chief Kamiakin," *Walla Walla Union Bulletin,* March 18, 1945; oral interview by authors with Charles Jenkins, June 12, 1970; Cain to Ferry, July 26, 1878, Secretary of State Papers, WSL.

[21]Report of Gustavus Sohon in John Mullan, "Report of Lieutenant Mullan, in charge of the Construction of the Military Road from Fort Walla Walla to Fort Benton," pp. 95-101, *HED*, 36th Cong., 2d Sess., No. 44, SS 1099; hereafter cited as Mullan's *Report*.

[22]Ibid. The various reports included in Mullan's road survey comprise a substantial body of data which stimulated public interest in the Palouse Country and contributed to the white settlement of the region.

[23]Report of P. M. Engle in Mullan's *Report*, pp. 105-06.

[24]Mullan's *Report*, pp. 14-15

[25]*Walla Walla Statesman*, October 27, 1865; Josephy, *The Nez Perce*, pp. 392-400; Meinig, *The Great Columbia Plain*, pp. 208-14, 221-22.

[26]Holt, "List of Pioneer Residents," *Spokesman Review*, January 15, 1922; Meinig, *The Great Columbia Plain*, pp. 243-51. Meinig provides an excellent examination of the white settlement of the Palouse Country and his analysis of sources demonstrates the rapid invasion of the region by whites in the 1870s and 1880s. For an excellent study of the effects of white settlement in the region, see Deutsch, "Indian and White in the Inland Empire," pp. 44-51.

[27]Deutsch, "Indian and White in the Inland Empire," pp. 44-45.

[28]For specific information regarding the settlement of the Palouse Country, see Lever, *An Illustrated History of Whitman County*. For a microcosmic study of the settlement of one European ethnic group in the region, see Richard D. Scheuerman and Clifford E. Trafzer, *The Volga Germans: Pioneers of the Pacific Northwest*. Also, see Fred R. Yoder, "Pioneer Social Adaptation in the Palouse Country of Eastern Washington, 1870-1890," *Research Studies of the State College of Washington* 6 (1938): 931-59.

[29]W. McMicken, "Report of the Surveyor-General of Washington Territory," in report of the Secretary of Interior, *HED*, 43rd Cong., 1st Sess., No. 1, SS 1601.

[30]*Morning Oregonian*, April 18, 1873; Frank T. Gilbert, *Historic Sketches of Walla Walla, Whitman, Columbia and Garfield Counties, Washington Territory*, p. 439. For information regarding the changes in land uses, see Helmut K. Buechner, "Some Biotic Changes in the State of Washington particularly during the Century, 1853-1953," *Research Studies of the State College of Washington* 21 (1953): 154-91; Vernon Young, "Changes in Vegetation and Sod of Palouse Prairie caused by Overgrazing," *Journal of Forestry* 12 (1943): 834 38; J. S. Colton, "A Report on the Range Conditions of Central Washington," *Washington State Agricultural College Experiment Station Bulletin* 60 (190): 5-21; George W. Sutherland, "A Half Century in Eastern Washington," unpublished manuscript, Manuscripts and Archives, WSU.

[31]For Villard's remarkable career, see Henry Villard, *The Early History of Transportation in Oregon* and Scheuerman and Trafzer, *The Volga Germans*, pp. 118-24, 130-31.

[32]*Palouse Gazette*, September 29, 1877.

[33]*Walla Walla Union*, April 22, 1871.

[34]Holt, "Pioneer Residents of Whitman County," *Spokesman Review*, January 15, 1922; Splawn, *Ka-mi-akin*, pp. 266-67; Nelie B. Huntley, "The Coming of the Pioneers," *Colfax Gazette*, May 8, 1931.

[35]Winans to Milroy, August 31, 1872, NA, WS, RG 75, LR; Annual Report, CIA, 1872, p. 343; Brown, *The Indian Side*, p. 398; Sutherland, "A Half Century in Eastern Washington,"

[36]Annual Report, CIA, 1873, p. 157.

[37]*Idaho Signal*, May 21, 1873.

[38]Ibid.; *Walla Walla Union*, June 14, 1873.

[39]Sophie Williams' interview in Relander, "Colville and Palouse Notes," p. 45; Harry Painter, "New Light on Chief Kamiakin," in *Walla Walla Union Bulletin*, March 18, 1945. Emily Peone stated that the priest who baptized Kamiakin was called "Crowine" by the Indians, but she was unable to identify the man's name. There

is no mention of this baptism among the mission records that have been examined, but there are many sources—diaries, letters, notes—yet to be discovered and analyzed for Kamiakin's baptismal record.

[40]Splawn, *Ka-mi-akin,* pp. 8, 9, 121, 123.

[41]The sordid affair is best detailed in various pieces of correspondence found in Brown Collection, Manuscripts and Archives, WSU, particularly letters between Roland Huff and Brown.

[42]Huff to Brown, September 29, 1949, Brown Collection, Manuscripts and Archives, WSU; Painter, "New Light on Chief Kamiakin"; Splawn, *Ka-mi-akin,* p. 409; Cull White, "Kamiakin," unpublished manuscript, Cull White Collection, Manuscripts and Archives, WSU; Emily Adams, "Rock Lake: Lake of Mystery and Legend, *Colfax Gazette,* December 14, 1978.

[43]Oral interviews by authors with Emily Peone, January June, 1981; L. V. Mcwhorter, "Report of Trip to Mouth of Palouse River, July, 1939," unpublished manuscript, McWhorter Collection, Manuscripts and Archives, WSU.

CHAPTER 9

[1]Ralph Burcham, ed., "Orofino Gold," *Idaho Yesterdays* 4 (1960); 2-9; Bancroft, *History of Washington, Idaho, and Montana,* pp. 234-35; Josephy, *The Nez Perce,* pp. 691-95.

[2]McWhorter, *Hear Me,* p. 99. After the war in 1858, George Wright was promoted to general. His recommendation to Superintendent Geary to permit miners to dig for gold on the Nez Perce Reservation was an abridgement of assurances the general had made to his Nez Perce scouts during the war in 1858.

[3]Ibid.; Josephy, *The Nez Perce,* pp. 412-14.

[4]Josephy, *The Nez Perce,* pp. 412-22.

[5]Ibid., pp. 423-26; McWhorter, *Hear Me,* pp. 106-07. For details of the agreement of the money paid the Nez Perces, see Josephy, *The Nez Perce,* p. 429.

[6]Chief Joseph, "An Indian's View of Indian Affairs," *North American Review* 128 (1879): 412-33; hereafter all entries are cited from the same article published in Cyrus T. Brady, *Northwestern Fights and Fighters.* Joseph stated that "In the treaty councils the commissioners have claimed that our country had been sold to the Government. Suppose a white man should come to me and say, 'Joseph, I like your horses, and I want to buy them.' I say to him, 'No, my horses suit me, I will not sell them.' Then he goes to my neighbor, and says to him: 'Joseph has some good horses. I want to buy them, but he refuses to sell.' My neighbor answers, 'Pay me the money, and I will sell you Joseph's horses.' The white man returns to me and says, 'Joseph, I have bought your horses, and you must let me have them.' If we sold our lands to the Government, this is the way they were bought."

[7]Oral interview by authors with Mary Jim, November 9, 10, 1979.

[8]Monteith to J. Q. Smith, March 19, 1877 in Josephy, *The Nez Perce,* p. 493. "Report of Civil and Military Commission to Nez Perce Indians, Washington Territory and Northwest," Annual Report of the Secretary of Interior, 1877, pp. 607-09. For the best published source on Smohalla, see Relander, *Drummers and Dreamers.* Sharkey, "The Wanapums and the Priest Rapids Dam: Fulfillment of an Indian Prophecy"; Trafzer and Beach, "Smohalla, The Washani, and Religion as a Factor In Northwestern Indian History"; and Chapter 7, Mooney, "The Ghost Dance Religion."

[9]"Report of . . . Commission to Nez Perce Indians," Annual Report of the Secretary of Interior, 1877, pp. 607-09.

[10]Ibid.; Howard, *Nez Perce Joseph,* p. 30.

[11]Josephy, *The Nez Perce,* pp. 489-90.

[12]"Report of . . . Commission to Nez Perce Indians," Annual Report of the Secretary of Interior, 1877, pp. 607-09.

13Ibid.

14Ibid.

15Annual Report of the Secretary of War, 1877, 1, pp. 115-16; hereafter cited as Annual Report, SW. Also see, Chester A. Fee, *Chief Joseph,* p. 97.

16Annual Report, SW, 1877, 1, pp. 587-90; Howard, *Nez Perce Joseph,* pp. 37, 43. On March 14, 1877 Howard ordered two companies of cavalry armed with two Gatling Guns to prepare for action. He then ordered his soldiers to occupy the confluence of the Wallowa and Grande Ronde Rivers. When the soldiers arrived, Ollokot visited Monteith and requested another council with government officials which was forwarded to the commissioner of Indian affairs. A similar request reached the ears of Howard who agreed to meet with Ollokot on April 20, 1877. Ollokot and Howard parleyed at Fort Walla Walla where they agreed to hold another council. The Palouses and Nez Perces were then summoned to the second Lapwai Council.

17Howard, *Nez Perce Joseph,* p. 54.

18Ibid., p. 63; McWhorter, *Hear Me,* p. 171.

19McWhorter Collection, Manuscripts and Archives, WSU, Folder 213, B/70; McWhorter, *Hear Me,* pp. 172-73.

20McWhorter Collection, Manuscripts and Archives, WSU, Folder 213, B/37; McWhorter, *Hear Me,* pp. 172-73.

21McWhorter, *Hear Me,* p. 172.

22Ibid.

23McWhorter Collection, Manuscripts and Archives, WSU, Folder 213, B/37.

24Ibid. and Folder 213, B/70.

25Howard, *Nez Perce Joseph,* pp. 58-64. Toohoolhoolzote told Howard: "You have no right to compare us, grown men, to children. Children do not think for themselves. Grown men do think for themselves." Toohoolhoolzote concluded that the government in Washington, D.C., could not speak for the Indians, but Howard quickly refuted his assertion.

26Ibid., pp. 64-66.

27Joseph, "An Indian's View of Indian Affairs," p. 57.

28Howard, *Nez Perce Joseph,* p. 69.

29McWhorter Collection, Manuscripts and Archives, WSU, Folder 213, B/70.

30Howard, *Nez Perce Joseph,* p. 71; McWhorter, *Hear Me,* pp. 184-94.

31Joseph, "An Indian's View of Indian Affairs," p. 19.

32McWhorter Collection, Manuscripts and Archives, WSU, Folder 213, B/69.

33Howard, *Nez Perce Joseph,* p. 72.

34Oral interview by authors with Mary Jim, November 9, 10, 1979.

35Lucullus V. McWhorter, *Yellow Wolf: His Own Story,* p. 42; Joseph, *The Nez Perce,* p. 511.

36Oral interview by authors with Mary Jim, November 9, 10, 1979 and April 25, 1980.

37Oliver O. Howard, *My Life and Experiences among Our Hostile Indians,* pp. 262-64.

38Ibid., pp. 271-79.

39*New Northwest,* June 21, 1878; McWhorter, *Hear Me,* pp. 195-96. An excellent study of the beginning stages of the Nez Perce War is John D.McDermott, *Forlorn Hope: The Battle of White Bird Canyon and the Beginning of the Nez Perce War,* pp. 3-12. The first raid on the Salmon River occurred on June 13, 1877.

40Burns, *The Jesuits and the Indian Wars,* p. 392; Ray, "Native Villages and Grouping," p. 132.

41Davenport Letter, *Walla Walla Watchman,* June 22, 1877.

42*Lewiston Tribune,* June 23, 1877.

43*Walla Walla Watchman,* June 22, 1877; Level, *History of Whitman County,* pp. 235-36; George Sutherland, "A Half Century in Eastern Washington," unpublished manuscript, Oliphant Collection, Manuscripts and Archives, WSU.

44*Lewiston Teller,* June 24, 1855.

45*Walla Walla Watchman,* June 22, 1877; *Walla Walla Union,* June 23, 1877; and

Lever, *History of Whitman County,* pp. 235-36.

46*Walla Walla Watchman,* June 21, 1877; Lever, *History of Whitman County,* pp. 359, 411; John D. Butler, "Reminiscences of an Old Timer," Oliphant Collection, Manuscripts and Archives, WSU.

47*Lewiston Teller,* June 24, 1877; *Walla Walla Union,* June 23, 1877; and *Walla Walla Watchman,* June 29, 1877; oral interview by authors with Leonard Jones, July 16, 1980.

48D. S. Bowman's Story is found in Lever, *History of Whitman County,* pp. 235-36.

49*Walla Walla Union,* June 25, 1877; Burns, *The Jesuits and the Indian Wars,* p. 385.

50Joset to Simms, July 4, 1877 and Joseph Giorda, "Blessing in Disguise," in Joset and Giorda Collections, Oregon Province Archives of the Society of Jesus, Gonzaga University, Spokane, Washington; hereafter cited as OJ.

51Ibid.; Sqalgalt to Howard, June 21, 1877, Giorda Collection, OJ; McWhorter, *Yellow Wolf,* p. 36 and McWhorter, *Hear Me,* pp. 170-71, 273.

52*Walla Walla Union,* June 23, 1877.

53Joset Diary, June 23, 1877, Joset Collection, OJ.

54Burns, *The Jesuits and the Indian Wars,* p. 396; Giorda, "Blessing in Disguise," Giorda Collection, OJ.

55*Walla Walla Union,* June 23, 1877.

56Giorda, "Blessing in Disguise," Giorda Collection, OJ. This manuscript contains a valuable letter from Chief Seltice.

57*Lewiston Teller,* June 27, 1877; Burns, *The Jesuits and the Indian Wars,* p. 397.

58Ewart to Joset, June 27,1877, Joset Collection, OJ.

59Crowley to Ewart and Davenport in Gilbert, *Historic Sketches,* pp. 436-37.

60McWhorter, *Yellow Wolf,* p. 63. McWhorter provided this discussion of Kosooyeen on the same page in *Yellow Wolf:* "This intrepid young man's prewar name was Wewass Pahkalatkeikt (Five Sun-Rayed Bile). It is contended by some Nez Perces that the proper spelling is Kosooyoom, but since Yellow Wolf and other contemporaries pronounced the name as first spelled, that form will be used. Kosooyeen was reputed by his compatriots to be a brave warrior and adroit scout. A fine-looking young man, he resembled in many respects Chief Ollokot; both were general favorites with the people. He belonged to Chief Hahtalekin's Paloos, but was more often with Chief Joseph's band, because of his sister's marriage to one of its members. At the last battle Kosooyeen escaped to join Sitting Bull, but, returning with other refugees, he was arrested at Pendleton, Oregon, and banished to Indian Territory. He died on the Nez Perce Reservation in the early thirties. The writer knew him only as Luke Andrews."

61McDermott, *Forlorn Hope,* p. 34; McWhorter, *Yellow Wolf,* pp. 48-49 and McWhorter, *Hear Me,* p. 224. The fact that some Upper Palouses were related to Looking Glass and others is verified by several Palouse and Nez Perce elders, particularly Mrs. M. Lawyer who is the most informed individual on the Nez Perce Reservation today regarding the genealogies of tribal families.

62No attempt is made here to narrate the details of the Nez Perce War of 1877. Entire volumes have been written detailing the conflict. For the best volumes on the war, see Mark H. Brown, *Flight of the Nez Perce;* Josephy, *The Nez Perce;* McDermott, *Forlorn Hope;* Fee, *Chief Joseph;* Helen Howard, *Saga of Chief Joseph;* Howard, *Nez Perce Joseph;* McWhorter, *Hear Me;* McWhorter, *Yellow Wolf;* Bancroft, *History of Washington, Idaho, and Montana;* and Merrill D. Beal, *"I Will Fight No More Forever": Chief Joseph and the Nez Perce War.*

63Peter Ronan, *Historical Sketches of the Flathead Indian Nation,* pp. 64-66; McWhorter, *Hear Me,* pp. 347-54; McWhorter, *Yellow Wolf,* p. 107; *New Northwest,* December 27, 1878. The only trouble encountered by the Palouses and Nez Perces occurred at the eastern end of the Lolo Trail at Fort Missoula, Montana. There the Indians met a few troops under Captain Charles C. Rawn, but no conflict developed after the Indians agreed to ride through the Bitterroot Valley without disturbing the white settlers or their property. Because Rawn refused to engage the

Indians or to impede their escape, his post was nicknamed "Fort Fizzle."

[64]Josephy, *The Nez Perce,* pp. 563-72, 77-78; McWhorter, *Hear Me,* p. 369.

[65]Gibbon's Report, Annual Report, SW, 1, 1876-1877, pp. 501-05; also see Gibbon's, "The Battle of the Big Hole," *Harper's Weekly* 39 (1895): 1215-16 and 1235-36; McWhorter, *Yellow Wolf,* p. 112; G. O. Shields, "The Battle of the Big Hole," in Brady, *Northwestern Fights and Fighters,* pp. 164-90.

[66]Peopeo Tholekt to McWhorter, July 1928 in McWhorter, *Hear Me,* p. 380.

[67]See Wounded Head's Narrative and Young White Bird's Story in McWhorter, *Hear Me,* pp. 372, 376.

[68]McWhorter, *Yellow Wolf,* p. 119.

[69]Ibid.

[70]Beal, *"I Will Fight No More Forever,"* pp. 161-229; Brown, *Flight of the Nez Perce,* chapters 16-20; *New Northwest,* August 24, September 14, October 12, 1877; Charles E. S. Wood, "Indian Epic Is Re-Told," *The Spectator,* September 14, 1929; McWhorter, *Yellow Wolf,* pp. 162-218; Howard, *Nez Perce Joseph,* pp. 226-69; McWhorter, *Hear Me,* pp. 404-77; Josephy, *The Nez Perce,* pp. 590-612; Narrative of Peopeo Tholekt, McWhorter Collection, Manuscripts and Archives, WSU.

[71]McWhorter, *Yellow Wolf,* pp. 187-205; McWhorter, *Hear Me,* pp. 478-82; Henry Romlyn, "The Capture of Chief Joseph and His Nez Perce Indians," *Contributions of the Historical Society of Montana* 2 (1896): 286; Josephy, *The Nez Perce,* pp. 612-18; Brown, *Flight of the Nez Perces,* chapters 22-25.

[72]McWhorter, *Hear Me,* pp. 480-90; Josephy, *The Nez Perce,* pp. 619-25; McWhorter, *Yellow Wolf,* p. 214-17; Charles E. S. Wood, "The Pursuit and Capture of Chief Joseph," in Fee, *Chief Joseph,* pp. 324-26. Primary sources on the meeting between Joseph and Miles include Affidavit of Tom Hill, "Memorial of the Nez Perce Indians, Residing in the State of Idaho to the Congress of the United States," *SED,* 62nd Cong., 1st Sess., No. 97, SS 6108; Lovell Jerome, "Indian Battle Retold," *The Otsego Journal,* July 17, 1930; Miles' Report, December 27, 1877, Annual Report, SW, 1, 1876-1877, p. 629; and Nelson A. Miles, *Personal Recollections and Observations,* p. 276.

[73]Howard's Report, December 27, 1877, Annual Report, SW, 1, 1876-1877, pp. 630-31.

[74]McWhorter, *Yellow Wolf,* p. 224.

[75]Ibid., p. 225; Joseph, "An Indian's View of Indian Affairs," p. 429.

[76]Wood, "An Indian Epic," *The Spectator;* Wood to McWhorter, January 31, 1936, McWhorter Collection, WSU, Folder 181.

[77]Joseph's speech was reportedly transcribed by Charles Erskine Scott Wood and translated by Nez Perce scout. The speech is found in Howard's Report, December 27, 1877, Annual Report, SW, 1, 1876-1877, pp. 630-31. In his article, "The Chief Joseph Myth," *Montana* 22 (1972): 2-17, Mark H. Brown presents a convincing case that Joseph never delivered the speech and that Wood fabricated the words. Also see C. E. S. Wood, "Chief Joseph, the Nez Perce," *The Century Magazine* 6 (1884): 141-42; *San Francisco Chronicle,* November 9, 1877. The most important part of the speech was presented as follows: 'Tell General Howard I know his heart. What he told me before I have in my heart. I am tired of fighting. Our chiefs are killed. Looking Glass is dead. The old men are all killed. It is the young men who say Yes or No. He who led the young men is dead. It is cold and we have no blankets. The little children are freezing to death. My people, some of them, have run away to the hills and have no blankets, no food; no one knows where they are, perhaps freezing to death. I want time to look for my children and see how many of them I can find. Maybe I shall find them among the dead. Hear me, my chiefs, I am tired; my heart is sick and sad. From where the sun now stands, I will fight no more forever."

[78]The number of Indians who surrendered at Bear Paws varies, but 431 arrived at Fort Leavenworth, Kansas, on December 4, 1877. More than 431 surrendered, for some of the Indians died of wounds and exposure during their journey into exile. No record exists telling us the number of Palouses who surrendered. For details

of the order to remove the Palouse and Nex Perce to the Indian Territory, see Annual Report, SW, 1876-1877, p. 15. For the best discussion of the removal, see chapter 24 of Beal, *"I Will Fight No More Forever";* Brown, *Flight of the Nez Perce,* pp. 410-11; Clifford E. Trafzer, "The Palouse in Eekish Pah," *American Indian Quarterly* 9 (1985): 169-82.

[79]S.T.T. to Editor, July 19, 1878, *Council Fire,* August, 1878.

[80]Ibid.

[81]Alan Osborne, "The Exile of the Nez Perce in Indian Territory, 1878-1885," *The Chronicles of Oklahoma* 56 (1978-79): 453-58; Annual Report, CIA, 1878, pp. 33-34.

[82]Whiteman to Hoyt, June 16, 1879, Office of Indian Affairs, Ponca Agency (PA), NA, LR, File W-1388/1879; Trafzer, "The Palouse in Eekish Pah," pp. 172-77.

[83]Husishusis Kute was considered the spiritual leader of the non-Christian Palouses and Nez Perces. When he returned to the Northwest, he first took a group of Indians to the Nez Perce Reservation in Idaho before joining other Palouses on the Colville Reservation in Washington. There he continued his religion and the Washani faith, commonly called the Seven Drums, is a live and viable faith to this day.

[84]"Visit of Commissioners Fisk and Stickley to Colorado and Indian Territory," *Tenth Annual Report of the Board of Indian Commissioners for 1878,* pp. 47, 51; "Speech of Senator Thomas C. McCreery on Transfer of Indian Department," February 10, 1879, *Congressional Record* 45th Cong., 3d Sess., No. 8, pp. 115-55; "Testimony of Chief Joseph, the Interpreter, and H. H. Gregg," October 7, 1878, *Senate Miscellaneous Documents (SMD)* 45th Cong., 3d Sess., SS 1835.

[85]Washington, D.C., *Evening Star,* January 16, 1879; *Washington Post,* January 16, 1879.

[86]*Council Fire,* February, 1879.

[87]Joseph, "An Indian's View of Indian Affairs." In May,1879, a month after Joseph's article appeared, the *North American Review* carried a rebuttal by General Howard entitled "The True Story of the Wallowa Campaign."

[88]The influence of the article cannot be overstated. See J. Stanley Clark, "The Nez Perce in Exile," *Pacific Northwest Quarterly* 36 (1945): 218 19, 228-29; Osborne, "The Exile of the Nez Perce," pp. 455-57, 468-70.

[89]*Council Fire,* October, 1879.

[90]McNeil to Hoyt, April 24, 1879, NA, OIA, Inspector's Files, M-989.

[91]*Council Fire,* June, 1883; Kate C. McBeth, *The Nez Perce Since Lewis and Clark,* pp. 97-101.

[92]For Atkins' orders to return the Palouse and Nez Perce to the Northwest, see *HED* 48th Cong., 2d Sess., No. 88, SS 2302; also see McBeth, *The Nez Perce Since Lewis and Clark,* pp. 97-101.

[93]Clark, "The Nez Perce in Exile," pp. 230-31; Berlin B. Chapman, "The Nez Perce in Indian Territory: An Archival Study," *Oregon Historical Quarterly* 1 (1949): 121; Ernest V. Chappell, *The Nez Perce in Kay County, Oklahoma,* p. 5; McWhorter, *Yellow Wolf,* pp. 288-92.

CHAPTER 10

[1]*Spokane Times,* May 29, 1879.

[2]Newspapers in the Northwest for the period between 1870 and 1890 are filled with articles and editorials regarding Indian removal. The same is true of the Annual Reports, CIA and the Annual Reports SW, 1870-1890. Specifically, see Deutsch, "Indian and White in the Inland Northwest," pp. 44 -51.

[3]Henry Villard, "Two Railroad Reports on Northwest Resources," *Pacific Northwest Quarterly* 37 (1946): 182.

[4]Ibid.; United States Bureau of Census, Tenth Census of the United States, 1880; *Palouse Gazette,* March 21, 1879.

[5]*Palouse Gazette,* February 2, 1878.

[6]See Howard's comments regarding suspected Palouse Indian involvement in the

Bannock War in the Annual Report, SW, 2, 1878, pp. 649-50.

[7]Ibid.; Howard, *My Life and Experiences,* pp. 35-51; *Palouse Gazette,* June 8, 1878; Ruby and Brown, *The Cayuse Indians,* pp. 283-84; George F. Brimlow, *The Bannock Indian War of 1878,* pp. 124-44.

[8]*Palouse Gazette,* July 6, 1878.

[9]Pambrun, *Sixty Years on the Frontier,* pp. 130-31.

[10]Waughaskie was the son of Umtippe, the man who carried the body of Nice Whitman from the river to her parents in 1840. Both men were of Cayuse descent, but Waughaskie married a Palouse Indian and was considered a Palouse himself. He was often identified as a Palouse chief, despite the fact that he was neither a Palouse, nor a chief. However, the error is understandable given the social structure of Sahaptin-speaking people who readily accepted individuals from other tribes.

[11]McWhorter, "Report on a Trip to the Mouth of the Palouse River, July, 1939," McWhorter Collection, Manuscripts and Archives, WSU.

[12]Splawn, *Ka-mi-akin,* pp. 311-17. Splawn served as interpreter for the seven Umatilla Indians at their trial in Yakima. They were all convicted of murder and sentenced to be hanged. They escaped from prison twice, and two men were killed during the second escape by gunshot wounds. The other two were hanged.

[13]*Palouse Gazette,* July 13,1878.

[14]Ibid., July 20, 1878.

[15]Ibid., July 26, 1878.

[16]Ibid., January 31, 1879.

[17]Ibid., July 6, 1878 and August 2, 1878.

[18]Ibid., August 2, 1878.

[19]Pambrun, *Sixty Years on the Frontier,* pp. 128-29; *Palouse Gazette,* July 2, 1878. The works on Smohalla include Trafzer and Beach, "Smohalla, The Washani, and Religion as a Factor in Northwestern Indian History"; and Relander, *Drummers and Dreamers.*

[20]Ibid. Pambrun disliked Thomash and the other followers of the Washani, and the old resident of the Plateau used his influence with the military to hold Thomash captive. However, beyond his personal influence with the military, Pambrun had no power to hold Thomash. Pambrun had no position within the government at the time Thomash was held.

[21]Pambrun, *Sixty Years on the Frontier,* p. 129.

[22]Oral interviews by authors with Mary Jim, May 1, 1977, April 2, November 10, 17, 1979, and April 25, 1980.

[23]*Walla Walla Union,* April 17, 1975; oral interview by authors with Isaac Patrick, May 8, 1981; Brown, *The Indian Side,* pp. 390-93. Because their sister married a prominent member of the Showaway family on the Umatilla Reservation, Wolf, Thomash, and their brothers were frequent visitors to that reservation. Wolf married a granddaughter of Owhi whose mother was the beautiful woman who had entered Wright's camp with Qualchin. This woman was married to Qualchin, and her name was Whiststalks. Through her and other family relations, Wolf was a member of a very powerful network within the Indian community. His descendents live on the Yakima, Umatilla, and Warm Springs Reservations.

[24]Mooney, "The Ghost Dance Religion," pp. 716-21.

[25]George Hunter, *Reminiscences of an Old Timer,* pp. 428-29; Hunter to Shurz, February 17, 1880 in Relander, *Drummers and Dreamers,* p. 109; Brooks to Wilbur, March 12, 1880, Yakima Agency Letterbooks, NA, WS, RG 75; hereafter cited as Yakima Letterbooks.

[26]Wilbur to Brooks, April 6, 1880, Yakima Letterbooks.

[27]Ibid.

[28]Ibid.

[29]Wilbur to Powell, April 19, 1880, Yakima Letterbooks.

[30]Annual Report, CIA, 1881, pp. 173-74.

[31]Monteith to Price, December 30,1882, NA, WS, RG 75, LR.

[32]Annual Report, CIA, 1884, pp. 173-74.

[33]Ibid.

[34]Ibid.

[35]Hunter, *Reminiscences,* pp. 364-65.

[36]Ibid., pp. 412-13.

[37]Howard, *My Life and Experiences,* pp. 350-51.

[38]Ibid. Howard made an agreement with Quetalakin of the Columbias to form a new reservation from the Okanogan River to the Columbia River. By Executive Order the Colville Reservation was established on April 19, 1879.

[39]Mooney, "The Ghost Dance Religion," pp. 716-20.

[40]In 1884 Agent Milroy characterized Kotaiaquan as "the chief of the most refactory band" on the reservation. Earlier that year Milroy demanded that Kotaiaquan's children attend the agency school. When he refused to send his children to school, Milroy arrested the leader and chained him to a cell for two weeks until he consented to send his children to school. Later that year, Kotaiaquan challenged Milroy again over the same matter which led to a short exchange of gunfire between agency police and Kotaiquan's band. See the Annual Report, CIA, 1885, pp. 200-01.

[41]MacMurray was one of the few whites to witness "a grand ceremonial service" of the Washani religion. See Mooney, "The Ghost-Dance Religion," p. 723; oral interviews by authors with Mary Jim, November 10, 17, 1979.

[42]Mooney, "The Ghost-Dance Religion," p. 723.

[43]MacMurray identified Kotaiaquan as Kamiakin's son, which was not true. More likely Kotaiaquan was the son of Showaway and therefore the nephew of Kamiakin.

[44]Annual Report, CIA, 1884, p. 174.

[45]Ibid.

[46]Hunter, *Reminiscences,* pp. 372-75; Register of Entries, Whitman County, Washington, 1885-1900, Pioneer Title Company, Colfax, Washington; Manring to McWhorter, November 8, 1939, McWhorter Collection, Manuscripts and Archives, WSU. Washington homestead entries for Palouse Indians near the mouth of the Palouse River include the following: "Young Charlie, Young Bones, Swenee, Kamiakin, Lean, Fisher, Toch Sites, Toch-o-toch-ite, Pol-o-cotts, Williams, Old Charley and Palouse Jack." Final patents for Indian homesteads were filled on July 17, 1894. Also, see "Umatilla Notes," Relander Collection.

[47]Hunter, *Reminiscences,* pp. 372-75. Hiyouwath was the grandson of Waughaskie and Juklous the grandson of Hahtalekin.

[48]*Northern Pacific Railroad Company vs. Fisher (Indian),* November 26, 1886, in Sam Fisher file, McGregor Land and Livestock Company, Hooper, Washington; hereafter cited as McGregor Company Records.

[49]*Register of Entries, Whitman County, Washington, 1885-1900,* Pioneer Title Company; Manring to McWhorter, November 8, 1939, McWhorter Collection, Manuscripts and Archives, WSU; Relander, *Drummers and Dreamers,* p. 103. For interesting details on individual Palouses and their relationship with one prominent white family in southeastern Washington, see the Margaret Pettyjohn Collection, Penrose Memorial Library, Whitman College, Walla Walla, Washington.

[50]*Northwest Magazine* 5 (1887): 33; Annual Report, CIA, 1890, p. 231; oral interview by authors with Isaac Patrick, May 8, 1981.

[51]Wilbur *Register,* June 30, 1893 and William C. Brown, *Journal, 1931-38* (including Hay Hay Tah interview), Brown Collection, Manuscripts and Archives, WSU.

[52]"Colville and Palouse Notes," Peter Dan Moses' Testimony, Relander Collection; Relander, *Drummers and Dreamers,* p. 108; Cule White Papers, Robert H. Ruby Collection, Moses Lake, Washington.

[53]*Spokesman Review,* May 4, 1909; oral interview by authors with Isaac Patrick, May 8, 1981. Husishusis Moxmox died by drowning in the Umatilla River on May 3, 1909.

[54]Kamiakin's son, Lukash, proceeded his family to the Colville Reservation where he married into the family of Chief Moses. The Columbia chief had searched for an appropriate suitor for his daughter, Sinsingt, and Moses wanted her to marry

a man of equal aristocratic heritage. He chose Lukash, a son of Kamiakin. Moses soon became the proud grandfather of a girl named Nellie. While on a trip to Spokane Falls, Lukash was murdered in an axe slaying by Puckmiakin, an Okanogan Indian, who dealt in the liquor trade. See the Annual Report, CIA, 1886, p. 232; oral interviews by authors with Emily Peone, January-June, 1981; Annual Report, Secretary of Interior, 1886, pp. 449-50.

[55]Annual Report, CIA, 1897.

[56]Ibid.

[57]Oral interview by authors with Andrew George, November 15, 1980.

CHAPTER 11

[1]Relander, *Drummers and Dancers,* pp. 115-16.

[2]Oral interviews by authors with Mary Jim, May 1, 977, April 2, November 10, 17, 1979, and April 25, 1980. The Palouse burial site (45FR36) is located in Franklin County, Washington. The site was excavated by archaeologists in the summer of 1964. The archaeologists determined the cemetery had been utilized from the 1840s to 1910. The site had several multiple burials of children indicating its use during epidemics. See Roderick Sprague, "The Descriptive Archaeology of the Palus Burial Site, Lyon's Ferry, Washington," *Washington State University Report of Investigations* 32 (1965). And for an excellent source on Palus Village, see L. V. McWhorter, "Report of Trip to Mouth of Palouse River, July 1939," unpublished manuscript, McWhorter Collection, Doc. 1529, Manuscripts and Archives, WSU.

[3]For information on Sam Fisher and his Appaloosa horses, see Frank G. Roe, *The Indian and the Horse,* pp. 154-55. The specific information on Fisher was found in the Sam Fisher file, McGregor Company Records.

[4]The remarkable story of the McGregors and their settlement of the Palouse Country is found in Alexander C. McGregor, *Counting Sheep: From Open Range to a Business on the Columbia Plateau.*

[5]Sam Fisher File, McGregor Company Records.

[6]Parrott to Walla Walla Register and Receiver, October 30, 1920 in Sam Fisher File, McGregor Company Records.

[7]*Harrison v. Fisher,* United States Land Office, Spokane, Washington, August 3, 1928, Commissioner of Indian Affairs George R. Wickham to Walla Walla Register and Receiver, October 23, 1922 in Sam Fisher File, McGregor Company Records.

[8]Ibid.; also see Relander, *Drummers and Dreamers,* p. 115.

[9]Sam Fisher File and Maurice McGregor to Department of Anthropology, Washington State College, January 10, 1923, McGregor Company Records, oral interview by authors with Sherman McGregor, March 17, 1979.

[10]Oral interviews by authors with Mary Jim, November 10-17, 1979. Big Island was one of two islands situated two miles upstream from present-day Leavy, Washington. Between 1957 and 1960 the burials were excavated by archaeologists. See Richard Daugherty, "Excavations in the Ice Harbor Reservoir, 1957-1960: A Preliminary Report," *Washington State University Report of Investigations* 10 (1961). For the information of Chief Big Sunday, see *Spokesman Review,* May 29, 1911.

[11]Oral interviews by authors with Mary Jim,November 10-17, 1979; Jack Briggs, "Who Took Indians' Land?," *Tri-City Herald,* April 31, 1980. Since Chowatyet's (Fishhook Jim's) homestead was still registered in 1959, the Army Corps of Engineers filed a condemnation suit to determine the ownership of the land. Ice Harbor Dam flooded eighty-seven acres of the Jim homestead valued at $3,800 — $43.68 per acre — which was divided among eighteen heirs. The corps determined that since Mary Jim and her family did not maintain year-round residence (she was away to gather food, visit relatives, and tend to her children), none of the Palouses were entitled to government housing, even though the government built homes for the Wanapums at Priest Rapids.

[12]"Colville and Palouse Notes," Relander Collection. A discussion of the elder's efforts to perpetuate the native religion of his people is found in Verne F. Ray, "The Bluejay Character in the Plateau Spirit Dance," *American Anthropologist* 39 (1937): 593-601; June Randolf, "Witness of Indian Religion," *Pacific Northwest Quarterly* 48 (1957): 139-45; oral interviews by authors with Emily Peone, January-June, 1981.

[13]William C. Brown, "Trip with Tomeo Kamiakin in 1928," notebook, Brown Collection, Manuscripts and Archives, WSU.

[14]Oral interview by authors with Ida Desautel, October 20, 1981.

[15]Paul M. Niebel, "Petitioners' Proposed Findings of Fact, Before the Indian Claims Commission, Docket No. 161," and I. S. Weissbrodt, "Petitioners' Proposed Findings of Fact, Before the Indian Claims Commission, Docket No. 224," Indian Claims, NA, RG 279; Click Relander, *The Yakimas: Treaty Centennial, 1855-1955,* p. 55; *Indian Claims Commission Decisions* 7, pp. 795-96.

[16]"Commission's Findings of Fact, Docket Nos. 161 and 224, July 28, 1959," *Indian Claims Commission Decisions* 7, pp. 795-96. Docket 222 was formally accepted by the commissioners on July 29, 1963. See also "Commissioners' Additional Findings of Fact, Dockets Nos. 161, 222 and 224, July 29, 1963," *Indian Claims Commission Decisions* 12, pp. 66-67, 302, 341-45, 355, 360. Also, oral interview by authors with Shirley Palmer, December 7, 1982.

[17]"Commission's Interlocutionary Order, Docket No. 161, 222, and 224, July 29, 1963," *Indian Claim Commission Decisions* 12, p. 391b. Ray had conducted considerable fieldwork among the Plateau Tribes in 1928 and 1937 and had worked with informants of all of the tribes involved in the litigation long before the claims commission was created. His own research was supplemented by an exhaustive review of primary source materials with particular emphasis on the work of Dr. George Gibbs, the ethnologist who had worked with Governor Stevens between 1853 and 1855. Ray testified on the aboriginal land use, extent of territory, and village locations for each of the tribes whose leaders were listed as signatories of the Yakima Treaty. According to his research the area exclusively claimed by the Palouse Indians in the middle of the nineteenth century covered an area roughly along the entire course of the Palouse River to the Washington-Idaho boundary, along the Snake River from Alpowa to the Palouse village of Khalotus (about fifteen miles downstream from Palus), all the land between these two rivers and the Deadman Creek watershed south of the Snake River. Within this vast area he documented the existence of thirty-four Palouse Villages. The remaining lands along the lower Snake River to Pasco, Ray ascribed to the Wanapum tribe.

[18]"Opinion of the Commission, Dockets Nos. 161, 222 and 224, April 5, 1965," *Indian Claims Commission Decisions* 15, pp. 227, 231b. The Claims Commission specified the boundaries of Palouse Country on the basis of "exclusive use and occupation in Indian fashion." For Palouse this was defined in the following terms. 'Beginning at the westernmost point of Kahlotus Lake, thence northerly to the divide separating the waters of Rattlesnake Canyon, thence northeasterly to Lancaster, Washington, thence easterly to Steptoe, Washington, thence southerly to Wawawai, Washington, thence westerly along the Snake River to a point opposite Devils Canyon, thence northwesterly along said canyon to the place of beginning.'

[19]Alalumti Kamiakin was born at the village of Almota (Alamotin) in January 1885 and was the daughter of Tom Pahween, a prominent Palouse leader from that village. Alalumti moved to the Colville Reservation when her family was forced there around 1895. For information on Cleveland's death, see "Chief Kamiakin, A Great Indian, Dies," *Wenatchee Daily World,* September 4, 1959; oral interviews by authors with Mary Jim, November 10, 17, 1979.

[20]The authors attended a first salmon ceremony, a root feast, and a naming ceremony of the Palouse and Wanapum Indians. The description contained here was of a root feast and naming ceremony celebrated on the Snake River in 1980. Mary Jim and several other Palouses still own land along the Snake River, although most of it has been flooded by reservoirs behind dams.

BIBLIOGRAPHY

MANUSCRIPT COLLECTIONS

Archdiocesan Archives, Seattle, Washington: Dellanoy Collection, including the Brouillet Letters.

Bancroft Library, University Of California, Berkeley: Joset Papers and Crawford Narrative.

Bieneke Library, Yale University, New Haven, Connecticut: Coe, Landsdale, Mason, Mercer, Miller, Spalding, Stevens, and Whitman Collections.

Department of American Indian Studies, San Diego State University, San Diego, California: Birkby, George, Jim, Jones, Kamiakin, Nightwalker, Patrick, Peone Interviews; Bartlett, Scheuerman, and Seeman Manuscripts; Palouse Indian Calendar; Kamiakin Genealogy.

Department of Botany, Washington State University, Pullman: Gill Field Ethnobotanical Notes.

Federal Records Center, Seattle, Washington: Simms Letters, General Service Administration Records, Record Group 75.

Houghton Library, Harvard University, Cambridge, Massachusetts: American Board of Commissioners for Foreign Missions Collections.

Hudson's Bay Company Archives, Provincial Archives, Winnipeg, Manitoba: Journals, 1831-32, Incoming Correspondence, 1827-29, District Reports, 1827-29, George Simpson Correspondence.

Huntington Library, San Marino, California: Cornelius Collection, Fort Dalles and Fort Simcoe Letterbooks.

Idaho State Historical Society, Boise: Nez Perce Agency Letterbooks and Nez Perce Allotment Book.

Library of Congress, Washington, D.C.: McClellan Collection.

Manuscripts and Archives, Washington State University Library, Pullman: Brown, DeSmet, Deutch, Kuykendal, McWhorter, Oliphant, Simms, Southerland, and Winans Collections.

Maryland Historical Society, Baltimore: Archer Collection.

McGregor Land and Livestock Company, Hooper, Washington: Sam Fisher File.

National Archives, Washington, D.C.: Records of the Bureau of Indian Affairs, War Department, State Department, Cartographic Division, Nez Perce War File, and Indian Claims Commission.

Oregon Historical Society, Portland: Geary, Gibbs, Nesmith Collections, Oregon and Washington Volunteer Soldiers' Papers.

Oregon Province Archives of the Society of Jesus, Crosby Library, Gonzaga University, Spokane, Washington: Cataldo, DeSmet, and Joset Collections.

Oregon State Archives, Salem: Oregon and Washington Volunteer Soldiers' Papers.

Pacific Northwest Collection, University of Washington Library, Seattle: Haller, Stevens, and Swan Collections.

Pioneer Title Company, Colfax, Washington: Register of Entries, Palouse Indian Homesteads.

Robert H. Ruby Collection, Moses Lake, Washington: Cull White Papers.

Special Collections, University of Oregon Library, Eugene: Palmer Collection; Nez Perce Agency Letterbook, 1871-79; Cayuse and Yakima War Papers.

Spokane Public Library, Spokane, Washington: DeSmet, Monteith, and Stevens Collections; Oregon and Washington Volunteer Soldiers' Papers.

State Historical Society of Washington, Tacoma: Interview of Spokan Garry's daughter.

Washington State Library, Olympia: Wool Collection; Governor's Letterbooks, 1853-55; Oregon and Washington Volunteer Soldiers' Papers.
Washington State Military Archives, Camp Murray, Tacoma: Washington Territorial Military Records.
Yakima Valley Regional Library, Yakima, Washington: Relander Collection.

ORIGINAL SOURCES AND SPECIAL STUDIES

Allen, Paul. *History of the Expedition Under the Command of Captains Lewis and Clark.* London: Longman, Hurst, Rees, Orme, and Brown, 1814.

Anderson, Butler P. "Letter in Regard to Chief Leschi, May 4, 1858." *Washington Historical Quarterly* 1 (1906-07):59.

Ault, Nelson A., ed. *The Papers of Lucullus Virgil McWhorter.* Pullman, Washington: Washington State College, 1959.

Barker, Burt B., ed. *Letters of Dr. John McLoughlin Written at Fort Vancouver 1829-32.* Portland: Binsford and Mort, 1948.

Bartlett, Grace. "The Appaloosa." Unpublished manuscript. Bartlett's private collection, Joseph, Oregon.

Bleknap, George P. "Authentic Account of the Murder of Dr. Whitman." The *History of a Pamphlet* 55 (1961):319-46.

Bischoff, William N. "The Yakima Indian War: 1855-1856." Ph.D. dissertation, Loyola University of Chicago, 1950.

Bjarke, Nels. *The Indian War, 1855-56, Pro and Con.* Pamphlet of speech by Judge James Wickersham, 1893. Tacoma, Washington, 1949.

Blanchet, Francis Norbert. *Historical Sketches of the Catholic Church of Oregon.* Portland: Catholic Sentinel, 1878.

Brouilett, J. B. A. *Authentic Account of the Murder of Dr. Whitman.* Portland, Oregon: Metropolitan Press, 1869.

Brown, William Compton. *The Indian Side of the Story.* Spokane: C. W. Hill Printing Company, 1961.

Chalfant, Stewart. "Ethno-historical Report on Aboriginal Land Occupancy and Utilization by the Palus Indians." Defense Exhibit 69, United States Indian Claims Commission, National Archives, Record Group 279.

Chittenden, H. M. and A. T. Richardson, eds. *Life, Letters and Travels of Father Pierre Jean DeSmet, S.J., 1801-1873, Missionary Labors and Adventures Among the Wild Tribes of the North American Indians, Embracing Minute Descriptions of their Manners, Customs, Modes of Warfare and Torture . . . .* 4 Vols., New York: Francis P. Harper, 1905.

Clark, Ella E. "George Biggs' Account of Indian Mythology in Oregon and Washington Territories." *Oregon Historical Quarterly* 56 (1955):293-325.

Coan, Charles F. "Federal Indian Policy in the Pacific Northwest, 1849-1870." Ph.D. dissertation, University of California, 1920.

Cox, Ross. *Adventures on the Columbia River.* 2 vols. London: H. Colburn and R. Bentley, 1831.

Coyote, Barney Old. "An Indian's Appreciation." *Indian Sentinel* 2 (1921):295.

Curtis, Edward S. *Indian Days of the Long Ago.* New York: World Book Company, 1915.

_____. *Indian Life and Indian Lore in the Land of the Head Hunters.* Yonkers, New York: World Book Company, 1915.

DeSmet, Pierre Jean. *Oregon Missions and Travels Over the Rocky Mountain in 1845-46.* New York: Edward Dunigan, 1847.

_____. *Origin, Progress and Prospects of the Catholic Mission to the Rocky Mountains.* Philadelphia: M. Fithian, 1843.

DeVoto, Bernard, ed. *The Journals of Lewis and Clark.* Boston: Houghton Mifflin, 1953.

"Doty's Journal of Operations." Documents Relating to Negotiations of Ratified and Unratified Treaties. National Archives, Record Group 75. Microfilm T494. Reel 5.

Douglas, David. *Journal Kept by David Douglas, During His Travels in North America, 1823-1827.* London: William Wesley and Son, 1914.

Drury, Clifford, ed. "A Letter by Henry H. Spalding from the Rocky Mountains." *Oregon Historical Quarterly* 51 (1950):127-33.

_____. "Gray's Journal of 1838." *Pacific Northwest Quarterly* 29 (1938):277-82.

_____. "Letters of Rev. H. H. Spalding and Mrs. Spalding, Written Shortly After Completing Their Trip Across the Continent." *Oregon Historical Quarterly* 37 (1936):111-26.

_____. "Spalding and Whitman Letters, 1837." *Oregon Historical Quarterly* 37 (1936):111-26.

_____. *The Diaries and Letters of Henry H. Spalding and Asa Bowen Smith Relating to the Nez Perce Mission, 1838-1842.* Glendale, California: Arthur H. Clarke Company, 1958.

Duggar, Sister Anna Clare. "Catholic Institutions of the Walla Walla Valley." Master's thesis, Seattle University, 1953.

Eby, Isaac N. and Emily Eby. "Diary of Colonel Isaac N. and Mrs. Emily Eby, 1856-57." Edited by L. A. Kibbe. *Pacific Northwest Quarterly* 33 (1942):297-323.

Eells, Myron. *History of Indian Missions on the Pacific Coast, Oregon, Washington and Idaho.* Philadelphia: American Sunday School Union, 1882.

_____. *Ten Years of Missionary Work Among the Indians at Skokomish, Washington Territory, 1874-1884.* Boston: Congregational Sunday School and Publishing Society, 1886.

_____. The Foundations of the Whitman "Myth." Walla Walla, Washington: Whitman College, 1898.

Elliott, T. C., ed. "David Thompson's Journeys in Idaho." *Washington Historical Quarterly* 11 (1920):97-103, 163-73.

_____. "David Thompson's Journeys in the Pend Oreille Country." *Washington Historical Quarterly* 23 (1932): 18-24, 88-93, 173-76.

_____. "David Thompson's Journeys in the Spokane Country." Washington *Historical Quarterly* 8 (1917): 183-87, 261-64; 9 (1918):11-16, 103-106, 169-73, 284-887; 10 (1919):17-20.

_____. "Journal of David Thompson." *Oregon Historical Quarterly* 15 (1914):39-63, 104-25.

_____. "Journal of Alexander Ross, Snake Country Expedition, 1824." *Oregon Historical Quarterly* 14 (1913):366-88.

_____. "Journal of John Work's Snake Country Expedition of 1830-31." *Oregon Historical Quarterly* 13 (1912):363-71; 14 (1913):280-314.

Elsensohn, M. Alfreda. *Pioneer Days in Idaho Country.* 2 vols. Caldwell, Idaho: The Caxton Printers, Ltd., 1947.

Fisher, Southerland G. "Journals of S. G. Fisher, Chief of Scouts to General O. Howard During the Campaign Against the Nez Perce Indians, 1877." *Contributions to the Historical Society of Montana* 2 (1869):269-82.

Franchere, Gabriel. *Narrative of A Voyage To The Northwest Coast of America, In the Years 1811, 1812, 1813, and 1814, Or the First American Settlement on the Pacific.* New York: Redfield, 1854.

Gibbon, John. "The Battle of the Big Hole." *Harper's Weekly* 39 (1895):1215-16.

Gibbs, George et al. "Report on the Indian Tribes of the Territory of Washington." *Secretary of War Reports of Explorations* 1 (1854):400-49.

Gibbs, George. "Tribes of Western Washington and Northwestern Oregon Published with Extensive Vocabularies," in W. H. Dall, *Tribes of the Extreme Northwest, Contributions to North American Ethnology, 1, for U.S. Geographical and Geological Survey of the Rocky Mountain Region.* J. W. Powell, Director. Washington, D.C., 1877:163-361.

Gilbert, Frank T. *Historic Sketches of Walla Walla, Whitman, Columbia and Garfield Counties, Washington Territory.* Portland, Oregon: A. G. Walling Co., 1882.

Gray, W. H. *The Moral and Religious Aspect of the Indian Question.* "A Letter Addressed to General John Eaton, Department of the Interior, Bureau of Education, Washington, D.C." Astoria, Oregon: Astorian Book and Job Print, 1879.

Greene, Glen Stonefield. "Prehistoric Utilization in the Channeled Scablands of Eastern Washington." Ph.D. dissertation, Washington State University, 1975.

Haller, Granville O. "Kamiakin—In History: Memoir of the War, in the Yakima Valley, 1855-1856." Manuscript A128, Bancroft Library, University of California, Berkeley.

_____. "The Indian War of 1855-56 in Washington and Oregon." Pacific Northwest Collection, University of Washington Library.

Haller, Theodore N. "Life and Public Services of Colonel Granville O. Haller." *Washington Historian* 1 (1899-1900):102-104.

Hamilton, William T. "A Trader's Expedition Among the Indians from Walla Walla to the Blackfeet Nation and Return in the Year 1858." *Contribution to the Historical Society of Montana* 3 (1900):33-123.

Hembree, Waman C. "Yakima Indian War Diary." *Washington Historical Quarterly* 16 (1925):273-83.

Hinton, H. P. "The Military Career of John Ellis Wool, 1812-1863." Ph.D. dissertation, University of Wisconsin, 1960.

Howard, Oliver O. *Famous Indian Chiefs I Have Known.* New York: The Century Co., 1907-1908.

_____. *My Life and Experiences Among Our Hostile Indians: A Report of Personal Observations, Adventures, and Campaigns Among the Indians of the Great West, With some Account of Their Life, Habits, Traits, Religion, Ceremonies, Dress, Savage Instincts, and Customs in Peace and War.* Hartford: A. D. Worthington and Co., 1907.

_____. *Nez Perce Joseph.* Boston: Lee and Sheperd, 1881.

Hunter, George. *Reminiscences of an Old Timer.* San Francisco: H. S. Crocker and Co., 1887.

Indian Claims Commission. "Evidence in Support of Proposed Findings of Fact of Petitioners in Docket Number 222 on Issues of Liability." United States Claims Commission. National Archives, Record Group 279.

_____. "Testimony of Verne L. Ray." United States Claims Commission. National Archives, Record Group 279.

Indian Claims Commission Decisions. Vol. 7, Part B and Vol. 12, Part A. Boulder, Colorado: Native American Rights Fund, n.d.

Jackson, Donald, ed. *Letters of the Lewis and Clark Expedition with Related Documents, 1783-1854.* Urbana: University of Illinois Press, 1962.

Joseph, Young Chief. "An Indian's View of Indian Affairs." (Often called "Chief Joseph's Own Story.") *North American Review* 128 (1879):412-33.

Kane, Paul. "Notes of Travel Among the Walla-Walla Indians." *The Canadian Journal* 5 (1856):417-24.

Kappler, Charles J. *Indian Affairs, Laws and Treaties.* 2 vols. Washington, D.C.: Government Printing Office, 1940.

Kelly, Plympton J. *We Were Not Summer Soldiers: The Indian War Diary of Plympton J. Kelly, 1855-1856.* Portland: Oregon Historical Society, 1980.

Kingston, Ceylon Samuel, ed. *Grassroot Cuttings; Sources of the History of the Territory of Washington.* Longview, Washington: Longview Daily News, 1954.

Kip, Lawrence. *Army Life on the Pacific; A Journal of the Expedition Against the Northern Indians, the Tribes of the Coeur d'Alenes, Spokanes, and Pelouzes, in the Summer of 1858.* New York: Redfield Publishing Co., 1859.

_____. *Indian Council at Walla Walla.* Seattle: Facsimile Reproduction (The Shorey Book Store), 1971.

Ledbetter, W. G. "Military History of the Oregon Country, 1804-1859." Master's thesis, University of Oregon, 1940.

McWhorter, L. V. *Hear Me, My Chiefs!* Caldwell, Idaho: The Caxton Printers, Ltd., 1952.

_____. *Tragedy of the Whak-Shum; Prelude to the Yakima Indian War, 1855-56; the Killing of Major Andrew J. Bolon.* Fairfield, Washington: Ye Galleon Press, 1958.

_____. *Yellow Wolf: His Own Story.* Caldwell, Idaho: The Caxton Printers, Ltd., 1940.

Masterson, James R. "The Records of the Washington Superintendency of Indian Affairs, 1853-1874." *Pacific Northwest Quarterly* 37 (1946):31-41.

Merk, Frederick, ed. *Fur Trade and Empire: George Simpson's Journal, 1824-1825.* Cambridge, Massachusetts: Belknap Press, 1968.

Miles, Nelson A. *Personal Recollections and Observations.* Chicago: The Werner Co., 1897.

Mooney, James. "The Ghost Dance Religion and the Sioux Outbreak of 1890." *Fourteenth Annual Report to the Bureau of American Ethnology* 14. Washington, D.C.: Government Printing Office, 1892-93.

Morgan, M. R. "Recollections of the Spokane Expedition." *Journal of the Military Service Institution of the United States* 42 (1908):489-96

Morton, Arthur S., ed. "The North West Company's Columbia Enterprise and David Thompson." *Canadian Historical Review* 17 (1936):266-88; 18 (1937):156-62.

Mullan, John. *Report on the Construction of a Military Road from Fort Walla Walla to Fort Benton.* Washington, D.C.: Government Printing Office, 1863.

_____. "Report on the Indian Tribes in the Eastern Portion of Washington Territory, 1853." Secretary of War, *Reports of Explorations* 1, 437-41.

_____. "Topographical Memoir and Map of Colonel Wright's Late Campaign Against the Indians of Oregon and Washington Territories." *Senate Executive Document,* 35th Congress, 2nd Session, no. 32, SS 984.

Nesmith, James W. "Diary of the Emigration of 1843." *Oregon Historical Quarterly* 7 (1906):329-59.

Newell, Robert. *Robert Newell's Memoranda: Travels in the Territory of Missouri; Travel to the Kayuse War; Together with a Report on the Indians South of the Columbia River.* Edited by D. O. Johansen. Portland, Oregon: Champoeg Press, 1959.

Nicolay, C. G. *The Oregon Territory: A Geographical and Physical Account of That Country and Its Inhabitants with Outlines of Its History and Discovery.* London: C. Knight, 1846.

Noyes, A. J. *In the Land of the Chinook.* Helena, Montana: State Publishing Co., 1917.

Office of Indian Affairs. *Report on Sources, Nature and Extent of the Fishing, Hunting and Miscellaneous Related Rights of Certain Indian Tribes in Washington and Oregon.* Los Angeles: Department of Interior, Division of Forestry and Grazing, 1942.

Oliphant, Orin J., ed. "Journals of the Indian War of 1855-1856." *Washington Historical Quarterly* 15 (1924):11-31.

Oral Interviews: authors with Mary Jim, Andrew George, Emily Peone, Patricia Jones, Arthur Kamiakin, Joe Thompson, Karie Nightwalker, Ray DeLong, Charlie Jenkins, Leonard Jones, Bill McNeilly, Ida Desautel, Shirley Palmer, and Isaac Patrick.

Oregon State University. "Nutritive Values of Native Foods of Washington State Indians." Oregon State University Extension Service Circular 809 (1972).

Osgood, Ernest S. *The Field Notes of Captain William Clark.* New Haven: Yale University Press, 1964.

Painter, Robert M. and William C. Painter. "Journals of the Indian War of 1855-1856." *Washington Historical Quarterly* 15 (1924):11-31.

Palmer, Joel. *Journal of Travels over the Rocky Mountains.* Cincinnati: J. A. and U. P. James, 1814.

Pambrun, Andrew D. *Sixty Years on the Frontier in the Pacific Northwest.* Ed., Edward J. Kowrach. Fairfield, Washington, 1978.

Parker, Samuel. *An Exploring Tour Beyond the Rocky Mountains in North America, Under the Commissioners for Foreign Missions, Performed in the Years 1835, 1836, and 1837.* Dublin: William Proteus, 1840.

Pfulf, Otto, ed. "The Battle of the Big Hole: An Episode in the Nez Perce War." *Frontier and Midland* 10 (1929):63-80.

Phinney, Archie, ed. *Nez Perce Texts.* New York: Columbia University Press, 1934.

Quaife, Milo Milton. *Adventures of the First Settlers on the Oregon or Columbia River.* Chicago: The Lakeside Press, 1923.

Ray, Verne. "Palus Tribal Territory." United States Claims Commission, Docket 222, National Archives, Record Group 279.

_____. "Economic Use of the Tribal Territory of the Palus Tribe." United States Indian Claims Commission, Docket 161, National Archives, Record Group 279.

Redfield, F. M. "Reminiscence of Francis M. Redfield: Chief Joseph's War." *Pacific Northwest Quarterly* 27 (1936):66-76.

Register of Entries, Whitman County, Washington, 1885-1900. Pioneer Title Company. Colfax, Washington.

Reimers, Henry L. *The Secret Saga of Five-Sack.* Fairfield, Washington: Ye Galleon Press, 1975.

Rich, E. E., ed. *Part of a Dispatch from George Simpson Esqr., Governor of Ruperts Lands, to the Governor and Committee of the Hudson's Bay Company, London, March 1, 1829. Continued and Completed March 24 and June 5, 1829.* Toronto: Champlain Society, 1947.

_____. *The Letters of John McLoughlin from Fort Vancouver to the Governor and Committee: First Series, 1825-38.* Toronto: Champlain Society, 1941-44.

Rigsby, Bruce J. "Linguistic Relations in the Southern Plateau." Ph.D. dissertation, University of Oregon, 1956.

Ross, Alexander. *Adventures of the First Settlers on the Oregon or Columbia River: Being a Narrative of the Expedition Fitted Out by John Jacob Astor to Establish the "Pacific Fur Company"; With an Account of Some Indian Tribes on the Coast of the Pacific.* London: Smith, Elder and Company, 1849.

_____. *The Fur Hunters of the Far West; A Narrative of Adventures in the Oregon and Rocky Mountains.* Norman: University of Oklahoma Press, 1956.

Scheuerman, Richard. "Kinship and Marriage Among the Palouse." Unpublished manuscript. Department of American Indian Studies, San Diego State University.

Secretary of War. *Reports of Explorations and Surveys to Ascertain the Most Practicable and Economical Route for a Railroad from the Mississippi River to the Pacific Ocean, Made Under the Direction of the Secretary of War, in 1853-55.* 12 vols. Washington, D.C.: Government Printing Office, 1855-60.

Shaver, F. A. et al. *An Illustrated History of Southeastern Washington Including Walla Walla, Columbia, Garfield and Asotin Counties.* Spokane, Washington: Western Historical Publishing Company, 1906.

Sharkey, Margery. "Revitalization and Change: A History of the Wanapum Indians, Their Prophet Smowhala, and the Washani Religion." Master's thesis, Washington State University, 1984.

Sheridan, Philip H. *Personal Memoirs* 1. New York: C. L. Webster, 1888.

Spaid, Stanley J. "Joel Palmer and Indian Affairs in Oregon." Ph.D. dissertation, University of Oregon, 1950.

Sprague, Roderick. "Aboriginal Burial Practices in the Plateau Region of North America." Ph.D. dissertation, University of Arizona, 1967.

Stevens, Hazard. *The Life of Isaac Ingalls Stevens.* 2 vols. Boston: Houghton, Mifflin and Company, 1901.

Stevens, Isaac I. "Letters of Governor Isaac I. Stevens, 1853-1854." *Pacific Northwest Quarterly* 30 (1939):301-37.

_____. *Narrative and Final Report of Explorations for a Route for a Pacific Railroad, Near the Forty-Seventh and Forty-Ninth Parallels of North Latitude from St. Paul to Puget Sound.* Washington, D.C.: Government Printing Office, 1855, 1860.

"Stevens Letters that deal with Indian Problems, 1857-58." *Washington Republican* (1857).

Stewart, W. M. "David Thompson's Surveys in the North-West." *Canadian Historical Review* 17 (1936):289-303.

Tappan, William H. "Reminiscences of Early Days in Washington." *Washington Historical Quarterly* 1 (1899): 19-22.

Thompson, David. *David Thompson's Narrative of His Explorations in Western America, 1784-1812.* Vol. 12. Toronto: Champlain Society, 1916.

Thwaites, Reuben Gold, ed. *Original Journals of the Lewis and Clark Expedition, 1804-1806.* Vol. 3, 4, and 8. New York: Antiquarian Press Limited, 1916.

Todd, Ronald, ed. "Letters of Governor Isaac I. Stevens, 1857-1858." *Pacific Northwest Quarterly* 31 (1940):403-59.

Told by the Pioneers. *Reminiscences of Pioneer Life in Washington.* 3 vols. Olympia, Washington: Works Progress Administration, 1937-1938.

Trimble, I. Ridgeway, ed. "Captain C. S. Winder's Account of a Battle With the Indians." *Maryland Historical Magazine* 35 (1940):56-59.

Uhlenbeck, C. C. *Original Blackfoot Texts.* Amsterdam: John Buller, 1911.

Uncommon Controversy. A Report Prepared for the American Friends Service Committee. Seattle: University of Washington Press, 1970.

United States Bureau of Census. Census, Ninth through Thirteenth, 1870-1910.

United States Commissioners of Indian Affairs, Annual Reports, 1824-1949. Reprinted by Microcard Editions. Washington, D.C., 1968.

Wallace, William H. and others. "A Brief Notice of the Recent Outrage Committed by Isaac I. Stevens, Governor of Washington Territory." *Western America: Frontier History of the Trans-Mississippi West, 1550-1900.* New Haven, Connecticut: Research Publications, Inc., 1975.

Warren, Eliza Spalding. *Memoirs of the West.* Portland, Oregon: Marsh Printing, 1917.

Washington Territorial Census, 1871. National Archives. Microfilm 276, Reel 8.

Weisel, George F. *Men and Trade on the Northwest Frontier, as Shown by the Fort "Owen Ledger."* Missoula: Montana State University, 1955.

Wendt, Bruce. "A History of the Warm Springs Reservation." Master's thesis, Washington State University, 1982.

White, M. Catherine, ed. *David Thompson's Journals relating to Montana and Adjacent Regions, 1808-1812.* Missoula: University of Montana Press, 1950.

Whitman, Marcus. "Journal and Report by Dr. Marcus Whitman of His Tour of Exploration with Reverend Samual Parker in 1835 Beyond the Rocky Mountains." *Oregon Historical Quarterly* 28 (1927):239-57.

Whitman, Narcissa. *The Coming of the White Women, 1836, As Told in Letters and Journals of Narcissa Prentiss Whitman.* Portland, Oregon: Oregon Historical Society, 1937.

_____. "Narcissa Whitman Diary, 1836." *Transactions of the Oregon Pioneer Association* (1890).

Winthrop, Theodore. *The Canoe and the Saddle or Klalam and Klickitat.* Tacoma, Washington: John H. Williams, 1913.

Wood, Henry Clay. *Status of Young Joseph and His Band of Nez Perce Indians.* Portland, Oregon: Assistant Adjutant General's Office, Department of the Columbia, 1876.

_____. *Supplementary to the Report on the Treaty Status of Young Joseph.* Portland, Oregon: Assistant Adjutant General's Office, Department of the Columbia, 1878.

Woodstock Letters; A Record of Current Events and Historical Notes Connected with the Colleges and Missions of the Society of Jesus. Woodstock, Maryland: Woodstock Press, 1872.

Yakima Agency Letterbooks. Washington Superintendency. Records of the Bureau of Indian Affairs, National Archives.

HOUSE AND SENATE DOCUMENTS

House Executive Document 91, 33rd Cong., 2d Sess., 1854-55.
House Executive Document 93, 34rd Cong., 1st Sess., 1855-56.
House Executive Document 118, 34th Cong., 1st Sess., 1855-56.
House Executive Document 5, 34th Cong., 3d Sess., 1856-57.
House Executive Document 76, 34th Cong., 3d Sess., 1856-57.
House Executive Document 38-39, 35th Cong., 1st Sess., 1857-58.
House Executive Document 114, 35th Cong., 2d Sess., 1858-59.
House Executive Document 50, 35th Cong., 2d Sess., 1858-59.
House Executive Document 65, 36th Cong., 1st Sess., 1859-60.
House Executive Document 29, 36th Cong., 2d Sess., 1860-61.
House Executive Document 1, 44th Cong., 1st Sess., 1875-76.
House Executive Document 1, 45th Cong., 2d Sess., 1877-78.
Senate Executive Document 26, 34th Cong., 1st Sess., 1855-56.
Senate Executive Document 66, 34th Cong., 1st Sess., 1855-56.
Senate Executive Document 41, 34th Cong., 1st Sess., 1855-56.
Senate Executive Document 40, 35th Cong., 1st Sess., 1857-58.
Senate Executive Document 1, 35th Cong., 2d Sess., 1858-59.
Senate Executive Document 32, 35th Cong., 2d Sess., 1858-59.
Senate Executive Document 2, 36th Cong., 1st Sess., 1859-60.
Senate Executive Document 1, 36th Cong., 2d Sess., 1860-61.
Senate Executive Document 43, 37th Cong., 3d Sess., 1862-63.
Senate Executive Document 14, 45th Cong., 2d Sess., 1877-78.
Senate Executive Document 257, 56th Cong., 1st Sess., 1900.
Senate Executive Document 97, 62d Cong., 1st Sess., 1911.

NEWSPAPERS

Alta California
Billings Gazette
Cheney Sentinel
Corvallis Oregon Statesman
Council Fire
Evening Star
Idaho Signal
Columbia Basin News
Lewiston Morning Tribune
Morning Oregonian
National Intelligencer
New Northwest
Olympia Pioneer and Democrat
Palouse Gazette
Portland Oregonian
Puget Sound Courier
Seattle Daily Times
Spokesman Review
The Spectator

The Yakima County
Tri-City Herald
Walla Walla Journal
Walla Walla Statesman
Walla Walla Union
Walla Walla Union Bulletin
Walla Walla Watchman
Washington Historian
Washington Post
Weekly Oregonian
Wenatchee Daily World
Wilbur Register
Yakima Democrat
Yakima Herald
Yakima Morning Herald
Yakima Republic

ORAL SOURCES

Carol Bull, Lapwai, Idaho
Ida Disautel, Nespelem, Washington
Andrew George, Wapato, Washington
Rose Jack, Wapato, Washington
Karie Jim, Parker, Washington
Mary Jim Nightwalker, Parker, Washington
Patricia Jones, Lapwai, Idaho
Arthur Kamiakin, Nespelem, Washington
Isaac Patrick, Mission, Oregon
Emily Peone, Nespelem, Washington
Joe Thompson, Mission, Oregon
Flora Wasis, Wapato, Washington
Jim Windell, Warm Springs, Oregon

BOOKS

Allen, A. J. *Ten Years in Oregon; Travels and Adventures of Doctor D. White and Lady, West of the Rocky Mountains; With Incidents of Two Sea Voyages Via Sandwich Islands Around Cape Horn.* Ithaca, New York: Press of Andrus, Gauntlett, and Company, 1850.

Armstrong, A. N. *Oregon: Comprising a Brief History and Full Descriptions of the Territories of Oregon and Washington.* Chicago: C. Scott and Company, 1857.

Bagley, Clarence B., ed. *Early Catholic Missions in Old Oregon.* 2 vols. Seattle: Lowman and Hanford Company, 1932.

Bailey, Robert G. *Hell's Canyon.* Lewiston, Idaho: R. G. Bailey Printing Company, 1943.

_____. *River of No Return.* Lewiston, Idaho: R. G. Bailey Printing Company, 1948.

Bakeless, John. *Lewis and Clark, Partners in Discovery.* New York: W. Morrow, 1947.

Ballou, Robert. *Early Klickitat Valley Days.* Goldendale, Washington: Goldendale Sentinel, 1938.

Bancroft, Hubert Howe. *History of the Northwest Coast.* San Francisco: A. L. Bancroft and Company, 1884.

_____. *History of Oregon.* San Francisco: The History Company, 1888.

_____. *History of Washington, Idaho and Montana.* San Francisco: The History Company, 1890.

_____. *Native Races of the Pacific States of North America.* San Francisco: The History Company, 1886.

Barber, Floyd and Dan W. Martin. *Idaho in the Pacific Northwest.* Caldwell, Idaho: Caxton Printers, Ltd., 1956.

Bartlett, Grace. *Wallowa: The Land of Winding Waters.* Enterprise, Oregon: Wallowa County Chieftain, 1967.

Beal, Merrill D. *"I Will Fight No More Forever": Chief Joseph and the Nez Perce War."* Seattle: University of Washington Press, 1963.

Beeson, John. *A Plea for the Indians; With Facts and Features of the Late War in Oregon.* New York: J. Beeson, 1957.

Berreman, Joel V. *Tribal Distribution in Oregon.* American Anthropological Association Memoir 47. Menasha, Wisconsin, 1937.

Bischoff, William N. *The Jesuits in Old Oregon.* Caldwell, Idaho: The Caxton Printers, Ltd., 1945.

Boas, Franz, ed. *Folk-Tales of Salishan and Sahaptin Tribes.* Lancaster, Pennsylvania: American Folklore Society, 1917.

Brady, Cyrus. *Northwestern Indian Fights and Fighters*. New York: The McClure Company, 1907.

Brimlow, George F. *The Bannock Indian War of 1878*. Caldwell, Idaho: Caxton Printers, Ltd., 1938.

Brosnan, Cornelius J. *History of the State of Idaho*. New York: Charles Scribner, 1935.

_____. *Jason Lee, Prophet of New Oregon*. New York: Macmillan, 1932.

Burns, Robert Ignatius. *The Jesuits and the Indian Wars of the Northwest*. New Haven: Yale University Press, 1966.

Burroughs, Raymond Darwin. *The Natural History of the Lewis and Clark Expedition*. East Lansing, Michigan: Michigan State University Press, 1961.

Campbell, Marjorie W. *The North West Company*. New York: St. Martin's Press, 1957.

Cannon, Miles. *Waiilatpu, Its Rise and Fall, 1836-1847; A Story of Pioneer Days in the Pacific Northwest*. Boise, Idaho: Capital News Job Rooms, 1915.

Carey, Charles H. *A General History of Oregon Prior to 1861*. Portland, Oregon: Metropolitan Press, 1935-1936.

Catlin, George. *Letters and Notes on the Manners, Customs, and Condition of the North American Indians*. 2 vols. London: George Catlin, 1841.

Chalfant, Stuart A. *Interior Salish and Eastern Washington Indians*. New York: Garland Publishing, 1974.

Chalmers, Harvey. *The Last Stand of the Nez Perce: Destruction of a People*. New York: Twayne Publishers, 1962.

Cheetham, Robert N. *David Thompson Sesquicentennial*. Sandpoint, Idaho: Bonner County Museum, 1960.

Chittenden, Hiram M. *A History of the American Fur Trade of the Far West*. 2 vols. Stanford, California: Academic Reprints, 1954.

Chuinard, E. G. *The Medical Aspects of the Lewis and Clark Expedition*. Corvallis, Oregon: Oregon State University Friends of the Library, 1965.

Clark, Ella. *Indian Legends of the Pacific Northwest*. Berkeley: University of California Press, 1953.

Clarke, Charles G. *The Men of the Lewis and Clark Expedition*. Glendale, California: Arthur H. Clark, 1970.

Clarke, S. A. *Pioneer Days of Oregon*. 2 vols. Portland, Oregon: J. K. Gill Company, 1905.

Cody, Edmund R. *History of the Coeur d'Alene Mission of the Sacred Heart*. Caldwell, Idaho: The Caxton Printers, Ltd., 1930.

Cohen, Felix S. *Handbook of Federal Indian Law*. Albuquerque: University of New Mexico Press, 1971.

Costello, Joseph A. *The Siwash, Their Life, Legends, and Tales, Puget Sound and Pacific Northwest*. Seattle: The Calvert Company, 1895.

Coues, Elliott, ed. *History of the Expedition under the Command of Lewis and Clark*. New York: Dover Publications, 1965.

_____. *New Light on the Early History of the Greater Northwest: The Manuscript Journals of Alexander Henry and David Thompson, 1799-1814*. 2 vols. New York: F. P. Harper, 1897.

Crawford, Mary M. *Nez Perces Since Spalding*. Berkeley, California: Professional Press, 1936.

Crosby, Alfred W. *The Columbian Exchange: Biological and Cultural Consequences of 1492*. Westport, Connecticut: Greenwood Publishing Company, 1972.

Culverwell, Albert. *Stronghold in the Yakima Country*. Olympia, Washington: Washington State Parks and Recreation Commission, 1956.

Davidson, Gordon C. *The North West Company*. Berkeley, California: University of California Press, 1918.

Defenbach, Byron. *Red Heroines of the Northwest*. Caldwell, Idaho: The Caxton Printers, Ltd., 1936.

Desmond, G. B. *Gambling Among the Yakimas*. Washington, D.C.: Catholic University of America Press, 1952.

DeVoto, Bernard. *Across the Wide Missouri*. Boston: Houghton Mifflin, 1947.

Dillon, Richard. *Meriwether Lewis: A Biography*. New York: Coward-McCann, 1965.

Downey, Fairfax. *Indian Wars of the United States Army, 1776-1865*. Garden City, New York: Doubleday, 1963.

Drury, Clifford M. *Elkanah and Mary Walker, Pioneers Among the Spokanes*. Caldwell, Idaho: The Caxton Printers, Ltd., 1940.

_____. *First White Women Over the Rockies*. 2 vols. Glendale, California: Arthur H. Clark, 1963.

_____. *Henry Harmon Spalding*. Caldwell, Idaho: The Caxton Printers, Ltd., 1936.

_____. *Marcus Whitman*. Caldwell, Idaho: The Caxton Printers, Ltd., 1936.

_____. *Marcus Whitman, M.D.: Pioneer and Martyr*. Caldwell, Idaho: The Caxton Printers, Ltd., 1937.

_____. *Tepee In His Front Yard*. Portland, Oregon: Binfords and Mort, 1949.

Dryden, Cecil Pearl. *Up the Columbia for Furs*. Caldwell, Idaho: The Caxton Printers, Ltd., 1950.

Dunn, J. P. *Massacres of the Mountains; A History of the Indian Wars of the Far West*. New York: Harper and Brothers, 1886.

Dunn, John. *History of the Oregon Territory and the British North American Fur Trade with an Account of the Customs of the Principal Native Tribe on the Northern Continent*. London: Edward and Hughes, 1844.

Durham, N. W. *History of the City of Spokane County*. 3 vols. Chicago: S. J. Clarke Publishing Company, 1912.

Edwards, Jonathan. *An Illustrated History of Spokane County, State of Washington*. San Francisco: W. H. Lever, 1900.

Ellis, Richard. *General Pope and U.S. Indian Policy*. Albuquerque: University of New Mexico Press, 1970.

Emmons, Della G. *Leschi of the Nisqualies*. Minneapolis: T. S. Denison, 1965.

Evans, Elwood. *Campaign of Major John E. Wool, U.S. Army, Against the People and Authorities of Oregon and Washington, 1855-1856*. New Haven, Connecticut: Research Publications, Inc., 1975.

_____. *History of the Pacific Northwest, Oregon and Washington*. 2 vols. Portland, Oregon: North Pacific History Company, 1889.

Ewers, John C. *The Blackfeet*. Norman: University of Oklahoma Press, 1958.

_____. *The Horse in Blackfeet Culture, with Comparative Material From Other Western Tribes*. Washington, D.C.: Government Printing Office, 1955.

Fahey, John. *The Flathead Indians*. Norman: University of Oklahoma Press, 1974.

Fee, Chester A. *Chief Joseph: The Biography of a Great Indian*. New York: Wilson-Erickson, Inc., 1936.

Ferris, Warren A. *Life in the Rocky Mountains, 1830-1835*. Salt Lake City: Rocky Mountain Book Shop, 1940.

Fremont, John C. *Report of the Exploring Expedition to the Rocky Mountains in the Year 1842, and to Oregon and North California in the Years 1843-1844*. Washington: Gales and Seton, 1845.

Fuller, George. *History of the Pacific Northwest*. New York: Alfred A. Knopf, 1931.

_____. *The Inland Empire of the Pacific Northwest, A History*. Vol. 1 and 2. Spokane: H. G. Linderman, 1928.

Galbraith, John S. *The Hudson's Bay Company as an Imperial Factor, 1821-1861*. Berkeley: University of California Press, 1957.

Gass, Patrick. *A Journal of the Voyages and Travels of a Corps of Discovery under the Command of Captain Lewis and Captain Clark*. Minneapolis: Ross and Haines, 1958.

Gibbs, George. *Indian Tribes of Washington Territory.* Fairfield, Washington: Ye Galleon Press, 1972.

Gibson, Arrell M. *The American Indian: Prehistory to Present.* Lexington, Massachusetts: D. C. Heath, 1980.

Gidley, M. *With One Sky Above Us.* Seattle: University of Washington Press, 1979.

Gilbert, Frank T. *The Whitman Massacre, With a Few Prior Historical Events.* Portland, Oregon: North Pacific History Company, 1888.

Glassley, Ray. *Pacific Northwest Indian Wars.* Portland, Oregon: Binfords and Mort, 1953.

Goetzmann, W. H. *A History of Oregon, 1792-1849, Drawn from Observation and Authentic Information.* Portland, Oregon: Harris and Holman, 1870.

Gray, William H. *A History of Oregon.* Portland, Oregon: Harris and Holman, 1870.

Greenhow, Robert. *The History of Oregon and California, and the Other Territories on the Northwest Coast of North America.* Boston: Charles C. Little and James Brown, 1844.

Guie, H. Dean. *Bugles in the Valley: The Story of Garnett's Fort Simcoe.* Portland, Oregon: Oregon Historical Society, 1977.

Haines, Francis. *Appaloosa, The Spotted Horse in Art and History.* Austin, Texas: University of Texas Press, 1963.

_____. *The Nez Perces.* Norman: University of Oklahoma Press, 1955.

_____. *Red Eagles of the Northwest.* Portland, Oregon: The Scholastic Press, 1939.

Hawley, James H. *History of Idaho.* 4 vols. Chicago: The S. J. Clarke Publishing Company, 1920.

Hazard, Joseph T. *Companion of Adventure.* Portland, Oregon: Binfords and Mort, 1952.

Hines, Gustavus. *History of the Oregon Missions.* Buffalo: G. H. Derby, 1852.

_____. *Life on the Plains of the Pacific.* Buffalo: G. H. Derby, 1852.

_____. *Oregon: Its History, Condition and Prospects.* Buffalo: G. H. Derby, 1851.

Hines, H. K. *History of the State of Washington.* Chicago: Lewis Publishing Company, 1894.

_____. *Missionary History of the Pacific Northwest.* Portland, Oregon: Marsh Printing Company, 1899.

Hodge, Frederick W., ed. *Handbook of American Indians North of Mexico.* 2 vols. Washington, D.C.: Government Printing Office, 1907-1910.

Hoopes, A. W. *Indian Affairs and their Administration, 1849-1860, With Especial Reference to the Far West.* Philadelphia: University of Pennsylvania Press, 1932.

Howard, Harold P. *Sacajawea.* Norman, Oklahoma: University of Oklahoma Press, 1971.

Howard, Helen A., and George D. McGrath. *War Chief Joseph.* Caldwell, Idaho: The Caxton Printers, Ltd., 1941.

Hulbert, Archer Butler, and Dorothy Printup Hulbert, ed. *Marcus Whitman, Crusader: 1802-1839; 1839-1843; 1843- 1847.* 3 vols. Colorado Springs: The Stewart Commission of Colorado College, 1936-1941.

_____. *The Oregon Crusade: Across Land and Sea to Oregon.* 6 vols. Colorado Springs: The Stewart Commission of Colorado College, 1935.

Hull, Lindley M. *A History of Central Washington, Including the Famous Wenatchee, Entiat, Chelan and Columbia Valleys.* Spokane: Shaw and Borden Company, 1932.

Irving, Washington. *Astoria, Or Anecdotes of an Enterprise Beyond the Rocky Mountains.* Boston: Twayne Publishers, 1976.

_____. *The Adventures of Captain Bonneville, U.S.A., in the Rocky Mountains and the Far West.* New York: G. P. Putnam, 1849.

James, J. A. *English Institutions and the American Indian.* Baltimore: Johns Hopkins University Press, 1894.

Jennings, Francis. *The Invasion of America: Indians, Colonialism, and the Cant of Conquest.* Chapel Hill: University of North Carolina Press, 1975.

Jessett, Thomas E. *Chief Spokan Garry.* Minneapolis: T. A. Dennison, 1960.

Johansen, Dorothy O., and Charles M. Gates. *Empire of the Columbia: A History of the Pacific Northwest.* New York: Harper and Row, 1967.

Josephy, Alvin M., Jr. *Chief Joseph's People and Their War.* Yellowstone Park, Wyoming: Yellowstone Library and Museum Association in Cooperation with National Park Service, U.S. Department of the Interior, 1964.

_____. *The American Heritage Book of Indians.* New York: Knopf, 1968.

_____. *The Nez Perce Indians and the Opening of the Northwest.* New Haven: Yale University Press, 1965.

Kane, Paul. *Wanderings of an Artist Among the Indians of North America, from Canada to Vancouver's Island and Oregon, through the Hudson's Bay Company's Territory and Back Again.* London: Longman, Brown, Green, Longmans and Roberts, 1859.

Kimmel, Thelma. *The Fort Simcoe Story.* Toppenish, Washington: The Toppenish Review, 1954.

Kirkwood, Charlotte M. *The Nez Perce Indian War Under Chiefs Joseph and Whitebird.* Grangeville, Idaho: Idaho County Free Press, 1928.

Knight, Oliver. *Following the Indian Wars: The Story of the Newspaper Correspondents Among the Indian Campaigns.* Norman: University of Oklahoma Press, 1960.

Kuykendall, E. V. *Historic Glimpses of Asotin County.* Clarkston, Washington: Clarkston Herald, 1954.

Lever, W. H. *An Illustrated History of Whitman County.* Np., 1901.

Lewis, William S. *The Case of Spokane Garry.* Spokane, Washington: Bulletin of the Spokane Historical Society, Vol. 1, no. 1, 1917.

Lyman, Horace S. *History of Oregon; The Growth of an American State.* Vols. 2, 3, and 4. New York: North Pacific Publishing Society, 1903.

Lyman, W. D. *History of the Yakima Valley, Washington, Comprising Yakima, Kittitas and Benton Counties.* Chicago: S. J. Clarke, 1919.

_____. *Lyman's History of Old Walla Walla County.* 2 vols. Chicago: S. J. Clarke, 1918.

_____. *The Columbia River: Its History, Its Myth, Its Scenery, Its Commerce.* New York: Putnam, 1909.

Lyons, Sister Letitia Mary. *Francis Norbert Blanchet and the Founding of the Oregon Missions (1838-1848).* Washington, D.C.: The Catholic University of America Press, 1940.

McBeth, Kate C. *The Nez Perces Since Lewis and Clark.* New York: Fleming H. Revell Company, 1908.

McDermott, John D. *Forlorn Hope: The Battle of White Bird Canyon and the Beginning of the Nez Perce War.* Boise: Idaho State Historical Society, 1978.

McDonald, Archibald. *Peace River, a Canoe Voyage from Hudson's Bay to the Pacific by the Late Sir George Simpson (Governor, Hon. Hudson's Bay Company) in 1828.* Ottawa: J. Durie and Son, 1872.

MacInnes, Tom. *Chinook Days.* Vancouver, British Columbia: Sun Publishing, 1926.

MacKenzie, Alexander. *Voyages from Montreal, on the River St. Lawrence, Through the Continent of North America.* London: T. Cadell, Jr. and W. Davies, 1801.

MacKenzie, Cecil W. *Donald MacKenzie, King of the Northwest.* Los Angeles: I. Deach, Jr., 1937.

Manring, B. F. *Conquest of the Coeur d'Alenes, Spokanes, and Palouses.* Spokane, Washington: Inland Printing Company, 1912.

Mannypenny, George W. *Our Indian Wards.* New York: Da Capo Press, Inc., 1972.

Marshall, William Isaac. *The Acquisition of Oregon and the Long Suppressed Evidence About Marcus Whitman.* 2 vols. Seattle: Lowman and Hanford Company, 1911.

Meinig, Donald W. *The Great Columbia Plain*. Seattle: University of Washington Press, 1968.

Mohr, Walter H. *Federal Indian Relations, 1774-1778*. Philadelphia: University of Pennsylvania Press, 1933.

Moulton, Gary E. *John Ross: Cherokee Chief*. Athens, Georgia: University of Georgia Press, 1978.

Morgan, Dale L. *The West of William H. Ashley*. Denver: Old West Publishing, 1964.

Mowry, W. A. *Marcus Whitman and the Early Days of Oregon*. New York: Silver Burdett and Company, 1901.

Nash, Gary. *Red, White, and Black: The Peoples of Early America*. Englewood Cliffs, New Jersey: Prentice-Hall, 1974.

O'Hara, Edwin V. *Pioneer Catholic History of Oregon*. Patterson, New Jersey: Anthony Guild Press, 1939.

Oliphant, J. Orin. *On the Cattle Ranges of the Oregon Country*. Seattle: University of Washington Press, 1968.

Oregon Improvement Company. *Eastern Washington Territory and Oregon*. Portland, Oregon: Oregon Improvement Company, 1881.

Palladino, Lawrence B. *Indian and White in the Northwest*. Lancaster, Pennsylvania: Wickersham Publishing Company, 1922.

Parkman, Francis. *The Jesuits in North America*. Boston: Little Brown and Company, 1867.

Payette, B. C., ed. *The Oregon Country Under the Union Jack*. Montreal: Payette Radio, Ltd., 1962.

Peltier, Jerome, and B. C. Payette. *Warbonnets and Epaulets*. Montreal: Payette Radio, 1971.

Prucha, Francis Paul. *American Indian Policy in Crisis: Christian Reformers and the Indian, 1865-1900*. Norman: University of Oklahoma Press, 1976.

_____. *American Indian Policy in the Formative Years: The Indian Trade and the Intercourse Acts, 1790-1834*. Cambridge, Massachusetts: Harvard University Press, 1962.

_____. *Indian Peace Medals in American History*. Madison: State Historical Society of Wisconsin, 1971.

_____. *Indian Policy in the United States*. Lincoln: University of Nebraska Press, 1981.

Ray, Verne F. *Cultural Relations in the Plateau of Northwestern America*. Los Angeles: Southwest Museum, 1939.

_____. *Sanpoil and Nespelem: Salishan Peoples of Northeastern Washington*. Seattle: University of Washington Press, 1933.

Relander, Click. *Drummers and Dreamers*. Caldwell, Idaho: The Caxton Printers, Ltd., 1956.

_____. *Strangers on the Land*. Yakima, Washington: Franklin Press, 1962.

_____. *The Yakimas: Treaty Centennial*. Yakima, Washington. Republic Press, 1955.

Richards, Kent. *Isaac I. Stevens: Young Man in a Hurry*. Provo, Utah: Brigham Young University Press, 1979.

Roe, Frank G. *The Indian and the Horse*. Norman: University of Oklahoma Press, 1968.

Rollins, Philip A., ed. *The Discovery of the Oregon Trail*. New York: Charles Scribner's Sons, 1935.

Ronan, P. *Historical Sketch of the Flathead Indian Nation*. Helena, Montana: Journal Publishing Company, 1890.

Ronda, James P. *Lewis and Clark Among the Indians*. Lincoln: University of Nebraska Press, 1984.

Rosebush, W. E. *Frontier Steel, The Men and Their Weapons*. Spokane: Eastern Washington State Historical Society, 1958.

Ruby, Robert H., and John A. Brown. *Half-Sun on the Columbia: A Biography of Chief Moses*. Norman: University of Oklahoma Press, 1965.

_____. *Indians of the Pacific Northwest*. Norman: University of Oklahoma Press, 1982.

_____. *The Cayuse Indians: Imperial Tribesmen of Old Oregon*. Norman: University of Oklahoma Press, 1972.

_____. *The Spokane Indians, Children of the Sun*. Norman: University of Oklahoma Press, 1970.

Rushmore, Elsie M. *Indian Policy During Grant's Administration*. New York: Marion Press, 1914.

Saum, Lewis D. *The Fur Trader and the Indian*. Seattle: University of Washington Press, 1968.

Scheuerman, Richard D., and Clifford E. Trafzer. *The Volga Germans: Pioneers of the Pacific Northwest*. Moscow, Idaho: University Press of Idaho, 1981.

Schiach, W. S., and H. B. Averill et al. *An Illustrated History of North Idaho Embracing Nez Perces, Idaho, Latah, Kootenai, and Shoshone Counties, State of Idaho*. Spokane: Western Historical Publishing Company, 1903.

Shea, J. Gilmary. *History of the Catholic Missions Among the Indian Tribes of the United States, 1529-1854*. New York: E. Dunigan, 1855.

Shields, G. D. *The Battle of the Big Hole*. Chicago: Rand McNally Company, 1889.

Skarsten, M. O. *George Drouillard: Hunter and Interpreter for Lewis and Clark and Fur Trader, 1807-1810*. Glendale, California: Arthur H. Clark, 1964.

Skinner, Constance L. *Adventures of Oregon*. New Haven: Yale University Press, 1921.

Snowden, Clinton A. *History of Washington*. 6 vols. New York: The Century History Company, 1909-1911.

Spier, Leslie. "The Prophet Dance of the Northwest and Its Derivatives: The Source of the Ghost Dance," *General Series in Anthropology*. Menasha, Wisconsin: George Banta Publishing Co., 1953.

_____. "Tribal Distribution in Washington," *General Series in Anthropology*. Menasha, Wisconsin: George Banta Publishing Co., 1936.

Spinden, Herbert J. *The Nez Perce Indians*. Lancaster, Pennsylvania: New Era Print Company, 1908.

Splawn, A. J. *Ka-mi-akin, Last Hero of the Yakimas*. Portland, Oregon: Stationary and Printing Company, 1917.

Steffen, Jerome O. *William Clark: Jeffersonian Man on the Frontier*. Norman: University of Oklahoma Press, 1977.

Stewart, E. I. *Washington Northwest Frontier*. 4 vols. New York: Lewis Historical Publishing Company, 1957.

Sutherland, Thomas A. *Howard's Campaign Against the Nez Perce Indians, 1878*. Portland, Oregon: A. G. Walling, 1878.

Swanton, John R. *Indian Tribes of North America*. Washington, D.C.: Government Printing Office, 1952.

Tannatt, E. F., ed. *Indian Battles in the Inland Empire in 1858*. Spokane, Washington: Shaw and Borden Company, 1914.

Tebble, J. W., and K. Jennison. *The American Indian Wars*. New York: Harper, 1960.

Thomson, Origen. *Across the Plains in 1852*. Greensburg, Indiana: O. Thomson, 1896.

Thornbury, William D. *Regional Geomorphology of the United States*. New York: John Wiley and Sons, 1965.

Tolan, Providencia. *A Shining From the Mountains*. Montreal: Providence Mother House, 1980.

Townsend, John Kirk. *Narrative of a Journey Across the Rocky Mountains to the Columbia River and a Visit to the Sandwich Islands*. Philadelphia: H. Perkins, 1839.

Trafzer, Clifford, E., ed. *American Indian Prophets*. Newcastle, CA: Sierra Oaks Publishing Co., 1986.

_____. *Indians, Superintendents, and Councils: Northwestern Indian Policy, 1850-1855*. Lanham, MD: University Press of America, 1986.

Tyler, Lyman. *A History of Indian Policy*. Washington, D.C.: Government Printing Office, 1973.

Tyrrell, J. B., ed. *David Thompson's Narrative of His Explorations in Western America, 1784-1812.* Toronto: Champlain Society, 1916.

Underhill, Ruth Murray. *Indians of the Pacific Northwest.* Riverside, California: Sherman Institute Press, 1945.

_____. *Red Man's America, a History of Indians in the United States.* Chicago: University of Chicago Press, 1971.

Utley, Robert M. *Frontiersmen in Blue: The United States Army and the Indian, 1848-1865.* New York: The Macmillan Co., 1967.

Victor, Francis Fuller. *The Early Indian Wars of Oregon.* Salem, Oregon: Grant C. Baker, State Printer, 1894.

_____. *The River of the West; Life and Adventures in the Rocky Mountains and Oregon; Embracing Events in the Lifetime of Mountain-Man and Pioneer; With the Early History of the Northwestern Slope.* Hartford, Connecticut: Columbia Book Company, 1870.

Villard, Henry. *The Early History of Transportation in Oregon.* Eugene: University of Oregon Press, 1944.

Walker, Francis A. *The Indian Question.* Boston: J. R. Osgood, 1874.

Wheeler, Olin D. *The Trail of Lewis and Clark, 1804-1904.* 2 vols. New York: G. P. Putnam and Sons, 1926.

Winther, Oscar Osburn. *The Great Northwest.* New York: A. A. Knopf, 1947.

_____. *The Old Oregon Country, a History of Frontier Trade, Transportation and Travel.* Palo Alto, California: Stanford University Press, 1950.

Wood, Erskine. *Days with Chief Joseph.* Portland, Oregon: Binfords and Mort, 1920.

_____. "Pursuit and Capture of Chief Joseph," in Chester A. Fee, *Chief Joseph: The Biography of a Great Indian.* New York: Wilson-Erickson, Incorporated, 1936.

Woodward, Arthur. *Indian Trade Goods.* Portland, Oregon: Oregon Museum of Science and Industry, 1965.

_____. *The Denominators of the Fur Trade.* Pasadena: Socio-Technical Publications, 1970.

ARTICLES AND REPORTS

Andrews, Clarence L. "Warfield's Story of Peo-Peo-Mox-Mox." *Washington Historical Quarterly* 25 (1934):182-84.

Atkinson, G. H. "The Choice of a Home by Settlers in Oregon or Washington or Idaho." *The West Shore* 6 (1880):38-40.

Bagley, Clarence B., ed. "Attitude of the Hudson's Bay Company During the Indian War of 1855-56." *Washington Historical Quarterly* 8 (1917):291-307.

_____. "The Cayuse, or First Indian War in the Northwest." *Washington Historical Quarterly* 1 (1906): 34-49.

Barry, J. Neilson. "Archibald Pelton, the First Follower of Lewis and Clark." *Washington Historical Quarterly* 19 (1928):199-201.

_____. "Lieutenant Jeremy Pinch." *Oregon Historical Quarterly* 38 (1937):223-27.

_____. "The Trail of the Astorians." *Oregon Historical Quarterly* 13 (1912):227-39.

Bartlett, H. E. "The Appaloosa Was Not the Nez Perce War Horse." *The Westerners New York Posse Brand Book* 14 (1967):88-89.

Beall, Thomas B. "Pioneer Reminiscences." *Washington Historical Quarterly* 8 (1917):83-90.

Beers, Henry P. "The Army and the Oregon Trail to 1846." *Pacific Northwest Quarterly* 28 (1937):335-62.

Berkes, Fikret, and Carol S. Farkas. "Eastern James Bay Cree Indians: Changing Patterns of Wild Food Use and Nutrition." *Ecology of Food and Nutrition* 7 (1978):155-72.

"Bibliography of Isaac I. Stevens." *Washington Historical Quarterly* 9 (1918):174-96.

Bischoff, William N. "The Yakima Indian War, 1855-56, a Problem in Research." *Pacific Northwest Quarterly* 41 (1950):162-69.

_____. "Yakima Campaign of 1856." *Mid-America* 31 (1949):163-208.

Bischoff, William N., and C. M. Gates. "The Jesuits and the Coeur d'Alene Treaty of 1858." *Pacific Northwest Quarterly* 34 (1943):169-81.

Brackett, W. S. "An Exploring Expedition in Northern Idaho." *The Northwest* 19 (1901):7-10.

Bretz, J. Harlan. "The Channeled Scablands of the Columbia Plateau." *Journal of Geology* 31 (1923):617-49.

Brown, Mark A. "The Joseph Myth." *Montana, Magazine of Western History* 22 (1972):2-17.

Buck, Amos. "The Battle of the Big Hole." *Contributions to the Historical Society of Montana* 7 (1910):117-30.

Buechner, Helmutt K. "Some Biotic Changes in the State of Washington, Particularly During the Century 1853-1953." *Research Studies of the State College of Washington* 21 (1953):154-92.

Burcham, Ralph, ed. "Orofino Gold." *Idaho Yesterday* 4 (1960):2-9.

Burns, Robert Ignatius. "Pere Joset's Account of the Indian War of 1858." *Pacific Northwest Quarterly* 38 (1947):285-314.

_____. "The Jesuits and the Spokane Council of 1877." *Pacific Historical Review* 21 (1952):65-73.

_____. "The Jesuits, the Northern Indians, and the Nez Perce War of 1877." *Pacific Northwest Quarterly* 42 (1951):40-76.

Butterfield, Grace and J. H. Horner. "Wallowa Valley Towns and Their Beginning." *Oregon Historical Quarterly* 38 (1947):285-314.

Calloway, D. H., R. D. Giauque, and F. M. Costa. "The Superior Mineral Content of Some American Indian Foods." *Ecology of Food and Nutrition* 3 (1974):203-11.

Cannon, Miles. "Snake River in History." *Oregon Historical Quarterly* 20 (1919):1-23.

Carriere, Gaston. "The Yakima War: An Episode in the History of the Oregon Missions, Refutation of a False Accusation." *Vie Oblate Life* 34 (1975):153-63.

Catlin, J. B. "The Battle of the Big Hole." *Montana State Historian's Annual Report* (1927).

Chadwick, S. J. "Colonel Steptoe's Battle." *Washington Historical Quarterly* 2 (1907-08):333-43.

Chaffee, Eugene B., ed. "Nez Perce War Letters." *Idaho Historical Society, 15th Biennial Report* (1936).

Chalfant, Stuart A. "Ethno-Historical Reports on Aboriginal Land Occupancy and Utilization by the Palus Indians." *Interior Salish and Eastern Washington Indians* 4. New York: Garland Publishing, 1974.

Clark, Ella E. "The Mythology of the Indians in the Pacific Northwest." *Oregon Historical Quarterly* 54 (1953):163-89.

Clark, Robert C. "Military History of Oregon." *Oregon Historical Quarterly* 36 (1935):14-59.

Clark, Stanley J. "The Nez Perces in Exile." *Oregon Historical Quarterly* 36 (1935):14-59.

"Clearwater Gold Rush." *Idaho Yesterdays* 4 (1960):12-15.

Coale, George L. "Notes on the Guardian Spirit Concept Among the Nez Perce." *National Archives of Ethnography* 48 (1958).

Coan, C. F. "The Adoption of the Reservation Policy in the Pacific Northwest, 1853-1855." *Oregon Historical Quarterly* 23 (1922):1-38.

_____. "The First Stage of the Federal Indian Policy in the Pacific Northwest." *Oregon Historical Quarterly* 22 (1921):46-89.

Colton, J. S. "A Report on the Range Conditions of Central Washington." *Washington State Agricultural College Experiment Station Bulletin* 60 (1904):5-21.

Cook, S. F. "The Epidemic of 1830-33 in California and Oregon." *University of California Publications in American Archaeology and Ethnology* 43 (1955):303-26.

Cox, Thomas R. "Tribal Leadership in Transition: Chief Peter Moctelme of the Coeur d'Alenes." *Idaho Yesterdays* 23 (1979):2-9, 25-31.

Culverwell, Albert. "Stronghold in the Yakima Country: Fort Simcoe and the Indian War, 1856-59." *Pacific Northwest Quarterly* 46 (1955):46-51.

Daugherty, Richard. "Excavations in the Ice Harbor Reservoir, 1957-60." *Washington State University, Report of Investigations* 10 (1961).

Davidson, Stanley. "Worker in God's Wilderness." *Montana, Magazine of Western History* 7 (1967):8-17.

DeLacy, Hugh. "Diary of the Yakima Indian War, June 12-August 29, 1856." *Washington National Guard Pamphlet* 2 (1961):104-16.

Deutsch, Herman J. "Indian and White in the Inland Empire: The Contest for the Land, 1880-1912." *Pacific Northwest Quarterly* 47 (1956):44-51.

Douglas, Jesse S. "Origins of the Population in Oregon in 1850." *Pacific Northwest Quarterly* 41 (1950):95-108.

Dozier, Jack. "Coeur d'Alene Country: The Creation of the Coeur d'Alene Reservation in North Idaho." *Idaho Yesterdays* 6 (1962):2-7.

_____. "The Coeur d'Alene Indians in the War of 1858." *Idaho Yesterdays* 5 (1961):21-32.

Drury, Clifford M. "I, The Lawyer." *The Westerners New York Posse Brand Book* 7 (1960):1-21.

_____. "Lawyer, Head Chief of the Nez Perce, 1848-1875." *Idaho Yesterdays* 22 (1979):2-12.

_____. "Oregon Indians in the Red River School." *Pacific Historical Review* 7 (1938):52-54.

Elliott, T. C. "David Thompson and Beginnings in Idaho." *Oregon Historical Quarterly* 21 (1920):49-61.

_____. "Steptoe Butte and Steptoe Battle-field." *Washington Historical Quarterly* 18 (1927):243-53.

_____. "The Murder of Peu-Peu-Mox-Mox." *Oregon Historical Quarterly* 35 (1934):123-30.

_____. "The Strange Case of David Thompson and Jeremy Pinch." *Oregon Historical Quarterly* 40 (1939):194-95.

Field, Virgil. "Washington Territorial Militia in the Indian Wars of 1855-56." *Official History of the Washington National Guard.* Vol 2. Tacoma, Washington: 1961-63.

Forse, Albert G. "Chief Joseph as a Commander." *Winners of the West* 12 (1936):1-6.

Freeman, Otis W., J. D. Forrester, and R. L. Lupher. "Physiographic Divisions of the Columbia Intermontane Province." *Annals of the Association of American Geographics* 35 (1945):53-75.

Galm, Jerry, Glen Hartmann, Ruth Masten, and Garry Stephenson. "A Cultural Resource Overview of the Bonneville Power Administration's Mid-Columbia Project." *Central Washington University Management Report* 1 (1981).

Garth, Thomas R. "Early Nineteenth Century Tribal Relations in the Columbia Plateau." *Southwestern Journal of Anthropology* 20 (1964):43-57.

_____. "Waiilatpu After the Massacre." *Pacific Northwest Quarterly* 38 (1947):315-18.

"Grievances of the Nez Perce." *Idaho Yesterdays* 4 (1960):6-7.

Gunther, Erna. "The Indian Background of Washington History." *Pacific Northwest Quarterly* 41 (1950):189-202.

Haines, Francis. "Chief Joseph and the Nez Perce Warriors." *Pacific Northwest Quarterly* 45 (1950):189-202.

_____. "Mackenzie's Winter Camp, 1812-1813." *Oregon Historical Quarterly* 37 (1936):329-33.

_____. "Nez Perce Horses, How They Changed the Indian Way of Life." *Idaho Yesterdays* 4 (1960):8-11.

_____. "Problems of Indian Policy." *Pacific Northwest Quarterly* 41 (1950):203-12.

_____. "The Nez Perce Tribe Versus the United States." *Idaho Yesterdays* 8 (1964):18-25.

_____. "The Northward Spread of Horses Among the Plains Indians." *American Anthropologist* 40 (1938): 429-37.

Hilgard, E. W. "The Yakima and Clickitat Regions." *The Northwest* 2 (1884):1-12.

Hoaglin, Lester L., Jr., and Herbert C. Taylor, Jr. "The 'Intermittant Fever Epidemic of the 1830's on the Lower Columbia River." *Ethnohistory* 2 (1962):160-78.

Horner, J. H., and Grace Butterfield. "The Nez Perce-Findley Affair." *Oregon Historical Quarterly* 40 (1939):40-51.

Horton, Helen J., and Steven J. Gill. "The Ethnobotanical Imperative: A Consideration of Obligations, Implications, and Methodology." *Northwest Anthropological Research Notes* 15 (1981):117-87.

Huggins, E. L. "Smohalla, the Prophet of Priest Rapids." *Overland Monthly* 17 (1981):208-15.

Hunt, Garret. "Sergeant Sutherland's Ride: An Incident of the Nez Perce War." *Mississippi Valley Historical Review* 14 (1927):39-46.

"Idaho's Indian Wars." *Idaho Yesterdays* 5 (1961):22-25.

Jackson, W. Turrentine. "Indian Affairs and Politics in Idaho Territory, 1863-1870." *Pacific Historical Review* 14 (1945):311-25.

Jacobs, Melville. "A Sketch of Northern Sahaptin Grammer." *University of Washington Publications in Anthropology* 4 (1931):83-292.

_____. "Historical Perspective in Indian Languages of Oregon and Washington." *Pacific Northwest Quarterly* 28 (1937):55-74.

Josephy, Alvin, Jr. "Nez Perces and the Appaloosa Horse . . . False History?" *The Westerners New York Posse Brand Book* 14 (1967):73-87.

_____. "The Last Stand of Chief Joseph." *American Heritage* 9 (1958):36-43, 78-81.

_____. "The Naming of the Nez Perces." *Montana, Magazine of Western History* 5 (1955):1-18.

Julian, R. C. "Wallula, Washington." *Pasco Express Souvenir Illustrated Edition* (1906).

Kelley, Pat, Eugene Hunn, Charles Martinsen, and Helen Norton. "Ascorbic Acid Content of Northwest Native Plant Foods." *Journal of the American Dietetic Association*. In press.

_____. "Composition of Northwest Native Fruits." *Journal of the American Dietetic Association*. In press.

_____. "Composition of Northwest Native Root Food." *Journal of the American Dietetic Association*. In press.

Konlande, J. E., and J. R. K. Robson. "The Nutritive Value of Cooked Camas as Consumed by Flathead Indians." *Ecology of Food and Nutrition* 2 (1972):193-95.

Lee, M., R. Roburn, and A. Carrow. "Nutritional Studies of British Columbian Indians." *Canadian Journal of Public Health* 62 (1971):285-96.

Lewis, W. S. "The Case of Spokan Garry, Being a Brief Statement of the Principal Facts Connected with his Career." *Spokane Historical Society Bulletin* 1 (1917):1-68.

Liljblad, Sven. "The Indians of Idaho." *Idaho Yesterdays* 4 (1960):22-28.

Longmire, David. "First Immigrants to Cross the Cascades." *Washington Historical Quarterly* 8 (1917):22-28.

MacMurray, J. W. "The Dreamers of the Columbia River Valley in Washington Territory." *Transactions of the Albany Institute* 11 (1887):241-48.

Martig, Ralph. "Hudson's Bay Claims." *Oregon Historical Quarterly* 36 (1935):60-70.

Meinig, Donald W. "Isaac Stevens: Practical Geographer of the Early Northwest." *Geographical Review* 45 (1955): 542-58.

Mills, Hazel E. "Governor Isaac I. Stevens and the Washington Territorial Library." *Pacific Northwest Quarterly* 53 (1962):1-16.

Mitchell, John H. "Oregon, Its History, Geography, and Resources." *National Geographic Magazine* 6 (1895):239-84.

Nash, Gary B. "The Image of the Indian in the Southern Colonial Mind." *William and Mary Quarterly* 29 (1972):192-230.

Nelson, Denys. "Yakima Days." *Washington Historical Quarterly* 19 (1928):45-51, 117-33, 181-92.

Nielsen, Jean C. "Donald McKenzie in the Snake Country Fur Trade, 1816-1821." *Pacific Northwest Quarterly* 31 (1940):161-79.

O'Connor, James. "The Flathead Indians." *Records of the American Catholic Historical Society* 3 (1883-1891):85-110.

Oliphant, J. Orin. "Encroachments of Cattlemen on Indian Reservations in the Pacific Northwest, 1870-1890." *Agricultural History* 24 (1950):42-58.

_____. "George Simpson and Oregon Missions." *Pacific Historical Review* 6 (1937):234-39.

_____. "Some Neglected Aspects of the History of the Pacific Northwest." *Pacific Northwest Quarterly* 61 (1970):1-9.

Osborne, Alan. "The Exile of the Nez Perce in Indian Territory." *The Chronicles of Oklahoma* 56 (1978-79):450-71.

Prosch, Thomas W. "The Indian War in Washington Territory." *Oregon Historical Quarterly* 16 (1915):1-23.

_____. "The Indian War of 1858." *Washington Historical Quarterly* 2 (1908):237-40.

_____. "The United States Army in Washington Territory." *Washington Historical Quarterly* 2 (1908): 28-32.

Randolf, June. "Witness of Indian Religion." *Pacific Northwest Quarterly* 48 (1957):139-45.

Ray, Verne. "The Bluejay Character in the Plateau Spirit Dance." *American Anthropologist* 39 (1937):593-601.

_____. "Native Villages and Groupings of the Columbia Basin." *Pacific Northwest Quarterly* 27 (1936):99-152.

_____. "Tribal Distribution in Eastern Oregon and Adjacent Regions." *American Anthropologist* 40 (1938): 384-415.

Richards, Kent. "Isaac I. Stevens and Federal Military Power in Washington Territory." *Pacific Northwest Quarterly* 63 (1972):81-86.

Romeyn, Henry. "Capture of Chief Joseph and the Nez Perce Indians." *Montana Historical Society Contributions* 2 (1896):283-91.

Santee, J. R. "Pio-Pio-Mox-Mox." *Oregon Historical Quarterly* 34 (1933):164-76.

_____. "The Slaying of Pio-Pio-Mox-Mox." *Washington Historical Quarterly* 25 (1934):128-32.

Schroer, Blanche. "Boat Pusher or Bird Woman? Sacagawea or Sacajawea?" *Annuals of Wyoming* 52 (1980):46-54.

Scott, Leslie M. "Indian Disease as Aids to Pacific Northwest Settlement." *Oregon Historical Quarterly* 19 (1928):99-107.

Sebring, F. M. "Indian Raid on the Cascades in March, 1856." *Washington Historical Quarterly* 19 (1928):99-107.

Smith, Alan H. "The Indians of Washington." *Research Studies of the State College of Washington* 21 (1953):85-113.

Spinden, Herbert J. "Myths of the Nez Perce Indians." *Journal of American Folklore* 21 (1908):14-15.

_____. "The Nez Perce Indians." *American Anthropological Association Memoirs* 2 (1908):165-274.

Sprague, Roderick. "The Descriptive Archaeology of the Palus Burial Site, Lyon's Ferry, Washington." *Washington State University, Report of Investigations* 32 (1965).

_____. "The Meaning of Palouse." *Idaho Yesterdays* 12 (1968):22-27.

Swanson, Earl H. "Association of Bison with Artifacts in Eastern Washington." *American Antiquity* 24 (1959):429-31.

Teit, James A. "Salishan Tribes of the Western Plateau." *Bureau of American Ethnology* 145 (1927-28):23-396.

Thompson, Albert. "The Early History of the Palouse River and Its Names." *Pacific Northwest Quarterly* 62 (1971):69-71.

Thompson, Erwin N. "Men and Events on the Lower Snake River." *Idaho Yesterdays* 5 (1961):10-15.

Todd, C. C. "Origin and Meaning of the Geographic Name Palouse." *Washington Historical Quarterly* 24 (1933): 192-96.

Trafzer, Clifford E. "The Palouse in Eekish Pah." *American Indian Quarterly* 9 (1985):169-82.

Trafzer, Clifford E. and Margery Ann Beach. "Smohalla, the Washani, and Religion as a Factor in Northwestern Indian History." *American Indian Quarterly* 9 (1985):309-24.

Trafzer, Clifford E. and Richard D. Scheuerman. "The First People of the Palouse Country." *Bunchgrass Historian* 8 (1980):3-18.

Trafzer, Clifford E., ed. "A Palouse Indian Speaks: Mary Jim Remembers." *Bunchgrass Historian* 8 (1980):20-23.

Tyrrell, J. B. "David Thompson and the Columbia River." *Canadian Historical Review* 18 (1937):12-27.

Villard, Henry. "Two Railroad Reports on Northwest Resources." *Pacific Northwest Quarterly* 37 (1946).

Weibel, George. "Fifty Years of Peaceful Conquest." *Gonzaga Magazine* 5 (1913-1914):18-25, 70-78, 125-33, 179-87, 232-41, 293-303, 344-56, 407-18, 455-64, 520-32.

Wells, Merle W. "The Nez Perces and Their War." *Pacific Northwest Quarterly* 55 (1964):35-37.

Whitner, R. L. "Grant's Indian Peace Policy on the Yakima Reservation, 1870-1882." *Pacific Northwest Quarterly* 50 (1959):135-42.

Will, Drake W. "Lewis and Clark: Westering Physicians." *Montana, Magazine of Western History* 21 (1971):2-17.

Woodruff, C. A. "The Battle of the Big Hole." *Contributions to the Historical Society of Montana* 7 (1910):97-116.

Yoder, Fred R. "Pioneer Social Adaptation in the Palouse Country of Eastern Washington, 1870-1890." *Research Studies of the State College of Washington* 6 (1938):931-59.

Young, Vernon A. "Changes in Vegetation and Soil of Palouse Prairie Caused by Overgrazing." *Journal of Forestry* (1943):834-38.

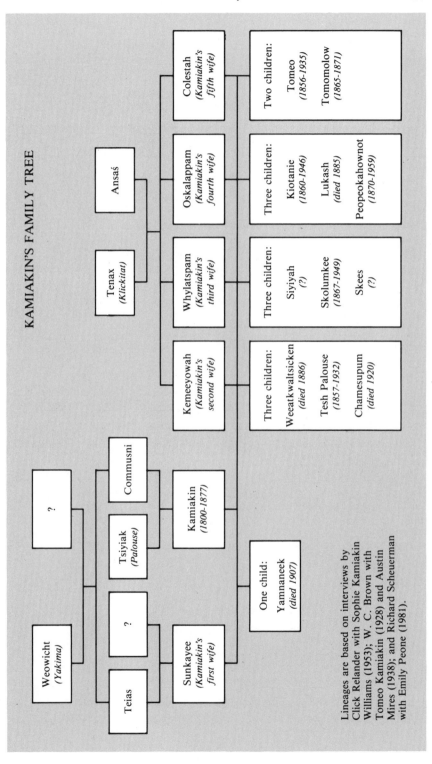

KAMIAKIN'S FAMILY TREE

Weowicht
(Yakima)

?

Teias

Tsiyiak
(Palouse)

Commusni

?

Tenax
(Klickitat)

Ansaś

Sunkayee
*(Kamiakin's
first wife)*

Kamiakin
(1800-1877)

Kemeeyowah
*(Kamiakin's
second wife)*

Whylatspam
*(Kamiakin's
third wife)*

Oskalappam
*(Kamiakin's
fourth wife)*

Colestah
*(Kamiakin's
fifth wife)*

One child:
Yamnaneek
(died 1907)

Three children:
Weeatkwaltsicken
(died 1886)
Tesh Palouse
(1857-1932)
Chamesupum
(died 1920)

Three children:
Siyiyah
(?)
Skolumkee
(1867-1949)
Skees
(?)

Three children:
Kiotanie
(1860-1946)
Lukash
(died 1885)
Peopeokahownot
(1870-1959)

Two children:
Tomeo
(1856-1935)
Tomomolow
(1865-1871)

Lineages are based on interviews by
Click Relander with Sophie Kamiakin
Williams (1953); W. C. Brown with
Tomeo Kamiakin (1928) and Austin
Mires (1938); and Richard Scheuerman
with Emily Peone (1981).

LIST OF MAPS

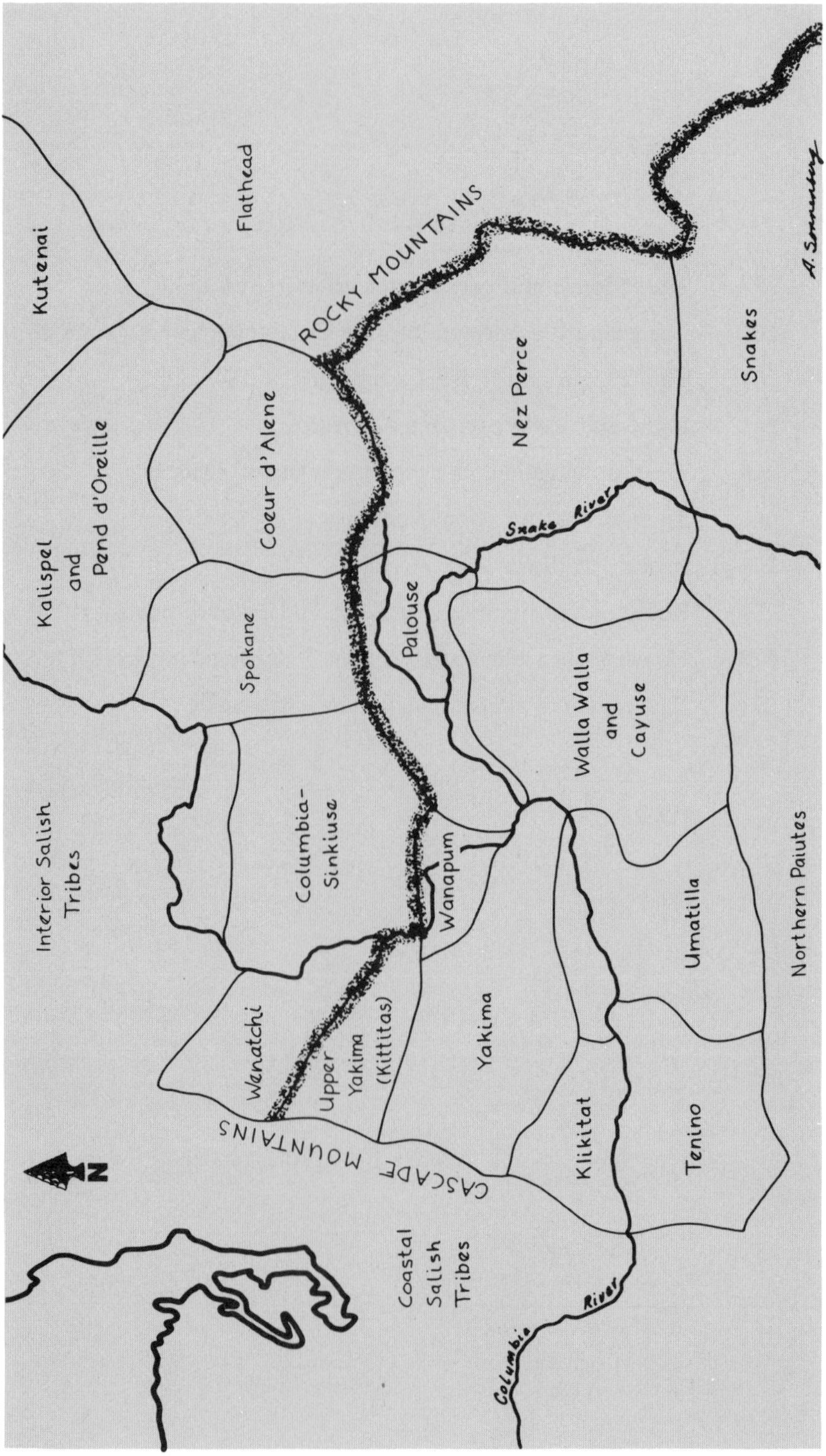

The Palouse and neighboring tribes, circa 1800

The Palouse homeland and the Columbia Plateau, circa 1820

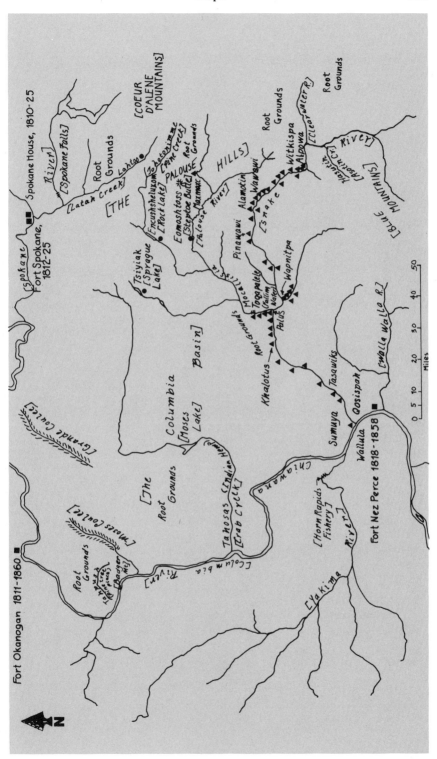

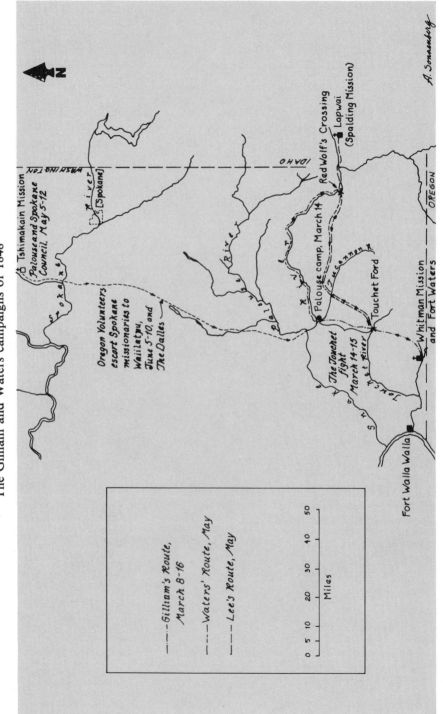

The Gilliam and Waters campaigns of 1848

Rains and Kelly campaigns of 1855

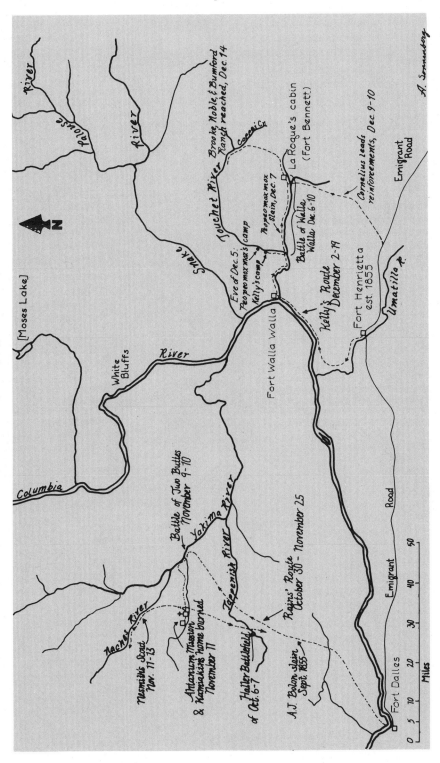

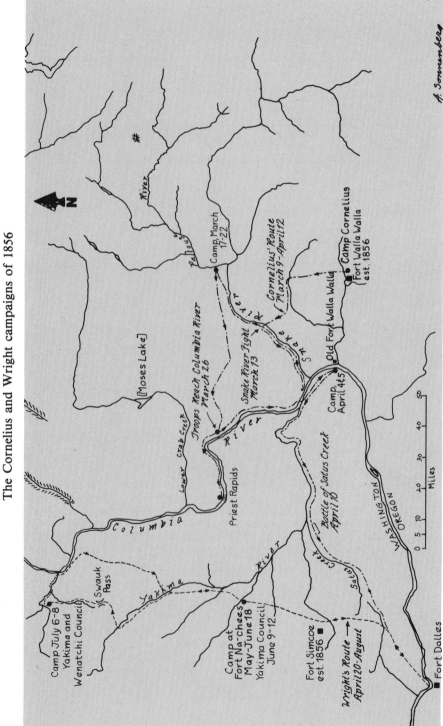

The Cornelius and Wright campaigns of 1856

The Steptoe and Wright campaigns of 1858

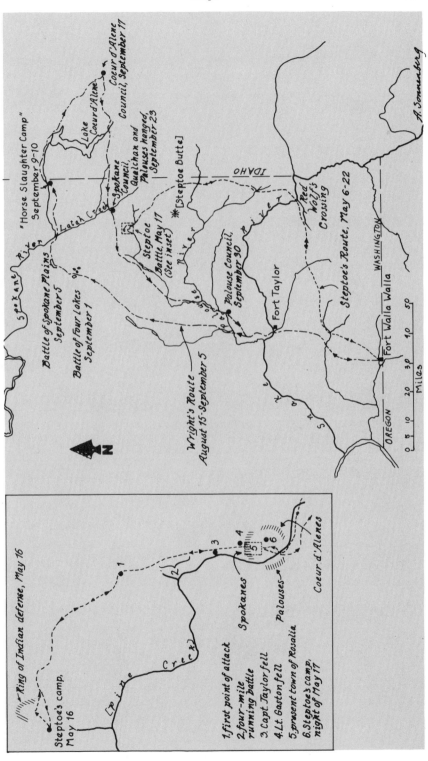

"Horse Slaughter Camp"
September 9-10

Coeur d'Alene
September 17

Lake
Coeur d'Alene

Coeur d'Alene
Council, September 17

Spokane
Council,
September 23

Qualchan and
Palouses hanged,
September 23

Spokane River

Latah Creek

IDAHO

*[Steptoe Butte]

Steptoe
Battle, May 17
(See inset)

Battle of Spokane Plains
September 5

Battle of Four Lakes
September 1

Palouse Council,
September 30

Red
Wolf's
Crossing

Fort Taylor

Steptoe's Route, May 6-22

Wright's Route
August 15-September 5

WASHINGTON

Fort Walla Walla

OREGON

Miles

0 5 10 20 30 40 50

A. Sonnenberg

N

Inset

"Ring of Indian defense, May 16

Steptoe's camp,
May 16

Pine Creek

Spokanes

Palouses

Coeur d'Alenes

1, first point of attack
2, four-mile
running battle
3, Capt. Taylor fell
4, Lt. Gaston fell
5, present town of Rosalia
6, Steptoe's camp,
night of May 17

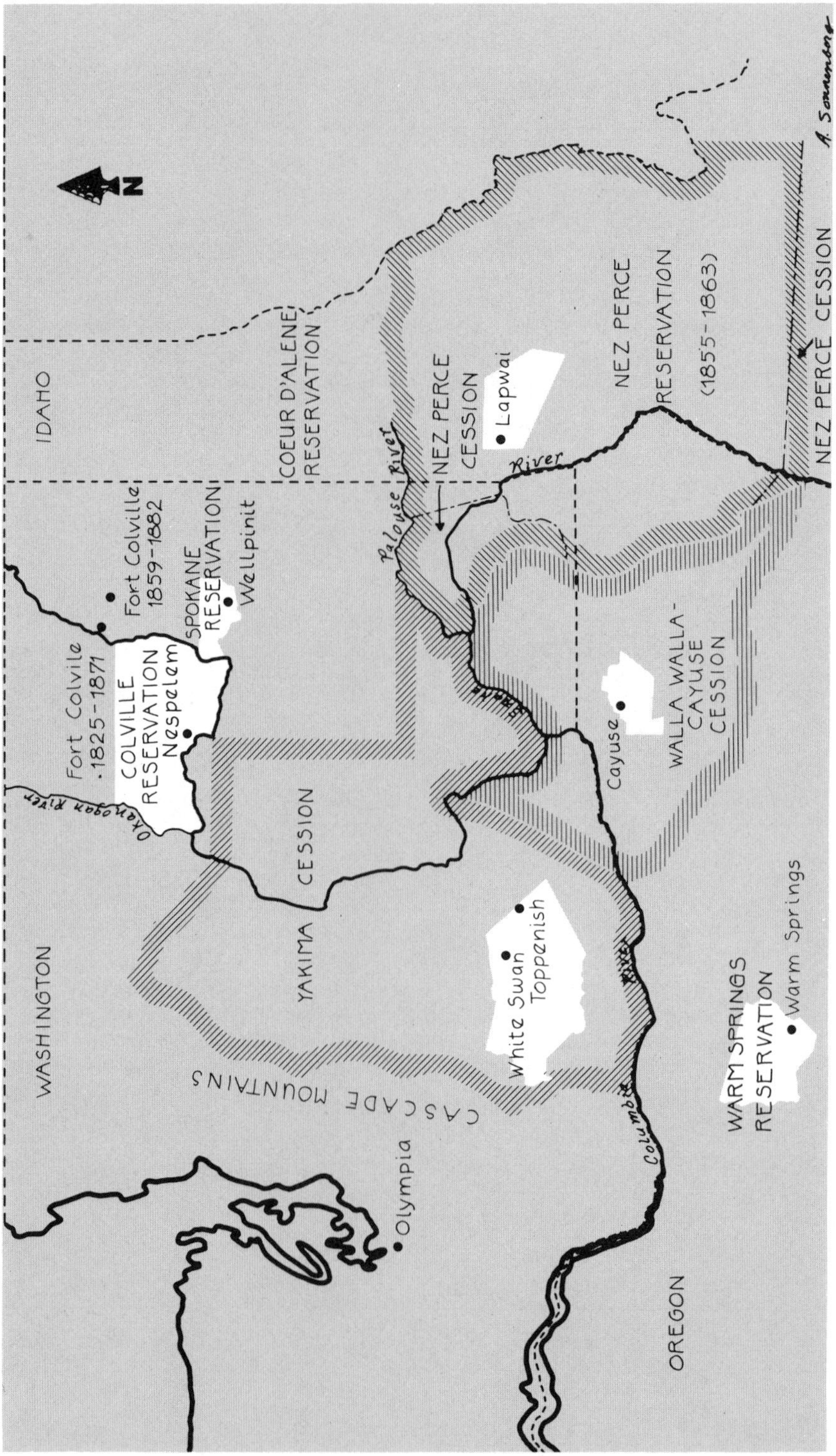

Inland Northwest treaty cessions

Route of the fighting Nez Perce and Palouse bands, 1877

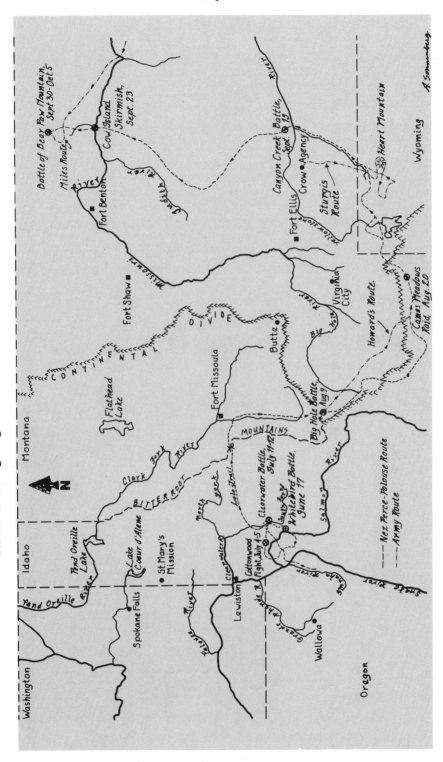

Howard's peace councils and the Palouse country, 1877

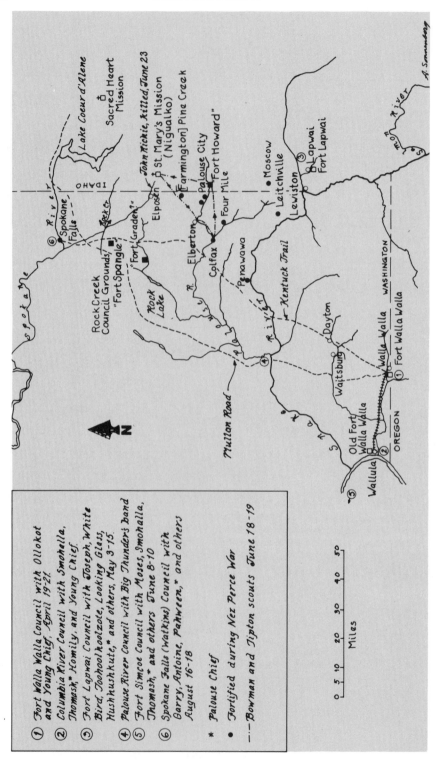

① Fort Walla Walla Council with Ollokot and Young Chief, April 19-21.
② Columbia River Council with Smohalla, Thomash,* Homily, and Young Chief.
③ Fort Lapwai Council with Joseph, White Bird, Toohoolhoolzote, Looking Glass, Hushhushkute,* and others, May 3-15.
④ Palouse River Council with Big Thunder's band
⑤ Fort Simcoe Council with Moses, Smohalla, Thomash,* and others June 8-10
⑥ Spokane Falls (Watkins) Council with Barry, Antoine, Pahween,* and others August 16-18

* Palouse Chief
● Fortified during Nez Perce War
--- Bowman and Tipton scouts June 18-19

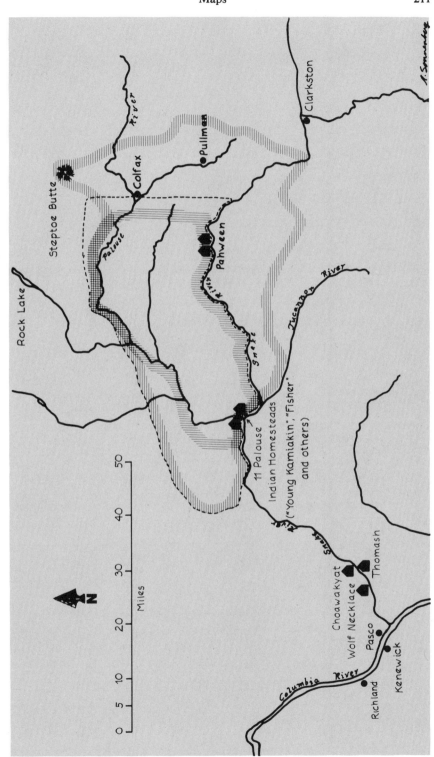

Palouse tribal claims and Indian homesteads

INDEX